D0722076

THINKING BEYOND WAR

Biographical Sketch

Lieutenant Colonel Isaiah "Ike" Wilson III is an Associate Professor with the Department of Social Sciences at the U.S. Military Academy, West Point, New York, where he serves as Director of American Politics, Public Policy, and Strategic Studies and as Director of the Beyond War Project. Prior to this professorship, Lieutenant Colonel Wilson served as a strategist in the U.S. Army.

Commissioned into the Army as a Second Lieutenant from the U.S. Military Academy at West Point in 1989, Major Wilson served for 10 years as an Army aviator. He earned a BS degree in International Relations from West Point in 1989 and holds an MPA from the Cornell Institute for Public Affairs, an MA in Government from Cornell University, and two Masters in Military Arts and Science (MMAS) from the U.S. Army Command and General Staff College (CGSC) and the U.S. Army School of Advanced Military Studies (SAMS). He earned his Ph.D. in Government from Cornell University in 2003.

Alternating throughout his military career between military troop-leading, staff-planning, and teaching assignments, Lieutenant Colonel Wilson has participated in numerous strategic-level and operational-level defense and security policy research and planning initiatives; he has published extensively on subjects related to organizational politics and national security and defense policy. During major combat operations in Iraq (March–May 2003), Lieutenant Colonel Wilson served as a historian, field interviewer, and early writer for the U.S. Army chief of staff's Operation Iraqi Freedom Study Group (OIFSG). The data and combat interviews collected during this initiative have since contributed to numerous significant advancements and reforms in U.S. Army acquisition and production programs geared toward enhancing soldier effectiveness and survivability in combat and have provided much of the empirical evidence informing many of the early published histories of the Iraq War.

Lieutenant Colonel Wilson most recently served as the Chief of Division Plans for the 101st Airborne Division (Air Assault) during the Division's participation in combat, counterinsurgency, and reconstruction operations in northern Iraq as part of Operation Iraqi Freedom (2003–2004), as well as during the 101st Airborne's reorganization and transformation (2003–2005).

At the time of writing of this book, Lieutenant Colonel Wilson was serving as an International Affairs Fellow (IAF), in residence with the Council on Foreign Relations (CFR) in New York City. Lieutenant Colonel Wilson is married to Lauren Ann Lee of Toronto, Canada. They have three children: David, Spenser, and Mae.

Thinking beyond War

Civil-Military Relations and Why America Fails to Win the Peace

Isaiah Wilson III

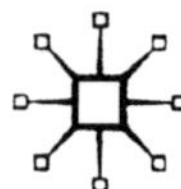

THINKING BEYOND WAR

First published in 2007 by
PALGRAVE MACMILLAN™
175 Fifth Avenue, New York, N.Y. 10010 and
Houndmills, Basingstoke, Hampshire, England RG21 6XS
Companies and representatives throughout the world.

PALGRAVE MACMILLAN is the global academic imprint of the Palgrave Macmillan division of St. Martin's Press, LLC and of Palgrave Macmillan Ltd. Macmillan® is a registered trademark in the United States, United Kingdom and other countries. Palgrave is a registered trademark in the European Union and other countries.

ISBN-13: 978–1–4039–8199–8
ISBN-10: 1–4039–8199–X

Library of Congress Cataloging-in-Publication Data

Wilson III, Isaiah, 1965–
Thinking beyond war : civil-military relations and why America fails to win the peace / Isaiah Wilson III.
p. cm.
Includes bibliographical references and index.
ISBN 1–4039–8199–X (alk. paper)
1. Civil-military relations—United States. 2. United States—Military policy. 3. Iraq War, 2003—Peace. I. Title.

JK330.W55 2007
322′.50973—dc22 2007005042

A catalogue record for this book is available from the British Library.

Design by Newgen Imaging Systems (P) Ltd., Chennai, India.

First edition: October 2007

10 9 8 7 6 5 4 3 2 1

Printed in the United States of America.

To My Sons and Daughter . . . that they may have liberty to study mathematics and philosophy, art and poetry.

Contents

List of Illustrations

Figures

Maps

Tables

Author's Note #1

The Meanings of War and Peace

This book is a work of heresy. It looks into the ideas and mechanizations of America's way of war, and after looking, takes a wrench to many parts of that long-standing machinery in an effort to dismantle some parts, tighten up others, or in some instances to tear apart worn-out pieces. In this book I question everything. A healthy skepticism of all that currently stands and defines our modern way of war and peace—our war and peace agendas, how our war and peace policies are formulated and "operationalized," how we implement those agendas—drives this inquiry. While much of the story I tell focuses on what we today regard narrowly as war and war-fare, the object of my heresy goes well beyond our modern notions of war—this is a focused study of *how America intervenes.*

An important aspect of this heresy is in the recasting of traditional terms and concepts. The modern lexicon of the U.S. military—its doctrinal terms and references—is an intentional target for recasting. The entire domain of security and war studies vernacular is a target throughout this book. In executing this heresy, I take liberties with the use of scare quotes, italics, and hyphenation to emphasize (intentionally "over" emphasize for point of re-teaching the reader) and/or to categorize certain aspects or functions of new concepts and constructions I offer.

Perhaps the best example of this approach is in my recasting of the concept and terminology of *war* itself. Integral to the argument of this book is the following: our nation's understanding of war is limited and only partial definition of the full and natural (seminal) definition of war. What Americans and the wider Western societies consider as war (military combatives) is actually only referencing one small part of the fuller and accurate definition and domain of war. By referencing this American/Western interpretation (misinterpretation) of war in scare quotes—"war"—I aim to distinguish between the interpretive concept and the natural or historically accurate (definitional) concept. It is also my way of holding the interpretation suspect.

Another bedrock of the argument is the consideration of *war as a domain of policy*, similar in process and purpose to any other type of public policy (and, consequently, subject to similar policy treatments), albeit peculiar in terms of practice. This interpretation of war as policy is not arbitrary. I chose to ground this book's interpretation and conception of war in the construct of Carl Von Clausewitz, the nineteenth-century Prussian military soldier and theorist. He defined war as "an act of force to compel our enemy to do our will" and further characterized war as "not merely an act of policy but a true political instrument, a continuation of political intercourse, carried on with other means." Simply put, for Clausewitz war was policy. This conception of war formally underpins all existing modern-era (post–Napoleonic era) Western military traditions and undergirds the U.S. modern lexicon and doctrine. My heresy does not begin here, in reiterating and emphasizing the Clausewitzian tradition. Rather, it begins with my intimation that despite the rhetorical homage modern U.S. military doctrine and practice pays to Clausewitz and his interpretation of war, modern-day U.S. policies of war do not marry with or live up to the Clausewitzian interpretation.

That argument must be left to the pages of this book. However, it was important to introduce the Clausewitzian interpretation itself now since it informs the manner in which I have chosen to craft the language of war as policy in this work. The liberal use of hyphens in my articulations of war as a domain of policy has proven to be an effective method for recasting traditional functions and aspects of war in postmodern parts of (functions, or divisions of labor within) a broader domain of war-policy. It also offers a useful tool for distinguishing between the various parts of war-policy. To demonstrate,

1. War, as a domain of policy, is offered as *war-policy.*
2. The domain of war-policy, like all policy domains, has several subcategories or functions:
    - *War-agenda-setting*;
    - *War-formulation and legitimization (planning)*;
    - *War-implementation.*

The war-formulation and legitimization stage of the policy domain is the main area of inquiry (and heresy) in this book. It happens to be the least studied and consequently most underappreciated and misunderstood function within the policy domain of war. It is also where most of America's current problems in its war-policy (the paradox of war) begins. The formulation category refers to all those functions and divisions of labor that deal with administration and resourcing—it is the *bureaucratic middle* of war-policy. War-*planning* is a major point of study in this book—an aspect of *war-formulation and war-legitimization.* Other functions falling within this subcategory are war-*wages* and war-*wares.*

War-implementation is a referent for war-policy in practice, the execution functions of war-policy. The term *Warfare* is intentionally and descriptively recast as War-Fare as an emphasis on this being just one particular function within war-policy—*actions taken in the execution of war-policy.* So too is the term and concept of the *Warrior* revised as the War-rior, as a way of distinguishing *those who implement war-policy* (i.e., the practitioner) from the practice of war itself.

The heresy goes further.

If I have done my job well in this book, the reader will come to see war as, in part, a martial (military) affair, but also inclusive of much more than military actions. As such, the reader will come to know of *war* as Clausewitz taught us to know it: as a means for reaching its goal—the political object—or rather, the war-purpose. From here it will not be difficult for the reader to begin to see that the martial functions—the military means of war-policy—are merely one category of functions making up war-policy (war-fare). And then it is easy to see that thinking of the war-rior as limited to the *military man* is wholly insufficient and incomplete. Truly, if war is policy and politics, by other means, then military means are only one part of the politics and the policy—soldiers are only one, albeit the most popularized, of the war-rior caste. When we can all see that the practice of war goes beyond the martial practices, the martial means, and even the martial war-riors (the soldiers)—we have crossed the conceptual Rubicon and can then begin the hard work of recasting war, war-fare, and the war-riors themselves. We can begin to give war-credit to those activities that have always merited the credit and to those persons who have been waging war-fare, albeit in a form and with a means nonmilitary.

If it is all war, then it logically follows that, redesigned in particular ways, everyone can be war-riors, despite their policy domain of origin. A doctor serving overseas with Doctors Without Borders, depending on how those humanitarian assistance activities integrate into an overall war-campaign, can be considered a war-rior—in fact, we must consider him or her as such, particularly if the conditionality of the humanitarian mission is a bona fide combat zone, where the doctors cannot implement their means and methods without "military assistance." Conversely, simply because a combat infantryman may be directed within a comprehensive war-plan (a campaign plan) to engage in civil restoration operations does not mean that the soldier is no longer a war-rior. *It is still war*, despite the lack of or lessening of the *close-with-to-destroy* functionality. We did just this during most of America's interventions in the 1990s—American soldiers engaged in "peace operations" (a doctrinal concept!) engaged in something "other-than-war," and indirectly sent a message to the soldier that what they were doing had little if anything to do with war-fighting. The message was actually not so subtle. Officers and soldiers participating in interventions in Haiti, Rwanda, the Balkans, and Kosovo did not receive combat credit for those experiences. Somalia (Operation Restore Hope) was a similar case, until the Blackhawk Down incident in Mogadishu and the death of 18 Army Rangers convinced the Pentagon that the situation in Somalia had turned to war and all those soldiers taking part in the operation were now combat veterans (once again, war-riors). Might many of those very same "other-than-war" war-riors from the 1990s experiences have made more appropriate senior leaders or "commanders" in some of the latter phases of Operation Iraqi Freedom (Iraq War, 2003–) if their Officer Record Briefs had clearly indicated their earlier-gained expertise as combat experience, thereby elevating them in the order of merit selections for future combat assignments and combat commands? Hard to tell. But it is an intriguing question—one that is addressed in this book.

Once the martial walls are torn down, the entire modern lexicon and body of doctrinal terms and scriptures are open for rethinking. This book recasts the terms and concepts of the "offense," "offensives," "offensive operations" into a *beyond-the-combatives* context. The offense is applicable to any policy function and all functions within the domain of war-policy. The term *offensive* is an adjective describing a particular character and tenor of an action, as in *to take the offense in closing with to destroy an enemy force*. But the offense can also be taken *to close-with-to-restore* stability, civic society, and civil infrastructures. The basic *Webster* definitions of the term and the concept have been captured by our military. The heresy is in returning this hostage term (and others!) to the broader war-policy communities.

In fact, the entire body of modern U.S. military tactical tasks (including *defeat*, *secure*, *isolate*, *contain*) are tactical tasks—extremely prescriptive terms limited in their use and understandings to martial tactical combat actions. If a staff briefer presents a course of action to a commander for decision and guidance, and that course of action calls for a unit to "seize" a particular objective, the lexicon is so ingrained and well understood within military circles that all that needs to be said is "Unit A seizes OBJ X in order to ———." The word *seize* is a package of action and intent, implying (even prescribing) a very specific type and quantity of capability for the action. Achieving this level of parlance and understanding within the profession of arms has taken decades, and the benefits have been significant—clarity and rapidity of action. However, when we recast the profession of arms into the more timely and appropriate construct of the profession of war, the lexicon immediately becomes overly dogmatic and restrictive. All of the effective meanings of the arms-based tasks and purpose terminology is immediately lost. The term *seize* has little to no meaning or mission in it when the term is used to prescribe a *close-with-to-restore*-type operation. In fact, if applied this way and spoken to a modern-era senior commander, without further explanation of the unique context, a tactical task term such as "seize" in a stability or reconstruction context could lead the decision maker to an erroneous understanding of the mission and an error of judgment, decision, and action. Expanding the context and meaning of these held-hostage terms and concepts from a profession-of-arms to a professions-of-war-context—transposing the language of battle into the languages of war-policy is an important first step in thinking and acting in a manner commensurate with the *beyond-war* contemporary operating environment.

War As a "Sign of the Times"

Critical theory, a specific model in critical theory literature—constructivism—underpins this study. The liberal use of scare quotes and hyphenations is a standard convention within the constructivist literature, as a method of emphasizing the arbitrary (constructed) nature of contemporary forms, practices, definitions, and concepts.

Looking at this study's prime question (*why is America prone to winning all its battles but losing its wider wars?*) through this critical theory lens, one sees war, both as policy and as action, as a social construct—an arbitrary construct, insofar as the prevailing image of war changes (should and must change) as society changes. War, as we know it, is *a sign of the times.* The argument here is that the present and prevailing U.S. (Western) construct of what constitutes "war" is rapidly being overruled by the contemporary realities of twenty-first-century war-fare. From a constructivist viewpoint, the material facts undergirding the international system and our contemporary ways of war "acquire meaning for human action only through the structure of shared knowledge in which they are embedded."[1]

The nonstandard research approach of this book demands some nonstandard uses of terms and some liberty with traditional grammatical renderings. It is my sincere hope that these liberties do not detract you, the reader, from appreciating the important journey offered in this book.

Let the heresy begin.

Note

1. Alexander Wendt, "Constructing International Politics," *International Security*, 20 (1): 73.

Author's Note #2

Intentions

This book is essentially a story of one war-planner's experiences with the challenges and opportunities—the realities—of postmodern-era war in general and of the Iraq War as a more recent and specific case. That story has many faces, many angles. It is a work of theory, in that it offers new propositions and hypotheses for explaining America's record of big losses in its "small" wars. The study is at the same time a work of history, charting the growth of this paradox within the nation's modern way of war to its present postmodern maturity. The story provides an addition to the already robust body of "early histories" of the Iraq War as part of a broader chronicle of U.S. military history. The emphasis this book places on war in practice in Iraq (the early history) also makes this aspect of the book a story of current practice in postmodern war-fare. Finally, as a theory-history-practice account of America in war and an accounting of America in war in Iraq, this book serves as a primer for a broad and cross-cutting (interdisciplinary) study of the American way of war and peace—a study titled Think-Beyond-War.[1]

Where the Book Fits in the Theoretical Literature

Thinking Beyond War takes an unconventional theoretical look at war-policy and war-fare. Most of the literature that defines the fields of international relations, international security, and security studies is dominated by one of two schools of theory—realism (the first among the two equals) and liberalism. Where realist accounts traditionally focus on questions relating to *why nation-states conflict* and attempt answers that tend to be more focused on material-power-based explanations, liberal renderings have tended to focus on the question *how can nation-states cooperate?* incorporating both material (traditional power politics explanations) and nonmaterial (suasive, nontangible) causal mechanisms into their theoretics.

This book asks a different kind of question (*Why do entities wage war-conflict the way they do? Why does America wage war the way that it does?*), and in so doing, it approaches the age-old question of international relations—why war?—from the indirect angle of *how we fight* and how those ways of warring may have a determinative impact on whether we wage war at all and, if we do, what the probable outcome may be.

This angle of questioning demanded a different way of theorizing. Critical theory is a sociological school of thought that has a relatively recent history of use in the field of political science. Even rarer are critical theory accounts related to issues of security studies and war studies. See Kier's *Imagining War* and Legro's *Cooperation under Fire* for two of a limited number of such accounts.[2] This book applies a specific critical theory model—*constructivism*—in search of explanations of and answers to the paradox within the American way of war and peace. The constructivist lens allows us to peer into the foundational questions of war and peace (*What is war? What do we mean by "peace"?*) and offers us a way of reconsidering war as a social construct—a *sign of the prevailing times.* This unique approach allows us to "think" of war-policy in an important new way: as both a product of the politics that prevail during any given time or societal condition and as a process that can determine (accurately or erroneously) future politics of war. When we look at the Iraq War, for example, while the questions of why we went to war in the first place are important, whether our manner of defining what constituted "the War" in Iraq versus the "postwar" might be a cause of our present "troubled policy" in Iraq is, in my opinion, an all-too-often ignored line of inquiry and one that holds much explanatory power *and* most of the potential solutions.

Where This Book Fits in "Early Histories" of the Iraq War

There are those who claim that history, true history, cannot be written so soon after an event.[3] As a military historian, I tend to agree. However, as historian Dave Palmer defended his own premature history of the Vietnam War years ago, I similarly defend my own contribution to the early histories of the Iraq War now—we live now, and undoubtedly we will be compelled to wage other wars before more definitive histories can be written on Iraq, even *before* the Iraq War is concluded.

Moreover, it is not like this work does not have a lot of companion works. The shelves of New Releases at bookstores across the country were being filled with Iraq War accounts, histories, personal journeys, and the like as early as four months after the start of the war in March 2003. I participated in one of the earliest of those early accounts[4]—an account that has provided a majority of the empirical data supporting histories that have followed. These early works have tended to fall into three categories: *war accounts*, the *other-than-war accounts*, and the *there-I-was accounts*, as I have termed them.

The *war accounts* are those books and related publications that have focused on a historical rendering of what we have collectively defined (erroneously so, I believe) as the "War"—activities taking place on the ground in and around Iraq from initiation of major combat operations on 19 March 2003 to the collapse of the Hussein state regime on 9 April 2003. *On Point* was the first among equals of this category, followed by similar accounts offered by Williamson Murray and Major General (Retired) Robert H. Scales, Jr. (*The Iraq War*) and General (Retired) Tommy Franks (*American Soldier*).[5]

The *other-than-war accounts* are those works that flooded the marketplace during and after the March 2003 commencement of hostilities—works that covered a wide range of accounts, from embedded reporter accounts of focus units and their commanders (Rick Atkinson's *In the Company of Soldiers*, 2003) to party-political renderings of the events leading up to and perpetuating the American war in Iraq (Richard Clarke's *Against All Enemies*, 2003; Bob Woodward's *Plan of Attack*, 2003).

There have also been several *there-I-was accounts*, and as soldiers and others serving on the ground in Iraq return home, we should expect to see more of these accounts. David Phillips, former senior advisor to the U.S. Department of State, has provided such an account (*Losing Iraq: Inside the Postwar Reconstruction Fiasco* [Westview Press, 2005]), as has Larry Diamond, recounting his personal experience as a senior advisor to the Coalition Provisional Authority (CPA) in *Squandered Victory*.[6] The most widely acclaimed of these accounts has come from reporter George Packer (*The Assassins Gate*).[7]

I intend this book as an addition to all three of these "camps"—and beyond, as a fresh retrospective of this war and the lessons it has to offer for those wars that will unfortunately but undoubtedly come after Iraq. The book is my personal recording of a *more complete*, but still incomplete, war account, covering my experiences as a military observer and official recorder[8] of the march-up-country phases of the war as well as my experiences as a Division war-planner in northern Iraq from June 2003 to March 2004—a period of the war that unfortunately came to be regarded as the "postwar."

I also intended this book to be *beyond* the body of works on the Iraq War that have focused as much (or more) on partisan assaults against the war-makers (and the peace-makers) as they have on plain-spoken histories or simple assessments of the intervention. A respectable number of books have focused on the question of strategic intent and choice behind the American *state's* decision to go to war in Iraq in 2003, and the United States' method for convincing the American *nation* (the public)—and the national publics of a number of coalition-of-the-willing nation-states—to follow. *Why did the Bush administration lead us to war in Iraq, when they did, and in the way they did it?* This is a vital question, especially since it now appears that much if not all of the intelligence used to justify the 2003 entry into war with Iraq was deemed "nonoperable" (Washington-speak for "not true") by spring 2004. However, I have never found this obsession with the strategic choices behind our war-policy in Iraq to contribute anything of a positive value to the war underway *in* Iraq today. Looking at the war from the foxhole makes the questions and criticisms over why we went to war in 2003 a rather senseless exercise—war-fighters, "peace-fighters," and the Iraqi citizens living the war today are beyond the question of why we came that was once, but is no longer, extremely important from a practical standpoint. The war still rages, despite our hope to regard ourselves as "in the postwar phases." We will have years to assign culpability or honors to the progenitors of the war-policy. However, today, winning the war and finishing it "well" is the important thing. We need more studies devoted to this purpose.

This book is one attempt.

Notes

1. The epilogue details the Beyond War Project.
2. Elizabeth Kier, *Imagining War: French and British Military Doctrine between the Wars* (Princeton, NJ: Princeton University Press, 1996); and Jeffrey W. Legro, *Cooperation under Fire: Anglo-German Restraint during World War II* (Ithaca, NY: Cornell University Press, 1995).
3. General (Retired) Dave R. Palmer prefaced what was, at the time of its writing, his own "early" or premature history of the Vietnam War. See Dave Palmer, *The Summons of the Trumpet* (New York: Ballantine, 1978).

4. See *On Point: The United States Army in Operation Iraqi Freedom* (Leavenworth: Combat Studies Institute, 2003).
5. Williamson Murray and Maj. Gen. (Ret) Robert H. Scales, Jr., *The Iraq War: A Military History* (Cambridge: Belknap Press, 2003), and Gen. (Ret.) Tommy Franks, *American Soldier* (New York: Regan Books, 2004).
6. Larry Diamond, *Squandered Victory: The American Occupation and the Bungled Effort to Bring Democracy to Iraq* (New York: Henry Holt and Company, 2005).
7. This author contributed to some of the discussions within this book that focused on the planning that went into the U.S. war-plans and the apparent absences of operational plans for what were at the time considered to be the "postwar" phases of the Iraq War. George Packer, *The Assassin's Gate: America in Iraq* (New York: Farrar, Straus, and Giroux, 2005).
8. From early April to late June 2003, I served as an organizer, data-collector, and early author on the OIFSG, an initiative organized and directed under the aegis of the U.S. Department of the Army, and then sitting Army Chief of Staff General Eric Shinseki. The OIFSG's mission was threefold: (1) deploy into Iraq and conduct field interviews and historical data collection of the war during the war-fight (under fire); (2) collect important insights and lessons from soldiers in the fight regarding "winners and losers" with reference to field equipment and other operationally impacting materiel, return with that feedback, and submit it to the ongoing Army Strategic Planning Board (ASPB) and budgeting processes in an effort to correct materiel wrongs and provide the soldiers a quick fix to many of those equipment failures; write the early history of the U.S. Army in the Iraq War. The book *On Point* is a product of that research initiative.

Preface

This is a story of war and peace and a broader study of how America intervenes.

America's way of war and peace (i.e., intervention) has long suffered an irony, a paradox. While the U.S. military has rarely met defeat in the battles and engagements of its tactical war-fights, the American nation has a long and spotty record of wins and losses in the wider wars it has waged. America has suffered big problems in its efforts to win in what the military has long termed "small wars." The Vietnam War is the modern, twentieth-century exemplar of America's small wars paradox. The Vietnam experience left us with a haunting epitaph—"we won all the battles but still managed to lose the war." Those old ghosts of the paradox currently haunt the U.S. war-efforts in Iraq, Afghanistan, and in every other theater of war the United States now finds itself engaged in, including the American homeland. These ghosts trouble our decision makers, planners, and military leaders to fashion a war-waging approach and war-winning strategy that will prove effective against global terrorism and what may be ahead on the horizon: a growing transnational insurgency directed against and questioning through the "politics of guns" and terrorism the viability, capabilities, and legitimacy of the nation-state-premised international system. These threats are now considered the prime threats to global security and prosperity.

These "ghosts of small wars past" can be seen all too clearly in our war in and for Iraq. The war in Iraq now rages well beyond the borders of that country and beyond the physical grappling that takes place between soldiers and insurgents on the ground. The U.S. military, along with those combat forces of America's coalition of the willing, initiated a ground war against the state regime and military of Saddam Hussein on 19 March 2003. That march up country and the "shock-and-awe" air campaign that preceded it ended on 9 April 2003 with the official collapse of the Saddam government. Yet, even as U.S. soldiers and elated Iraqis tore down the statues and posters of the old regime, the ghost of America's small wars past began to rise with their all-too-familiar haunts. If by 1 May 2003, President Bush could publicly claim *mission complete*, what was to come next? Was *mission complete* the same as "the war is over"? Did this mean that American could return home? If it was *mission complete* by 1 May, why were U.S. and coalition forces "digging in" into more static areas of operation by late June 2003? What was the American public to think of the war by April 2004—a year after the declaration of *mission complete* but, ironically, by this time the most deadly month for soldiers and Iraqis alike? And what are Americans to think today? What are the Iraqis and the wider international community to think?

It is, at the time of this writing (2005), some 27 months after the 1 May 2003 declaration of *mission complete*. America's war in Iraq still rages, even as the Iraqis now wage their own war for a future democratic Iraq. The questions and confusions of the war have come home to roost. The purple index fingers symbolic of the Iraqi people's tactical electoral victory (January 2005) mix with the purple hearts now (by early 2007) donned, posthumously, by more than 3,500 dead American soldiers and by reportedly more than 40,000 surviving but wounded soldiers, and now combine with a growing "red-versus-blue" coloration of American public opinion over the nation's stakes and interests not only in this war but also in this new age of global war against terrorism. To the average American this war in Iraq is looking more like that past war in Vietnam, raising public concerns over the war to a level and tenor that just might catalyze the very outcome—loss of the war—that no one intends.

The possibility of losing our war in Iraq goes well beyond the context of losing Iraq. A loss of this war could spill over into the worst problems in our future interventions and overall national security policies. The suasion of American soft and hard power could suffer in the eyes of the international community, lowering America's legitimacy as a global power. This decline in America's reputation as a benevolent hegemon could not come at a worse moment in history since the dawn of World War II. It took nearly two decades for the United States to cast out the ghost of its Vietnam experience. I worry that our nation, and the world, does not have another 20 years to spend in reflection of "what went wrong." Time is clearly of the essence in the context of the war-fight in Iraq. Coalition soldiers and Iraqi civilians are dying at a rate of about three and 100 per day, respectively. The possibility of a safe and secure democratic Iraq of no threat to its own people or its neighbors seems more uncertain with every human loss. A sectarian-based civil war may be on the horizon in Iraq, with spillover impacts of a scope and scale currently beyond our comprehension.

And now that this war in and for Iraq has become inextricably linked to our nation's global war on terrorism (GWOT) and a wider assault on the nation-state system, getting it right in Iraq will prove telling for the future effectiveness of U.S. power, prestige, influence, and security. Ours is not only a paradox within our ways of war-fighting; it is a wider dilemma. The paradox lies beyond our capacity to wage battle and war-fare—it lies in our capacity to *wage and win peace*. Ours is a problem of impotence in how, where, and why we intervene.

Neither our nation nor the world can afford to simply describe this paradox within the Western (and particularly American) way of war and peace. We must go beyond mere descriptions of the problem and search for explanations for why it persists and for how the paradox can be overcome. Centrally important is the imperative to explain this paradox not only to the "usual suspects" of military, defense, security, and foreign policy wonks and experts but also to the laity. Convincing the average American of the problem with the nation's current approach to war-fare and peace-fare is a necessary and perhaps a sufficient mechanism as well for finally getting our nation "over" its large problem with waging and winning what it for too long has considered "small wars."

Why *Thinking Beyond War*?

Thinking Beyond War is much more than a book title. In these three simple words, I believe our nation can finally find an effective way out of its longtime difficulties with waging war to win the peace—with *military interventions.*

Meeting and overcoming the complex challenges of this new age of intervention demands that we all reconsider everything we believe we know and have known about war and peace. First, we must find opportunities (and take those opportunities) to think about this new age of intervention and our future roles and stakes therein, and we must learn to think anew. A revolution in military affairs has been the obsession of many military and war *aficionados*, especially since the end of the cold war era in 1990–1991. Making this so-called RMA a reality demands nothing short of a revolution in how we think about war, as policy and as practice, and how we elect to conduct ourselves in our intervention policies.

From My Father's Wars to Wars of My Own

The subject of this book is not so much something that I searched out as it is something that searched me out. My first conscious memory of war, and really the paradox I now study and write about, was in 1970, when I was about five years old. My father had just returned from his second tour of duty in Vietnam. A combat veteran of World War II, postwar occupation in Germany, the Korean War, and Vietnam, my father was, now as I reflect upon it as an adult and as a soldier myself, the image of America's modern-age idea of war and way of war-fare. He was part of that first "greatest generation" that "saved the world" from fascism and communism and protected our nation and its interests abroad by "closing with to destroy" the enemy. My father had just moved us to Lexington, Kentucky, and though Lexington was no Berkeley or Kent State, the "antiwar" movement had reached even this remote corner of the home front by 1970. The Tet Offensive had come and gone. U.S. military forces had survived this surprise, exacting a terrible human toll on our North Vietnamese opponent. After Tet, the Vietcong insurgents in South Vietnam had been defeated as an effective and organized fighting force. However, it was becoming all too clear that despite not only surviving TET but also winning all the battles of the Tet Offensive, by 1970 America was losing the war in Vietnam. The images of this impending loss were evident on Lexington's Third Street one sunny day in 1970.

On this particular day, my father, my mother, and I were on our way from getting me a haircut. In fact, it may have been my first. As we drove down Third Street, I noticed my father slowly stop our car. I leaned over between the front seats (seat belts were not yet the convention much less the law) to see whether we were at a red light. I saw up ahead of us a large group of men in the middle of the street surrounding something that was ablaze. My father, despite the clearly fearful objections of my mother, got out of the car, moved to the back, opened the trunk, and pulled out a blanket that we always kept there for emergencies. Next, he approached the agitated crowd, passed through them, and proceeded to put out whatever was on fire, and then on his hands and knees placed fragments of whatever had been burned delicately into the blanket. As he returned to the car, the crowd behind him seemed dumbfounded. My mother was by now beyond her concern for my dad's and our safety and clearly angry. I remember a lot of cursing going on the rest of the trip home, with most of the four-letter words directed by my mother toward my father and his "careless bravado." When we reached home, my father took the blanket into the living room and started a fire in the fireplace. He then took what looked like small scraps of singed cloth one by one from the blanket and delicately placed them in the fireplace. My mother kept me at a distance from what all of a sudden seemed like one of the Masses we attended every Sunday.

What I learned later was that my father had stopped the burning of the American flag during a protest and then had returned the remnants of that desecrated flag to our home where he put it to rest. When I asked my father, many years later, what he was thinking, all he could tell me was "I'll be damned if I was going to let those sonsofbitches burn something that I fought to defend."

I do not relay this story because of my disgust at a flag being burned. In fact, although I would prefer that protesters avoid discourse that involves the burning of the American flag, I can and do appreciate such an act as a legitimate display of civil disobedience in a free and democratic society—an American right, albeit one that I would prefer Americans choose not to avail. Nor am I telling the story to rebuke that growing chorus of "antiwar" activists and partisan politicos who are perhaps making too much of the present opportunity to compare our sticky situation in Iraq with our past quagmire in Vietnam. I am not "antiwar." To me, as a soldier and public policy scholar, claiming to be "anti" war would be similar to saying that I am against public policy and as such against the idea that the government has a legitimate role in providing for the social good. This does not mean that I am "pro" war either. Any soldier who is "for" war should not be a soldier. This would be the equivalent of a surgeon, highly trained and specialized to perform the act of surgery, awaiting with great anticipation and glee the next opportunity to put someone under the knife. Doctors do not eagerly await their next traumas. Neither do professional soldiers hope for their next wars, for it is the soldier who has the most to lose in war-fare.

This boyhood memory, more than I would like to admit, today links me and my own experiences of war in the Balkans and in Iraq with my father's own experiences in war. And as that memory of the flag burning in the streets of Lexington, Kentucky, burns in my own mind's eye, it has helped illuminate some important aspects of those past times and conditions of my father's wars through contrast and comparison with the character of those wars that I have experienced firsthand in recent times. When I think on what compelled me to write this book and on what drives me to search for solutions to America's war-policy paradox, the motivation is complex and multifaceted. But when you peel back all the layers, it goes back to that flag, and that act by my father, and what all that represented in terms of the war in Vietnam itself and elsewhere.

The years between the TET Offensive and the First Gulf War in 1990–1991 found America engaged in an internal struggle to repair its collective psyche and regain its confidence. At the same time the nation was striving outwardly through its foreign policies to buttress and reinforce the reputation of the country as an effective power in the eyes of the international community. The paradox of our American way of war, as witnessed and evidenced in the Vietnam experience, took its toll on the country at the macro level. It took its toll at the individual level as well. My father, a seasoned noncommissioned officer, was one of those veterans who had served in three of America's earlier wars, returning as the hero from the first (World War II), as the forgotten soldier from the second (Korea), and from his last (Vietnam), seen as the war-monger and the baby-killer. The personal battle my father waged from the time of his final return from Vietnam in 1970 until his untimely death in 1985 reflected his internal struggle to reconcile his experiences in World

War II and Korea with what he experienced when he returned from Vietnam. Had war changed all that much between what it was during World War II or the Korean War and what it had become by the time of the Vietnam War? What haunted my dad in his persistent nightmares was that the actions he and his fellow soldiers had taken on the ground in Vietnam, to win that war, had been similar to, if not the same as, the ways in which he and others had fought to victory in World War II and Korea. Yet, they had returned from the former experiences with a win for the nation (the world) and as the victor, but from Vietnam they had returned as the villain. How could we return with a loss when we had defeated and destroyed the enemy on the ground in battle after battle? These ironies of war plagued my father and countless Vietnam veterans like him, driving many of them to psychological collapse and early deaths. As a young man, watching my father, my family, and my nation struggle to survive this loss and to come to terms with the paradox made this paradox my own "little war."

The country saw a lot of healing in the 20 years after our withdrawal from Saigon in 1975. Vietnam veterans finally received some relief from their purgatory, indirectly, through witnessing the rebirth of American strategic power in the Gulf War of 1990–1991 and the triumphal receptions America's soldiers received from a grateful nation at that war's end. Our military rolled up its sleeves and began the hard work of remaking America's armed forces in its own attempts to exorcise the demons of Vietnam from its military doctrine and ways of war-fare. The effort paid off in many significant ways, with the Gulf War of 1990–1991 being the exemplar of the return of American *battle-waging* prowess. During the mid- to late 1980s, and in the midst of the Reagan-American renaissance and rebirth of American military power, I was just beginning my military career as a cadet at West Point. Graduating in 1989, by the outbreak of Operation Desert Storm I was a First Lieutenant in the U.S. Army and training as an Apache Attack Helicopter pilot at Fort Rucker, Alabama, and Fort Hood, Texas. The military victory of that "100-hour war" had an enormous psychological effect on me and the generations of soldiers born and coming of professional age during the late 1970s and 1980s, and it had an organizational impact on America's armed forces. The lessons we all learned from that "Certain Victory" in the Gulf War shaped for us a "new view" of war and war-fare. Actually, that new view was not all that new but rather a high-tech variant of our older way of war-fare, the one that had brought us victory in World War II. The Gulf War victory symbolized our final departure from that *small war* in Vietnam. It reflected the final exorcizing of the devil of unconventional war-fare and the resetting of the American military, and the country, on what was considered a "better path" of "conventional war-fare" that brought victory in our great wars.

Time, experience, and study have since shown me the drastic errors that lie in viewing war and the lessons from war in this narrow way. Asking *how we fight* is pointless if the question is not asked and answered in the context of *why we fight*. That higher context—the quality-of-peace objective—is what purposes war and our actions in war (war-fare). Why we wage war as reflected in how we wage war defines our intervention policy; that policy defines for the world who we are as a nation.

In retrospect, my own personal experiences since the end of the Gulf War mirror those of my father following the end of World War II. For him, the victory against Germany and Japan (my father served in both theaters) was immediately followed by the ambiguities and challenges of nation-rebuilding and occupation duties. Trained as a war-fighter to close-with-to-destroy enemy forces, my dad found himself all of a sudden more like a cop, walking a beat in France and occupied Germany. And then a mere four years later, he was once again the war-fighter, leading troops in Korea. His experiences reflected what the nation and the world were experiencing on the macro scale. In a very short period, from 1945 to 1950, the state of war, if not its very nature, changed dramatically. By 1950, the nuclear age was already past its dawn, collective security was the new security paradigm, containment was the new security strategy, and the cold war was upon us.

The Korean War has become known as our *forgotten war*. But my father and other veterans like him never forgot that experience. While the war reflected much of the characteristics of World War II, Korea presented a new and unique dimension of war that was as unfamiliar to our nation as it was to my dad. Similar to World War II, the Korean War was a conventional war stereotypical of the modern age. It was a war of ground combatives pitted against national armies over national stakes. Yet at the same time, this kind of war was different from its most recent predecessor. Sure, this war was still of the same family of modern wars, but Korea was a "distant cousin," a "black sheep" of that family. Korea was the world's first adventure in this new world order of collective security. The stakes, as such, went broadly beyond the parameters of the Korean peninsula. Korea was a small piece within the larger puzzle of the cold war. Losing Korea meant losing much more than a country as it could prove to be the first of a series of dominos to fall to global communism. In this new global context, what would have been considered, quite accurately so in 1945, a small or limited war was now a war of tactical battles with grand strategic implications.

Even so, the fighting done by my father and other fathers in Korea was still war-fare as they had grown to know it. In Korea, they could still leave the fighting to the soldiers and their generals, and the diplomacy and the politics to the politicians. My father returned from Korea in 1952 and married my mother that same year. He returned seen by the public as the same hero, having done his best fighting the forces of communism, despite only bringing home a "tie." During the 1940s, our way of war was enough to yield the decisive win. By the 1950s, those same ways could muster only a stalemate. By the 1960s and by the Vietnam War, our fathers were doomed to failure no matter how valiantly they fought the enemy on the ground.

Cut back (or more accurately, forward in time) to the 1990s and my own wars.

In hindsight, the Gulf War victory was very similar in terms of context to the nation's and my father's experience in World War II. Just as World War II became the example of a proven military doctrine and a metric for an effective national *way of war* for my father's generation, the Gulf War became a similar measure for us. Just as that earlier generation immediately faced the complexities and ambiguities of a new age after "winning" World War II, our own faced a similar situation in the aftermath of our victory in the Gulf in 1991. The decade that followed presented the United States with a whole series of "Korea-like" conflict situations. Somalia, the Balkans, Rwanda, Haiti, Kosovo, and other similar crises found America engaged in acts similar to the tactical war-fights of the past but now within a different context altogether, one that did not measure up to or reflect what we had been taught defined war and war-fare. These "other than wars" of the 1990s were, like Korea before them, wars of local intimacy, wars of tactical actions that manifested grand strategic implications and consequences. Like Korea before it, these new "other-than-war" wars seemed to yield stalemates at best. None of these wars had an immediate or direct impact on American security. In none of these efforts did it appear that we could actually "win" (achieve and sustain a stable peace) by military means alone.

In hindsight, neither did Korea. Maybe this is why we learned to label these wars as "small wars"—not because of their inherent limited scope and scale but because of the small impact we saw these wars having on our own interests and our own futures. My father could return from the Korean War seen as the same hero he was on his return from World War II, despite only being able to fight to a stalemate, because a tie in Korea was "good enough" in regard to America's own immediate and direct national security. The "welcome homes" from the small wars of the 1990s, and my own return from Bosnia-Herzegovina in 1996, were judged and publicly regarded as so distant from the vital U.S. national interest that the interventions were not even regarded as wars at all, and those who waged those "other-than-wars," upon their returns, were not even thought of as combat veterans coming home. These "deployments" were seen as nonwars with consequences of a strategic and political importance, but not much in terms of consequences for national defense and security.

Those of us who "fought" these nonwars during the 1990s were not even graded on wins or losses. And perhaps that is a good thing, since the official record tells a rather bleak story, a tale of war-fare that saw "too little" of American power and reputation applied "too late" to crisis situations, and when it was applied, applied "not long enough" to make an effective difference. When I returned home from my overseas tour in Europe, where I had been involved in support of our intervention in the Balkans, I returned with the sense that the tactical actions my soldiers and I had taken on the ground had had an effective impact, but also with the feeling that those tactical actions and activities had not measured up to, and would not measure up to, a substantial strategic win. Moreover, I was left with the sense that every tactical action that we failed to make in these "nonwars" was having some unforeseeable consequence on the strategic environment and America's reputation in that environment. It seemed at the time that these "other-than-war" experiences and our tactical actions in them were in some way impotent in their capacity to solve the broader systemic problems underlying them. How impotent, why, and at what future cost were still questions of curiosity by the late 1990s. On 11 September 2001 these questions took on a stark relevance.

Beyond 9/11

Since the attacks of 9/11, we have all suffered from this impotence, this now *post-modern* paradox. By any measure, the combat actions taken by our soldiers and "other-than-war" operators on the ground and within every "hot" theater of operation in this global war on terrorism have had substantial positive results. The tactical prowess of our war-fighters, at the war-fighting level, remains unmatched and unmatchable. The same holds true for America's unmatchable skill at winning the peace locally (i.e., village by village). Yet, it also cannot be disputed that America's intervention policy and war and peace strategies have so far failed to bring about lasting peace, security, and prosperity.

Rome was not built in a day. And that is a fact that all of us need to remind ourselves of when we question why we have not "won" the war in Iraq, in Afghanistan, and at home. And if we are blatantly honest about it, if we reconsider our war-experience during World War II as a war that actually began with Hitler's rise in the mid-1930s, progressing through the reconstruction of battle-torn Europe and the reintegration of Germany into the international community of nation-states, the "decisive victory" of World War II was not a four-year venture in pure combatives that achieved an "unconditional surrender." Rather, World War II was a holistic war of uncertain victory over a period of 20 years (1935–1955), by rough estimate. In light of this, should we be surprised that there is still instability in Afghanistan, six years after the initial defeat of the Taliban regime, and still an insurgency raging in Iraq, more than four years after the initiation of combat operations in that country (and a declaration of "mission accomplished" by the U.S. president, George W. Bush). We absolutely have to be more honest with ourselves regarding what it will truly take to finish and finish well and completely in these major operations.

What is troubling to me, however, and what is and should be of growing concern and suspicion among a majority of Americans when it comes to Iraq in particular and the GWOT more generally, is that there does not appear to be any coordinated rhyme or reason to how we are prosecuting operations, whether it be close-with-to-destroy or close-with-to-restore operations, in this theater of war. Moreover, the grand strategy, which could tie what we are doing in Iraq to what we are doing in other theaters of operation (including the American homeland), and purpose of those actions and activities through an integration with war-policy that is grand and as publicly transparent as possible remains absent. A CBS News Poll conducted 11–16 June 2005 indicated 59% public disapproval of the war in Iraq (2007 reveals a similar public opinion, with a reported 57% of Americans seeing the United States losing the war). That public disappointment in the war-policy comes in the face of extremely high marks being given by the public in support of its soldiers in the field. The irony of this is sharp and deserves close attention.

Unlike in Vietnam, where my father and veteran soldiers like him received the scorn of a disappointed, confused, and ungrateful American public, I and my comrades have been received warmly and continue to be held in a sort of protective bubble even as public concern and scorn turn against the war-policy itself. Even though I am happy to not have to endure the pain and suffering my dad endured, I am still similarly confused and disappointed, as he was back then, about the impotence of our intervention policies. The blood and money we shed in our war-fights and peace efforts suddenly appear not good enough to *win the peace*.

Those of us who have served on the ground have seen daily the destruction of enemy forces, the rebuilding of governments and local economies and schools and civic life. It is unbelievably frustrating having seen and participated in such local "successes" to witness the limits of those individual tactical acts in their capacity to "turn" or convert local wins into countrywide victory. Even though I know that winning will take much more time and effort, I also know that the manner in which we are approaching the implementation of our intervention policy in Iraq as well as other operational theaters is yielding local and regional "stalemates." I fear that if we do not think of new ways of leveraging these local actions into theaterwide and strategic wins, this stalemate situation (winning the lethal battles against insurgents and terrorists but muddling through in our efforts to reconstruct stable civil societies and to "counter" the rise of global insurgency) might lead to losing Iraq, the wider war and the peace intended to follow, and ourselves as a nation in the process.

In a letter to his wife Abigail dated 12 May 1780, during some of the darkest days of the American Revolution—this young country's insurgency against the British government—John Adams wrote the following:

> I must study politics and war that my sons may have liberty to study mathematics and philosophy.

My father struggled with the irony of war and peace his entire adult life. It seems that I will do so as well. In a small way this book serves as a letter to the American public and republic. In the effort, I hope to ignite a spark among those who read this work to commit to rethinking and acting anew in our understandings and approaches to how we intervene, through our actions in war and in peace, so that the generations that follow may have liberty to know more than war and the politics that determine it.

Acknowledgments

I am above all grateful to the "peace-makers" (blessed be they), whether they be the soldier, the humanitarian worker, or the peace-keeper, for their devotion to peace, prosperity, and humanity. The opportunities I have had to bear witness to their good works—*their pure and noble courage*—I will forever cherish. It is my hope that this work does theirs the justice it deserves.

We live in trying, tumultuous, and dangerous times. The physical dangers that come on the battlefields and the peace and humanitarian fronts we readily and easily recognize. But these are also times that challenge and test our minds, our hearts, and our souls. Overcoming all the challenges and risks that are limiting our capacities to intervene rightly and justly and therefore adding to the threats against our republic demands intellectual courage as much as it does physical, heroic courage; perhaps more so. Standing up and speaking the truth, with absolute candor, to power has been and remains a risky business. Much of the risk is of our own making. The promise of rich and successful careers, power, and glory combines with the threat of losing those riches to create and foster environments within all of our fields of practice that make standing up as the change-agent—the heretic—a dangerous and often career-ending enterprise.

These days, it is hard to be the professional. Yet professionals (and professions) do still exist. There is still an American republic. And again, the opportunities I have had to witness these individuals in action, and to fight alongside a few of them, has given me hope that effective change will come our way—that it is not too late to effect a change, to change our course as a nation and as a legitimate force of intervention.

I have chosen not to mention any of these individuals by name. As quiet professionals, they do not need or want such recognition, and as agents of change, we cannot afford to put them at career risk—we need their good works to continue.

To the Iraqi people, and all those who are living in countries and nations struggling to create an environment of life, liberty, prosperity, egalitarianism, peace, and security for themselves and their posterity, I offer my humble thanks and my continued commitment to the community we share in this important global cause.

I owe a special thanks to the Council on Foreign Relations. During the 2005–06 period I served as an International Affairs Fellow (IAF) in-residence at the Council's New York City office. The time afforded to me during this fellowship year to research, to think—and to rethink—greatly contributed to the completion of the writing of this book. While any faults or flaws that may lie in this work fall fully on my shoulders, the opportunities afforded to me by the CFR clearly contributed to any successes that may come from this work.

Last, but always, to my wife Lauren and my kids, David, Spenser, and Mae, thank you for your love and for giving me a wonderful life outside of my public responsibilities. I hope that this humble work helps in some way to make America, ripe with the potential for greatness, truer to its ideals and, as such, a better place for you to live and thrive.

Part I

Beyond War

The chapters in this part presage the discussion of a "new age" of war with the important review of where we find ourselves at present—still *waging modern war*.[1] Before thinking anew, we must first reconsider the old—and the current—ideas, traditions, doctrines, practices of, and justifications for *modern war* and its conduct.

A popular and seminal debate has raged among military scholars and practitioners for at least the past 20 years; it is a discussion that continues to this day: are we experiencing a period of revolutionary change in geostrategic relations, a change that has brought about a *revolution in military affairs* (RMA)? The fact that we are even having the wide debate over the RMA is testament to at least a growing perception of a gap between *war* as we have known it and practiced it in the "past" and an older, premodern conception of *war* as reintroduced to us, particularly since September 11, 2001. For the purposes of this book, whether this tectonic rumble meets the prerequisites of a bona fide RMA is irrelevant. What counts is that the debate validates and legitimizes the notion that some sort of change is upon us, negatively impacting our war-waging and peace-winning effectiveness.

Chapter 1 introduces the idea of a paradox within the American (and Western) ways of war and peace—a paradox between how the nation intervenes and the effectiveness or success of those interventions. This chapter raises several important questions that become the subject of discussion in later chapters of the book. One of these important questions is whether the paradox even exists; if so, how do we know it when we see it? Another key question raised in this first chapter centers on the current case of the U.S. war in Iraq, asking, if the paradox exists and is present in Iraq as it was in our earlier experiences in Vietnam, can this paradox be overcome.

Chapter 2 explores the *three generations of modern war and war-fare*, describing the evolution of U.S. and Western military theory, doctrine, and practice from the seventeenth-century *age of dynastic war* up to the twentieth-century *age of mechanized warfare*. This walk through history reveals the birth of the modern-day (and present day) paradox, born of unwitting parents: the organizational structural and procedural design of our war-making systems and the cultural proclivities of the modern military services and professionals.

Chapter 3 goes beyond modernity, exploring the transition from modernity, benchmarked by the end of the cold war, to the dawn of the postmodern age of war and peace, presented here as that period during the 1990s that found the United States taking its first intervention policy steps in its *unipolar moment* as the lone standing superpower leading up to the terror attacks on the U.S. homeland on September 11, 2001. The attacks of 9/11 confirm the *dawn of the postmodern age*, the birth of a policy of democratization as the established the *national security strategy of the United States* and dawn of a new American way of intervention. This chapter examines this transition and offers some propositions for a new theory, organization, and operational approach to guide and legitimize U.S. intervention policy for the twenty-first century.

Chapter 4 then provides a discussion on modern-era military planning, offering some propositions on postmodern planning.

Chapter 1

The Paradox of the American Way of War and Peace

"You know you never defeated us on the battlefield," said the American colonel. The North Vietnamese colonel pondered this remark a moment. "That may be so," he replied, "but it is also irrelevant."

Summers, *On Strategy*, 1, conversation in Hanoi, April 1975

We're fighting a war up here too . . . . We're just not whining about it!

Planner's Journal, conversation in Mosul, Iraq, September 2003

For Americans, the Vietnam War has become our own "Greek Tragedy"; our Pyrrhic victory,[1] where despite a record of dramatic victory over enemy forces, conventional and guerrilla, on the ground in battle after battle, American soldiers and their nation lost the war and, more importantly, the peace that was intended to follow. Surviving that loss and recovering from it as a nation, physically and psychologically, took over 20 years. Many of our own did not survive; others survived but never fully recovered. All in all, we overcame. Yet, we never really fully understood exactly what happened to us in that war. Why did we lose? How could we lose—a superpower facing a premodern and unsophisticated army—as a great nation fighting in only a "small war"?[2] How could we have lost, particularly after winning every battle and engagement in the war?

Time passed, and as it did, we as Americans learned to live well enough. We learned to live with and accept what had happened to us "over there" and to move on.

Our *certain victory* in Operation Desert Storm, 1990–1991, excused us from any further thinking on why and how we lost in Vietnam two decades earlier.[3] Defeat of Saddam Hussein's army in only 100 hours of armored ground war-fare was proof enough to convince us all that we had recovered well and completely from whatever went wrong in that past war. We convinced ourselves that Vietnam was an anomaly. As a war, it was anathema to the traditional sorts of wars nations such as America intended to fight. We had convinced ourselves that our loss in Vietnam was as much of an anomaly as was the war itself. We placed Vietnam in the category of limited or "small" wars and in so doing all but openly declared the entire category suspect of the types and character of wars worthy of a great power like the United States' participation and commitment.

This American sentiment framed the manner of when, where, and how we intervened in the "crises" (note: not *wars*) of the 1990s, or post–cold war era. Somewhat as a direct consequence of seeing this decade of conflict characteristic of something "other" than traditional wars and war-fare, America's intervention record during the 1990s is one well described as *incomplete finishes*—"too little, too late, and for not long enough." Somalia, Rwanda, Haiti, the Balkans, and Kosovo are, in hindsight, examples of the unintended consequences of this too little, too late approach to U.S. intervention policy, and after the wake-up call of 9/11, we can see that the World Trade Center bombing of 1993, the attack on the Murrow Building in Oklahoma City, the calamities to New Orleans and the Gulf Coast brought about by Hurricane, and other similar "other-than-war" incidents "at home" are also a testament to a too little, too late view of the new reality surrounding us.

Today, we find ourselves stretched to the extreme in war-fights in Iraq, Afghanistan, at home, and, truly, across the four corners of the globe if we are to take the rhetoric of this being an era of *global war on terror* literally. Increasingly, the public language surrounding these wars and putting context to them is taking on a tenor more and more similar to that of the Vietnam War era—of the very type of complex unconventional wars that Vietnam was and the sort of wars we as a nation had sworn we would never fight again.

Public Opinion on the Iraq War

Polls show a dramatic (and rapid) degradation of public support for the war in Iraq since the initiation of major ground combat operations in Spring 2003. At the time of this writing (late July 2005), a *Washington Post*-ABC News Poll showed a declining trend in public approval of how the president has handled the situation in Iraq, with a shift in support ranging from about 68 % approval in June 2003 to around a 58 % disapproval rating as of June 2005. The disapproval rating was 72% in May 2007 as per the CBS News/*New York Times* Poll of May 18–23, 2007.[4]

Most interesting is the crossover point in public support, which seems to have occurred in Spring 2004—about the same time of the first large-scale U.S. force rotation, the Battle of Fallujah, and around the time of the transfer of sovereignty to the Interim Iraqi Governing Council, June 30, 2004. The potential correlation between these critical *transitions* and the "transition" of public support for the administration to disapproval is an intriguing point of study. A second polling example (*Washington Post*-ABC News, July 8, 2005) focused on the cost of the war in Iraq; the poll surveyed respondents by asking them to make a cost-benefit-based decision—*has the war been worthy of the casualties, and, more generally, worth fighting in light of overall cost?* The results were stark. Those 58 % of public respondents who found the loss of American soldiers a worthy sacrifice back in April 2003 (regime collapse and "mission accomplished!") had dwindled to only 25 % by May–June 2005. Those 34 % who in April 2003 found the casualties of this war unacceptable had expanded to 73 % by June 2005.

Overall, by mid-Summer 2005, public opinion polls in the United States were indicating upward of 58 % of the public finding the war in Iraq not worth fighting. Those polls also showed an America divided, increasingly by opinion over the war, into "red" (i.e., Republicans) versus "blue" (i.e., Democrats) partisan factions.

Staunch die-hard Republicans seemed to side with the administration (73 % in support of the war), while the equally but ideologically oppositely extreme Democrats saw the war negatively (83 % against the war). The rise of an "independent" opinion against the worthiness of the war (63 %) is perhaps the most informative result of these polls, since it implies that the growing American sentiment against the war in Iraq might be more than a partisan-political disagreement. Americans may truly be turning away from the administration's policy and practices in Iraq for systemic and substantial reasons. For those who have always been prone, for various reasons, to draw the parallels of this war to Vietnam, such indicators of public sentiment add more to their extrapolations. For those of us who have held firm to our skepticisms and reluctances to make the comparison, such indicators force us to finally take harder looks at the possibility of this war becoming another Vietnam.

The Paradox of the American Way of War and Peace

What do I mean by "the paradox of the American way of war"? Simply put, the paradox describes our national tendency, in what we regard as limited or "small wars," to *win all the battles but still lose the war*. This tendency was sealed in public sentiment in the aftermath of our experiences in limited war-fare in Vietnam. That sentiment has returned in the context of our latest and ongoing foray in "small warfare"—Iraq. This time, the paradox was popularized during the 2004 presidential campaign in a slogan coined by Senator John Kerry, the challenger to President Bush and a critic of America's approach to the war in Iraq : "[W]hy did we have a plan to 'win the war' in Iraq, but none to 'win the peace'?"[5]

Both slogans, past and present, aptly describe the paradox, but neither provide a useful *explanation* for its existence or for its persistence. That is not to say that efforts were not made, post-Vietnam, to provide some answers to the loss of that war, nor that similar efforts are not being made today to pinpoint causes of our "tenuous position" in Iraq.

The paradox goes well beyond Iraq, and Vietnam before. The paradox is systemic and chronic and extreme in its consequences on this nation's capacity to *fight and win*. Many scholars have studied the existence of this paradox, despite not labeling the phenomenon as such. An evocative body of research has emerged over the past five years or so that has addressed the phenomenon in the form of questions as to why Great Powers seem to be losing, with greater frequency, small wars to small or nonstate actors and, more specifically, why (and how) democracies tend to lose small wars. A majority of these studies have been in the form of longitudinal (quantitative, large sample size) studies—macro studies attempting to capture and chronicle the existence of this phenomenon.

A recent study by Patricia Sullivan, Associate Professor of Political Science at Georgia State University summarizes the "paradox" this way:

> Despite their immense war-fighting capacity, major power states failed to attain their primary political objective in almost 40 % of their military operations against weak state and non-state targets since 1945. Why do strong states frequently fail to achieve even limited objectives when they use military force against vastly weaker targets? Evidence from recent research suggests that war outcomes are largely a function of strategic

> selection (war initiation), military-industrial capabilities, combat effectiveness, and strategy choice. But none of these factors can explain why a major power would ever lose an armed conflict with a weak target.[6]

Sullivan's longitudinal study using an original data set of 127 post–World War II major power military intervention cases of her own construction is a powerful contribution to the subject literature as it empirically confirms to some degree the existence of the paradox itself. Rather than focusing on the usual suspect causes—strategic selection and choice, military-industrial capabilities, and combat effectiveness—Sullivan focuses her attention on the key variable of war-aims as a prime cause for why strong states lose wars to weaker opponents.[7] By war-aims, Sullivan is intimating that the type of war waged—whether the war is a "total and symmetrical war" versus a "limited and asymmetrical war of limited political objective"—matters and carries much if not all of the explanatory water for the paradox. Another highly acclaimed study by Gil Merom focused on the micro variables (domestic sources) that might explain the paradox—in his words, "how democracies fail in small wars in spite of their military superiority."[8]

Sullivan and Merom, and the scholarship their works represent, ground their propositions in the notion that the type of war really matters, and in doing so intimate that strong states—Great Powers and democracies such as the United States—do better against foes when the wars are "total" in scope and political objective and when those wars are fought against foes that respect and abide by the "conventions" of modern military art and science. In short, strong democratic states do well in conventional wars, more so than they do against nontraditional foes using nonconventional methods. In intimating this, I argue that both bodies of scholarship are promoting rather than dispelling a collective misunderstanding of war and war-fare and, as a consequence, unintentionally feeding the paradox.

The Other Side of War—Holistic War

This study, in addition to examining the "military side" of war-policy, also explores what I will call "the other side of war-policy"—the paradox of America's ways of "peace." In so doing, I am intimating a new idea of what constitutes "war" itself and implying a new relationship between war (as a policy process) and peace (as the political objective from which the policy process of "war" derives and finds its ultimate purpose). This new concept of war and peace—holistic war—denies past considerations of an antithetical relationship between war and peace and the separate functions of war and peace. A holistic war construction sees beyond the arbitrary distinctions of capabilities traditionally defined as those of "limited wars" versus "total wars" versus nonwars (other-than-wars) and promotes the development of a new paradigm that sees war in terms of its political purpose instead of its mere martial functions. When we view war and peace in this way, we can see peace as the ultimate political objective that determines and defines the value of all tools of national and international power, not only the military instrument of power, but also nonmartial tools at the nation-state's (or nonstate actor's) disposal. By seeing war in a holistic manner, we can appreciate the military warrior and the peace activist/operator as one-and-the-same united by policy purpose (political war-aim, that being peace) in spite of being separate in their policy roles and functions.

So far, the discussion of the paradox has been limited to the anemia of our martial war-winning effectiveness. But thinking holistically, we can appreciate that not only does the paradox negatively affect the martial side of war-policy, but the nonmilitary functions of war-policy. Just as the United States and most Western advanced military states are suffering in their capacity to turn big wins in their military strategies—their "war-policies"—so too are they failing to "win the peace" beyond the local levels. While there have not been to date any longitudinal studies similar to Sullivan's or qualitative case study analyses similar to Merom's focused on exploring the effect of the paradox on America's (and Western society's) peace operations, it is strongly proposed here that a similar paradox haunts the peace community in its efforts to convert localized (village-to-village) successes into countrywide, strategic "peace wins."

This book argues that unless we address the impacts of the paradox on both sides of America's intervention policy, our interventions will continue to fail to win the peace in spite of their separate successes at "winning" at the locales. In order to attain peace and stability that is lasting, legitimate, and sustainable, military functions and capabilities must be realigned and interwoven with nonwar (other-than-war) functions and capabilities for the creation of a holistic approach of peace and war.

"No More Vietnams"

Can We Prevent Iraq from Becoming Our Next Vietnam?

Was Saddam Hussein accurate when he said to the United States and its broad and united coalition in 1991 that "this [Gulf War] is the mother of all battles?" Was Saddam right and were we wrong? And are we now paying for it in Iraq and beyond? Have we thought too little and far too "small" of the type of war Vietnam was for us and inadvertently placed ourselves, and perhaps those who willingly followed us, on another pathway to a similar *march to folly*, this time in Iraq? Is it too late to change course and avoid the history lesson of the ages? Can we reconcile our *song of arms*[9] with our national ideals and with our reasons for singing the song in the first place, in Iraq and beyond?

This book is an attempt to explain why, in our American way of war, we seem to have a tendency to fail to secure the peace in our war-efforts—our intervention policies—despite our capacity to win all of the battles for peace along the way. It attempts to explain this "paradox" in a way that goes beyond the usual explanations that tend to center on either partisan-political-based criticisms or on the technical and arcane tactical descriptions of the paradox *in-action*. The descriptions and explanations offered here focus on the "how" behind our way of war—the mechanics of operational war-planning and war execution—and how those mechanics can impact, both positively and negatively, the effectiveness of our purposes and strategies in war. Our paradox is a failure in the American process of war. This book examines that process in search of causes and possible solutions.

The Paradox of the American Way of War in Vietnam

Answers to the Vietnam War-loss (or better said, *loss of the peace*) ranged from explanations that spoke to a "regression in military thought" among military practitioners, in the views of the limits of the armed forces' mission, to explanations based on the sheer "dereliction of duty" of senior military leadership and their collective failures to "speak the truth to Power" to the civilian decision makers deciding the war.[10] Between these bodies of analyses came volumes of rich descriptive histories on the war, perhaps one of the best "soldier accounts" being offered by Dave R. Palmer in *Summons of the Trumpet*.[11]

On Strategy and Its Unintended Consequences for the American Way of War and Peace

Colonel Harry Summers' accounting of the Vietnam War-loss, *On Strategy*, had and still has an enormous impact inside and outside military circles. In the work, Summers spoke to a situation of "tactical victory, strategic defeat." In doing so, he introduced the frustrations and the anecdotes of the paradox from the U.S. Army's perspective: "that as far as logistics and tactics were concerned we succeeded in everything we set out to do . . . . [y]et in the end, it was North Vietnam, not the United States, that emerged victorious."[12] Summers's answers centered on failures to factor in the will of the American public into the war-policy and on *application errors*—errant and imprecise and inadequate allocations and applications of military power to established political objectives. The work also explored the notion that part of the cause of defeat was in a failure of strategists to see Vietnam as a war, a near-sighted condition perpetuated by academic limited war theorists such as Robert Osgood and Thomas Schelling. The "limited war signaling strategy" these theorists adopted and offered to the Johnson administration saw the war, and limited wars like it, as an essentially diplomatic instrument, a tool for signaling and bargaining with the enemy, rather than for fighting.[13] To paraphrase Summers's explanation, the "seeing" of the war as a nonwar, in light of what we as an army had come to know war to be, first, by limited theory scholars and then by the policy makers they advised, contributed to the tactics-strategy mismatch, the paradox, and the loss of the war in Vietnam.

The Summers description of the tactics-strategy gap during his experiences in Vietnam applies similarly to my own experiences with the Iraq War, both as a scholar and as a war-rior. Yet, the conclusions that Summers drew from his earlier experiences with the "paradox" and the lessons our military drew from those conclusions, I propose, have been the wrong lessons learned—lessons that perpetuate rather than dispel the bane of the paradox on our contemporary approaches to war and its peace-objectives.

Gathering Wrong Lessons and Rebuilding an Army upon Them

As Summers correctly noticed, until the writing of his book in the 1980s, most Vietnam War "histories" ended with the Tet Offensive of 1968. He saw this limited historical recording of the war as a contributor to a common knowledge and understanding of the war-loss in Vietnam as an American loss of a guerrilla (i.e., small) war, "a loss caused by a failure to appreciate the nuances of counterinsurgency war."[14] Colonel Summers also correctly noted that the war persisted for an additional seven years after the Tet Offensive. What Summers concluded from this broader chronology of the war are conclusions that I argue were in error at the time of publishing of *On Strategy*. Those errant lessons were then accepted by the U.S. Army and used to legitimize radical reforms to U.S. Army doctrine, organization, and tactics; the conclusions continue to plague us in Iraq, Afghanistan, and other potential operations in the global war on terror.

The impact of Colonel Harry Summers's analysis of the Vietnam War-loss on the reformation of the U.S. Army and the American way of war and the impacts of those reforms on today's challenges in American war-policy cannot be understated, nor should they be underappreciated by the public. Summers was right in recognizing the "whole" historical chronology of the Vietnam War but was wrong in his characterization of earlier "histories" that defined the war up until Tet as a "counterinsurgency war" that we "won" as opposed to his categorization of the latter (post-Tet) seven years of the *war* as a "conventional" war that we lost. I argue that Summers was as wrong in this sort of "limiting" of the characterization of war as were the "limited war theorists" who narrowly defined the war as only useful as a tool of diplomatic signaling. This split characterization of the Vietnam War, as first-half, guerilla war, second-half, conventional war led Summers (and the U.S. Army that followed his conclusions) to an even more consequential conclusion: that the "key to understanding our failure did not lie in counterinsurgency theory, but in the long-since-discarded theories of conventional war."[15]

What Summers may have done is unwittingly contribute to the delinquency of a nation and its armed forces, a nation with a long tradition of seeing war as separable halves—conventional wars and limited wars. As Summers concluded in his foreword to the 1995 edition of *On Strategy*, "[T]he quintessential 'strategic lesson learned' from the Vietnam War is that we must once again become masters of the profession of arms . . . [t]he Persian Gulf War a decade later was proof positive that the Armed Forces of the United States has done just that."[16]

In this book, I argue that these conclusions rather than solving for the "tactical victory, strategic failure" paradox, instead, has contributed to its continuance.

Today's "Postmodern" Paradox

As I have seen it, and as the war in Iraq continues to demonstrate to us, the true quintessential strategic lesson *to-be-learned* from the Vietnam War experience, and now Iraq, is that in addition to, once again, becoming masters of the *profession of arms*, we must become the masters of the *professions of war and peace*.

Where yesterday's paradox was one of seeing war as two separate halves of a single military instrument of power, today's paradox is one of not knowing of war beyond the martial tools, of not knowing war as one of many policy processes that seek a quality of peace as a product of that process, as well as a result of the politics that form that policy, and of not knowing of war as a domestic policy as much as it is a foreign one. Today's paradox reflects to a great degree an outdated lock-in to the modern laws of war, which saw war as limited to the jurisdictions of the military combatant and all other activities as nonwar, or "other-than-war." This modern-era perception of what constitutes a "war" gathers reinforcement when we look back at the victories of World Wars I and II, and more recently the Gulf War of 1990–1991. These wars were "great wars" because they were wars largely fought by and between nation-states for traditional material, territorial, and moral reasons and because they were large-scale wars of conventional fighting forces—tanks, artillery, and mass troop formations. Yet, the modern era shows a record of hundreds of more "other-than" category "incidents" that by any commonly accepted tactical assessment merited credit as "wars" but nevertheless remained known as nonwar, police actions, small wars, and the like. One could say a reason why our "Forgotten War" in Korea was all but forgotten is because of its ambiguity (was it a war or a "police action"?) and because of its less-than-decisive conclusion (stalemate). That may also be the reason for our view of our other "other-than-war" experiences: in the Balkans, Somalia, Haiti, Rwanda, Kosovo, and in other like "crises" during the 1990s. These "wars" were surely not "great" wars, but by all established theories and definitions of war, these were wars too.

Today's paradox of the American way of war and peace is a legacy of our failings to draw and learn from the *entire war* in Vietnam, as well as a legacy of our refusals to regard the small wars we waged and fought throughout the decade following the post–Gulf War victory as "wars." It is a legacy passed down through the professional ethos of the U.S. armed forces, a culture that defines war and the war-rior based on the lethal and martial functions of battle, with offensively "closing with to destroy" enemy forces as its defining tenet—its purpose—rather than the core function of its myriad functions intended to bring about attainment of the political peace-objective. It is a legacy that was revived and justified in Colonel Summers's conclusions in *On Strategy*: that the war-loss in Vietnam was more due to the U.S. Army's over-emphasis of counterinsurgency war-fare and, consequently, its lack of emphasis on traditional conventional war-fighting. This oversimplified characterization of the war-loss in Vietnam gave the U.S. armed forces the excuse it was looking for to ignore the hard lessons gathered during the guerilla operations (i.e., that the purpose or political objective of all wars is the attainment of the peace-objective—the winning of hearts and minds and the suasion of populations) and instead to focus its attention and resources—for the next 30 years—on renewing its conventional tactics, techniques, and procedures (TTPs) in mechanized, major combat operations (MCO).

Not to be misunderstood, getting back to the old modern conventional basics was a valuable and important lesson learned from the Vietnam experience and the Summers insights of that experience. These lessons yielded important battle victories in the Gulf War and have provided the United States with the preeminent conventional fighting force on the planet. Nevertheless, while learning those conventional lessons was a necessary step toward defeat of America's paradox, it was always insufficient as an overall cure in and of itself to the paradox. Our war in Iraq is the most current case in point.

The Paradox of the American Way of War and Peace in Iraq

The rapid, and seemingly *decisive* at the time, combat operations of the ground campaign in Iraq, March–April 2003, were exemplar of the tactical prowess of the U.S. military. At the theater-strategic and national strategic levels, victories in battles and engagements also seemed to have validated much of the doctrinal revision and institutional reorganization undertaken by the U.S. Army following the end of the American war in Vietnam, "validated" during the Gulf War, and continued during the 12-year interregnum between Desert Storm and Operation Iraqi Freedom

(OIF). Every battle during the major offensive phases of OIF was "won" by U.S. and coalition forces. However, almost simultaneous with the collapse of the Hussein regime came a slowing and wandering of the U.S. war-plan and war-effort in Iraq. By the end of the first year, a full 10 months later than the administration and the Department of Defense expected U.S. military forces to be in Iraq, pundits, practitioners, policy wonks, and the public alike were openly questioning the progress of our actions in the war. Today, polls show a dramatic decline in public confidence of the war's "winnability" and, consequently, a significant rise in public skepticism over how good an original idea it was to initiate war in Iraq in the first place. In less than two years after President Bush declared mission accomplished in Iraq, we went from "we won!" to "are we winning yet?" to "can we win at any rate?" This "losing" sentiment comes in the face of unquestionable "wins" on the ground at the tactical levels of the war, both in terms of destruction missions against insurgent and terrorist forces and in terms of reconstruction activities throughout the country.

As Colonel Summers asked in his war, I ask in mine, "[H]ow could we have succeeded so well, yet [be failing] so miserably?"[17]

Are We Organizationally Prone to Paradoxical War-fare?

Can the question be answered as an unintended consequence of a recently adopted preemptive approach to war? Or can it be answered as a manifestation of an American *cult of the offensive* in our national security policy? Does cause and culpability lie with the Bush administration and Bush Doctrine itself—the agenda for America's preemptive war in Iraq? Does fault lie with the armed forces, and its derived capabilities-based war-fare approach, divined in the 2001 *Quadrennial Defense Review* and the 2002 *National Military Strategy*, in the aftermath of the 9/11 attacks on the American homeland?

Surely, some of the causes can be found in the agenda (how it was set, why it was set the way it was set) and in the implementation plans (the Pentagon's and Office of the Secretary of Defense' (OSD's) force design, organization, and resourcing for the war-effort). Many agenda-setting and implementation explanations have already been offered.[18] However, like their predecessor works of the post-Vietnam years, most of these works offer opinions (all too often, partisan-based) and describe the conundrum and point the accusing finger rather than provide any useful explanations for why the paradox persists in our war-policy toward Iraq or practical solutions to the paradox. Few if any of these explanations *satisfy* from a policy science point of view. Fewer even address the general public's concerns. That is, no recent explanation identifies a cause (or series of causes) that can actually be affected through a policy reform. This book seeks to provide a fresh alternative.

The cultural legacies of our modern organizations for war-policy, war-planning, and war-fighting may have entrenched us in a recipe for war that no longer satisfies our appetites in war. The very way we have structured ourselves for war and developed our cultural understanding of what war "is" vice what it is not has undoubtedly effected how we plan for war and our many forms of intervention policy, what we plan for in war, and what we do not plan for—even how we have determined to "fight." Whether those "cultural understandings" and how they have been embedded in our war-policy institutions have lessened or added to the paradox of our way of war and peace is a significant yet often ignored research question and one that, if addressed in a comprehensive way, could provide some useful answers.

Do We Control the Paradox or Does the Paradox Control Us?

In this book, I offer that though we have the power to capture and control the paradox within our way of peace and war, what we have witnessed surely throughout the twentieth century and during this first-half of the first decade of the twenty-first century—and currently in Iraq—reflects an inability to see the errors in our organized ways and a failure to control the paradox within our organized ways of war.

A study of the organizational evolution of U.S. military—its doctrinal and procedural developments, as well as its force designs and war-waging capabilities—offers insights (empirical and anecdotal) that strongly relate (correlate) the prevailing nature of the paradox to organizational and cultural causes.

The American Institution of War—*A Sign of the Times*

Institutions matter because they persist. That is one reason why we build them—to preserve that which we hold dear. For examples of this, we can offer the more profound and obvious institutionalization of our American Creed and ways of governance and civil society in our Declaration of Independence, Constitution, and Executive, Legislative, and Judicial branches of government. We have institutionalized our collective sense of liberty, rights, and due process under the rule of law within our Bill of Rights. We have preserved our desires for freedom of speech in the First Amendment and the laws, ethics, and informal conventions of our media. Even at a personal level, institutions matter. Families "institutionalize" their histories in genealogies, photos, and scrapbooks. They ensure the preservation of the family legacies and traditions through last wills and testaments, and even through the birth of their children. Again, we institutionalize in order to protect and preserve. This is why our institutions matter.

We do the same when it comes to protecting and preserving our national way of war and peace. Our modern "military traditions" are our "American family legacy" of our war-experiences, war-wins, and war-losses. During the earliest days of this United States, the Army was the nation, as an idea, in physical (institutional) form—it was the nation even before there was a nation. This tradition adds a unique aspect to the institution of the U.S. military and its relationship to the American republic. Just as our children and their public behavior are a reflection (good or bad) of their parents and "the family," so too is our way of war and peace (our way of intervening) a direct reflection of who we are as a nation. For Western military societies, our combined ways of war are a reflection of who we are as a "family of nations." How we behave in war reflects us.

But sometimes institutions persist even when the prevailing times call for and warrant a change. The resiliency of our American "institutions" is due to a built-in "flex" intended by the Founders—to allow for gradual change while also providing for stable preservations of bedrock ideals and principles. The American family is no longer a reflection of "Leave it to Beaver" 1950s traditions (though some would have it so). It has even evolved beyond its "Nuclear Family" portrait of just a decade and a half ago. Some family traditions are always to be preserved—a truth for families, the national family, and our Western family of nations—if we are to remain "the Smiths," "the Americans," and "the West." But those traditions that time proves no longer useful or outdated or even as suspect and uncivil in contemporary society should and must be discarded, all on behalf of cleansing the institutions and updating them for contemporary times and conditions. The amendment process within our Constitution is such a cleansing mechanism—an institution designed to "modernize" American civic society without weakening its bedrock foundations. The incorporation of these sorts of change mechanisms within our institutions has been key in keeping America "free" or at least keeping us moving along on a path toward greater inclusion and toward our ideal-type self-image as a nation. Such mechanisms have helped to preserve balance between our ideals and our behaviors—they have helped avoid paradox between ideals and actions. If our nation had avoided these sorts of "cleansings," we might have remained a slave nation much longer; women may have lingered as "noncitizens" denied the vote.

Families have similar mechanisms—they must or risk stagnation in old outmoded traditions, some of which no longer remain consistent with American societal norms. Many families hold on too long and too hard to past "sensibilities"—"marry only within the family religion, the family 'color,' the family political party tradition"—often causing rifts among families and internal splits within a single family that reach a point of conflict, maybe even "death of the family."

We must look at and consider our war traditions in a similar way. Much of our modern military traditions deserve and demand preservation, protection, and promotion into the next era. They have served us well in the past, continue to do so today, and have a great promise of continuing to do so in the future. They reflect the "right" ideals and credos of what it means to be an American or a member of Western society and, in that sense, are a useful and effective and morally legitimate means of exampling the American and Western tradition to other societies. Some of our traditions have become "overcome by events" and are no longer an accurate *sign of the times* but rather ghost of a past that needs to be put to final rest least we be haunted by their hollow lessons. Letting go of these dysfunctional traditions and exorcizing ourselves of these "ghosts" is essential for the life and future effectiveness of our war-waging institutions and for the society that those institutions represent, protect, and defend. Moreover, clearing the mechanisms of our way of war is essential in avoiding paradox between war-policy and war-actions, assuring a potential for war-winning remains within that way of war, and ensuring that our war-policy is consistent with American traditions and seen as legitimate in the eyes and hearts of the international community.

I argue that today we live in one of those paradoxical times—where our old ways tell us to hold true and firm to how we have seen and practiced war in the past despite the messages we are receiving from foe and friend alike telling us that we must determine "another way" or risk stalemate, loss, and destruction. Here is just a snapshot of some of those warning signs:

- a longtime trend within our armed services, but particularly within its land war (Army and Marine Corps) organizations, to restrict the definition of war and warfare to the services' core competencies of "closing with to destroy" enemy forces rather than on "fighting and winning America's wars," which entail "close-with-to-destroy" and "close-with-to-restore" (full-spectrum) activities;

- a doctrine that, during the post-Vietnam reformation of the U.S. Army and its sister armed services, separated unconventional war from conventional war to the point of a general restriction of wars to martial activities (combatives and those activities that directly support military combat operations) and a limiting of the military's jurisdictions to traditional martial war-fighting;
- a military lexicon of TTPs increasingly limited to "the offensive" and lethal, "march-up-country" battle and engagement techniques;
- the emergence of war-waging units, capabilities, and force-planning (design) methodologies oriented toward organizing for "martial battle" rather than holistic war-fare;
- a legacy of planning philosophies and methodologies designed to support traditional, modern-age notions of war and war-fare;
- intervention policy anemia—an inability to "finish well and completely" in our interventions, a failure to attain a sustainable quality-of-peace or "stability" objective in our overall interventions despite our effectiveness in the tactical actions of "intervening" at the local level. This "policy anemia" is challenging us not only in our wars abroad but also in our ability to "wage peace" at home in our domestic policies;
- the dominance of our national military traditions over America's war-policy legacies and traditions resulting in a militarization of American intervention policy—at home as well as in our "foreign" policies abroad.

War Is More than Just the Combatives

"Early Histories" of the Iraq War have all paid due homage to the "pure and noble courage" of the American soldier and the unmatchable power of America's tactical "war-fighting" prowess and effectiveness. The Herculean efforts of the "soldier on the ground" are testament to that prowess and, at the same time, a validation of the paradox and its negative consequences. Our tactical expertise at waging "combatives" at the tactical level is ironically and tragically our saving grace from the absolute defeats that can come from the paradox as well as a major cause for the paradox itself. The very question our nation poses after its strange small war defeats—*how did we lose when we won all the battles?*—belies this point. Our tactical prowess deafens us to the rest of the story the paradox has to tell and blinds us from seeing much beyond the victories we achieve in localized battles and engagements. Each battle, seen singly, perpetuates our misperception of victory and "mission accomplishment," as we far too easily extrapolate one single victory within a very particular local tactical action, by assumption-making, beyond that local context and toward a broader sense of victory for the wider war. Assuming such an extrapolated victory never makes it so. Assuring a strategic-level victory (impact) from the victories we achieve in our tactical actions does not come from "hopes" but rather from deliberate planning—operational-level planning.

The blindness that comes with the paradox is severe and chronic. It can blind us completely from appreciating threats that mount, adapt, and evolve right before our eyes. General Wallace, commander of the mighty U.S. Army's 3rd Infantry Division ("Rock of the Marne") that *thunder-runned* to Baghdad and rolled over Saddam's elite Republican Guard force stated during Operation Iraqi Freedom Study Group (OIFSG) interviews that the unconventional enemy force (the Saddam Fedayeen) we encountered during the march-up-country phases of the war was "not the enemy we war-gammed against."[19] Our superior capabilities as a conventional force over Saddam's own elite conventional army made it obvious that the enemy to war-game against was the conventional force we fought against and defeated in only 100 hours of ground combat back in 1991. Perhaps we failed to war-game against the whole enemy because the whole enemy was never part of the war-idea or the war-plan? Perhaps we failed to war-game against a potential (probable) insurgent and transnational terrorist threat in Iraq because such an enemy was the stuff of unconventional wars, not conventional ones, the stuff of small rather than Great Wars?

Similarly, General Franks talked about the phenomenon of "catastrophic success" when he described in hindsight in his memoir the ambiguity that immediately followed the rapid isolation and destruction of the Saddam state apparatus. What General Franks was trying to describe was this very tragic legacy of our tactical prowess—the propensity to lose sight of the whole war because of our hyper focus on our unmatchable abilities to rapidly "win" the tactical battle (the war-fight rather than the war-policy). The credo of "fighting and winning our nation's wars" takes on a tactical context and a tactician's pallor due to the sheer power and surety of our history of and organization for tactical success. A reality of war that goes beyond that tactical tradition and conception of what constitutes "the war" as opposed to those things "other-than" the war is in jeopardy of suffering the paradox.

Closing the Gap between War and Nonwar

During my travels in and around Iraq with the OIFSG, I saw the face of war—as we have traditionally known it as well as new looks—a new face of war that in many ways is anathema of our national idea of war.[20] Our American way of war and peace is out of synch with the signs of these new times. This is particularly true in Iraq.

During major combat operations (March 19–April 9, 2003), the war on the ground near-perfectly matched the American and Western tradition. Large-scale armored and mechanized forces, combined with special operations forces, rolled northward toward Baghdad *moving to contact* with similarly organized and tempered Iraqi military forces in a set-piece series of linear battles and engagements. The march-up-country phases of the war were a perfect American *Anabasis*—a condition of war-fighting almost tailor-made to the conventional traditions of the American way of war.[21] In this sense, the "war" as we knew it from late March to early April was a limited war—limited largely to the martial activities relating to the destruction of Iraq's conventional military forces and the defeat of Saddam Hussein's formal state governing apparatus. The march up country was all about closing with the enemy to destroy him and closing with the civilian noncombatant populations to remove and protect them from the combatants. These early phases and stages of the war were familiar to us. This was a soldier's war of a type and character that we have a rich tradition of winning.

On April 9, 2003, the formal regime of Saddam Hussein collapsed under the weight of American and coalition military power. On May 1, 2003, President Bush declared mission accomplished and as such sent a warning order to all U.S. military forces in Iraq that their war was soon to be over. But it was not over on May 1, 2003. It would take a full three to four months—not until August 2003—for all military and civilian forces in Iraq to receive official confirmation that their "war" in fact had not ended and would continue.

I contend that it was this notion (that the war was about the destruction of Saddam's military and state) and this idea (that the "war" was over with the April 9 regime collapse), combined with the three to four months of "uncertainty" and recommitting the force to a longer tour of duty in Iraq that followed, that set America on a path of stalemate rather than on one of victory.

Failing to See the War beyond the Combatives

Why was our military, unmatchable in the battles of the initial phases of the war in Iraq, suddenly impotent in its ability to control the countrywide looting, to "mop up" pockets of resistance, to restore the production and distribution of countrywide essential services to prewar (Saddam-era) levels, to protect the civilian populace from crime, terror, and intimidations? For the military on the ground in Iraq a related question was the important one: why was the military still there—in Iraq—when the war had already been won by them? Had not the military done its job? The Ba'athist state was gone and Saddam was on the run. We had defeated if not destroyed Saddam's army (easier than we had anticipated, which left senior leaders a bit contemplative, but why look a gifted horse in the mouth!). Was not the military "mission complete"? The U.S. military, as of May 1, 2003, fully anticipated that it would vacate Iraq within the next three months. The U.S. military fully anticipated a full transfer of command and authorities to either a U.S. State Department agency or perhaps even to the Iraqi National Congress (INC)—an authority organized for "postwar" activities such as reconstruction and nation-building. All these anticipations, when combined with similar expectations with the U.S. Department of State, other federal agencies, and among the free Iraqi leadership as well, added up to a differentiation between the "war" and the "postwar"—a distinction between the war itself and the peace that was to follow with the collapse of the Hussein government.

Our split idea *of* the Iraq War—the war "then" (March–April 2003) and the war "now" (post-May 2003)—has never matched with the realities of the War, on the ground, in Iraq. There never was any semblance of a clean and precise dividing line between war and nonwar—between war and "the peace to follow"—in Iraq, nor has there been in any war of any other time. How we as a nation (and a Western family of nations to a similar degree) have split war and peace into separate policy domains is as arbitrary as thinking of the policy of war out of context of its purpose of peace. War is, and always has been, a process that derives from a higher purpose—peace itself. Seeing military force as an instrument of war and "other" "forces" as instruments of "other-than-war" is wrong-headed and grossly inaccurate. Peace is the ultimate political purpose of a war-policy. And the military, rather than being an instrument of war is better understood as *a war-instrument of peace*, albeit a particularly lethal instrument of peace-achievement. The military instrument of power is but one of a full spectrum of instruments of varying degrees of suasive power. *It is all war*, when we reconsider all of the actions and the activities that take place—must take place—to achieve the true strategic objective of war-policy, an acceptable state of peace.

What we have endured thus far in Iraq, and what we have caused the Iraqi people to also endure, is a crippling of the overall war-effort through a hamstringing of both the combatives and restorative phases of the war. This has come about from a failure to integrate these activities at the operational level. American combat forces are perhaps less effective than their potential because *close-with-to-destroy* operations are not integrated and synchronized well enough with preventive reconstruction activities. The converse may also be true. Civil and civic reconstruction could possibly be more effective and sustainable today if these activities where better synchronized with lethal *close-with-to-destroy* activities.

Better applications of military power, as part of an integrative civil-military way of intervention, could make more effective use of the limited resources (both civilian and military) that our nation and family of nations have determined to spend on the war in Iraq and could, through their integration, establish conditions where more expensive lethal applications of power could be avoided.

The Iraq War as *Case in Point*

This book argues that there was no operational plan for what we deemed as the Iraq "postwar." It hypothesizes that, in Iraq today, as in our past wars, we continue to plan for war as we have remained designed to know war since World War II. Failing to plan for the wholeness of this war and those before it is as much our *sin of omission* as it may be of deliberate commission. According to Vietnam War scholars, up until Tet America defined the war as a small, counterinsurgency war. From an organizational and cultural viewpoint, I am offering that because we saw the war this way, we fought that war as a "small" war. Those same scholars then recognized in the late 1970s that the latter seven years of Vietnam War was not a counterinsurgency but rather a conventional war similar to the Korean War and World War II and more reflective of our national war traditions. The popular sentiment today within martial circles stems from this post-Vietnam revision stating that from a military standpoint the war was "lost" because even though the war had become a conventional war by 1968, the U.S. military continued, errantly, to wage a counterinsurgency war.

Today's "experts" are taking part in a similar folly of semantics, referring to the Iraq "War" as first, a conventional war but now a counterinsurgency war. I say why the qualifiers? The Iraq War is a "War"—period. It has many aspects and characteristics. One size fits all and "all-or-nothing" ideas of and approaches to the war have plagued our ability to keep up with the changes in war-fighting techniques on the ground and have placed our war-policy on the brink of failure. America's problem in war is that America goes into a war wanting to fight more than wanting to restore the peace. America goes to war committed to only a particular type of war-waging—either we are fighting a conventional war or an unconventional war, or else we are waging a nonwar, keeping the peace or whatnot. But do we get to decide on what kind of war the war will be? We get a vote, but so does the enemy and the people who are amid the combatants and who endure the war in hopes of the peace that is to come. America truly believes she has a choice in the type of wars she wages, but she has never had such a choice. War is war, a collage of a wide and varied assortment of types of war-activities—some of them conventional, some unconventional (guerilla or "small"), and others humanitarian-assistance-based and nonlethal.

This view of the war and its loss gets a bit closer to the organizational and cultural design thesis offered in this book. The notion that *how we fight* is bounded and restricted by our cultural understandings of the war itself (what kind of war is it? what kind of war is it "not"?) and of the organizational designs, processes, and procedures that are born of those cultural proclivities is reflected in these limited war views and revisionist histories of the Vietnam War experience and consistent to the propositions of this work.

However, I see our national cultural bias as contributing more significantly to a less-than-complete and less-than-effective American way of war and peace. Our cultural biases of how we define war's vice activities other-than-war are engrained in how we design ourselves for war-fare and how we plan for war-fare. Those designs and those biases promote a situation of "bounded choices" and bounded actions for our war-planners and war-fighters. Moreover, they even limit our vision in determining what activities legitimately constitute war-activities and even limit who we can consider "the war-riors." In this sense, the premises of this book go even further beyond the revisionist scholars of the Vietnam era who, despite recognizing the power that organizational design and organizational culture can have on effecting the progress and outcomes of war, fell far short of acknowledging how those strictures bound our understandings of what constitutes war, nonwar, and even peace.

Beyond the Iraq War

The Iraq War, while a major case under study and a major part of the storyline, is not the only nor is it the main subject of this book. The Iraq War is an important case descriptive of the paradox that plagues America's intervention policy effectiveness—its ability (or lack thereof) to convert tactical wins into sustainable strategic-level victories and its inability to win and sustain a lasting quality of peace. The Iraq War in this sense is a means to this end—a way of describing the paradox and a way of highlighting the significance of the consequences that come in the wake of this paradox for national, regional, and international security. Thinking through our failures to overcome the paradox in our war-policy toward Iraq is an important first step in addressing and overcoming the more systemic problem: *overcoming the anemia that plagues our overall policy approach to domestic and foreign intervention.* Thinking beyond war in general—and beyond this war in Iraq—is vital to our doing better in our interventions that are surely to come in the near future.

Plan for the Book

In this book, I attempt to introduce the paradox of the American way of war and peace to a broad forum, explain its negative impacts, offering the reader some ideas and methods—some hope—for overcoming its ill effects. I endeavor to tell the story in a way that is both accessible to the general readership but also of policy-relevant value to the scholars who theorize about our ways of war, policy makers who design and "sell" our ways of war, and practitioners (civilian and military) who carry out our war-policies. By mixing storytelling (i.e., narrating tales of my own personal experiences as a war-planner in Iraq) with analysis (i.e., application of theory, historical analysis, and practicum to the stories told) I hope to convey to an equally mixed readership, an equally interesting and useful (policy-relevant) story.

The Iraq War serves as both a main subject and a proxy (case study) for a more important subject of the book—the general paradox in America's overall *way of intervening*. Therefore, while the story hopefully satisfies the current public hunger for explanations of and answers to America's dilemma in Iraq, the book in telling this story seeks to go beyond Iraq and toward answers that may hopefully allow us to say *No More Iraqs*, just as we said *No More Vietnams* years ago, but this time with a hope—and a plan—for making it so.

What this chapter has done, in effect, is introduce a *theory* for why America is suffering a paradox in its present war in Iraq (why we cannot seem to finish it and finish it "well") and, moreover, in its overall way of war and peace—my theory. In this introduction, I have shown you my cards—what I contend are the reasons for our current muddling through in Iraq and other "small wars" like Iraq. Whether or not you as the reader agree with what I offer as a possible cause will definitely determine whether or not you choose to stay with me to the end of this story. Whether or not you believe me will depend on the preponderance of supporting evidence I am able to bring to bear—to convince you that what I have to offer as both cause and partial solution merits some greater- and higher-level consideration. Historic example and analysis and the incorporation of anecdotal narration (storytelling) will be my main tools of compellance.

What follows then, in a series of numbered chapters organized into four related parts, is a brisk historical walk through the modern ages of U.S. and Western warfare, all the way up to our present situation in Iraq and a bit beyond this point of history, peering over the edge of where we are today in Iraq and our modern way of war and peace to see what may lie ahead. This retelling of the history of our way of war and peace will center on how we have institutionalized ourselves for war in the past, for the present, and how we are currently leaning in our designs for the future. Those designs (past and present) have had and are having a negative effect on our ability to wage, win, and finish unconventional (postmodern) wars and, if not changed, have the potential for a similar negative impact in the future. This book will tell that history, reinforcing its relevancy and hopefully its appeal, by weaving in episodes of a more recent history, with examples of my experiences with postmodern war in Iraq, as a researcher, as a planner with the 101st Airborne in northern Iraq (July 2003–March 2004) during that Division's first combat tour in Iraq, and as chief of planning and operations for the Transformation (reorganization) of the 101st Airborne Division (Air Assault), from September 2003 to March 2005—the reorganization of this war-fighting organization leading up to its return to Iraq in Fall 2005.

It is my sincere hope that this story provides a wide readership with a new look at American intervention policy—at American war-fare—a better understanding of it, and an inspiration to think and act *beyond* our present traditions and to press our leadership to do the same, now, on behalf of a way of waging, winning, and finishing our wars more effectively and in a manner commensurate with the American republic and its democratic ideals.

Chapter 2

Modern War Revisited: Three Generations of Modern War-Fare

In making the point that war-fare in general and the American way of war and peace in particular have reached a generational crossroads—a significant if not revolutionary benchmark in that evolution—one must first frame this proposed change by locating it within a broader historical context.

This chapter revisits, briefly, what we will call the *last three generations of modern (Western) war-fare*. Placing the subject of military evolution in a generational context is an effective way of describing the living, organic, and human process that is the process of continuity and change in war-fare. It has been said that the history of man is a history of war. As societies have evolved, so too has their social enterprise of war-fare. The generations theme is significant in another sense. It refers indirectly to an emerging school of military thought—fourth-generation war-fare (4GW)—that proposes the nature of war-fare has once again crossed over into an era that reflects globalizational changes in geopolitics, geoeconomics, and sociocivilizational interactions. Whether this new school of thought offers a new legitimate theory of politics and war is debatable. What this new body of thinking and thinkers offers, however, are the building blocks of a new "postmodern" set of operating principles, characteristics of a new contemporary operating environment (COE) and the beginnings of a potentially new and more effective ordering principle for waging war-policy in this twenty-first century. The 4GW community is beginning to have a substantial impact on contemporary military thought and action, with young generations of military officers finding solace in many of the fledgling theoretical propositions being offered by 4GW advocates. I also find much utility in many of the 4GW hypotheses, and so in this book I will explore the impact of organizational culture and institutional structure on war-policy effectiveness from a 4GW angle of inquiry and analysis.

To consider the possibility of a "fourth" generation of war-fare would imply three "prior" generations.

Revolutions and "Generations" of Modern War

The argument of this book—America's tragic propensity toward losing the peace despite winning in battle—is premised on two major ideas. The first is that institutional structure and the organizational culture that lie within this structure define our prevailing and dominant ideas and understandings of war and peace and our national way of intervening through war-fare for the attainment of a peace-objective. *Organization and culture matter* is the first important variable. The second is that despite the war's constantly changing and adaptive nature, at times, change in a society's concept, organizational design, and operational way of war can become out of synch with the changing international environment—the changing geopolitical, geoeconomic, geocultural, and social environment.

This book further argues that the paradox within America's way of war and peace is the direct result of this phase mismatch between the changing nature of the environment within which man, societies, and, in this modern age, nations interact and the organizations, norms, principles, rules, and processes through which men, societies, and nation-states wage peace or war with and against each other. At periods of dramatic phase mismatch, where advancements in war-fare occur and outpace a society's political, economic, cultural capacity to command and control those changes, we tend to see historically recorded shocks to the status quo within the international system. At other times, we see striking improvements in a society's command and control of and innovations in war-fare—changes that often have led to revolutionary changes in political-, economic-, and cultural-societal arrangements (the dawn of new ordering principles). In all these instances, history's benchmark for these events is large-scale wars, collapse of political-societal systems (empires, dynasties). Scholars refer to these events as evolutions in war-fare, revolutions in technological affairs (RTAs), or revolutions in military affairs (RMAs). RMAs are the rarer and most historically noteworthy, since RMAs most often mark the end of a prior era of international relations and the dawn of a new age of political-military relations and a new ordering principle framing that new age's relationship between *man, the state, and war.*[1]

RMA scholars approach the issue of continuity and change in geopolitical and military affairs from various angles, and the body of their scholarship reflects their vast contribution to academia and the practical policy world in gaining a better understanding of war and peace policymaking and a more effective way toward intervention policy. War-fare is an evolutionary process, therefore, making the question of continuity or change irrelevant. The more relevant question is based on the issue of "evolution" versus "revolution" in military affairs brought about by advances in political, social, cultural, economic, and technological affairs. Table 2.1 that follows summarizes what I have interpreted as the more significant adaptations and innovations marking episodes of "evolutionary" versus "revolutionary" change in political-societal and military affairs.

It is interesting to note that those truly "revolutionary" developments appear to have occurred when the military leader was also the head of state (maintained an "imperial" and *centralized control* over what Michael Howard called elements of the "triangular dialogue" between operational requirements [and doctrine developed in response], financial limitations [resources], and technological feasibility)."[2] Frederick the Great (king of Prussia), Napoleon (emperor of France), and, to a lesser extent, Gustavus Adolphus (king of Sweden) were all examples of soldier-kings at the leading edge of (a contributing cause of) a revolutionary epoch of political and military affairs. Actors enabled by position to control all those evolutionary developments in the political, economic, technological realms and the authority to apply them to war-fare seemed to be the prerequisite of a true RMA.

Table 2.1 Evolutionary versus Revolutionary Change

	Strategic	Operational	Tactical
	Gradual rise of secular state system (Bretenfeld).	Limited, positional (maneuver) war-fare (Adolphus, Frederick the Great—late sixteenth century to early eighteenth century).	
Evolutionary Change (key "transitory" periods and episodes)	Rise in importance of coalitional war-fare (Breitenfeld → Allies defeat of Napolean in Waterloo Campaign in 1815).	Recognized importance of protraction as an operational technique of war-fare (American Revolution, Wellington's experiences in Spain, 1811).	Swiss innovations in artillery(lighter guns). Prussia's development and use of the "oblique order."
		"Fortified compound war-fare" (American Revolution, Napoleon's Spanish Campaign). This might have emerged as a revolutionary development if not for the fact that this change took place in what was considered at the time the periphery.	Foraging to magazines to resupply back to foraging (logistics), importance of reserve (gradual realization and development from Adolphus to Napoleon).
		Reemergence of "open war-fare" (Napoleon).	Rising importance of ambush and skirmishing (militia and irregulars).
		"Debate"over strength of "offensive" versus "defensive" war-fare (1830s–present).	
		Privatized armies to cantonal system to people's armies (levée en masse).	
Revolutionary Change	Dynastic war-fare to national war-fare (final change typified in French Revolution and Napoleonic system of war-fare).	Rise of formal PME (Frederick the Great).	Swiss mix of musketry and pike → combined arms concept (Adolphus).
		Corps organization (task organization at corps level and below—ca. 1805).	Decisive battle concept (Napoleon).

Source: Isaiah Wilson III.

Another interesting thing to note is that *revolutionary changes* seemed to occur during times of war or national crisis, while *evolutionary changes* seemed to occur during times of relative peace. This is in support of Dr. Stephen Peter Rosen's thesis in his book *Winning the Next War*, a seminal work in the literature on RMA.[3]

Our present-day "modern" military forms, doctrinal ways, and overall way of war were born of at least two revolutions in political-military and societal affairs. The military revolution of the seventeenth century marked a shift in the organizing principle of international affairs from one based on the dynastic rule of kings and queens to one based on territorially sovereign nation-states. The Treaty of Westphalia (1648) ended 30 years of dynastic wars and saw the rise of the modern European state system—a system based on "secular" power politics and heralding the end of the Holy Roman Empire. War-fare, consequently, shifted from dynastic war-fare to national war-fare.

The origins of modern armies drew upon larger, nonmilitary developments in European societies. The following quotation succinctly describes this seventeenth- and eighteenth-century military revolution, or RMA:

> The growing capacity of European governments to control, or at least tap, the wealth of the community, and from it to create the mechanisms—bureaucracies, fiscal systems, armed forces—which enable them yet further to extend their control over the community, is one of the central developments in the historical era which, opening in the latter part of the seventeenth century, has continued to our time. In the eighteenth century, this process was to gather increasing momentum, but until then it was a very halting affair. Its progress can be traced as clearly as anywhere else in the gradual acquisition of state control over the means of making war—over that violent element in European society which . . . had in the early seventeenth century virtually escaped from control and was feeding itself, so that the historian has to speak not so much of "war" of "wars" as of . . . a melee.[4]

As Howard reveals, a third peculiar and necessary precondition for the occurrence of a true RMA is for the governing authority—society—whether it be in the form of a society ruled and ordered by dynastic authority or in the form of a nation-state, to have attained an organizational and operational degree of effective and legitimate control over the wares and the ways of war-fare. These three "preconditions" support arguments touting that there have been to date at least three generations of war-fare born of two revolutions in military affairs and that today we may be witnessing a fourth-generation, marked by a third information-age RTA manifesting the latest RMA.

The 4GW school of thought and I differ slightly but significantly in our categorization of these three generations of modern war-fare (table 2.2).

While 4GW centers on war-fare, this book's alternative rendering of the generational shift in military affairs focuses more broadly on war-policy—war as a form of public policy reflective of a particular age or generational epoch of geopolitics and geosocial relations. This alternative model, consequently, promotes a premodern and modern framework categorizing varying relationships between man, society, and war. While the 4GW school focuses its fourth-generation inquiry and policy recommendations on an age of asymmetric war-fare and of small independent action cells (the dawn of an age of new means of war-fare), the alternative model posed here focuses attention on not only new indirect means and methods of war-fare (new

Table 2.2 Competing Generational Theories

	1GW	2GW	3GW
4GW	Age of Napoleon	Age of firepower	Age of maneuver and ideas
Alternative theory	Dynastic age of war-policy, Swiss/Prussian system of war-fare	Nation-state age of war-policy, Napoleonic system of war-fare	Nation-state age of war-policy, Industrial (mechanized) system of war-fare

Source: Isaiah Wilson III.

ways and means of implementing intervention policy) but more importantly on an entirely new paradigm for intervening—a new holistic concept of peace and war-policy. This new concept and its operational paradigm will be discussed in chapter 3.

The First Generation

According to the "generations" advocates, 1GW began with the age of Napoleon and the Napoleonic era of politics and war-fare. I choose to adjust the generational timeline and frame and categorize the first generation as the dynastic age of politics and war-fare, which began a full century earlier than the 4GW school of thought. As will be described in this chapter and the following, this alternative generational framing may prove determinative in the formation of a bona fide theory of fourth-generation war or, as I prefer to describe it, *postmodern age* of war.

The premodern or first-generation age of war and war-fare marks the period of time when the Western world emerged from the Middle Ages and the Renaissance in all aspects of Western social and political life that came with that emergence leading up to the profound social and political revolution that occurred in France in the 1800s—a revolution that shook Western Europe and gave rise to an entirely new national state system and way of war and peace. This was the generation of generalship and the soldier-king—the dynastic age of Western war-fare, a period of generalship that was personal and influential.[5] This was also the era that gave rise and definition to a particular form of war-fare and war-policy: limited war or wars of position. During this era, we see limited war-fare being practiced as an art form, progressing to a disciplined science of war-fare (through fortification and siege war-fare), and finally rising to its ultimate pinnacle of artistry and supreme scientific excellence under the hand of the great soldier-king, Frederick the Great of Prussia. Under King Frederick and others like him such as Sweden's Gustavus Adolphus, armies grew more professional and disciplined, moving from for-profit, for-hire mercenary forces (a mercantilist system of war-policy and war-fare) to people's or national armies fighting for God, king, and country more than for the spoils and profits of war. As a result, we witness a rise in the efficiency and effectiveness of governments to legitimately control and manage their armies and the political and societal mechanisms that kept them going.

During this epoch, we see a resurgence of the infantryman and infantry (foot-soldier) tactics and techniques and due to this resurgence a return to a system of war-fare and war-policy premised on the combined arms concept (a mix of various tools of war-fare such as cavalry and dismounted infantry, coupled with cannonry or "field artillery"). The premodern age was of centralized control over war-policy (agenda-setting, policy formulation and legitimization, and implementation) and of centralized execution, with the soldier-king leading; it was a humanistic age of war-fare.

The Second Generation

The second generation of war-fare marks the start of the modern age of war-policy. Social and political revolution (the French Revolution) sets the conditions and establishes the rationale for a RMA that gives rise and prominence (preeminence) to the Napoleonic way and system of war-fare. The French Revolution brought forth a wide and diverse array of changes in political, economic, and cultural aspects of French society—it led to revolutionary changes in the relationships between French society, the state, and its war-waging purpose, methods, and means.

The Napoleonic age of war-policy reflected this political-societal revolution. The army, rather than serving the monarch, was to serve the nation, with universal conscription in all ranks and a talent-based rather than patronage-based system of service and advancement being the significant tools for securing and sustaining a national army. The national army was to evolve into a national purpose-driven military, ideologically motivated (rather than driven by religious or pure power politics rationales) and sustained through the development of a political and economic system that afforded a reliable flow of resources, funds, and troops—adding to the professionalization of the military, creating a force that defined itself increasingly so based on its national purpose rather than on a mercantilist rationale for its organizational relevancy. The creation of the Continental System in 1806 reflected the evolution and marriage of the national state and its national military power and the development of a war-policy that purposed the utility of its military powers and prowess not on the martial functional capability of that tool of power but upon the political, economic, diplomatic, and social purposes and interests of the French nation-state.

When we analyze how this war-policy translates into an operational system of war-fare, we find how the French under Napoleon structured, organized, and institutionalized the innovations of a revolutionary French state and society into its national military systems. The Napoleonic system of war-fare was of centralized command but decentralized execution—the national and revolutionary composition and context of the army along with the rise in sheer size of armies (dawn of the million-man mass armies) demanded decentralization (liberty), while the sheer size and complexities of war-policy and war-fare demanded a centralized command of this multifaceted and multifunctional instrument of social and political national power. Improvements in technology were a necessary albeit insufficient enabler of this centralized command–decentralized execution balance act. The power and qualities of charisma, energy, and "genius" were other necessary but insufficient conditions for success of the Napoleonic age of war-policy and system of war-fare.

The Third Generation

The third generation of war-fare sees the modern age of war-policy evolving, with a RTA that comes with the Industrial Revolution of the late 1800s and early nineteenth century leading toward the dawn of the mechanized age of war-fare. This is the era of large machine wars, where we see the waging of two world wars (World War I, World War II) a multitude of great power wars by proxy (i.e., Arab-Israeli Wars of 1967 and 1973), and the dramatic increase in technocratization and bureaucratization as a consequence of the growing complexity of modern war-fare. This is the age when we witness the rise of the military power as the first of a nation-state's influence and power at the international level. This is the age of power politics and of realism, both in terms of a theory of international relations and in terms of how nation-states designed, resourced, and purposed its intervention (war) policy.

It is during the early years of this epoch (1806–1827) when Carl Von Clausewitz captures Western military modernity in theory, with the publishing of *On War*. *On War* to this day grounds Western military thought and practice—the foundation of the American way of war-fare. Clausewitz defines "war" as an act of force to compel one's enemy to do their will. He further describes war as politics by other means—a form of policy with a public function and purpose; a purpose that is reflective of a paradoxical relationship between government, its people, and its tools of political power.

During this era, we find the nation-state system at its zenith in terms of both its single-state (unilateral) productive power and its destructive capacity. Destruction of the enemy on behalf of the reestablishment of the status quo ante—the territorial sovereignty of a nation-state aggressed upon by another nation-state—was still the prime motive and function of war-fare and military force. Defense (in battle as well as defense of the nation and nation-state) was considered the stronger form of war, a "shield made up of well-directed (via well-purposed policy) blows," whose goal was preservation and stability.[6] During this age, we also witness the evolution of alliance war-fare from the episodic (mercantilist-based) expressions of coalition war-fare exampled during the waning years of Napoleon and the Napoleonic system, toward more long-standing alliances, from treaties to formal partnerships and regional and international regimes (i.e., UN, NATO, World Bank, IMF, etc.).

The broad U.S.-led international coalition war waged against Saddam Hussein's Iraq and won through the rapid and decisive actions of a combined (i.e., multinational) and joint (i.e., single-nation, multiservice) mechanized force against a mass mechanized Iraqi force exemplifies the glory of the machine age of modern war-fare and perhaps the pinnacle of nation-state war-policy effectiveness. Soon after the triumph of Operation Desert Storm (Gulf War-I) in 1991, we see NATO's final victory over the Warsaw Pact and the end of the cold war. What followed is continued academic debates and wild policy adventures into the strategic ambiguities of the post–cold war (postmodern?) geostrategic international environment.

From Generations to Policy Domains

The Three "Domains" of Modern War

Three generational evolutions of *man and the state* gave rise to the evolution of three "domains" of war-fare: the strategic level of war, the operational level of war, and the tactical level of war. These three *separate but interrelated* policy domains are the modern-day manifestation of a long evolutionary process. Understanding the definitions of these domains, their interrelatedness, and the evolutionary process itself is important to understanding the organizational story behind the modern paradox of the American way of war and peace.

Defining the Three Policy Domains

For better or worse (and beyond the subject of argument here), the philosophy and works of Carl von Clausewitz provide the baseline of Western military thought and U.S. military practice. His treatise on war was, by his own definition, a continuation of politics and policy by other (military) means.[7] For this reason, I choose to discuss and define what is more commonly considered in military circles as the *three levels of war* in terms of *three policy domains.*

The Tactical Domain

In the war vernacular, implementation or execution of policy falls within the context of *tactics.* According to Thomas E. Griess, tactics is "the planning, training, and control of the ordered arrangements (formations) used by military organizations when engagement between opposing forces is imminent or underway."[8] Taken from the Greek word *taktos* (ordered or arranged), tactics is the art of fighting battles. The nineteenth century saw the need to distinguish between two levels of tactics: *grand tactics* and *minor tactics.* Grand tactics spoke to the tactics of large organizations; minor tactics related to small organizations and/or organizations consisting entirely of one military arm (i.e., infantry, cavalry, or artillery).[9] Being the most practical and identifiable domains of policy, implementation, or tactics, is left at this level of definition. Three important points must be made with regard to the implementation level of policy and war before moving on to the more complex and, for this study, the more relevant domains:

1. While war (policy) is an act of force to compel our enemy to do our will,[10] it is vital that we remember that "essentially war [policy] is fighting, for fighting is the only principle in the manifold of activities generally designated as war."[11]

   That is to say that the de facto policy is the implemented policy.
2. To risk overstressing the point, execution is a key determinant in the prosecution of "good" policy.

The operational and strategic domains are more elusive, each in their own way. Since the concept of an "operational level of war" is a modern (twentieth century and later) formal concept and is largely defined in context of the tactical and strategic levels of war, let us first consider the strategic level.

The Strategic Domain

While the term *strategy* derives from the Greek word *strategos* (the art and skill of the general), the modern definition of strategy transcends the military realm. Even within the military policy subfield, military leaders generally work closely with civilian officials in the field of strategy.

Thomas E. Griess provides a useful and usable definition of strategy: "the planning for, coordination of, and concerted use of the multiple means and resources available to an alliance, a nation, a political group, or a commander, for the purpose of gaining an advantage over a rival."[13] While some have defined strategy as "position,"[14] others see strategy as "perspective"—an organization's way of doing things, its "concept of the business."[15] As addressed in chapter 1, strategy has become a multidimensional word, with multiple, often confusing, and even contradictory meanings. The word *strategy* is used variously *as a fixed doctrine or merely a plan* (what today, we would call "operations") *to describe actual practice or a body of theories.*[16]

The following definitions summarize some of the more prominent works (ideas and definitions of) in the fields of classical and modern thought on the subject of strategy:

Clausewitz:[17] The use of the engagement for the purpose of the war. The strategist must therefore define an aim for the entire operational side of the war that will be in accordance with its purpose. He will craft the plan of the war, and the aim will determine the series of actions intended to achieve it; he will, in fact, shape the individual campaigns and, within these, decide on the individual engagements. . . . [T]he strategist, in short, must maintain control throughout.

Jomini:[18] The art of making war upon the map, and comprehends the whole theater of operations. . . . [S]trategy decides where to act . . . grand tactics decides the manner of execution and the employment of the troops [pp. 69–71]. The art of bringing the greatest part of the forces of an army upon the important point of the theater of war or the zone of operations [p. 322].

Sun Tzu:[19] [Offensive strategy] 1. in war the best policy is to take the state intact; to ruin it is inferior to this; 2. to capture the enemy's army is better than to destroy it; 3. to subdue the enemy without fighting is the acme of skill; 4. what is supreme in war is to attack the enemy's strategy (attack plans at their inception); 5. next best is to disrupt his alliances; 6. the next best is to attack his army; 7. the worst policy is to attack cities (attack cities only when there is no alternative); 9. if the general is unable to control his impatience and orders his troops to swarm up the wall like ants, one-third of them will be killed without taking the city. Such is the calamity of these attacks; 10. thus, those skilled in war subdue the enemy's army without battle. They capture his cities without assaulting them and overthrow his state without protracted operations (they conquer by strategy).

Liddell Hart:[20] The art of distributing and applying military means to fulfill the ends of policy.

Luttwak:[21] the use of engagements for the object of the war.

Joint Publication (JP) 3.0: The art and science of developing and employing instruments of national power in a synchronized and integrated fashion to achieve theater, national, and/or multinational objectives.

Field Manual (FM) 3.0: The art and science of developing and employing armed forces and other instruments of national power in a synchronized fashion to secure national or multinational objectives. (Paragraphs 2–4)

What all these definitions of strategy teach us is that strategy is the purposing of military as well as all other tools of influence and power (policy apparatuses) to a higher political and societal goal or endstate.

The Operational Domain

By the dawn of the second generation of war-fare, or the modern age, we see an expansion of war as a form of policy and a function of national politics and a growing complexity of war-fare with technological advancements. With this expansion comes a formal institutionalization of a new domain of war-policy: the operational domain. The industrial age of war brings with it a Weberian bureaucratic ordering and organizing of the war-policy systems of most if not all advancing industrializing national states during the late 1800s and early 1900s. War is bureaucratized, mechanized, and divided and defined by a separation of war-fare through division of labor functions.

Table 2.3 summarizes what some of the seminal works in the fields of strategic and military operations have to say about operational art, science, and planning.

The lesson this table reveals about the operational domain of war policy is fivefold. First, the operational domain is about planning and process, albeit to serve the purpose of the commander and/ or the ruler (leader or leadership) in the making and execution of strategic decisions. It is focused on the operationalization of strategic endstates into realistic actions and obtainable (sustainable) objectives.[22] Second, the operational level of war is about the relating of aims, capabilities, and resources available in particular time, space, and purpose configurations. War takes on a particular geometric, geographical, and temporal form in the operational (policy formulation and legitimization) realm.[23]

Third, the operational domain synchronizes and/or sequences individual or intermediate actions and objectives, systematically, into coherent operations, campaigns, theater strategies, and grand war plans. National, regional, coalitional, nongovernmental assets are interrelated and synchronized through operational art and science. Fourth, the specific operational art and science of war policy has evolved over time, with different periods of modern war-fare typifying a particular formula of operational art and science.[24] That is to say the ways and means of working war-aims into achievable military objectives have changed over time, largely the result of improvements in technological means available and the consequential development of organizational and operational processes, procedures, doctrines for commanding and controlling these advances in techniques in ways that are contributory to the realization of strategic aims through tactical actions.[25]

The fifth revelation is the most informative. The evolution of the operational domain of war-policy during this modern era appears, by all standing definitions, to define operations, operational art and science, and the operational domain of war-policy *in military terms and/or a martial context.* Why this modern emphasis on the military tool of national power, particularly when advances in political-social, economic, and technological relations provide man and the state an enormous degree of command and control over all instruments of national power, as well as immense flexibility and choice over which tool of policy to use in the carrying out of its public policy interests? With this sort of increased command and control and improvements in policy tool choice, why would national decision makers choose to privilege military war-fare over more benign and less lethal policy instruments? Some of the answers can be obtained when we look from another angle of inquiry at the evolution of modern war.

The generational evolution of war reveals four critical points. First, the evolution from eighteenth to twentieth century witnesses a shift from the agenda-setting, policy formulation, and execution of war policy being vested in one leader or a

Table 2.3 The Operational Level of War

Sources	Operational Art / Operational Level of War
FM 3–0 (June 2001)	The use of *military* forces to achieve strategic goals through the design, organization, integration, and conduct of theater strategies, campaigns, major operations, and battles. (paragraphs 2–5)
FM 3–90 Tactics	*Operational framework—the arrangement* of friendly forces and resources in time, space, and purpose with respect to each other and the enemy or situation. It consists of the area of operations, battlespace, and battlefield organization.
JP 3–0	*Operational art*—the employment of *military* forces to attain strategic and/or operational objectives through the design, organization, integration, and conduct of strategies, campaigns, major operations, and battles. Operational art translates the joint force commander's strategy into operational design, and, ultimately, tactical action, by integrating the key activities of all levels of war.
MCDP 1–2 (USMC)	The link between strategy and tactics; our aim at the operational level is to get strategically meaningful results from tactical efforts; involves deciding when, where, for what purposes, and under what conditions to give battle—or to refuse battle—in order to fulfill the strategic goal; operations govern the deployment of forces, their commitment to or withdrawal from combat, and the sequencing of successive tactical actions to achieve strategic objectives; although the operational level of war is sometimes described as large-unit tactics, it is erroneous to define the operational level according to echelon of command; regardless of the size of a military force or the scope of the tactical action, if it is being used to directly achieve a strategic objective, then it is being employed at the operational level. (pages 5–9)
AFDD 1.0 (USAF)	*Operational level of war—the level* of war at which campaigns and major operations are planned, conducted, and sustained to accomplish strategic objectives within theaters or areas of operations. Activities at this level link tactics and strategy by establishing operational objectives needed to accomplish the strategic objectives, initiating actions, and applying resources to bring about and sustain these events. These activities imply a broader dimension of time or space than do tactics; they ensure the logistic and administrative support of tactical forces, and provide the means by which tactical successes are exploited to achieve strategic objective.
NDP 1 (USN)	The operational level concerns forces collectively in a *theater*. (page 16)
Luttwak, *Strategy*	Operational-level ~ normally dominates the tactical; details of topography and disposition; the overall interaction of the rival schemes of warfare determine outcomes; events conditioned by the *broader interaction of the armed forces as a whole within an entire theater of warfare.* (page 88)
Jacob W. Kipp (Svechin, *Strategy*)	*Operational art*—path to the ultimate goal broken down into a series of operations separated by more or less lengthy pauses, which take place in different areas in a theater and differ significantly from one another due to the differences between the immediate goals one's forces temporarily strive for; an act of war if the efforts of troops are directed toward the achievement *if* [*sic*] a certain intermediate goal in a certain theater of military operations without any interruptions; a conglomeration of quite different actions, namely drawing up the plan of the operation, logistical preparations, concentrating one's forces at the starting position, building defensive

Continued

Table 2.3 Continued

Sources	Operational Art / Operational Level of War
	fortifications, marching, fighting battles *which* lead to the encirclement or destruction of a portion of the hostile force andthe forced withdrawal of other hostile forces, either as a result of a direct envelopment or as a result of a preliminary breakthrough, and to the capture or holding of a certain line or geographical area. Operational art also dictates thebasic line of conduct of an operation, depending on the material available, the time *which* may be allotted to the handling of different tactical missions, the forces *which* may be deployed for battle on a certain front, and finally on the nature of the operation itself. (page 69)
Schneider (*Vulcan's Anvil*)	*Operational art—the employment* of *military* forces to attain strategic goals through the design, organization, and execution of campaigns and major operations. (page 2) "Attributes" (definitions)—distributed operation; distributed campaign; continuous logistics; instantaneous C2; operationally durable formation; operational vision; distributed enemy; distributed deployment. Three overarching features—Size; Balance; Comprehensiveness.
British Definition(s) (DGD&D)	The skillful employment of *military* forces to attain strategic goals through the design, organization, integration, and conduct of campaigns and major operations; requires the commander to identify the military conditions—or Endstate—that constitute his given strategic objective; to decide the operational objectives that must be achieved to reach the desired Endstate; to order a sequence of actions that lead to fulfillment of his operational objectives; and to apply the military resources allocated to him to sustain his sequence of actions.

small body of ruler-generals (soldier-kings) to a growing separation of war and war-fighting into separate entities—the placing of war policy in the hands of the ruler and the placing of power of execution of war plans (tactics and techniques) in the hands of the general.[26] By the turn of the twentieth century, the compartmentalization of the domains of war expands even further, with theorizing over issues of strategy falling to the purview of academics, policymaking falling to civilian leaders, and execution of war policy remaining with the uniformed experts.

Second, we see the emergence of a formally recognized "operational" domain of war, first defined simply in terms of logistical lines of communication (supply) but eventually expanding to include the command and control of forces within particular geographic theaters of war/operation and the array of forces in time, space, and purpose for realization of the higher war (grand strategic) aims.

Third, we find a shift from tactical-driven (execution-based) strategies to capabilities-driven strategizing (planning): the rise of force development and modernization (research and development, programming and budgeting, acquisition and procurement) of weapons systems and related technologies, normally specific to a particular military arm or service.

Fourth, we see the expansion of the domains, by the twentieth century, to include grand strategy (multinational, extranational, and extragovernmental) and national strategy. We see the expansion from national strategy to the military strategy and then toward theater-specific campaign strategies and the development and husbanding of service-specific, force-based stratagems advocating particular operational methodologies and tactical techniques and procedures.

The evolution, particularly in Western political-military society, and the resultant complication of the issues of strategy, operations, and tactics derived logically from the growing complexity of war policy itself. What could once be studied, written about, understood, taught, planned, put into practice, and more often than not won through a single decisive battle or engagement by individuals (soldier-rulers)[27] evolved into a complex policy issue that expanded well beyond the power and capacity of a single person—or nation—and, equally, could not be determined through a single battle. By the mid-twentieth century, it had become all too clear that war-policy could rarely be determined even through a series of battles and engagements (operations and campaigns).

So What? What Can We Learn From This Genealogy of Modern War-fare?

Edward Luttwak, arguably one of the preeminent experts of modern military strategic thought, found in his long years of study a paradox in the logic of strategy.[28] As in "normal" politics and policy, there is a horizontal and a vertical dimension to strategy making. In the horizontal dimension, one finds war and strategy's true nature—policy and plans, the result of contention between adversaries "who seek to oppose, deflect, and reverse each other's moves" in war.[29] Along the vertical, one sees the multidimensional nature of strategic policymaking—the vital interplay between the different levels of conflict—the tactical, technical, and operational. As in policymaking, there is no natural harmony between these aspects of strategy. The paradoxes that define the overall process of strategy are only rationalized as policy is rationalized—through the operationalization of strategic aims and vision into tangible and executable plans and policies.[30] The operational domain facilitates the effective dialogue between strategy and tactics; it permits the dialectic to take place in a functional and effective way.

If Clausewitz' notion of war is taken literally as a form of politics with a function commensurate with any other public policy, albeit a peculiar and particularly socially abhorrent policy function, and if we then take war, as policy, and superimpose on war the three stage model of policymaking, then we can see clearly the relationship between wars' three domains (strategic, operational, tactical) and the three stages of the policy-making process (agenda-setting, formulation and legitimization, implementation).[31] The three stages marry accurately with the three modern domains or levels of war. Reflecting on our discussion of the evolution of the operational domain of modern war-fare and more specifically on the peculiar martial character of the modern-age concept and definition and organization of the operational domain of war-policy, we can see the manner in which our modern concept of and organization for war has unintentionally, limited the development of our (Western) national war-policy systems and structures to military functions and martial forms of war-policy.

Why is the United States and its national security strategy strongly martially oriented? A significant reason is the manner in which war-policy and war-fare have evolved organizationally. That organizational development reflects a modern idea of and biased functional approach to war and war-fare that has emerged over at least three centuries of evolutions and revolutions in political-military and technological affairs. The American way of war and peace—America's intervention policy—reflects a misunderstanding and misapproach to war that comes from a modernization process that has been flawed by design from inception. Despite the best choices taken by the let's assume, "best intentioned" of national security (intervention policy) decision makers, the sheer design of the nation's (and the "West's") intervention (war) policy processes will, to varying degrees, result in a flawed and suspicious martial policy solution to most intervention policy challenges and opportunities.

Chapter 3

The Dawn of the Postmodern Age of War

Are we in a new age of war and peace—*a postmodern era*? If so, how would we know and why would, or should, we care? One important reason lies in the possibility that our national idea of and organization for war and peace may reflect more of a legacy of our past ideas and actions rather than a new and effective vision of and way toward our future. Since the tragedy and wonderment of our national prowess at war and peace during World War II, the sad truth is that our national peace-winning (i.e., war-finishing) capacity has slowly declined in effectiveness. World War II was a total and decisive war for the United States. The Korean War was, and still remains, a strategic and operational stalemate. Vietnam was an absolute war-loss for America due to its failure to turn a situation where its fighting forces won every battle and engagement on the ground against the Vietcong and the North Vietnamese regulars but still lost the war. Over three decades after this loss, America's confidence in its war-waging capability and will and its suasive power at attaining and maintaining the peace in its intervention policy have declined.

The 1990s saw a worsening of the situation. During America's moment as the world's sole-surviving hegemonic power, it either drowsily engaged in global crisis situations (acted too late with too little) or "slept entirely," ignoring or simply missing its moment (responsibilities) to intervene where and when its power and reputation as a benevolent hegemon were perhaps needed more than ever before. The Balkans Crises of 1990–1994 is a case in point of the former. Rwanda is a precise example of the latter. This anemic record of U.S. interventions during the 1990s appears to have fed a perception among U.S. friends and potential foes that the United States had become "soft" on military expeditions and critically casualty-averse. Some scholars and policy practitioners have even offered that a contributing factor that might have encouraged confidence in those who levied attacks against the U.S. on September 11, 2001 was this impression—a misperception and miscalculation on the part of the terrorists, as it turned out—that the loss of a mass number of Americans in such an attack would compel the United States to capitulate on all counts.

The growing anemia of U.S. intervention policy has contributed to a growth in instability, globally, and an increase in the security dilemma facing the United States.

Our apparent inability to plan and wage a war-policy that is capable of winning peace—and maintaining that hard-won peace—has made us less secure. Iraq is the latest and most poignant case in point. However, while most writing and speaking on the Iraq War have focused their barbs and analytical attention on the strategic choices of the Bush administration as a primal cause for our nation's current strategic quandary in Iraq, few if any have focused on the structural and cultural causes for our national propensity for getting it wrong in our intervention policy endeavors. Strategic choice arguments also miss an important point: the paradox within the American approach to intervention is not a G. W. Bush administration phenomenon but existed long before. If no action is taken to examine—and possibly change—how this nation is organized, postured, structured for war and peace intervention, then the paradox and its consequences for U.S. national, regional, and global security will persist.

From Modernity to Postmodernity

A Review of the Evolution of U.S. Military Thought and Practice

The previous chapter detailed the history of organizational change that led to the United States' modern-age understanding of and approach to (i.e., "way") of war and peace. That revisit from an organizational viewpoint reveals a systematic and institutional separation of the functions of war-fare from the quality-of-peace political objectives of war-policy. The splintering of process from purpose reached its most dramatic point in the early 1900s, with the Industrial Revolution and the rise of the United States as a substantial industrialized power. World War II was the necessary mother of invention and innovation in political-military affairs that elevated the United States as the preeminent power and its industrialized and mechanized way of war as the prominent Western form. While World War II and the cold war that followed exampled this modern way of war and peace in practical terms, the theory of Max Weber validated the modern bureaucratization and divisions of labor that are emblematic of today's way of war and peace and culpable in the promotion of the paradox. The theory of Carl von Clausewitz reiterated the vital importance of defining the military functions of war (his "military object") based upon the political objective in war. Clausewitz made this clear point:

> Wars cannot be divorced from political life; and whenever this occurs in our thinking about war, the many links that connect the two elements are destroyed and we are left with something pointless and devoid of sense.[1]

In the four theoretical chapters of his seminal work on the modern form and way of war, *On War*, Clausewitz articulated war as process and peace as its defining purpose. In four additional chapters, he applied his theory of modern war to the Wars of Napoleon, with his own experiences during those campaigns as important first-hand observational evidence that added to the story. While the first four theoretical chapters were honest and true to the book's title, the applied science chapters of the work would have better fallen under a different manuscript title—*On Battle*. Clausewitz' story of the Wars of Napoleon exampled war-fare of those days—a martial way of war-fare, with the *grand armee* the most readily available instrument of choice to the Emperor General Napoleon. The story was intended, I contend, as no more than a soldier's memoir. What our modern history of Western war reveals, however, is that Clausewitz' originally written and intended theory of war has not been the blueprint for the building of the modern Western forms of war-fare. Instead, Clausewitz' application of his theory to the very specific and peculiar case of Napoleonic war-fare in nineteenth-century Europe became the model for defining the modern idea of war and centering of the modern forms of war-fare in the martial functions of combat and battle.

It is this gross misinterpretation of the Clausewitzian story of Napoleonic war-fare for a modern theory of war that has over time been institutionalized and legitimized. The entire U.S. National Security policy system is a reflection of this misinterpretation—a policy system flawed by organizational design and an organizational culture that, though it may rhetorically appreciate the role of diplomacy, economics, and information, and social-political aspects of war, still fails to formulate and implement war-policy in such an integrated manner.

The organizational evolution of the Western way of war and peace sees an unintended separation of war's function from its overriding peace-objective and a privileging of the military instrument of policy as not only the first among equal tools of power but also as the tool that actually defines the American idea of what constitutes "war"—as "the absence of peace" rather than the more accurate understanding of war as a process of peace-policy.

The institutionalization and bureaucratization of war based on separated functions (divisions of labor) rather than on the unifying and defining peace-objective has fostered the very "stovepiping" problem that the 9/11 Commission revealed in its inquiry into the intelligence failures that contributed to the U.S. government's failure to predict and prevent the 9/11 terror attacks.[2] The stovepiping phenomenon is not limited to the intelligence community, and it is far less of a naturally occurring phenomenon than it is a human error in organizational architecture. The problem is chronic and systemic.

The Next (Fourth?) Generation

Where Might Postmodernity Take Us?

There are many pathways this generational evolution of the Western way of war and peace could take.

The historic linear "progression" could intimate a further division of labor—a further specialization of war and peace by separated purpose and function. There is evidence, empirical and anecdotal, that this is already happening in the U.S. Government. Over the past 100 years, the U.S. military organization has "evolved" from one holistic War Department to two separate organizations (the War Department and the Navy Department), to two separate "Services" (U.S. Army and U.S. Navy), to the formal organization of a third service (U.S. Air Force). Today, we have two new unified commands (Space Command, Northern Command). Within the U.S. Army, for further example, the division of labor and branch specialization have expanded from three (combat, combat support, combat service support arms) to at least 11 specialty fields or "functional areas," ranging from the traditional operational fields of infantry and cavalry to operational research and Acquisition Corps.

Similar specializations within other domains of national power (diplomatic, economic, informational, etc.) are evident as well, adding to the divided-we-fall stovepiping dilemma cautioned officially in the *9/11 Commission Report* in 2004. This evolved modern form has led to across-the-board (across the separate stovepipes) redefining of careers, functions, and purposes. Some recent scholarship has also recognized this separation dilemma and has even proposed that this trend has already led to a *deprofessionalization* of many of this nation's stalwart professions (i.e., the medical profession, the military profession) and an abhorrent and increasing decline in the effectiveness of our nation's effective-based (purpose-driven) professions.[3] This pathway could simply lead to a furtherance of the paradox that comes from such separations and should therefore be avoided or "turned" at all cost.

A second pathway could find this next (fourth?) generational evolution turning the way of war and peace back to premodern forms, functions, and purposes. The fourth-generation war-fare (4GW) school of thought seems to ground its argument in this idea. The 4GW concept carries some explanatory water. A working definition of 4GW is seen as

> [e]ncompassing attempts to circumvent or undermine an opponent's strengths while exploiting weaknesses, using methods that differ substantially from an opponent's usual mode of operations.[4]

4GW advocates, from a strategic standpoint, see the 4GW contemporary operating environment (COE) as one of asymmetry and asymmetrical threats. They see this environment as one that witnesses the loss of a nation-state's monopoly on war and a return to a world of cultures and states in conflict, typified by internal segmentations within all-before stable nation-states along ethnic, religious, and special interest lines within a national society.[5] From an operational perspective, the 4GW school of thought sees the function of war-fare as a true act of psychological aim that seeks major psychological impacts on the adversary's will to fight and national public opinion and the acknowledgment of the asymmetrical nature of resourcing war-fare to effect in this new age—acknowledging the disproportionate nature of results to investments. From the tactical perspective, 4GW is a return to an age of and practices in the human, personal, moral, and positional factors emblematic of premodern war-fare—the era of strategic wars of position and maneuver. This return to an age of *the sling-and-the-stone* conception of 4G war-fare, coupled with the ongoing revolution in technological affairs (RTA) yields an interesting marriage of ideas, opportunities, and challenges.[6] While 4GW advocates see the enhancing power of technology (information technology [IT] in particular) as an enabler of small unit, soldier-focused tactical ground actions with strategic impacts, they also accept and caution against the potential for a RTA coup d'état of a revolution in military affairs—the potential for 4G war-fare to be overtaken by advancements in technology.

What we see along this 4GW pathway is a focus on forms and functions of war-fare–a mix of the old and new weapons to combat—but very little if any reflection on the impact of this alternative form and functional design of war-fare on the purposing of fourth-generation war-policy. This, I offer, is a critical flaw in the 4GW pathway. A simple back-to-the-past functional conception of war (a focus on war-fare alone) misses the critical point of what advocating for a return to a premodern organization of war and peace might manifest. Might not a full return to premodern ways and means of war-fare unintentionally argue for a centralization of command and control (purpose and direction of war-fare) similar to the premodern forms? Such a course of action and innovation would admittedly yield a more efficient and effective command and control over the war-fare and might even have greater promise in bringing about a holistic way (full spectrum) of intervention policy. However, the cost might be the unintended, unwarranted, and unbridled accumulation of power in the hands of one single, undem-ocratic power. This path might unwittingly set the conditions for a return of the soldier-kings and dynastic political-military-societal arrangements—a fostering of illiberal regimes and illiberal democracies.

While I am in agreement with the 4GW school of thought on the nature of the COE and the advent of a return to premodern forms and functions of war-fare (not so much of our own volition but more so by the choice of our adversaries), neither I nor 4GW advocates, I would contend, are promoting a return to the illiberal regimes of the premodern era.

Quite the contrary.

If left to the natural winds of continuity and change in military affairs, the sheer nature of the COE—its threats against the sanctity and stability of the modern nation-state system—this fourth-generation trend could actually lead to the very clashes of civilizations that some scholars have pondered,[7] a *devolution* rather than a revolution of political-military affairs that fosters an increased militarism or the decline (collapse?) of the nation-state international system and the return of authoritarian regimes. Cynics may say that the United States is already moving unwittingly along such a fault line, driven through a mix of bad choices and fear of terrorism to tear apart America's institutional systems of separated powers and checks and balances, without a comprehensive and deliberate (logical?) analysis, on behalf of defense and security of the American homeland and the national interests abroad. No one truly knows how much damage has been incurred upon the American democratic system of divided and separated (but representative) government—its liberal forms and purposes—by the dramatic institutional and organizational changes our nation has taken since 2001 to restructure governmental and military power. The current U.S. security policy (the Bush Doctrine) and *National Military Strategy* (a strategy of preventive and, if necessary, preemptive liberalization and democratization) strongly hint at the direction in which the nation is headed. Our recent policy behavior seems to privilege American unilateralism and consequently may confirm the rise of an unintended American empire (under the control of an imperial presidency) and the demise of the liberal American republic. There has to be another path forward.

A Postmodern Alternative

The Dawn of a Postmodern Way of War and Peace

In economics, returns of scale describe what happens as the scale of production of any sort of enterprise (firm or government or association) increases. A return of scale refers to a technical property of production: what happens to output if we increase the quantity of all input factors by some amount. If output increases by that same amount, there are constant returns to scale (CRTS), sometimes referred to simply as returns to scale. If output increases by less than that amount, there are decreasing returns to scale. If output increases by more than that amount, there are increasing returns to scale.[8] There are basically two varying rates of scale each yielding an outcome, one positive and the other negative: economies of scale and diseconomies of scale. Economies and diseconomies of scale refer to the saving in cost of production of a good or service, or the loss in those production costs, respectively. That is due to mass production or an organization's capacity to mass produce. Economies and diseconomies of scale also refer to an economic property of production: what happens to cost if we increase the quantity of all input factors by some amount. If costs increase proportionately, then there are no economies of scale; if costs increase by a greater amount, then there are diseconomies of scale; if costs increase by a lesser amount, then there are (positive) economies of scale. Economies of scale tend to occur in industries with high capital costs in which those costs can be distributed across a large number of units of production (both in absolute terms and, especially, relative to the size of the market).

The exploitation of economies of scale helps explain why companies grow large in some industries. It is also a justification for free trade policies, since some economies of scale may require a larger market than is possible within a particular country. Economies of scale also play a role in a natural monopoly. Typically and theoretically, because there are fixed costs of production, economies of scale are initially *increasing*, and as volume of production increases, eventually *diminishing*, which produces the standard U-shaped cost curve of economic theory.

If we think of government and nation-states and the nation-state-based international system in these economic terms, we can see an individual nation-state as a company (a production firm), the nation-state system as a network of producing firms (of varying economies of scale), and the international system as an industry—a multinational corporation of sorts. If we review the evolution of the modern Western way of war and peace though this economic lens and if we consider the goods for production as "security" and the means of production as a nation-state's public policy production capacity (its national security system), then we can begin to appreciate the enormous diseconomies-of-scale dilemma the United States currently faces, as the preeminent producing firm of national, regional, and international security—a problem of scale and capacity that other nation-states less robust in capacity suffer even more.

To be more correct and consistent with the economic theory, security as a form of public produce is more an example of a network externality, with what we see in the comparison here as an example of economies of scale external to the firm, or industry-wide scale economies. The issue of the production of national, regional, and international security is an example of a network externality because of security's nonfungible nature: a product that cannot be easily deprived of free riders (those who do not pay for their fair-market share of security are not easily denied of the product) and is driven by demand-side economies. What we see then at the macro (global, international) scale is a decline in efficiency and effectiveness of the nation-state-premised international system to produce the goods (security) at the rate and quality demanded by users within the market. What we have termed an international system of idiosyncratic and asymmetrical threats can be seen, in economic terms, as a decline in the nation-state system's capacity to mass produce security at an acceptable cost of production. When we look at the United States—one, albeit the first among equal security-producing firms—we see the same failure of production. The United States in the micro and the traditional (modern-era) international system in the macro are suffering a diseconomies-of-scale problem. The sheer scope, scale, and nature of the security dilemma defining of this twenty-first-century COE defies the effective and efficient command and control of any single nation-state—even the great power and capacity of the United States. The paradox lives within this diseconomies-of-scale environment. Unilateral security strategies in this light can be seen as dead, an anachronism of modernity. Of course, firms still produce despite their lessening efficiency and effectiveness in producing to demand rates and requirements, as do national governments. But that does not make the production effective enough, and eventually the firm will go bankrupt and out of business. Political scientists may say that this is where the analogy to economics ends, since governments are not companies and consequently cannot simply go out of business. I argue that this is a myth and a falsehood. Nation-states also go "out of business" at times; we call them *failed* or *failing states.* Unlike the firm, liquidation is often in the form of violence.

The current unilateral-based, martialized national security and military strategies of the United States of America may be an example of a firm holding on too hard and for too long to "go-it-alone" strategies that can no longer be carried forward effectively and efficiently through one single means of production: the military. Continuing to produce in this sort of return-of-scale environment, like in the politics of the firm, typically leads to market failures—in our case here, natural monopolies or oligopolies of the means of production. In the case of the United States, some argue that we are on a trend to becoming the very example of an illiberal democracy our national security strategy rhetorically argues to guard against. The flaws in our organizational idea of and way of war and peace may have turned us into our own worst enemy—an enemy of our own state and of the nation-state international system.

Bringing the State Back in

Integrating National Instruments of Power and then Going Global

How can a return to an *economies-of-scale* balance of production in security (national, regional, international) be attained particularly given the globalized nature of today's geostrategic environment?

A "corporate merger" is in order. In order to *bring the state back in*[9] and in control of contemporary international politics, bureaucratically separated capacities within individual nation-states should be reintegrated, repurposed (along quality-of-stability and peace-political objectives) and then reorganized for policy implementation. On the macro (global) scale, war-policy (agenda-setting, formulation and legitimization, implementation) would need to be incorporated—through a likely evolution that would continue the progression from wars of alliances to wars of coalitions, to wars of collectivities (of defense and then security), to perhaps some sort of international *communitarian*-based war-policy.[10] The multilateralism approach is a necessary part of this evolutionary progression, but until the holistic communitarian endstate is finally attained, this approach will continue to prove insufficient for bringing the state back in and in control of international relations and returning to the nation-state a reliable and legitimate (in the eyes of its national public) means of national security production.[11]

Integrating U.S. Tools of Power

The basic point and purpose of a security policy and intervention strategy is to ensure the national ends of that policy through the proper ways of policymaking and means (resources) available for implementation.

As chapter 2 discussed, there are myriad modern definitions and conceptions of strategy: the most functional one, particularly from a policy perspective, would be that offered by John Lewis Gaddis.[12]

The Gaddis paradigm, unlike others, articulated an additional factor into the standard and traditional ends-ways-means paradigm: an expression of the relationship between national intentions (in its war-policy) as articulated through that nation's available capabilities (its ability to perform or carry out some type of activity of a series of functions toward a grand purpose or objective). Gaddis's definition, unlike most other definitions, relates strategy to the political goals of a political society and relates the national creed and its interests to those abilities and the structures of those abilities of a nation that give it power and legitimacy in the use of that power. This *intentions-to-capabilities* factor is particularly important in an age of globalization and information, where the transmission of policy intent is nearly immediate and largely beyond the command and control of the transmitter.

Today, the U.S. *National Military Strategy* is based upon what defense and force planners regard as a capabilities-based model. But what exactly does this mean in regards to war-policy? Given the separated-by-function organizational structure of the modern U.S. war-policy system, a capabilities-based approach to war-policy and strategy is subject to multiple definitions—multiple systems—of capabilities, as varied as the number of separate and distinct stovepipes that make up the U.S. National Security system. Is the overall U.S. intervention capacity a simple and straight additive of all these separated capabilities? The answer is no. First, effective policy attains a synergistic effect—a policy result that is more in combination than the sum total of its individual contributing parts. An integrative policy is a more effective intervention policy. Second, as per the modern U.S. model, the military domain of war-policy is, regarded as the first among separate but equal domains of war-policy instruments and is resourced as such at the expense (zero-sum) of the others. The martial domain of U.S. intervention policy is the more mature, and as a consequence our national tools (instruments) of military power are the more advanced and resourced. This reality adds to the imbalance and overmilitarization of current U.S. intervention policy, as the vicious and tragic cycle of overresourcing the U.S. military at the expense of State Department tools of progress (i.e., diplomacy, etc.), commerce and trade (i.e., economic development), and so on perpetuates a U.S. martial way of war and peace.

United we stand divided we fall is more than a national slogan. It is indicative of the current state of U.S. security affairs and is descriptive of this nation's chronic anemia in its intervention prowess, both at home and abroad.

Making the situation even worse, a mythology has grown around these arbitrary functional divisions that further divide our war-functions from their peace purposes—myths that separate organizations make use of to both maintain their separate and "unique" identities and to reinforce and justify their separate organizational relevancy. The most poignant example is the false divide between the warrior (soldier) and "war-fare" and the peace operator and peace operations.

These myths are reinforced by institutional designs, successful interventions at local levels, and dominant cultural wants and desires (ethos) of the military fields and the peace fields of study and practice. These myths lead to false debates (i.e., a constabulary force carries out peace operations better than the military), and these false debates contribute to a false national understanding of what constitutes war and what does not. These myths defy the realities of the contemporary world and operating environment—it ignores (wishes away) the realities of what the enemy can do and what the enemy is doing. More specifically, allowing these myths and misunderstandings to persist deprofessionalizes the military as well as all other functionaries that play a key role in security, defense, and foreign policy by allowing the players to define themselves and their entire organizations upon a preferred function rather than by public purpose. Two related examples illustrate this point. The first example is of the U.S. military and its organizational and cultural preference for battle and major combat operations (MCO). When the U.S. armed forces articulate its understanding and support of the Weinberger-Powell Doctrine that the purpose of the U.S. military is to fight and win America's wars, what it is really stating is its understanding of its core purpose as being fighting and winning in tactical battle. This is because the U.S. military has mistakenly defined "war" by its combative functions—a vitally necessary but woefully insufficient part of a nation's war-winning policy. The statement made by a senior-ranking U.S. Army commander performing peace-enforcement duties in the Balkans in the mid-1990s—that the Army does not do windows—was much more than just an errant and politically incorrect statement; it reflected a sentiment that contributed to a too little, too late U.S. intervention in the Balkans and in other "other-than-war" wars of the 1990s and a resultant global instability and level of crisis that might have been averted or lessened by a more holistic and robust U.S. intervention policy during his period. A second example is found within the peace fields. There is a myth that the effectiveness and protectedness of peace operations is the result of the separation of peace operators (and their operations) from military operations and operators. As the myth holds, peace operations, and more specifically humanitarian assistance operations, gain and maintain legitimacy in the hearts and minds of the local populations by (1) maintaining their neutrality; (2) maintaining their impartiality; (3) maintaining their independence; and (4) maintaining their separateness from military affairs.[13] This is many respects may hold true, at least under "modern" conditions.

But the postmodern COE presents one additional reality that may negate all four of these traditional imperatives for maintaining a wall of separation between military and "peace" operations, forms and functions: the enemy and the COE itself "militarize" the persons, organizations, and activities of peace operations as much as or more than simply affiliating with the military and their martial operations may have done in the past. *The postmodern COE is a war-zone*, as defined by our enemy and his activities (his war-fare). Unilateralism, from an effectiveness standpoint, is dead, in spite of the fact that a policy and strategy of unilateralism may still bear some partisan-political fruit for senior leaders and parochial benefits (spoils of war, institutional relevancy, organizational "glory") for senior leadership within military and "other-than-war" fields. In spite of our separate and peculiarly particular functions and forms, all public policy functionaries are commonly purposed based on a quality-of-peace and stability political objective (endstate). In this sense, we are all "the war-riors" working toward a common endstate. Reintroducing this common purpose to all agencies within and throughout the U.S. interagency system is a vital step toward the creation of a holistic and purpose-driven national security and intervention policy regime.

Holistic Campaign Planning: A New Way

As the Gaddis paradigm shows, the art and science of war-policy planning provides the systematic ties that bind separated forms and functions into a coherent single-purpose war-policy and integrative strategy.

How we plan for war reflects *how* we know of war and *what we know* of war. In World War II, our nation declared unconditional surrender as its measure of success and effectiveness. Consequently, our nation's armed forces planned and prepared for the war in a manner consistent with that unconditionality. There was no enddate given to U.S. and Allied forces—only an endstate of unconditional surrender on all fronts. To meet those established measures of effectiveness, nothing less than the entire nation was necessary for waging and winning the war.

In Korea, our nation, as part of a UN collective defense effort, intervened in a civil war of strategic and ideological consequences but failed to declare this intervention as a "war." If you were to ask the academics, policy makers, and agenda-setters of the time, they would tell you Korea was a "conflict" or a "police action" but assuredly not a bona fide war. If you were to ask the ground-pounder, Korea was a "war." While the Army and the Marine Corps engaged in full-scale conventional war-fare on the ground in Korea, strategic-level war-riors waged what they termed as something "other." Despite the tactical actions on the ground, the Korean War ended in a stalemate. Our war-plans for the Korean "Conflict" reflected something less-than-war and consequently produced something less-than-victory.

Vietnam witnessed the *tactics-strategy* divide in stark terms and terminology. Vietnam, for America, was at first a "small war" against black-pajama-clad guerillas and later a conventional war against a North Vietnamese invasion force of 130,000 men and 18 divisions supported by tanks and artillery. Vietnam was first a war anathema to our "modern sensibilities" and later an exemplar of modernity. Our military and our nation were determined to know about the Vietnam war in these exact opposite terms. Seeing the war as a "limited war of signaling" rather than a war of "fighting" presented the U.S. military a "way out" of its strange and embarrassing defeat. By declaring the first half of the war that ground combat forces fought as a guerrilla war but the latter half as a war against a bona fide conventional force, military leaders could assign its war-loss to a respectable conventional army and, as such, could argue that it had never lost to a rabble, insurgent force. Losing was one thing, but defeat at the hands of an insurgent was so unacceptable that the "war" had to be redefined in a way that could allow us to decide to whom we lost.

For all these wars and "other-than-war" wars, our plans reflected our prevailing "idea" of war.

On Planning

Planning is a mix of science and art, for any profession or field of policy. It bridges that conceptual gap between what we want out of intervention (our goals) and how we go about getting it (our actions). Planning spans the practical chasms that block our chances and capacities of reaching our objectives (policy endstates) through the actions we take in the war-fight. It marries the institutions of war with our instrumentation for war. Planning can balance the ends and means of our intervention-policies, and in doing so, it can legitimize those policies. A lack of planning can lead to the exact opposite: confuse those on the receiving end of our intervention-policies (foes, friends, and ourselves) of our true intentions because of the inconsistency between what we say and what we do. A lack of planning can delegitimize our actions and even ourselves as a nation.

The Planning for Operation Iraqi Freedom

A Campaign Plan "Flawed By Design"[14]

There are two dictums that are commonly understood by those in the planning community. The first is that *planning does not occur in a vacuum.* The second is that *no plan survives first contact.* The planning that led to the execution of Operation Iraqi Freedom (OIF) violated the first dictum and relied far too heavily on the latter. The result was an Iraq War campaign plan that was not—a campaign plan by name only, which was more reflective of a major combat operational plan than a holistic war-plan and a plan in which the actions and outcomes of the majority of its activities were left more to hope (and the vote of the enemy) than to deliberate prior preparation.

Dr. Conrad Crane of the U.S. Army War College refers to the flawed planning behind OIF as a result of "many plans, but not one."[15] I have referred to this condition as an anemia of U.S. war operational planning, resulting in the campaign plan that was not.[16]

Overall, the campaign planning for the Iraq War suffered then and continues to suffer from three major flaws:

1. Incomplete planning, re: purpose, that is, the Iraq War was fought based on the attainment of a limited military object (the overthrow of Saddam Hussein) rather than on the broader political objective of creating a stable and prosperous Iraq that will pose no threat to its neighbors and that will be friendly to U.S. interests.
2. Incomplete planning, re: timing, that is, the Iraq War was forward-planned toward the attainment of a limited military object (overthrow of Saddam Hussein) instead of a more comprehensive political objective. As such, the timing of the campaign plan (i.e., when diplomacy would end and MCO would begin) was arrived upon from an eye focused on a preemptive military timetable

instead of a more protracted and preventive "holistic" (D-I-M-E, or *diplomatic, informational, military, economic*) timetable.
3. Incomplete planning, re: authorization, allocation, and distribution (spacing) of forces, that is, the Iraq War was in fact a war that America would end up waging with the forces it had available rather than the force it needed. Limiting the war short of its natural parameters has left the United States poorly and inadequately positioned—strategically, operationally, and tactically—to fight the war to a complete *quality-of-peace* win, never having the right amount of force, the right mix of forces, or the right array of forces on the ground in Iraq.

In short, OIF is a case in point of the paradox within the American way of peace and war. It is an example of *a systemic failure to develop an operational plan* for the war in Iraq prior to the initiation of major combat operation on March 19, 2003.

Drawing Limited Lessons from Total Wars—OEF and OIF-1

The failure to plan story begins much earlier than 2001, but a snapshot from the U.S. war against the Taliban and Al Qaeda in Afghanistan in October 2001 is an appropriate and accurate staring point. Operation Enduring Freedom (OEF) set several bad precedents that contributed to the delinquency of planning for and the execution of war in Iraq since 2003. The U.S. expedition in Afghanistan in 2001 was a limited operation of primarily military objective—dislodging of the Taliban regime, disruption and if possible the destruction of the Al Qaeda, and the capture or killing of terrorist mastermind Osama bin Laden. Afghanistan was a major military operation *of military objective*. It was a combative action born of the mother of necessity—the terrorist attacks of 9/11. There was no original intention for a U.S. reconstruction effort, and therefore no original Phase-IV plan. In fact, there was no Phase-IV planning of any kind, and little of what could be considered as campaign planning.[17] The command, control, and execution was as ad hoc as the "war" itself. While tactical actions during OEF proved the unmatched innovativeness and adaptability of the American soldier at the level of tactical execution, the U.S. modern forms of war-fare and the capacity for the United States to combine the old (i.e., modern, even premodern) ways of war-fare with those of the present and the future (i.e., postmodern's fourth-generational), the decisiveness of U.S. and coalition MCO has yielded less than a decisive victory. In spite of the battle victory, the effort has only attained at best a strategic stalemate.

OEF is another case in point of the paradox. Adding insult to this injury, we witness that the failure during Operation Anaconda (popularly regarded as the Battle of Tora Bora) to isolate, contain, and then capture or kill bin Laden, key members of the Al Qaeda network, and remnants of the Taliban regime reflect a failure to achieve the strategic purpose of the major operation—a failure to complete the mission. Since Tora Bora, the United States and the international community have found themselves engaged in de facto Phase-IV activities if not outright official Phase-IV operations and nation-building writ-large. Because the original expedition was not premised upon a scope and scale of operations that encompassed stability, reconstruction operations, and a rebuilding of Afghanistan as a free, stable, and democratic-like nation-state, all Phase-IV operations have been the result of a scramble. International organizations (IOs) and nongovernmental organizations (NGOs) have equally been disillusioned by the Phase-IV chaos. The lessons these nonmilitary, nongovernmental agencies have gathered from the OEF Phase-IV experiences have been ironically 180-degrees opposite to what the U.S. military and Bush administration have gathered and learned. Many of these same IOs and NGOs that suffered through the chaos of a poorly planned Phase IV for Afghanistan have been wary and reluctant to cooperate in Iraq's reconstruction. Adding to their wariness has been the continued competition for scarce resources (manpower, materiel, attention, etc.) between the OEF and OIF missions. In short, the peace community's lessons gathered have been lessons of reluctance. The U.S. military's (and administration's) lessons were more positive and more consequential in terms of today's impoverished situation in Iraq.

The tactical successes of the battle approach in Afghanistan were adopted, almost in total, and applied to the situation in Iraq—an entirely different and more complex situation than Afghanistan. The tactical and operational successes of OEF all but validated (stating it modestly) the SOF "plus" precision-guided munitions (PGM) "plus" indigenous ground forces (IGF) force design as the U.S. government preferred strategy of choice. This interpretation of OEF (that the operation was "won" through tactical, ground-level innovations) seems to have been interpreted as an adequate proxy for a military strategy for OIF, perhaps even for the entire war-policy. The paucity of the Iraq War campaign plan—the denial of the real and broader war that a war in Iraq was by its nature destined to be on behalf of a preferred war of limited military object (overthrow of Saddam)—finds some of its causal roots in the lessons rightly gathered from Afghanistan but wrongly applied to the situation that would become the Iraq War.

The evolution of military planning begins in earnest in late 2001 with initial guidance coming from the Joint Staff (at the time in the heat of OEF planning and operation management) that control of Phase-IV operations in Iraq would fall to the leadership of either the U.S. State Department or Iraq's exile government (the Iraqi National Congress [INC]). By June 2002 and in the aftermath of the tactical success of OEF, this was changed—the lead agency for campaign planning for the Iraq War, including Phase-IV planning, would be the Office of the Secretary of Defense (OSD) and the Pentagon.[18] Central Command (CENTCOM) planning began in June 2002, with ECLIPSE II as the eventual base concept plan for OIF and its predecessor OPLAN COBRA II actually serving as the plan that led the execution of MCO. The bulk of this planning was conducted at Combined Forces Land Component Command (CFLCC) levels—Third Army Headquarters initially in Tampa, Florida and then Camp Doha, Kuwait.

The CFLCC planning sequence paralleled that of CENTCOM with the intent of ensuring an effective integration and synchronization of these two key echelons of planning and theater-strategic intervention policy implementation (execution)—a process in the military known as "nesting."

Among the key factors affecting the planning and later the execution of OPLAN COBRA II (what would eventually become the campaign plan for OIF) was the determination of how many units would deploy before combat operations were to begin and how many axes of advance ground forces would use to execute the major combat operation. This consideration proved highly political and, as a consequence, toxic to the hopes of creating, resourcing, and executing a holistic campaign plan that was reflective of the complete complexity of the operations, activities, challenges, and opportunities that would define the entire domain of the Iraq War.

Part of the early planning considerations for how many forces would be deployed prior to the initiation of MCO rested on the traditional tension between the historic American penchant for large-scale, deliberate deployments of overwhelming forces and the more efficient approach of "just-in-time" operations. There were at least two factors that weighed in and impacted the decision to deploy a heavier and more full-spectrum forces or a lighter and more fleet and agile force. The first major factor was purely operational—logistics requirements for large-scale Army and Marine Corps formations and the availability of relatively limited strategic lift capacity (due to competing war-fights in Afghanistan and other operational theaters around the globe) stiffened those arguments for a deliberate (protracted) deployment. A strong operational counterargument was the potential gains in operational surprise over enemy forces that could possibly be gained by a quick no-notice strategic deployment. The second major factor impacting the force-generation decision was political. By Fall 2002, U.S. diplomatic efforts in the United Nations demonstrated to the world that an American-led campaign to remove Saddam Hussein from power was becoming a probability more than simply a possibility.[19] The administration in Washington, DC, by this time saw a grave danger to the United States and its friends and interests within the wider Middle East region festering in Iraq with every moment of delay in offensive preventive action. The need for a military preemptive intervention against this threat by Fall 2002 had become the political agenda undergirding all intervention planning. These two key factors set the course for America's intervention policy toward Iraq—an intervention derived from a limited political-military objective of ending Saddam Hussein's regime in Iraq.

From this tension developed three options of planning courses of action: a deployment scheme similar to DESERT STORM (1990–1991), an almost no-notice deployment in which the war would start with very few forces on the ground in Kuwait, and a hybrid that combined elements of both former approaches.[20]

Most official accounts that have been published or delivered in lectures since the inception of the war in 2003 have offered that few if any of the operational planners, particularly those on the military side of the planning, thought that the Saddam regime would immediately collapse under the pressure of simultaneous attacks along multiple lines of operation (avenues of advance). Nevertheless, much planning and rehearsal time and resources were expended on developing plans for this remote possibility. The option of simultaneous attack for a rapid decisive effective regime collapse was, again, reflective of both a political desire for an immediate addressing of the grave and growing threat posed by the Hussein regime and an American tradition for quick (and, if possible, costless) decisive victories in its war-fights and interventions. Three iterations of planning took place, each reflective of different sets of operational conditions but all influenced by the political intent for a quicker than later resolution of the Hussein problem. Each included the idea of simultaneous attack from the air and on the ground, with the number of units available serving as the key variable in those calculations. The first iteration was regarded as the "generated start option," which assumed a buildup of forces until all the forces required had arrived in theater before the initiation of MCO (i.e., before initiation of the "war" as it was to be seen by planners and decision makers alike). Planners then developed a second option—the "running start"—which reflected assumptions of launching combat operations with minimum forces and continuing to deploy forces and employing them as they arrived in the operational theater.[21] The final option derived from the war-gaming took place in regard to the running start option. During simulation trials of the "running start" plan, planners determined that the minimum force required under the running start option was inadequate. As a result, a "hybrid plan" was developed that better reflected the forces required to effectively meet the objective of the intervention policy—collapse of the Hussein regime.

An Inadequate Plan

The hybrid plan, which was developed by military planners in response to their realizations through simulation and war-gaming, that more forces were required—demanded—by the anticipated conditions on the ground during the intervention was not the decided plan for resourcing, nor for eventual execution. What did ultimately become the campaign plan for OIF was a "compromise" solution between the running start and hybrid options that provided more forces than planned under running start scenarios but fewer than estimated as required for the hybrid plan. This compromise plan reflected little to none of the force requirements of the first and original "generated start" courses of action. Most of the officers taking part in this planning process preferred the simultaneous attacks afforded by the hybrid plan, once the decision process relegated the options to a zero-sum calculation between this alternative versus the paucity of the running start option. Nevertheless, the policy implemented was one that reflected the desires and determinations of what was acceptable by the administration and logistically feasible given the political timings of the military campaign.

The number of forces required was the single most important variable around which all planning variants revolved. The question over how much force is required to either stay the present course or change the course but the stay the fight in Iraq to win continues to define the Iraq War and the future role of the United States in it. The official U.S. Army "early" history of ground war in Iraq, *On Point*, acknowledged the preeminent importance of this forces-required question and also noted the persistent operational and strategic ambiguity that derived from an inability of force planners, operational planners, and decision makers alike to come to an agreement on the right approach (i.e., operational approach or "way") to executing the war-strategy. By *On Point* accounts, "the end was never in question—remove the regime; but the specific method, or way, required to achieve this strategic goal was the subject of contentious debate. Without agreement on the way—simultaneous or sequential—there rarely was agreement on the amount of force or means required."[22]

This early assessment was then, as it is today, woefully inaccurate. This assessment reflected an assumption that the end driving the intervention policy planning ("remove the regime") reflected the correct or appropriate political objective of the intervention. The fact of the matter has proven to be this: removal of the Hussein regime, though a necessary condition to "victory" was insufficient in and of itself as the means toward the greater end of achieving a sustainable and legitimate quality of stability and "peace" in Iraq. Moreover, the chosen method, or way, of intervention—MCO by use of military force—was to prove not only insufficient but in hindsight a contributing cause to the rise in insurgent and anti-American (anti"occupation") sentiment and condition in Iraq. While *On Point* and similar early histories correctly acknowledge the errors in the military planning for MCO against Saddam Hussein, all either ignore or simply fail to recognize the wider failures of planning and execution: the failure to plan for and execute an intervention policy and the civil-military plans and strategy for that policy that reflect and address the complete array of objectives, requirements, responsibilities, challenges, threats, and opportunities of the war that was to be "at hand" in a war in Iraq.

The plan for the major combative operations to bring about the end to Hussein's regime was not a plan for peace—it was, as planned, nothing more than a military plan for destruction and annihilation. Failing to plan for the whole war—failing to plan for the peace to follow the "war"—has left us in the quagmire that is America's war in Iraq.

"A Plan to Win the War, But Not the Peace"

The prevailing idea of the Iraq postwar was just that—that it was post- or after the fact of the war. As defined and explained to the public, and to the military, the war in Iraq was to begin with initiation of ground invasion on March 19, 2003 and was to end on or around April 9, 2003 with the final collapse of the Hussein state regime. Activities beyond regime collapse was "other-than-war"—postwar—and, as such, the purview and responsibility of some other entity than the U.S. military.

This United States' view of the jurisdictional divisions of the war had been made clear to me as early as March 2003, during the formation of the Operation Iraqi Freedom Study Group (OIFSG). When several of us on the Group's advance party asked "higher" about the scope of the Group's mission, we were told to focus our interviews, research, and recordkeeping on the ground war, to cover Phase I (Preparation) through Phase III (Decisive Operations) but to stop there. When several of us pressed the issue further, offering our concerns as historians with writing a "history" of the war that did not cover the war's entirety, we were further told that our mission was to end with the collapse of the regime. We could mention Phase IV (Transition) in passing as we concluded the book but should go no further—beyond the military's Phase IV was a story that went beyond the military's story, and, therefore, beyond our mandate.

By the time I arrived in Mosul, Iraq, on July 8, 2003 to assume my duties as chief of plans for then Major General David Petraeus and the 101st Airborne Division (Air Assault),[23] it was becoming more and more obvious that the war was not over and that the OISFG story I had been a party to telling would be a premature and incomplete one. In the last week of April—two weeks after regime collapse—the 101st Airborne had been re-missioned for "liberation" duties in Mosul and the northern provinces. The Marine Corps had been deployed earlier and had since run up against some "substantial challenges" in their attempts to pacify the north. By the time lead elements of 101st Airborne Division (2nd Brigade Combat Team—Stryker Brigade) had arrived in Mosul, the Marines had withdrawn "under pressure" (i.e., under fire) to the Mosul airport. On June 4, the Division faced a citywide riot in Mosul. By the June 17, the 101st had conducted a major air assault operation in its western sectors near the Jordanian and Syrian borders and destroyed a terrorist camp killing over 70 foreign-originated jihadist and former Hussein regime loyalists.

This was how "the postwar" looked like in the north—presumed at that time as one of the more pacified areas of the country. If this was not war, then what was it?

The lack of a coherent, complete, and comprehensive war-plan for the post-April 2003, postregime collapse actions and activities that would have defined a wider campaign plan for Iraq left the country and the U.S. intervention policy in strategic ambiguity and each war-fighting unit in Iraq by May–June 2003 without clear marching orders. Each separate division was left on their own to divine and develop their own campaign plans and approaches for conducting stability and reconstruction operations in their individual assigned areas of operations (AOs). The result was a completely under-coordinated and unsynchronized stability and reconstruction situation throughout Iraq, with each of the 18 provinces or governorates comprising the country of Iraq falling under the control of at least 5 separate multinational division (MND) controlling agencies—and, therefore, at least 5 separate and all-too-often distinct "campaign" approaches to security, stability, and reconstruction operations and activities. What we see in Iraq in terms of uneven developments in the restoration of security, essential services, governance, and the economy is largely the result of an unevenness in the planning for and execution of these operations by separate occupying forces in separate areas of operation and occupation—each approaching the mission based on their own definition of the mission, concept of operations, understandings of the social-political-economic situation, and their own separate interpretations of the grand strategic purpose of the war itself. All occupying forces (the commanders, their units or organizations, and the quantity and quality of their resources available) were not created equal, thereby contributing to the imbalances we see. Even those provinces or governorates that have experienced relative success in postcombat stability and reconstruction operations evidence a very sporadic development.

The two more successful areas of operation during the first year of the war—the northern provinces under the 101st Airborne and the southern provinces under the British occupation forces—each have suffered dramatic degradations in security, stability, and reconstruction efforts in the two years since those initial occupations. Once pacified and stabilized cities such as Mosul and Tall Afar and Basra had once again (by Winter 2005) devolved into epicenters of insurgency and transit stations (safe havens) for transnational jihadist (Islamic terrorist) activities. Initial failures to develop and implement a countrywide and comprehensive (i.e., full spectrum of consequences) campaign plan caused the U.S. and coalition intervention policy and war-strategy to stall. This culmination created and then exacerbated a seam between an effective war-fight and the absence of a plan of attack for winning the peace that was to follow. When removing a tick from a body, we all know that it is not enough to only remove the visible part of the insect from the surface of the skin—one must remove the infestation entirely from the body, else what is left invisible below the surface of the skin will become infected, thereby spreading the infection to the whole body. The same is true in intervention policies designed to affect regime change. As such, the battle plan to remove the Hussein regime merely removed one part of that regime from the body politic of the Iraqi nation. Lethal remnants of that regime were left to linger, fester, and metastasize into the chronic fever of insurgency and transnational terrorism that exist today.

Flaws in conceptual planning that determined the purpose of the U.S. intervention in Iraq in 2003 led to the flaws in operational planning (failure to plan to win the peace) that continue to deny decisive victory for the Iraqis, the United States, and its coalition. Those operational planning flaws have heavily informed and influenced U.S. force-planning reconceptualizations and organizational redesigns since Fall 2003. Many of these redesigned units are now returned to war-fights either in Afghanistan or Iraq—redesigns that may reflect more of the modern-age flaws that have denied us success and victory thus far in both interventions rather than new and more effective postmodern force designs and structures reflective of the COE.

A Modular Approach to Force Design and Implementation

The Need to Reorganize for Holistic War

Are American war-waging forces adequately designed and oriented for twenty-first-century war-fare? That question was an important one for the OIFSG to consider back in 2003. It is an important question today, as the U.S. Army—the nation's entire war-waging machinery—undergoes reorganization, a reform process labeled by the Department of Defense as Transformation. The question was even made relevant to U.S. Army forces fighting on the ground in Iraq in late 2003, when, in September 2003, the Army's new chief of staff, General Pete Schoomaker unveiled his vision for Army Transformation—a reorganization to a "Modular Force" configuration—and in fall 2003 directed two of his war-fighting divisions at the time still in the fight in Iraq (the 3rd Infantry Division and 101st Airborne Division-Air Assault) to immediately begin transformation. As chief of plans for the 101st Airborne Division, I inherited responsibility for the planning of that Transformation, adding this plan's requirement to the family of plans we were already developing to wage and win the war and the "postwar" in our sector of the war—northern Iraq. I remained chief architect for the planning and implementation of the 101st Airborne Transformation Initiative until March 2005.

Working on new war-fighting designs of the Division and developing new innovations to our war-fighting capabilities as a light-infantry, air assault combat organization, in the context of my early 2003 observational study of what worked and what did not during the OIFSG and now in the context of the "fight" at hand provided some very unique context and an intriguing environment for change. Scholars have written several works on revolutions in military affairs—those rare episodes in history that evidence radical and systemic alterations of military doctrine, organization, tactics and techniques, technologies—and the impact of those changes on greater society. Was the work we were about in Iraq, fighting and changing-changing and fighting, such a revolution? After seeing the transformation in practice in Iraq, and back stateside, and after leading the effort to bring about an effective revolution in our military affairs for two years, I still remain the "healthy skeptic," and so should you.

Though our military has made many great strides forward in this latest reform initiative, the fact that our organizations for war continue to remain structured and oriented ("tasked and purposed") as combat "versus" "all other supporting" organizations indicates that we still have a long way to go before we achieve a true revolution in military affairs (RMA). We are at the doorstep and that is something to be positive about. However, until we can bring ourselves to cross through the doors—kick them down—we will continue to suffer the paradox.

Today, our military, in spite of its well-earned reputation as an effective learning organization, is still romanticizing war-fare as the function of direct applications of martial combatives and the forms of armored cavalry. The forms and functions we invest in today could prove to be our modern-day Maginot Line and methodical battle, leading America on a string of "strange defeats."

New organizational designs and formations are only one part of true transformation. The dawn of a new age of postmodern intervention policy—war-policy—will be largely predicated not only on new technological solutions but also on a new quality of "soldiering" that is born and cultivated from the education of a new breed of holistic postmodern warriors.

The Postmodern War-rior

The Need to Educate for Holistic War

How the U.S. Military is designed to educate its officers in strategy and planning will determine success, or failure, in its efforts to produce and sustain strategic planners—uniformed professionals, experts in advice-giving on matters related to national policy, national strategy, and experienced in the operational planning and tactical execution of martial actions intended to translate strategic goals into tangible effects.[27] The military services' education processes and systems design shows signs of pending "failure," indicated by

- separate approaches to strategic-level education, operational-level education, and tactical-level education;
- differentiated career paths for officers trained in strategy versus operations and tactics;
- a seniority-based approach to the education and experience of officers in national and grand strategy;
- Military-centric approach to education of strategists ("Military" strategist);
- service-bifurcated education systems (joint education, by exception);
- a military-centric approach to future roles, functions, and missions for military strategic planners.

Today's complex strategic environment calls for the synthesis of expertise in the three domains of war into one entity: the uniformed strategic planner. To meet this educational end, the current educational ways and means must be assessed, evaluated; weak spots and points of failure must be identified—all on behalf of retooling the system in ways that facilitate the development of Army experts in national strategic planning.

I propose that postmodernity demands some specific structural and procedural treatments to what not only I but many authoritative figures in the rising revolution in educational affairs movement offer is an antiquated modern-era education system "flawed by design" and therefore ill equipped to consistently produce the quality and quantity of strategic planning experts demanded by the security challenges that face the Army, the military services in general, and the nation on the whole. These four proposals are as follows:

1. removal of arbitrary functional-based branch qualification requirements for specific promotion ranks within military and civilian occupational fields of practice;
2. formalization of advanced military studies (i.e., operation and theater-strategic planning) in the professional education of all military officers and equivalent civilian operators;
3. implementation of a dual-track uniformed strategic planner education system, incorporating civilian and interagency academic and experience-based education into the pedagogy;
4. congressional enforcement of a holistic change to how security professionals are educated (i.e., academically schooled + tactically trained + operationally experienced) and incorporation of a joint (i.e., military service-integrated), interagency, intergovernmental (i.e., federalist), and multinational (JIIM) educational construct more reflective of the postmodern COE.

Developing a new postmodern approach to education demands that we first understand how the modern form came into being and how the evolution of that modern-age form has led to this postmodern need for change. This evolution in how we educate our "warriors" (i.e., civil-military, security experts) parallels the same organizational evolution expressed in chapter 1.

This postmodern age of intervention policy—this information age of war-policy—calls for a reconsolidation of the art and science of war-policymaking and implementation. In a democracy such as the United States, though intervention policy must continually and always remain subservient to and determined by the civilian leadership (i.e., the elected leaders), planning and execution of holistic interventions must be conducted through collaborative efforts of military and civilian operational experts. The type and nature of holistic campaign plans needed during this new postmodern era will undoubtedly demand the creation and fostering of a new breed of experts cross-educated, cross-trained, and experienced in holistic war-policy—with a comprehensive appreciation of all domains and realms of post modern war-fare.

Conclusions

The Return to Considering War as a Form of Policy

What this chapter has presented is a brief introduction of some of the "evolutions" that, in my opinion, herald a new age of intervention policy and war-fare. This story of "evolutions" clearly shows, first, a devolution of war and peace into separable aspects (parts), with war being defined more by its combative (martial) or battle functions rather than its overriding and defining purpose—the peace-objective. The modern incarnation of organizational forms, functional processes and procedures and conceptions reflects this separation of function from purpose—a separation of forms and functions for implementing intervention policy from its original intended quality-of-peace-objectives that has led to a prevailing misconception within the

American polity over what constitutes war and peace. The modern concept of war and war-fare has elevated the role of the military and combatives to an end in and of itself and one that is separate from its original peace-objective (purpose). It is important to reiterate that this separation of war's activity from its peace-objective is largely unintentional—the result of organizational flaws and organizational cultural bias that today defines war as "the absence of peace" and peace, conversely, as "the absence of war." This separation is in direct violation of the very nature of war and peace, in direct violation of the Clausewitzian principles that underpin the modern American and Western ways of war and peace, and, as a result, a direct contributor of the paradox within our national ways of war and peace. When it comes to U.S. intervention policy—*when, where, how, and why America intervenes*—this national misinterpretation is a root cause of our propensity to win in battle but lose in our efforts to win and secure the peace.

War as Policy

The theory of a new, postmodern era of war and peace presented in this book sets the argument solidly upon the original intended theory and definition of war prescribed by Karl von Clausewitz in his seminal work, *On War*, published in 1832. This new theory takes the old theory literally, that war defined is "an act of force to compel one to do your will" and war described is "a continuation of politics by other means." This new theory sees war as a form of public policy (albeit a peculiar and abhorrent form of public policy) and, therefore, as a function of peace. While the attainment of a quality of peace is the political objective of war (or any other public policy function), war is one of several policy processes intended and designed for the attainment of that peace-objective. As is true with any public policy, the practice of the policy (process) in and of itself is largely meaningless when considered absent from its defining policy purpose—strategy is meaningless in the absence of the political goal behind that strategy. So it is with war-policy. The "act of compellance" alone is meaningless out of context and content of the original purpose and intent behind the policy to compel. Once again, Clausewitz warned over a century and half ago,

> [W]ars cannot be divorced from political life; and whenever this occurs in our thinking about war, the many links that connect the two elements are destroyed and we are left with something pointless and devoid of sense.[28]

The modern (Western) conception of war and peace typifies the very sort of divorce that Clausewitz warned against. The result of this failed marriage between war-policy and peace-objective as evidenced in stark relief over the past 15 years (post–cold war era) in particular has been a short but poignant history of incomplete interventions, a muddling through in U.S. intervention policy that has failed to secure a lasting quality of peace in nearly all of its post–cold war expeditions. Iraq is merely the latest in a long trail of "incomplete finishes"—a by-product of flawed war-policies. Adding to the tragedy is the failure to win and secure the peace-objective in spite of heroic actions on the part of soldier and peace operator alike on the ground and in spite of carrying out the day-to-day duties and details of intervention policy implementation. In spite of our unmatched prowess at implementing policy at local levels, be it attaining victory over enemies of the peace in local engagements (battles) or ably providing aid and security to those in need in our humanitarian efforts from village to village, those valiant efforts still tend to fall short of attaining any sort of widespread quality of security, stability, or prosperity (i.e., a quality of peace) that can then be maintained and sustained and built upon. Wars tend to widen due in part to our national inability to contain war-fare through securing and then expanding the peace-objective in our intervention policy and strategies—real prevention. The paradox is emblematic of this systemic failure—a flaw in the modern war-policy process.

This policy framework—the stages of the public policy process—categorizes the policy process into four domains or "stages": agenda-setting, formulation and legitimization, implementation, and evaluation. These four stages form a policy development cycle; it serves as a very useful model for simplifying the complexities of policymaking as well as for examining and analyzing any given real-world policy. A "balanced" policy would be the product of an equilibrium between the intended goals of the policy at national or higher levels, with the policy programs that are formulated within bureaucratic agencies and processes within the policy-making system that are realized, as originally intended, after implementation. A balanced policy would find the actual policy impact on the ground perfectly or near-perfectly reflecting the actual intentions of the policy vision as set at national or higher decision-making levels. Such perfections occur in theory but rarely if ever in real practice. The degree to which reality deviates from this theorized equilibrium is what becomes most interesting from a policy science point of view. When we consider war-policy, the degree of mismatch can have dire and dramatically tragic effects.

Applying the four-stage model to modern-era war-policy in general, we can examine and preliminarily evaluate the presence and impact of the paradox. By posing a hypothesis, IF war is a peace-policy process, AND if that process is currently premised on a faulty (partial) idea of the policy endstate of war-fare, THEN we may be witnessing and feeling the impacts of the following:

- We may be crediting too much public policy success (credit) to our military's ability to win in tactical battle (and, similarly, placing too much hope for a viable peace "victory" on the localized efforts of so-called peace operations)—the "tactification" of U.S. intervention policy, feeding the paradox within our intervention policy.
- Our entire national security policy system (regime, a la Krasner[29]) may be militarized by design and overly "offensive" in its orientations for implementation. Consequently, all "security challenges and opportunities" facing us may be seen as proverbial "nails" demanding the use of only (predominantly) the military "hammer" to deal with it. The hammer may still be the "appropriate tool"—remember, a hammer has two ends: one for banging, but the other for a whole other set of functions. The hammer can be a tool for direct action as well as indirect action—the purpose of both actions is "peace attainment/sustainment."
- Part of our flawed structure includes a flawed lessons-gathered/lessons-learned evaluative process. Perpetuating the ill-lessons-learned phenomenon, ironically, is the unmatchable prowess and pure and noble courage and innovative spirit of the "soldier"—who makes do, goes to war, and is largely successful (in a local tactical context) "with the Army he has" rather than the one he deserved all along." When all is said and done, the histories record that our Army that went to war

must have been the "good-enough" solution, as the soldiers were able to "meet the mission." The course of failure is complete in large part by the can-do spirit of our own implementers, with their Macgiver-like actions to make less work better on the ground feeding the misperception among decision makers that nothing is broken and therefore nothing needs fixing.

- We may in fact be witnessing the rise of a new "generation" of war-fare and experiencing the negative impacts of the collision between this emergent new age of war-fare (i.e., 4GW) and the traditional (modern-era) generation. The paradox within America's way of war and peace may be a manifestation of this revolutionary (or perhaps devolutionary) tectonic shift.

To summarize, getting the concept of the war wrong in the first place led the United States and its coalition of the willing to errant decisions on war-plans (deliberate plans for battle but sparse plans, if any, for the wider war itself), force allocations (too few boots-on-the-ground for the battles that would ensue after the fall of Saddam, too few "other-than-military" forces available), and force configurations (adequate joint configurations but poor to completely absent representation of interagency, intergovernmental, multinational, or NGOs, agencies, and expert personnel). Ultimately, the misconception led to an overly offensive-based and military battle-focused conception of and approach toward the war. Our failure to *think beyond* the modern conceptions of war (i.e., war "versus" peace) and our failure to then redesign our plans, processes, and organizations so that we can *act beyond* those modern understandings and perceptions of war have left us yet again in the strategic position of losing this wider war in (and around) Iraq, despite our valiant efforts on ground everyday.

The dawn of a postmodern age of war and peace is well upon us. Yet America sleeps. Waking to this new dawn and rapidly adjusting to its light is vital if we are to maintain our reputation and sheer capacity as an effective—and legitimate—force of intervention.

Chapter 4

On Planning: A New Methodology for Postmodern War-Fare

Was there or was there not a "plan to win the peace" in Iraq? This simple question has boggled, beguiled, and bewildered the collective mind and our collective understanding (or rather lack thereof) of what has gone wrong in our war-policy and military strategy in Iraq. This question underpinned a heated U.S. presidential campaign in 2004 and continues to fuel partisan divides within Washington, DC, within the Pentagon, and well beyond the political beltway adding confusion and frustration in the hearts and minds of the American public. Much of the debate over whether there was a plan for the postcombat phases of the war has taken place within a veil of ignorance over what "a plan" really is or what "planning" really means? The issue divides us and continues to deny us in our efforts toward fixing the problem, and ultimately, we do not even know what we are taking about.

In this chapter, I intend to clarify the subject of "planning." In so doing, I hope to shed informative light on the subject of plans and planning in general (what is it? why is it important?) and the impact of plans and planning before, during, and after initiation of major combat operations (MCO) (entry into war) in Iraq (did we or did we not have a plan for the whole war? so what?). Finally, I provide insight on the relevancy of the "question of planning" on U.S. intervention policy beyond Iraq. This chapter intends to educate the reader on the significance of planning (policy formulation) in the development of war-policy and strategy: it is in the planning where the course is set and where resource authorizations, allocations, and distributions are determined for the effective implementation of the policy, an execution of intentions that reflect (and therefore legitimize) the original stated policy. Getting the planning wrong is a prerequisite for getting the policy wrong and ultimately for failing to win.

What does it take to win a war? More important, what does it take to win the peace that is to follow? We know about the intangibles of a war- and peace-winning strategy—you should have goals, public support, moral authority, political will, patience and determination, clarity of mission, leadership, and so on.

But getting to the bare bones of the fight on the ground for war and for peace and from a capabilities-based standpoint, how much, from a material point of view, is "good enough" for ensuring a victory in a war-fight and subsequent peace?

Understanding the Modern Construct

Joint Operational Planning

The modern age way of war and peace all but formally defines war-fare and war-policy planning as a martial affair—an exercise relegated to the domain of military art and science. To understand the present paradox and gain an appreciation for its persistence, we must understand and appreciate the modern-era planning process and concepts that underpin and perpetuate its existence. The joint campaign planning process, as articulated in Chapter Five of *Chairman, Joint Chief of Staff Manual (CJCSM) 3500.05*, provides us with that base description and understanding.

The modern planning construct, in short, reflects a parallel planning process—one driven predominantly during crisis situations by the commander of a particular operation (i.e., the commander of a joint task force [CJTF]) but during periods of relative stability or "peace" (noncrisis moments) a deliberative planning process driven more by the estimates and planning of staff, working from constantly evolving planning guidance from the commander based on a combination of commander and staff intelligence estimates and updates. This planning process is a four-stage process. The first stage, mission analysis, is the foundation of all effective planning. The commander and his or her staff endeavor to define the tactical and operational problem (the root-and-stem causes and effects of the crisis at hand or pending/looming). This problem definition is predicated on a thorough assessment of the situation (friendly, threat, neutral party, environmental, political-societal, etc.) through a process formally known as an intelligence preparation of the battlefield (IPB). This situational understanding is gained through a detailed process of fact determination, the development of assumptions (to fill the gap where facts are not readily available), the analysis of and synchronization with higher command missions and intent (to ensure commonality of purpose and direction), the determination of operational limitations and constraints, the determination of sources of one's own force and power as well as that of the enemy (known as "centers of gravity" in the military vernacular), and the identification of key tasks to be performed in accomplishment of the missions (specific, implied, and essential tasks). Mission analysis uses this knowledge to conduct initial force structure analyses—in hopes of fashioning the right and appropriate complement and composition of forces and capabilities commensurate with mission success; this data is also critical in risk assessments, the determination of intermediate military objectives (that lead toward the accomplishment of the overriding political peace-objective), and the determination of political endstate.[1] Campaign plans are effective or ineffective largely due to proper or incomplete mission analyses, respectively—a cyclical, dynamic assessment and fact-determining process.

The second formal stage of the planning process is course of action (COA) development. During this stage, the staff and commander integrate commander intentions with staff estimates to determine various alternative ways in which the CJTF can accomplish, at an initial minimum, the essential tasks associated with a particular mission or series of missions that comprise a major operation. Each COA includes at least five elements that answer five key operational questions: the type of operation(s) to be conducted (What), the time and timing of the operation(s) to be conducted and their enddates (When), the assigned areas of operation (AO) within the joint operations area (JOA) (Where), the purpose of the operation(s) (Why), and the method of conducting the operation(s) using major available resources (How). The end product of COA development is a set of distinctive courses of action, approved by the commander and available for further analysis and comparison (war-gaming).

The third major stage in the planning process is COA comparison (analysis). It is designed to determine or reveal which COA has the highest probability of success against an enemy or threat COA that most concerns the commander. The end product of this process is a decision briefing delivered by the planning staff to the commander complete with staff recommendations of the preferred COA. These recommendations are arrived upon by analysis that centers on five validity test criteria (suitability, feasibility, acceptability, differentiation, completeness),[2] followed by a cross-comparison of alternative COAs based on some arrived-upon sets of criteria.

The final stage of the planning process is selection and modification of the COA. This is the result of war-gaming and comparative analysis of the options available to the commander for mission accomplishment—it provides the base focus for all staff and executing agencies for mission execution and forms the baseline for operations plan (OPLAN) and operations order (OPORD) development.

What has just been described details the standard, doctrinal (commonly approved or accepted) methodology and conception for planning for the *waging of war*. While this book calls into stark question the adequacy of the modern planning paradigm for effectively meeting the challenges and opportunities of postmodern intervention, what is not under scrutiny is the solvency of the war-waging capacity of this process. This modern planning process has more than proven its worth over decades of crisis interventions. What is under scrutiny is the effectiveness of this planning paradigm for the *winning of the peace*.

Again—and it is vitally important to reiterate this point—the planning sequence just described is a proven success in planning to wage war-fare, but by design, it is limited in the following critical ways:

- military-centric;
- overly sequential in conception and orientation;
- response-oriented;
- evolving toward better "joint" (i.e., integrated, intermilitary service) operations but still far shy of the type and degree of joint, interagency, intergovernmental, and multinational (JIIM-based) integrated operations to fight wars to a peace-objective win.

In short, this joint campaign planning process reflects the same limitations of the modern-era organization structures. Our planning processes perpetuate a limited or truncated national idea of what constitutes the jurisdictions of war versus the jurisdictions of peace, denying us all a proper and complete understanding of war as a process of peace along a continuum of consequences and opportunities that demand the integration and synchronization of all available resources—civilian and military, governmental and private—for successful completion of war's purpose, which is the attainment and sustainment of peace.

Postmodernity demands that we begin to consider an entirely new question other than *how should America fight?* That new postmodern question is *how do we win the peace?* This postmodern question implies the need for a new postmodern approach to planning.

What Does It Take to "Win the Peace?"

The war in Iraq is the most recent in a long debate over how much manpower and materiel, not to mention time, is required to win decisively in our nation's wars and interventions. The debate is the offspring of the traditional "guns-versus-butter" argument that is important for any democratic nation to undertake prior to, and throughout, a war-policy process (agenda-setting, policy formulation and legitimization, implementation, evaluation).[3] This latest war in Iraq, however, has raised this discussion to a new level of importance. This is the case, in part, because of the elusiveness of the "decisive victory" that defense and military planners were convinced would come with the collapse of the Hussein regime on April 9, 2003, and the boots-on-the-ground ("BOG") insurgency and anti-insurgency in which the United States and its military forces have found themselves since the declaration of "mission accomplished" on May 1, 2004.

Was there a plan for the peace? Some say yes, but others say no. This chapter will focus on the way in which we have traditionally conducted the force planning (determination of resource requirements, the allocation and distribution of those resources) for war, raising the overdone question of *why no winning plan for Phase-IV operations in Iraq?* to a new level of relevance by revealing a more important secondary question: *do the same correlates ("wages") of modern war adequately apply to postmodern war?*

Determining the proper correlates for postmodern war depends on determining the proper mathematics (the "calculus") of planning and resourcing for postmodern interventions. Before we determine this, we must first understand the modern system correlates—largely and predominately martial- and combatives-based—and understand from where they derive and gain their privileged position as the dominant wares and wages for determining success or failure in modern war.

While the new Office of the Secretary of Defense (OSD) construct appropriately recognizes the prevalence and importance of planning and implementation phases and stages in the war-policy process that precede and proceed the war-fighting ("dominant") phases of campaigning, the modern realities are as follows: the "decisive phase" of the campaign is still regarded as the *dominant* phase—a mainly military and combative affair. This simple fact bears a substantial impact on the effectiveness of how America prepares, plans, and executes its intervention policy in this postmodern age of war and peace. While modernity may have legitimized this notion of the decisive battle as determinative of victory or defeat of the war-policy itself, postmodernity shows us time and again that the act of force remains an integral component toward the attainment of the peace-objective but is no longer decisive in war. Yet, when we consider the resourcing of our intervention capacities and the emphasis of program acquisitions and production that determine our current and future force designs for intervention, we see that modernity still reigns over the demands of the postmodern contemporary operating environment (COE). War remains a martial affair. Winning wars still equates to victory in battles—in combat. Our military services take the lion's share of defense, security, and foreign policy budgets alike each year at the direct expense of other agencies and capabilities (nonmilitary, other-than-military); this is critical to success under postmodern conditions (i.e., winning and sustaining the peace).

The OSD "revised and updated" six-phase campaign construct applied to the Iraq War, 2003–, reveals the prominence of planning efforts, force planning, and resourcing that went toward the major combat (war-fighting) phases of Operation Iraqi Freedom (OIF) as compared to the relative paucity of those phases (stabilize, enable civil authority) coming after the May 1 declaration of mission accomplished. It also shows the limitations of the modern campaign planning approach—with the majority of activity beginning at crisis moment (activation of war-plans), relegating the attention and resources given to more preventive (i.e., peace-time engagement) planning and actions to marginal importance.

Our challenges in Iraq stem from this modernity-postmodernity gap in operational planning. We essentially approached the intervention from a modern mindset and focused on *the war that was to be planned for and won*—the defeat of Saddam and his Baa'thist regime. Postmodernity proved this calculus of war as woefully incomplete and inappropriate. Like a carpenter using the wrong tools for the job at hand or the architect designing a house on faulty blueprints, U.S. policy makers laid errant blueprints, military and civilian planners took those errant blueprints and derived and developed their own, separate, implementation plans, and the nation set upon executing its intervention policy in Iraq—near completely devoid of a comprehensive understanding or appreciation of the war for what it was and would prove to be by its postmodern nature—a war for the hearts and minds of the Iraqi people, a war of ideas and of nation-building.

As blatant and dramatic as these errors are, they are predominately structural, and, as such, are fixable.

The war we initiated in March 2003, from a postmodern viewpoint, was a war that we embarked upon at least a decade earlier (ca. Desert Storm, 1990–1991). In order to have arrived at the more accurate force requirements for this war, our planners and decision makers would have had to have seen the war in this fuller scope and scale. The war we resourced was far more limited than this war that fell upon us beginning in March 2003. Consequently, we have never embarked on the war in Iraq in its entirety—we are yet to wage the real holistic war in Iraq and are beginning to realize it. This realization may unfortunately be too little and too late to make a change to our present course in our policy and strategies toward the war in Iraq that will allow us to stay the fight for peace completion.

Getting the Right Force Mix

Hindsight is 20/20. It allows one to see through both the natural fog of war that may have been present at the time of the actual war-fight as well as beyond the blindness that can come from looking too hard, too close, and too narrowly at the planning problem at hand prior to the initiation of the war-fight. That is not to say that one cannot chart a predictable and reliable course through the fog and self-imposed frictions of war and prewar through planning. On the contrary, deliberate planning can help one to get the initial array of forces "right" for the anticipated objectives that make up the war-plan. Planning and mission-type orders are a traditional doctrinal mainstay of the modern Western military way of war; it is the bedrock of our military art and science. The military decision-making process (MDMP) is a planning approach or model—a policy-making schema—that helps military planners to receive a higher mission order (at the highest level of analysis, a war-policy agenda as set by the National Command Authority), analyze the intent (purpose, method, endstate) of the higher order/policy through mission analysis, develop various courses of action (COAs) for the array of available forces (traditionally limited to combat forces) and the application of those forces, war-game those options (COA analysis) to determine the most feasible, acceptable, and suitable of the options for maximum effective implementation. This process is one of many available to the military war-planner, at all echelons, for guiding perhaps one of the more critical aspects of war-planning and execution: the request for appropriate forces from higher headquarters for execution of the missions at hand and the allocation (assignment of certain forces to certain mission tasks or "trooping to tasks" in the military vernacular) and distribution of those resources (human and materiel) to various units for execution of the plan.

Ensuring Our "Intended" Strategic Goals through Our Tactical Actions

From a strategic point of relevancy, getting the "troop-to-tasks" calculus, at least within the "ballpark," is essential for ensuring the type of ends-ways-means balance that is defining of a war-strategy that has a hopeful chance, by design, of ensuring a high probability of success of tactical actions on the ground effecting the strategic impact that was originally intended. From the ground perspective, getting the right mix of forces and the right distribution of available troops to perform the tasks at hand is imperative for the success of the mission (for winning the battles and engagements) and for surviving to "fight and win" another day. There is a third layer to the force-planning calculus that resides at what we call the *operational level of war*. At this level of war-policymaking, separate tactical-level (implementation-level) missions and activities get tied together—integrated and synchronized into a particular "operational set of activities"—in a particular context of time, geographical space ("battlespace"), and purpose. This "operationalization" stage of war-planning is the *tie that binds* otherwise-disparate activities together into a common purpose and direction, providing a *synergistic effect* (a solution greater than the sum of its individual parts or activities).

The dynamics of battlefield troop-to-tasks force tailoring has its own unique logic. Again, that logic has at least three dimensions: temporal, geographic, and purpose-based. Traditionally, war has also been usefully divided into two operational types: the offense and the defense. The logic follows, then, that with each type of war (offense or defense) comes a different character and condition of the three dimensions of war (time, space, purpose). Modern, mechanistic-age war-fare has typically formed based upon a linear battlefield architecture, with a spatial (geographic) orientation of "deep, close, and rear" AO and an operational concept and construct that model war as a linear progression of action-reaction-counteraction moves on the part of belligerents—a trade of offensive and defensive (and counteroffensive) moves. Modern-age war-fare is predicated on the power and effectiveness of maneuver (fire + movement) and the rapid and high-tempo nature of maneuver war-fare. Finally, modern war and war-fighting have been traditionally refined by the martial arts and sciences—and for the purpose of "closing with to destroy" an enemy.

The relevant questions, from a force-planning standpoint, are these: Does the calculus of modern war-fare suffice in this postmodern environment? Do we need a new calculus of peace?

The Modern Legacy—The Correlation of Forces and Means

What sort of force does it take to fight and win in today's postmodern war-environment? How can we increase the probabilities of success in our wars of the postmodern age? The modern age (mechanized age, second and third generations) of war was more easily reducible to a linear framework and calculus than this new postmodern (postindustrial, digital, informational, cybernetic, fourth-generation) age of war has already proven itself to be in the first five years of the twenty-first century. The science of the former was more quantifiable, reducible to numbered calculations, and more susceptible to valuations of success versus failure from an attritional evaluation. Not to say that this postmodern age of nonlinear and non-contiguous battlespace is beyond the numbers game. On the contrary, numbers matter as much, perhaps more so, than they did during the linear age. The significant difference is not in the nature of the comparative war-environments (quantitative or qualitative, by base nature) but rather by the "mathematics." While the linear age of war-fare was more predictable by way of additive and algebraic calculations, this new nonlinear age is the stuff of advance graduate-level calculus and differential equations. War has become as much an equation of derivatives (derivations of traditional forms and uses of military capabilities for extramartial purposes) as it remains the game that it has always been—a simple and straightforward equation of addition and subtraction, peace won through a direct application of mass against an opposing force, F = MxA (force equals mass multiplied by directional velocity or "acceleration").

Predicting the type and quantity of military force required to obtain and sustain a high probability of success ("victory") over an opponent was largely relegated to the methodology of correlation of forces and means (COFM), a quantitative process for estimating the likelihood of attack success, based on an assessment of projected resource allocations and the monitoring and attritional accounting of current operations. Though the COFM was designed for application at the operational (divisions and corps) and higher levels of war-planning, the implications of these analyses were intended to impact and inform the actual distribution of combat forces at the tactical levels. The modeling, like all modeling, was to be adjusted to the situation for practical relevancy, based on "METT-T" (mission, enemy, tactics and terrain, troops, time). The COFM methodology has a long history in Western military history but particularly in the annals of the U.S. Army and the army of the former Soviet Union. It still maintains a relevancy, albeit somewhat depleted since the end of the cold war, in both a vernacular sense (commanders and their staff planners still refer to their troop-to-tasks array of force work as "COFM") and a practical sense (there are still aspects of postmodern war that are "linear" in nature). As matter of fact, the original COFM approach still plays a significant role in qualitative methods developed by

Table 4.1 Modern versus Postmodern COFM

	Modern-Age COFM Factors	Postmodern-Age COFM Factors
Mission	Defined in terms of "operations," distance, and attrition.	All modern-age factors are still relevant, with inclusion of the following: • theater-strategic spatial orientation, campaign geometry; • theater-strategic distances; • "intention-based" warfare (purpose).
Enemy	Defined in terms of "strength of opposing forces" and resources allocated.	All modern-age factors are still relevant, with inclusion of the following: • "black-list" pattern and link analysis; • "gray-list" (neutrals, associational groupings, i.e., tribes) pattern and link analysis; • "white-list" (friendly forces) pattern and link analysis; • extramartial and nonmartial diplomatic, informational, economic resources at disposal.
Tactics and terrain	Defined in terms of "attack strike sectors and frontages" and movement rates.	*Same as above plus* • "human" terrain analysis; • return of "defense" zones; • urban and subterranean terrain analysis; • "steady-state" (positional) rates; • "deep operations" = cultural-based (anthropological) operations.
Troops	Defined in terms of "strength of friendly forces" and resources allocated.	*Same as above plus* • non- and extramartial players (civil-military); • indigenous groupings—that is, clans, tribes, kin-based relations, and so on.
Time	Defined in terms of "phase completion time."	*Same as above plus* • incorporation of nonlinear "stages" and/or "domains" temporal framework; • consideration of "tempo" in terms of a bidirectional rheostat rather than a unidirectional factor fail-safed to the accelerative position; • incorporation of "transitional" phase and stage analysis; • long, protracted timelines.

Source: Major Isaiah Wilson III, PhD, February 8, 2005.

the U.S. Army, including the MDMP, Battle Damage Assessment Process, COA analysis, and war-games.

Despite its continued applicability and relevancy to those aspects of postmodern war that are "enduring," in the sense of "unchanging" or "eternal," the legacies of the modern COFM-based war-planning and analysis may have an unintended negative impact on our ability to "see" postmodern war in its own uniqueness. This blurred vision of the nature of postmodern war-fare may blind us in the planning calculus of force allocation and distribution and, consequently, deny us a winning strategy for the postmodern war-environment, or at least extend the time we end up committing to fighting and finally winning in these postmodern conflicts (table 4.1).

What the data in table 4.1 hints at is a proposition for upgrading the long-standing and traditional COFM factors of analysis in a manner that better reflects *postmodernity*. Doing so, it is hoped, will lead to a more realistic and reliable method for modeling the force requirements for postmodern war-fare, for better predictions on what it takes to "fight and win" wars of traditional combatives (of the modern age) and wars for lasting peace of the contemporary age.

Getting the COFM "Right"—The Case of OIF, Phases I–III

What was the force required to fight and win the MCO of Phases I–III in Iraq, March–April 2003? The short answer, in the hindsight of "victory," is *exactly the amount of force we allocated*. History will show that we got the calculus 100 % right for the MCO fight of OIF-1.

Because hindsight is 20/20, our Army will suffer the worst for this rosy historical recording of that war-fight. Nevertheless, when we focus the analysis to just these three operational phases of the war, the war-planning—the COFM—actually "adds up" to the win (collapse of the Hussein regime) we achieved on April 9, 2003. The modern calculus held up in the face of the battles we faced during the MCO phases. How so? By the nature of the Phase I–III war-fight, that is how. This fight was a close fit to the same types and styles of traditional, linear, march-up-country offensives the U.S. military has grown superior and confident in waging over the past six decades; it is a war-fight all combat units have fought and won time and again at the combat training centers (CTCs). There were significant "exceptions" to the modern rules of war we faced and overcame during those phases. A significant portion of the "enemy" we actually faced on the ground turned out, in fact, not to be the "enemy we had war-gamed against" (Lieutenant General Wallace, V Corps commander).[4] In some respects, our undercalculations in the prewar COFM (discounting the Fedayeen fight) were balanced out (negated as a differentiating factor) by our "over-counting" of the strength and disposition of the Iraqi conventional forces. Even with this positive turn of the fog of war in our favorable direction, there were "close-call" moments of near-operational culmination (i.e., periods of time when major combat units were either "red" on Class III and Class V or actually in the "black" on these critical supplies, high-risk miscalculations of the nature and impact of the terrain—physical and human—and weather, etc.). Overall, however, the number and type of "combat power" available to combat commanders on the ground proved necessary *and* sufficient for success.

Getting the COFM "Wrong"—The Case of OIF, Phase- IV Operations

How could our defense and war-planners have gotten the "war" so right and the "other-than-war operations" so wrong in Iraq? There has been plenty written and talked about regarding that question. Unarguably, the plan to win the war has proven itself almost incapable of providing a winning of the peace. Why? In a recently published essay, "American Anabasis,"[5] I argued that an institutionally reinforced commitment to the "old ways" of knowing war and doing the business of war denied us, collectively as a nation and its military, planning for and fighting the war that faced us in Iraq as soon as the regime fell in Baghdad.[6] Here, I stand by that assertion and provide a slightly different way of evidencing the claim. I argue that the "old ways" of calculating the type and amount of forces required to "fight and win"—the traditional ways we have viewed post-MCO—proved still necessary but broadly insufficient as an equation for winning. What table 4.2 below provides is a "first-cut" expansion (not a replacement) of the modern military lexicon for war as an update to the modern ways and means of Western war-fare in order to better reflect the realities of "postmodern," fourth-generation war-fare (4GW) and therefore to improve our operational effectiveness in postmodern war-fare.

The purpose, geometry, time, and space characteristics of the first three phases of OIF-1 were such that the "modern" lexicon, doctrine, tactics, techniques, and procedures (TTPs), and even force design still proved necessary *and* sufficient as a war-waging and war-winning strategy and force-planning design. Phases I–III of OIF-I were "march-up-country" phases of a traditional and conventional sort. America's *Anabasis* was not all that different from Xenophon's 3,000 years earlier. But this "reality" and condition set dramatically changed on April 9, 2003, when the Saddam regime tumbled. U.S. and coalition forces, however, remained on the original *Anabasis*, directing preparations for the "march" out of country. The dramatic change of the situation in Iraq (from dynamic and rapid MCO to a condition of steady-state, protracted combat, stability, and support operations) brought with it a whole new set of numbers and equations that needed to have been added to the modern COFM. The "New Math" is still a work in progress. Not knowing what we did not know in terms of the new conditions and requirements of Phase IV contributed and perpetuates to this day a spiral of "unknowing." At a minimum, the postmodern COFM factors offered here need to be added to our traditional and standing doctrine; we must set ourselves on a crash course of learning this "New Math."

A Postmodern Anabasis

Some Planning Considerations

What table 4.2 reflects is an attempt to pose some preliminary macro-level questions that should drive a relook and expansion of the modern military lexicon and doctrinal base. Macro factors, such as *mission, enemy, terrain and troops, culture* (METT-C) are useful planning parameters.

Mission. The modern-age lexicon still promotes the Napoleonic prescripts of the linear march to the sound of the guns and, most significantly, the vital importance

Table 4.2 A "4GW" Correlation of Forces and Means

	Modern Military Lexicon	Postmodern (4GW) "Civil-Military" Lexicon
What is a "battle and an "engagement" in a postmodern war?	*Battle*: A series of related tactical engagements that last longer than a single engagement, involve larger forces, and could affect the course of campaign. They occur when division, corps, or army commanders fight for significant objectives.	The concept must expand to cover any and all activities and functions performed at the ground, field, and tactical (i.e., "implementation") levels within the civil-military theater/area of operations.
	Engagement: In air defense, an attack with guns or air-to-air missiles by an interceptor aircraft, or the launch of an air defense missile by air defense artillery and the missile's subsequent travel to intercept. In the Army, an engagement is a small tactical conflict, usually between opposing maneuver forces.	The martial and lethal concept and definition of "battle" or "engagement" remain relevant but now must also include nonlethal actions at the implementation levels and activities expanding beyond (but also still incorporating) martial activities.
Who/what is the "enemy" in a postmodern war?	*Enemy*: The enemy is any individual, group of individuals (organized or not organized), paramilitary or military force, national entity, or national alliance that is in opposition to the United States, its allies, or multinational partners.	The concept and definition must be expanded to include any "information gap" in one's own forces and capabilities, those of allies and partners, nongovernmental organization capabilities, indigenous groups (i.e., tribes, kin-based groupings), and civic organizations.
		The concept and definition also must incorporate "terrain" and "weather" factors and "time available."
How must we view the "terrain" in a postmodern war?	The terrain is generally thought of in terms of geography and atmosphere (land and weather) and is to a lesser degree considered in terms of aggregate populations (pattern analysis).	Human terrain (and its combined effect when integrated with a particular type of physical terrain) is of increased importance. Individual "high-value targets" (HVTs) are also of particular importance ("black-listed," "gray-listed," and "white-listed" individuals).
What do the traditional tactical tasks of "destroy, defeat, isolate, seize, secure" mean in postmodern war?	*Destroy*: 1. A tactical task to physically render an enemy force combat-ineffective unless it is reconstituted. 2. To render a target so damaged that it cannot function as intended or be restored to a usable condition without being entirely rebuilt. Artillery requires 30% incapacitation or destruction of	The concept and definition of all tactical tasks must be expanded to incorporate activities at the implementation levels that are beyond the martial and that raise to parity with "close-with-to-destroy" functions, functions related to "closing with an 'enemy' to restore," etc.

Continued

Table 4.2 Continued

	Modern Military Lexicon	Postmodern (4GW) "Civil-Military" Lexicon
	enemy force. (See also defeat.) See *FMs* 1–111, 5–100, 6–20, 71-100, 100–5, and 100–15.	
	Isolate: A tactical task given to a unit to seal off (both physically and psychologically) an enemy from his sources of support, to deny an enemy freedom of movement, and to prevent an enemy unit from having contact with other enemy forces. An enemy must not be allowed sanctuary within his present position. (See also encirclement.) See *FMs* 7–7, 7–8, 17–95, and 71–123.	All tactical tasks must be reconceived in terms of "effects" rather than mere actions or physical capabilities assigned to a particular tasks or mission.
	Seize: A tactical task to clear a designated area and obtain control of it. (See also contain.) See *FM* 100–40.	
	Secure: In an operational context, to gain possession of a position or terrain feature, with or without force, and to make such disposition as will prevent, as far as possible, its destruction or loss by enemy action. In the Army, a tactical task to gain possession of a position or terrain feature, with or without force, and to deploy in a manner that prevents its destruction or loss to enemy action. The attacking force may or may not have to physically occupy the area. See *JP* 1–02, NATO.	
What are "combat forces" in a postmodern war?	The definition is generally limited to traditional, conventional military forces and military technical skill sets.	Must be reconsidered in terms of force or effects "packages" and should include all "capabilities" (military, civilian) at a nation's or other nonstate entity's access and disposal.
	Combat forces: infantry, armor, artillery, air defense, attack aviation.	
	Combat support (CS): engineer, military police, signal, military intelligence.	Combat forces must be military-civilian effects packages, capable of full-spectrum operations, but organic design or force-tailoring—all full-spectrum assets and enablers

Continued

Table 4.2 Continued

	Modern Military Lexicon	Postmodern (4GW) "Civil-Military" Lexicon
		must be "on hand" to remain in command of one's own Observe, Orient, Decide, Act (OODA) "Loop" decision and actioning cycle and to retain an initiative and capacity to exploit an enemy's OODA cycle.
	Combat service support (CSS): ordinance, transportation, quartermaster.	
What are "operations" in a postmodern war? What are "deep" operations in postmodern war?	*Operations*: (*JP* 1–02, NATO) A military action or the carrying out of a strategic, tactical, service, training, or administrative military mission; the process of carrying on combat, including movement, supply, attack, defense, and maneuvers needed to gain the objectives of any battle or campaign. In the Army, a broad category of related tactical activities such as offense, defense, and retrograde.	Must be expanded in terms of concept, definition, and planning processes to include *all* actions and missions (civilian, military, combined civil-military), for full-spectrum "effects-based" objectives.
	Deep operations: In the Army, deep operations are those operations directed against enemy forces and functions that are not in contact at the forward line of troops (FLOT), line of departure, or friendly perimeter and are between the FLOT or perimeter and the forward boundary of the unit conducting the operation. These operations employ long-range fires, air and ground maneuver, and command and control war-fare to defeat the enemy by denying him freedom of action, disrupting his preparation for battle and his support structure, and disrupting or destroying the coherence and tempo of his operations. (See also decisive point, forward boundary, and simultaneous attack in depth.) See *FMs* 1–112, 6–20–30, 100–5, and 100–15.	"Deep" operations must be reconceived froma linear concept, construct, and operational method to a nonlinear concept centered on "depth of local embeddedness within, and understanding of, an indigenous area and its terrain" (human and geographic). Deep operations more often refer to cultural engagement operations (acculturation activities).
What is "offense" versus "defense" in postmodern war?	*Offense*: A principle of war by which a military force achieves decisive results by acting with	Offense must be redefined not by specific tactical tasks (i.e., destruction functions) but rather

Continued

Table 4.2 Continued

	Modern Military Lexicon	Postmodern (4GW) "Civil-Military" Lexicon
	initiative, employing fire and movement and sustaining freedom of maneuver and action while causing an enemy to be reactive.	by operational and strategic purpose(i.e., type of war, such as anti-insurgency versus counter-insurgency).
	Offensive operations: Combat operations designed primarily to destroy the enemy. They may be undertaken to secure key or decisive terrain, to deprive the enemy of resources or decisive terrain, to deceive or divert the enemy, to develop intelligence, and to hold the enemy in position. Forms of offensive operations include movement to contact, attack, exploitation, and pursuit. The offensive is undertaken to seize, retain, and exploit the initiative. (See also attack, movement to contact, and reconnaissance in force.) See *FMs* 1–111, 6–20, 7–20, 7–30, 17–95, 71–100, 71–123, 100–15, and 101–5.	All actions should have an "offensive"character and capability and a "defensive" character and capability to ensure, by definition, a full-spectrum capacity.
	Defend: A combat operation designed to defeat an attacker and prevent him from achieving his objectives. It employs all means and methods available to prevent, resist, or destroy an enemy attack. Forms of defensive operations are area and mobile. Choices of defensive operations are in-depth and forward. The defensive techniques are to defend in sector and to defend a battle position. See *FMs* 7–30, 71–100, 71–123, 100–5, and 100–15.	Countertype operations are by their nature "defensive" in orientation and purpose.
	Defensive operations: Operations conducted with the immediate purpose of causing an enemy attack to fail. Defensive operations also may achieve one or more of the following: gain time; concentrate forces elsewhere; wear down enemy forces as a prelude to offensive operations; and retain tactical, strategic,	Anti-type operations are by their nature and design "destruction-oriented" operations.

Continued

Table 4.2 Continued

	Modern Military Lexicon	Postmodern (4GW) "Civil-Military" Lexicon
	or political objectives. (See also area defense, defend, and mobile defense.) See *FMs* 7–30, 71–100, 71–123, 100–5, and 100–15.	
What is "decisive" in postmodern war?	*Decisive engagement* (*JP* 1–02): In land and naval war-fare, decisive engagement is an engagement in which a unit is considered fully committed and cannot maneuver or extricate itself. In the absence of outside assistance, the action must be fought to a conclusion and either won or lost with the forces at hand. In the Army, in some situations, this is a desired result in order to hold key terrain, defeat a specific enemy force, or secure a specific objective. In this situation, the unit can receive additional forces or support to be able to disengage.	Decisive is no longer determinable by the single engagement or "battle."
	Decisive point: 1. A point, if retained, that provides a commander with a marked advantage over his opponent. Decisive points are usually geographic in nature but could include other physical elements, such as enemy formations, command posts, and communications nodes. 2. A time or location where enemy weakness is so positioned that overwhelming combat power can be generated against it. It could be an enemy weakness that can be exploited or a time when the combat potential of the enemy force is degraded. (See also critical point.)	The "line of operation" connected by "decisive points" is less the case (a poor model). "Domains" of operation (nonlinear, noncontiguous, holistic—civil and military, state and non-state, national and extranational) networks correlated via multifunctional decisive "nodes" is a better fitting model.
	Decisive terrain: Key terrain that has an extraordinary impact on the mission. It is relatively rare and will not be present in every situation. To designate terrain as decisive is to recognize that the successful accomplishment of the	Decisive "terrain" is more than likely human-based and perceptual rather than terrain-oriented and material.

Continued

Table 4.2 Continued

	Modern Military Lexicon	Postmodern (4GW) "Civil-Military" Lexicon
	mission, whether offensive or defensive, depends on seizing or retaining it. The commander designates decisive terrain to communicate its importance in his concept of operations, first to his staff and, later, to subordinate commanders. (See also key terrain.) See *FM*s 34–130 and 101–5.	
What is "war?"	"War" defined by *Webster's Dictionary* is a state of open and declared, hostile armed conflict between states or nations, or a period of such conflict.	The root of the English word "war," *werra*, is Frankish-German and means confusion, discord, or strife. The verb form *werran* means to confuse or perplex. (*The Internet Encyclopedia of Philosophy*)
	"An orderly affair in which states are involved, in which there are declared beginnings and expected ends, easily Identifiable combatants, and high levels of obedience by subordinates" (John Keegan, *A History of Warfare* [NewYork: Vintage, 1994]).	It is Clausewitzian, not in terms of the "applied science" of *On War*, but rather in terms of the "theory" of war in *On War*: "a true endeavor to compel on to do your will . . . a continuation of politics and policy by other [ALL] means" (my emphasis).
	War is determined in terms of state versus state- armed military confrontation (lethal or threat of lethal conflict). Offensive-, lethal-, and martial-oriented by modern Western doctrine and convention.	War is determined in terms of "intentions" (neutral/agnostic, friendly, benign, disharmonious, antagonistic, belligerent) instead of potential actors (state versus state).
	War is the antithesis of "peace."	War is policy as well as practice, with "combatives" being only one practice in a wide spectrum of "practices."
		War is no longer viably defined in the comparative of the "war state." Peace and war are seamless (peace is a "better" or more acceptable state of war).

Source: Major Isaiah Wilson III, PhD, February 10, 2005.

of the decisive battle. Victory rested in the hands of the general who could muster combat forces upon certain decisive points leading to rendering of the enemy to a decisive battle at a time and place of the general's choosing with the greater genius (the third eye capable of seeing the decisive points of the battle and of directing forces toward those decisive points faster and more effectively than the opponent).

We see the mastery of nineteenth-century grand tactics during the Napoleonic era. The linearly formed corps-organized army is the defining tool of war; it is the instrument of power capable of bringing the enemy to decisive battle. The "fourth generation" of war-fare (this postmodern age) sees expansions of the tools of war, the geometry (scope and scale) of war-fare, and, consequently, an expansion in the stakes and interests (goals and purpose) of war. The availability of more wares of war (and more new wares of war) allows war's players and stakeholders more flexibility in determining their war-aims; superpower national states now can have attainable global interests. We have never been closer to the ideal-type models of total war that military theorists have postulated about throughout history than we are today. Expansions of war-policy have, however, removed all potential for the attainment of decisive victory through the single decisive battle. It is posited here that the postmodern age defines the possibility of victory through the successful waging of nothing less than theater-strategic civil-military campaigns. The martial and lethal concept and definition of the 'battle" or the "engagement" remain relevant but now must also include nonlethal actions at the implementation levels and activities that expand well beyond, but at the same time incorporate, martial activities.

The Enemy, Culture, and the Terrain. The modern doctrine and its lexicon define and "see" the enemy as individuals or groups of individuals (military or paramilitary) of nation-states or national alliances. Modernity still defines war not only as purely martial but also as a lethal game played between nation-states. We all know better but have been slow to update the definition; we have been slow to change how we think of "the enemy" and who we see as "an enemy." All modern understandings still apply (a continuity of war-fare, war is a human enterprise) but now must also include an "information or intelligence gap" we face in regard to ourselves, the organic threat, the population of concern, and the physical (natural, man-made, materiel) and psychological (cognitive, informational). Our Western lack of knowledge of, understanding of, and appreciation for human organizing models other than the national state (i.e., tribes, kin-based associations, clan-based organizations, cyber-organizations, etc.) become our greatest self-made "enemy." Human terrain and its combined effects when integrated with a particular type of physical and psychological terrain are of increased relevance and importance. The importance of the *individual* threat (not just "group" threats) is critical in 4GW. Religion, culture, and ethnicity are types of "terrain" that must be considered and incorporated in postmodern IPB planning.

Troops. What are "combat forces" in a postmodern war? Unlike in modern wars where combat is limited to military combatives, to closing with to destroy an enemy military or paramilitary force and where military combat troops are organized accordingly into "combat," "combat support," and "combat service support" units, postmodern wars expand the way we think of the "soldier," the "combatant," and therefore alters how we should think of troops and "trooping to tasks" as well as how we should organize troops for war-fare (transformational reorganization). A 4GW concept of troops and trooping-to-tasks calls for a focus on multifunctional force or effects packages, packages that include all capabilities (instruments of power, national and "other") at a nation's or other nonstate entity's access and disposal. Combat force packages must be *organized* as *military-civilian effects packages.*

If, and then until nonmartial organizations are reconfigured with their own *combat maneuver* capabilities (fire + mobility + command and control capability + ample "education" [formal academic learning, training, experience-based learning] in war-fighting), all postmodern war-fighting will require military forces and capabilities for effective application of civil-military war missions and *pre- and post*mission survivability. War operations must be reconsidered as full-spectrum, "effects-based" operations with full-spectrum objectives. There are no longer any tactical actions that do not have operational or strategic impacts. It is *all* civil-military! We must organize for every "fight," be it close-with-to-destroy missions or close-with-to-restore missions, full-spectrum and civil-military in composition because the enemy gets a vote and because there is never a situation of perfect information or "perfect knowing." We must array ourselves in ways that allow us to apply full-spectrum force at our whim. That will require dramatic, revolutionary changes in how we acquire, produce, build, organize, and prepare all our forces for war (people, equipment, education, etc.).

What Is Postmodern War-fare?

Operational/Theater-Strategic Perspective

From the theater-strategic and operational perspectives, postmodern (4GW) war-fare is

- nonlinear;
- noncontiguous (time, physical/psychological space, purpose);
- "four"-dimensional (x-axis, y-axis, z-axis = "cultural," and time)
- full-spectrum (the "grapple" and the "marathon"); and
- purpose- and intent-based (not task-defined, not "capabilities-based").

War and its postmodern version remain a Clausewitzian affair. The theory of war offered by Clausewitz is still extremely relevant to war in the postmodern era. There are deliberate efforts within and outside the U.S. Army to develop a new theory and joint operational design for war in the postmodern age. We need the new joint operational design but already have our theory—the very one Clausewitz gave us in *On War* and the one Eastern theorists such as Sun Tzu gave us over 2,500 years ago. War remains, as the *Webster's* dictionary tells us, "a state of usually open and declared armed hostile conflict between states or nations," and as Clausewitz and Sun Tzu declared before, an endeavor to compel one to do your will and a continuation of politics and policy by other means. Wars and their postmodern variants are never capable of being "won" without offensive actions, but still the defense remains the *stronger form of war*. War is policy and the practice of that policy, not mere "combatives;" combatives are only one part of war's whole and one activity in a wide array of practices. Defensive war is always the stronger (i.e., more legitimate) form, but that is not to say that defensive war equates with nonoffensive war-fare. On the contrary, if war's aim is defensive, then it is ethical and legitimate to "go on the offensive" on behalf of the *strategic defense*. Prevention and preemption strategies, reconceived in this sort of postmodern way, can now be appreciated for their broader potentials. "Peace-time" military engagement and preventive defense strategies of the 1990s should be revisited due to their inherent "postmodern" characteristics and potentiality. Finally, postmodern war is seamless.

Peace is a relative state of being with no context outside of the "war-state," and vice versa. Peace becomes the "better state" of the perpetual state of war.

This new way of looking at war and war-fare surely demands a full and comprehensive review and revision of standing international laws and conventions governing and guiding modern war and war-fare. The new postmodern conventions are already upon us, and we are now playing a catch-up game of epic proportions and implications.

What We Really Want to Know but Are Afraid to Ask

Did General Eric Shinseki Have the COFM "Right" in February 2003?

We end as we began: with the question, how much is good enough for fighting to a win in postmodern war? The traditional correlation of forces and means methodology has served us well in the past and is still relevant. But does it predict accurately the requirements for "finishing well" in the peace stages of a postmodern war-strategy?

In February 2003, then Army Chief of Staff General Eric Shinseki, in an attempt to answer a question posed to him during a House Armed Services Committee (HASC) testimony on how many troops he would estimate required for the war in Iraq, offered the following:

> Something on the order of several hundred thousand soldiers are probably, you know, a figure that would be required. We're talking about post-hostilities control over a piece of geography that's fairly significant, with the kinds of ethnic tensions that could lead to other problems . . . . [I]t takes a significant ground-force presence to maintain a safe and secure environment, to ensure that people are fed, that water is distributed, all the normal responsibilities that go along with administering a situation like this. . . .

These words proved prophetic and have since proven quite the irritant to the current administration. They have unfortunately fed the mechanizations of partisan-political play and banter more than they have been used to serve as a beginning toward an operationally useful and essential analysis of what went wrong in our calculus for the war in Iraq and a readjustment of our force-planning methodologies for wars of a postmodern era, such as Iraq.

So, how many troops would have been "enough" to win the peace in Iraq? According to a recent Rand study led by James Dobbins,

> [I]n most successful occupations, ranging from post-1945 Germany to post-1999 Kosovo, the figure [of required troops] has never been lower than one soldier per 50 people.

In Iraq, and by that historical calculus, that would have meant 500,000 troops or three times the number the coalition has had available to date. In early 2005, former National Security advisor Zbigniew Brzezinski, offered 500,000 as the magic number of required forces on the ground to retake the operational initiative (the "offensive") in Iraq:

> While our ultimate objectives are very ambitious we will never achieve democracy and stability without being willing to commit 500,000 troops, spend $200 billion a year, probably have a draft, and have some form of war compensation.

Truth of the matter is this: There have never been more than 160,000 coalition soldiers to control a population of 25 million Iraqis. Even adding in 20,000 private security contractors, that still amounts to only one soldier for every 139 Iraqis. But if we have been undercounting the requirement since the beginning of the war, as most say we have, what are we to think of this "500,000" number? Where did that come from and is it even adequate—"good enough"? There are at least two separate calculations that may have given birth to the 500,000 troop requirement. One rationale may have come from the ratio of 1 soldier for every 50 local people, a ratio cited in the Dobbin's Rand report and recognized as the rough planning factor used during Clinton-era interventions. Based on the population of Iraq, this 1:50 formula would yield the 500,000 troop requirement figure. Another possible justification may have derived from a rough COFM analysis of the estimated number of insurgent forces in Iraq and the references to traditional force-planning ratios used in the past for anti-insurgencies, which propose a required 10:1 ratio—10 soldiers ("counterinsurgents") to every 1 insurgent—to retain the initiative and improve the probability of a win. At the time of the Brzezinski article, Pentagon officials were publicly stating that there may have been between 20,000 and 50,000 insurgents countrywide as of the December 2004 timeframe. By a simple, linear-age COFM calculation, this range would justify a U.S./coalition force BOG count of between 200,000 and the now popular 500,000 soldier requirement.

So what does this really tell us? Frankly, not much, at least not in terms of a tactical or operational relevancy to the type of war we are presently engaged in on the ground in Iraq.

Correlating the Forces and Means for Postmodern War-fare

The requirement of 500,000 soldiers for the "peace"-fight in Iraq was and still is a number reflective of a linear-, mechanized-, and modern-age understanding of and approach to war and war-fare. This calculus reflects a mission analysis (definition of the tactical and operational problems) that is still far too linear and "contiguous" in its spatial orientation and too "combat-centric" in the traditional war-fighting sense.

A requirement of 500,000 combat soldiers may be an accurate troop-to-tasks design for those tasks related directly to anti-insurgency operations (close-with-to-destroy insurgents, setting stable security conditions in Iraq), particularly if the estimates on the current number of the insurgency are even somewhat reliable. But that would only cover one small part of a much larger, complex, and multifaceted civil-military mission set in Iraq. This sort of straight-line COFM might be necessary, even sufficient, for force-against-force anti-insurgency strike operations but entirely insufficient for the broader "counterinsurgency" campaign that is arguably more defining of the type of war U.S. forces should be supporting in Iraq today. Determining the number of BOG required from only an anti-insurgency perspective risks minimizing the war itself to an anti-insurgency war in terms of military purpose, in spite of our stated strategic purpose in Iraq. Regardless of the stated policy (what we may "want" the war in Iraq to be), what gets resourced for the fight—what gets done on the ground—reflects the "real" policy. A narrow determination of forces required can inadvertently create policy reality on the ground that in no way reflects the full intent of the desired policy at national levels. The way in which we resource the fight on the ground is the real determining policy for whether or not we can "win" in Iraq and the determinant for how long U.S. forces will have to remain on the ground in Iraq. Our war-policy has suffered and continues to suffer from a discounting of the full context and scope of this war and from a consequential undercounting of what type and number of "BOG" are required to win this broader war for Iraq.

A more accurate and operationally effective requirements estimate will likely balloon the number of required military forces (combat, combat support, combat service support) significantly, well beyond the earlier estimates of 500,000. That is not a popular estimate, but it is one more earnestly reflective of the postmodern conditions in, and our stated endstate for Iraq. If there are in fact above 50,000 bona fide insurgents (a mix of home-grown insurgents and Al-Qaieda affiliated foreign fighters) in Iraq today, the 500,000 combat soldier requirement would be a *minimum* required number of BOG for just the destruction of this threat. Additional terrain- and conditions-based factors would have to be added into the equation, such as unrestricted, slightly restricted, or severely restricted (to include urbanized terrain), for a more accurate count. The more complex and compound the terrain (urban? mountainous? transborder?), the higher the COFM requirement. So, even in this sense, with the added terrain factors, we see the 500,000 force requirement already as a *bare minimum* for just stabilizing the current situation in Iraq, well short of the number of combat troops needed to retake the anti-insurgency offensive.

And that only speaks to the "war" functions. What about the "peace" side of the war in Iraq? If we stick to the modern-age MDMP, we would be less likely to even consider nonmilitary and extramartial forces in our calculations. We begin to see clearly that this COFM must be more nuanced and detailed than a simple straight-line combat count. The peace side of postmodern war-fare has to integrate into the requirements equation not only required combat troops but also what we in the military call supporting arms technical units (combat service and combat service support units) and supporting arms technically trained experts. These nontraditional specialty arms include the more obvious military police units, engineer units, civil affairs and psychological operations (PSYOP) units, military intelligence units, and the more obscure, such as foreign area experts, linguists, information operations specialists, communications experts, and so on. These additional "operations-other-than-war" military forces add to the aggregate military force requirements.

We must also begin to add into the calculations interagency and multiagency forces—"other governmental agencies" (OGA) and the like—as special operating forces (SOF) assets critical to postmodern-age compound war-fare. All of these combat support, CSS, and multiagency "forces" require "force protection" assets to be added to their organizations in order to ensure not only their survivability in today's COE but also, as a consequence, to ensure mission effectiveness. Besides this, all forces within theater must be serviced and resupplied continuously; the logistics support forces required must be added to the COFM and must also be "hardened" and made "combat-ready" to be capable of effectively fighting, surviving, and winning in their support functions.

In today's battlefield environment, all forces must be full-spectrum capable, either by organic design or through force tailoring (packaging). All units and forces, civilian and military, must be capable of fire and maneuver for mission accomplishment and force protection, in an environment that has no clear demarcation lines between zones of war and zones of peace. The full-spectrum realities of the COE add significant complexity, fog, and fiction to war. This is not war-fare as we have known it. *It is war-fare as we must learn to know it.* Achieving effectiveness in this environment will demand more force than that which is recommended by the old traditional COFM analysis.

Mr. Wolfowitz, the deputy defense secretary, called General Shinseki's February 2003 estimate of several hundred thousand troops needed in postwar Iraq "wildly off the mark."[7] Mr. Wolfowitz' contradiction was and is *correct.*

However, it is not in the sense the Pentagon was hoping for. All guesstimates have been "wildly off the mark," not as a sin of commission but rather a *sin of omission.* Simple modern mission analyses, and the correlation of forces and means estimations that come with it, are woefully inaccurate by design—forcing models that have become antiquated and as such only partially useful for accurate and reliable planning for present and future wars. Wolfowitz' estimate that no more than 100,000 "troops" would be required to win the "postwar fight" was clearly a figure born more from political hope than the operational realities on the ground. The more recent estimates that linger around the 500,000 mark are less hopeful and more attuned to the realities facing us on the ground. Yet, as this chapter has shown, even this large number will likely prove insufficient for sealing a decisive win in this war, at least not in the near term.

Moreover, time may not always be on the side of the Western coalition and the fledgling Iraqi national state. If, say, a 500,000 "troop" requirement was "good enough" (and it is not!) in 2003 to fight and win the anti-insurgency as well as to take the initiative in a full-scale counterinsurgency, then that number and type of force would be what is needed on the ground today, in 2007. The postmodern COFM must take into account the variable of time and space (when and where the required number and type of "forces" [civil-military] are needed to *close with to destroy* vice *close with to restore*) in a predictive, preemptive, and preventive manner, else all that the calculation will reveal is what we actually need*ed* on the ground to win the whole war, more than likely too little, too late.

Finishing our war in Iraq, to completion and at a time and in a manner of our choosing, demands an entirely different computation of what is required to win the war and the peace, of what may prove itself in the end as the first, but surely not the last, 4GW of the twenty-first century.

We're Fighting a War Too, We're Just Not Whining about It!

> Therefore I say: Know the enemy and know yourself; in a hundred battles you will never be in peril. When you are ignorant of the enemy but know yourself, your chances of winning or losing are equal. If ignorant both of your enemy and yourself, you are certain in every battle to be in peril. Such people are "mad bandits." What can they expect if not defeat.[8]

Sun Tzu's warning is telling and defining of America's challenge in winning in postmodern war. Largely the result of *legacy* organizational designs that linger, and continue to serve a relevant purpose when it comes to the core war-fighting roles and functions, the U.S. Army is finding itself locked in a modern understanding of itself and its expanded jurisdictions in postmodern, holistic war-fare. During the early offensive phases of OIF-1, the U.S. Army knew the "enemy" well enough to avoid the peril that Sun Tzu speaks of. Even when that enemy evolved to become the compound enemy that "we did not (exactly) wargame against,"[9] the Army maintained enough overmatching firepower and tactical expertise to overcome its collective ignorance of the nature and purpose of the new threat.

Besides, during the initial combatives phases, "knowing the enemy" was easily defined as just needing to know, *how many and where?*; no broader understanding was required in order to "destroy." The U.S. Army was able to avoid possible early culmination (due to scarce resources available to fight the fight), to overcome the odds, and to "win" in bringing about the collapse of the Hussein regime, because the Army knows itself very well in terms of its combative roles and functions—*fight and win America's wars.* However, since the regime collapse in May 2003, the U.S. Army has been in a constant state of peril, in every "battle" it has faced; perhaps it is in peril of losing the "war," even after supposedly winning it.

The difference is in the *knowing.*

Can We Wage More Effective Postmodern War in the Future?

What the 101st Airborne Division (Air Assault) did "right" during their first tour of duty in Northern Iraq, 2003–2004 was approach its actions throughout the war "holistically." The Division's operational approach to the war (the way its commander "defined" operational aims and objectives, the way its planners planned and arrayed capabilities for the attainment of those aims and objectives, and the way in which its tactical leaders carried out their daily missions) reflected a full-spectrum approach. The capacity of the 101st to "think" and act beyond the common understanding of war—to obtain a broader and more in-depth knowledge of the compound threat (organic and inorganic)—allowed the Division to achieve relative success in northern Iraq, while U.S. forces elsewhere were experiencing relative setbacks.

A Failure in Operational Planning

Understanding the operational domain of war is essential to understanding war itself. To better understand the mediocre record of America's experience in the Iraq War, one must reconsider both the actions on the ground and the overall goals and aims of the nation's war-policy in light of how these two aspects of the Iraq War policy were integrated and interrelated at the operational level.

Initiating the ground invasion phase of a war-policy without a full operational plan for winning the "peace" could prove the fatal knot for U.S. foreign and security policy, not only regarding Iraq but also for the future credibility of U.S. war-efforts relating to the global war on terrorism (GWOT). Though noted for its preeminent war-fighting operational art and science, very few outside of military circles study the formulation aspects of that war-policy. There are eight essential elements of U.S. military operational design, elements by which a war-plan can be measured and evaluated (see table 4.3).

The attempt here is to extend the context of this mechanized-age framework to cover more of the full spectrum of war and therefore extend the analytical utility of this framework for effective postmodern war-planning. Reconstructing the context of these elements to the fuller temporal and environmental realities of the war in Iraq and then reapplying the framework to tactical and operational activities in the

Table 4.3 The Eight Elements of Operational Designs

	Doctrinal Definition	Combat Operations	SASO/Civil-Military Operations
Endstate	The set of required conditions—diplomatic, informational, military, and economic—that achieves U.S. national interests in a situation.	Army operations Initially focus on a military endstate (a set of military conditions) that marks the point When military force is no longer the principle Strategic means.	There may be a broader strategic endstate that includes not only military conditions but also a variety of diplomatic, informational, and economic conditions. The relative emphasis in the combinations of U.S. national elements of power shifts throughout a conflict.
Objective(s)	Clearly defined, decisive, and attainable aims that direct military operations.	Usually defined in terms of tactical tasks (seize, secure, destroy, defeat, disrupt, interdict, etc.).	Ambiguous and of long duration; operations appear to be best described in terms of "purpose" (allow, cause, create, protect, support, etc.).
Centers of gravity	Characteristics, capabilities, or localities from which a military force derives its freedom of action, physical strength, or will to fight.	At the tactical and operational levels of war, most often defined in terms of an enemy military force or military capability, the destruction of which will lead toward decisive victory (press the enemy into culmination).	More often defined in terms of human capital—the "hearts and minds" or "will" of the people—and/or the physical terrain that contains it (major urban centers, etc.).
Decisive points	Physical elements or events in time that offer a commander a marked advantage and greatly influence the outcome of an action. They offer a commander a clear advantage when correctly exploited. They are also key to attacking or destroying the center of gravity.	Most often defined in terms of key and/or decisive (dominant) physical terrain (a road/rail juncture, a ridgeline, a port, etc.).	Similar to decisive points under combat operations but also includes psychological and ideational factors/influences, directly or indirectly affected through information operations and PSYOP.
Lines of operation(s)	Link a force with an objective or a series of objectives to focus military activity toward	Traditionally, arrayed linearly, sequentially, and in terms of military functionality.	Noncontiguous, simultaneous and duplicative, more often nonmilitary in nature

Continued

Table 4.3 Continued

	Doctrinal Definition	Combat Operations	SASO/Civil-Military Operations
	the endstate (geographical, logical, or both).		(military as a supporting or enabling function).
Operational reach	The distance and duration for which a unit can successfully employ military capabilities. Reach is influenced by relative combat power, logistics, capabilities, and the geography surrounding and separating opponents.	Normally thought of in terms of military power and the battlefield operating systems (BOS)—maneuver, fires, intelligence, etc.	Same as combat operations but also includes one's ability (capability and capacity) to understand local cultures, rituals, norms, etc. and to access those issues.
Culmination	*Offense*: The culmination point is that point in time and location when the attacker's effective combat power no longer exceeds that of the defender. *Defense*: The defender reaches culmination when the defending force no longer has the ability to go on the attack or defend successfully.	Traditionally defined in terms of military power and logistical support.	Though often determined in the end by the availability of military power to implement particular civil-military activities, culmination more often than not is defined in terms of civilian power.
Timing/ phasing/tempo	Simultaneity is the ideal in the American way of war. Simultaneity in time overwhelms opposing commanders with a wide range of immediate decision requirements. Simultaneity in space presents opposing forces with devastating consequences throughout the depth of the battlespace. Simultaneity in purpose orchestrates the linkage between all activities in the operational framework, ensuring that all activities are directed toward the ultimate endstate.	Timing, phasing, and tempo are "rapid, decisive operations" (RDO).	It is anathema to the traditional American way of war in that SASO/CMO is characterized by long, sustained operations, with the decisive operation normally judged temporally in months and years (rather than hours or days) and judged physically in terms of reconstruction (rather than destruction).

Source: Isaiah Wilson III.

theater of war (execution) reveals a critically flawed operational application of force in Iraq.

The framework is not the problem. The problem is in the way *engagements, battles, major operations,* and *campaigns* are defined. The conception of these terms in purely military context is part of that problem. The definition of the "strategic center of gravity" as the political objective "versus" the "operational center of gravity" as the "military" center of gravity. The distinction is more than just an issue of semantics. It is symbolic of a legacy approach to the operational art and science of modern Western war-fare and symptomatic of what is "ailing" postmodern U.S. war-policy, specifically its war-experience in Iraq.

During the initial phases of the Iraq war (March–April 2003), the framework measured up quite accurately against the reality of the situation in the field, at the operational level. The formal military apparatus, to include Saddam Hussein as head of that military machine and his Ba'athist Party as the mechanism, was the operational center of gravity for that despotic state. However, even in these initial months, the Saddam regime was *not the strategic center of gravity,* at least not in accordance with the stated agenda of the Bush administration. The *Iraqi people themselves, and the establishment of conditions in Iraq* that would facilitate a safe and secure environment and consequently become fertile ground for freedom and democratization, were the real strategic center of gravity. Saddam Hussein and his regime had to be eliminated as a means to that end (an intermediate operational center of gravity that had to be isolated, seized, and destroyed). Unfortunately, the prevailing view of the war and its war-aims were limited to seeing the Iraqi Army (the elite formations of the Republican Guard more specifically) as the single military objective and the capture or killing of Hussein as the strategic endstate.

This overly simplistic conception of the "war" led to a cascade of incidences that in turn led to the undercutting of the war-effort: too few troops, too little coordination with civilian and governmental/nongovernmental agencies (U.S. State Department, as one example), and too little allotted time to achieve "success." In short, getting the operational and strategic centers of gravity analysis wrong has contributed to America's too little, too late acknowledgment of the war for what it was even before the initiation of ground combat operations: a war for the freedom of the Iraqi people, a people's war, an insurgency/counterinsurgency. Legitimization of this formulated war-plan for Iraq may have required more detailed explanation to the American public, given its fuller context and as a result its more extensive commitments.

The current meandering pace and direction of civil-military operations in Iraq can be categorized and expressed in terms of this elemental framework. Some details on three other of these elements suffice as ample illustration.

Operational Reach. Our typical notions of operational reach normally speak to extended, longitudinal distances, the capacity to defeat or destroy an enemy force from extended distances. In stability and security, transition and reconstruction (SSTR) operations, operational reach retains this horizontal meaning but takes on a broader context. While we conceive of "deep" operations in two-dimensional terms, in SSTR and civil-military operations, "deep" is actually a more appropriate term for operations that focus on the embedding of a force "into" and "within" the local environment: into the local cultures, religions, rituals, histories, and so on. SSTR are by definition operations of "depth"—a truer meaning of deep operations and deep maneuver than modern militarists traditionally think of the term and the concept. What we understand to be deep operations in combat operations would be better termed and regarded as "long-range" or extended distance operations. Deep should reference depth and therefore apply to the degree of integration of a force into a local environment.

So thinking of "deep operations" in this context, conditions during SSTR present the operational planner with a unique set of challenges. The first and foremost demand placed on the SSTR planner is getting to know not only the enemy but more importantly the locals. Getting to know the locals implies an in-depth knowledge and association with the resident population as time permits. Such an in-depth understanding requires operations of long, sustained timelines. It certainly takes time for a nonindigenous force to "embed" within an indigenous community.

If the Iraqi ethno-sociopolitical life was not complicated enough, the added heterogeneity of the northern Iraqi societal landscape made it so. The Arab-Kurd divide is only the tip of an underlying iceberg of contrary, competing, and repeated clashes of cultures in and around the principle city of Mosul. Tribal genealogies—political, cultural, and fictive—add to the already-complicated cultural landscape. Determining the effective mix and relationships among various tribal groups, ethnic groups, and political parties within the AOs was essential to establishing an effective governing apparatus, adequately functioning public service systems, and effective state of security in the region. The creation and maintenance of enemy force "blacklist," neutral and/or potentially suspect local population "gray list," and, perhaps most importantly in many respects, a "white list" of community members supportive of the coalition force and "pro-progress" Iraqi reconstruction efforts have proven essential to campaign plan success in northern Iraq. The Division began to see a distinctive improvement in local community cooperation and coordination with U.S. forces after approximately three months in and around Mosul. Three months of "familiarization" with the local environment and communities was probably a rapid timetable for acclimation ("acculturation"). At the seventh month of the Division's 12-month tour of duty, the planning staff of the Division began to reap the longer-term and longer-reaching benefits of its expertise in local ways, norms, and mores.

Timing, Phasing, and Tempo. Planning under SSTR conditions requires—demands—operational patience and flexibility. During dynamic, rapid decisive combat operations, the determination of initiative (who has it?), effect (what is it and what do we want it to be?), and "victory" or "defeat" are most often decided within seconds, minutes, hours, or at most days. In SSTR, these determinants are measured across much longer horizons. And the measures are much more elusive, subjective, and the stuff of perception—whichever side of the fight best capable of reinforcing the rationale and logic of their campaign with tangible examples of success often being the victor.

The shift from the rapidity and violent swiftness of dynamic combatives to the deliberateness of SSTR is a dramatic one. The immediate transition from dynamic to steady-state operations can set the conditions—good or bad—for the remainder of the campaign. The transition is not for those faint of heart or weak of mind and imagination. Failure to see the marker indicating the time to shift from dynamic to steady-state war-fare—and the failure to make that transition—can delegitimize a force with the local population, creating systemic rifts in trust and partnership that can persist throughout the remainder of the campaign and forestall successful completion of the campaign's strategic aims.

The transition from broadsword operations to rapier operations facilitated by the 101st Airborne Division (Air Assault) in late April and early May of 2003 as it first assaulted the city of Mosul and then occupied all of northern Iraq should be viewed as a new chapter of the textbook on how to transition from full-scale combatives to peace-enforcement operations. Within the first 30 days of occupation, the Screaming Eagles identified potential local leadership, established mechanisms, and set conditions for ballot selections of local and regional government, and reestablished order and public services throughout the city of Mosul and its outlying areas. The Division was able to maintain its reputation as a lethal fighting force (not to be crossed) as it donned the persona of peacemaker and civil servant. The Division was able to retain its legitimacy in the eyes of the majority as a force capable of fighting and winning, but also capable of protecting and serving.

The relative success of transition in the northern Iraqi area of operation should in no way be used as a measure of effectiveness for other forces within other AOs in the Iraqi theater of war. No SSTR experiences are alike. However, history will likely show that at least some of the success experienced by the soldiers and leaders of the 101st Airborne Division (Air Assault) was due to their actions before, during, and after transition from MCO to SSTR, as opposed (in contrast) to the problems experienced by other multinational divisions (MNDs) in theater, which for a multitude of reasons were unable or unwilling to balance lethal and nonlethal engagement.

Endstate. It comprises the required conditions—diplomatic, informational, military, and economic—that achieve U.S. national interests in a situation. The doctrine tells us this but our collective actions (or lack thereof) too often defy the notion. Perhaps one of the more scathing commentaries of this war, particularly if the peace that was and is meant to follow never comes, will be that the United States, its military and civilian agencies, and its "coalition of the willing" all failed to properly and adequately plan the campaign for Iraq from the projected and intended strategic endstate. Early initiatives to "stick to timeline" for national elections have since proven to be an indicator of the success of the coalition and the Iraqi people to evolve from a state of war toward a better state of peace and stability in a very short period. Enddate imperatives seem to have overwhelmed concerns with the stability and sustainability of endstates in Iraq's future governing structures.

Are We Winning Yet? Comparing Operational Designs

Current (legacy) understanding and definitions of what are "operations" and what constitutes "operational science and art" are stark and rigid in there relegation of the definition to "capabilities" and, further, to *military capabilities.* Even at the U.S.

Army's elite School of Advanced Military Studies (SAMS), a long-standing debate continues to roar over what constitutes operations and perhaps more importantly (based on what the dominant answer to the first question is) whether or not a non-state actor/entity can be considered as having an operational approach to war, an operational art to its war-fighting.[10] The debate is not without theoretical substance and underpinnings.[11] Beginning with current U.S. Army doctrinal definitions of operational art (*FM 3–0*) and moving through the prevailing contributions of dominant contemporary military theorists, the following are the doctrinal (i.e., currently accepted) indicators of operational art:

1. *Does the action involve military forces?* If it does not, then it is not operational art. This does not mean, however, that operational art is limited to only military forces. Agencies and assets outside of military forces can and often do play a role in operational art, but they must be employed in conjunction with military force for the action to qualify as operational art.

2. *Is the action designed to achieve a strategic goal?* At first glance, all military actions are designed to achieve a strategic goal or at least to contribute indirectly to its attainment. The difference is that in operational art an action's primary purpose is to achieve a strategic goal. A successful battle may or may not achieve strategic goals, but successful operational art always does so.

3. *Is the action intentional?* It is possible, at least hypothetically, to achieve a strategic goal without intending to do so. This is more appropriately referred to as "luck," not operational art. Operational art consciously aims at the achievement of strategic goals.

4. *Does the action include at least one theater strategy, campaign, major operation, or battle?* These are the building blocks of operational art, and if they are not present, then you probably have an engagement, but nothing more. Since they form the basic elements of operational art, they are worth defining:

> *(Theater) Strategy*: the art and science of developing and employing armed forces and other instruments of national power in a synchronized fashion to secure national or multinational objectives. (*FM 3–0*, paragraphs 2–4)
>
> *Campaign*: a related series of military operations aimed at accomplishing a strategic or operational objective within a given time and space. (*FM 3–0*, paragraphs 2–5)
>
> *Major Operation*: a series of tactical actions (battles, engagements, strikes) conducted by various combat forces of a single or several services, coordinated in time and place, to accomplish operational and sometimes strategic objectives in an operational area. (*FM 3–0*, paragraphs 2–5)
>
> *Battle*: a set of related engagements that last longer and involve larger forces than an engagement. (*FM 3–0*, paragraphs 2–12)
>
> *Engagement*: a small tactical conflict between opposing maneuver forces, usually conducting at brigade level and below. (*FM 3–0*, paragraphs 2–12)

5. *Are the components of the action (strategies, campaigns, major operations, and battles) organized in time, space, and purpose so that each component makes a unique contribution to the achievement of the strategic goal?* Each component of the campaign should support the achievement of the strategic aim. If one or more do not, then it is wasted effort, not operational art. In execution, this may prove unavoidable so the real issue rests on the intended and foreseeable consequences of each

component. *FM 3–0* explicitly warns against components of an action that are not organized in time, space, and purpose to achieve the strategic aim. In such a situation, operational art has disappeared and the result is "a set of disconnected engagements with relative attrition the only measure of success."

6. *Are all the components of the action (strategies, campaigns, major operations, and battles) integrated so that their cumulative effect leads to the achievement of the strategic goal?* Even if all the components contribute to the achievement of the strategic goal but their cumulative effect falls short of that goal, the action misses the mark of operational art. Again, since perfect advance knowledge is rarely a possibility in war-fare, this question deals primarily with the intended and foreseeable cumulative consequences of the components.

7. *Does the action move beyond planning to execution?* If the action never moves beyond planning, then it has the potential to become operational art but falls short of the definition until it is actually executed.

Ironically, it is the U.S. Government writ-large that seems to be having difficulties measuring up to its own prescribed criteria for what defines an effective operational art. The U.S. Army fails its own test because the test is a flawed creation, the product of a flawed organizational understanding and appreciation of what constitutes war and the operational art of war. The military capabilities focus of the checklist is the first flaw of concern, for all the reasons given earlier. To briefly restate, a capabilities-based approach is more than (*should* be more than) a simple additive summation of individual materialistic parts.

Not until November 2003 did the Coalition Provision Authority (CPA) in Baghdad develop and publish a formal campaign plan for "Phase-IV" operations in Iraq. Even then, the CPA plan, due to the organization's ignorance (i.e., lack of education, experience, and training) in operational planning, was compelled to define progress and success in the simplest way: by time. Due in part to a lack of knowing how to plan for the war, the CPA redefined the war (in spite of the war's stated end*state*) by a largely arbitrary end*date* (June 2004). V Corps Headquarters in Baghdad (CJTF-7 Headquarters, the operational-level command and control—and planning—headquarters) did not fall into the "time trap" but did "operationalize" its own derivative campaign plan based on its own organizational design flaws; the Army defined the campaign approach for Phase IV in distinct and separate ("stovepiped") lines of operation: offense "versus" defense/deterrence, "versus" stability "versus" support. The Army defined its approach and therefore the "war" it would fight based on capabilities and methods (a means-based planning approach that contributed to a means-based approach to implementation).

The 101st Airborne Division, like other divisions in theater, developed its own theater-strategic-level campaign plan. It was the first Phase-IV operational plan within the theater.[12] Unlike its successor plans, the 101st plan focused on "effects" rather than on time and/or physical capabilities at hand. Success and progress were determined and judged relative to purpose and effects. The timing and shifting of method (application) were not predetermined *by time* but rather from the purpose (aims) and the conditions at any given moment *in time*. Resident capabilities were applied at the tactical level through innovative operational methods, to achieve strategic endstates (see figure 4.1).

True postmodern operational artistry is the same as what it was: prelinear and mechanistic age of war-fare. It is about achieving a *synergistic effect* over an adversary (and over an adversarial environment) through the *application of force*, of which the military arm is but one of many. With that said, one must recognize the reality of our U.S./Western contemporary operating situation: few if any organizations other than the U.S. military (the U.S. Army in particular, given its dominant relevancy in *land campaigning*) have the capability, the capacity, and the experience to "operationalize" full-spectrum, postmodern war-fare. The U.S. Department of State, despite its better concepts for waging and winning in postmodern war, does not yet have a formal operational science or art; it does not have its own separate operational planning process or approach. Even if it does, it suffers in terms of returns-to-scale—the organization cannot cope as adequately and effectively as the U.S. Army can in planning for and commanding and controlling multifunctional and multiechelon forces on the expansive "battlefields" of the COE. It is a similar story for other nonmilitary, governmental, and nongovernmental defense and security organizations. In that regard, the U.S. Army must take lead in postmodern civil-military

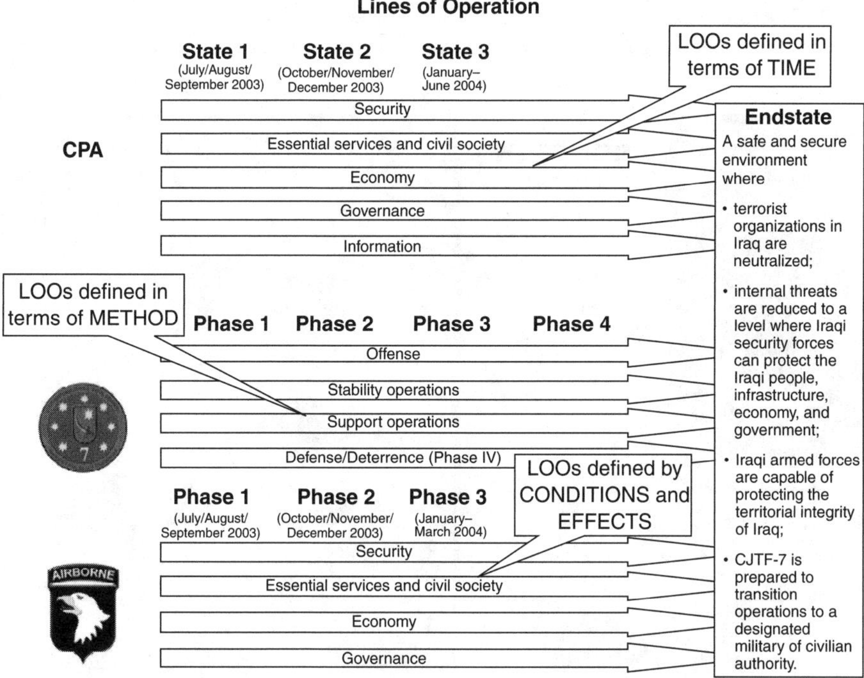

Figure 4.1 Dueling Operational Conceptions and Designs

Source: Official 101st Airborne Division planning briefings (unclassified versions and/or declassified materials), June 2003–May 2005.

operations, applying the martial science and art to provide a power-based enforcement (effective implementation) capability to the diplomatic, informational, economic, and humanitarian and reconstruction (nation-building) domains of war. The U.S. Army must take its old utensils, develop new ones, and combine both—the martial with the extramartial—in order to finish eating the soup placed at the nation's table.

Full-Spectrum War-Fare

Offensive Operations, Counterinsurgency, Counterterrorism, Reconstruction

As the 101st Airborne continued to gain experience in full-spectrum operations, the Division developed a better operational understanding of what, conceptually, the U.S. Army had defined as *full-spectrum operations.* While contemporary U.S. Army doctrine identifies full spectrum as composed of *offense*, *defense*, *stability*, and *support* operations, the 101st experience revealed both a different array of operations and timing/sequencing of those operations (see map 4.1).

Experience in northern Iraq, and arguably within the entire country, proved something other than the theoretical linear and sequential progression from offensive operations to SSTR. While the war's beginning marked the beginning of offensive operations, there was no definitive end to "offensive" operations. In truth, there was no way of, and no reason to, determining a beginning or ending to offensive

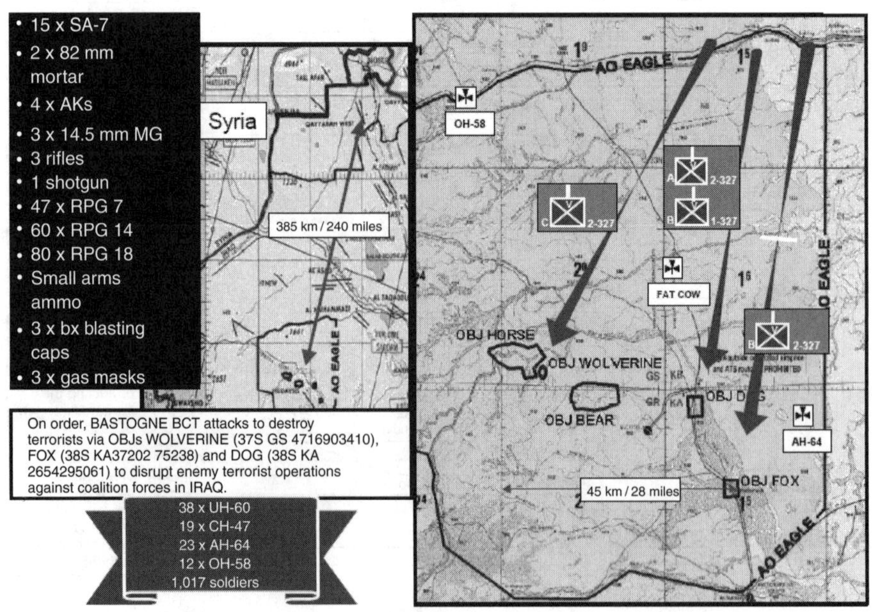

Map 4.1 Operation McClellan, August 30, 2003

Source: Official 101st Airborne Division planning briefings (unclassified versions and/or declassified materials), June 2003–May 2005.

operations. The nature of those offensive operations—the point of attention—proved a dynamic and ever-changing thing. Traditional "close-with-to-destroy" type offensive operations were continuous but were only one aspect of the "offense." Close-with-to-restore local industrial, commercial, and essential service infrastructure was another continual form of offensive operations. The reconstruction agenda was synonymous with the offensive. Counterterrorists and counterterrorism operations tended to be periodic; precision strike operations were conducted as shaping operations to "contain" the internal challenges of pushing forward the reconstruction efforts from the external terrorists threat. All of these activities, challenges, threats, and operations were seamless; they were the thesis and antithesis of war and peace. All, combined, were definitive of an environment of insurgency.

Relearning to Eat Soup with a Knife

To make war upon rebellion is messy and slow, like eating soup with a knife.
T. E. Lawrence, Seven Pillars of Wisdom, 132

Though a war of rebellion it was, predicted by some military planners even before it officially began, the war in Iraq was not "officially" regarded as a war of rebellion, and therefore a U.S.-supported counterinsurgency until December 2003—almost one year after initiation of combat operations in Iraq, and after the 101st Airborne had been conducting counterinsurgency operations in northern Iraq for eight months. Reluctance in even defining the situation for what the conditions on the ground defined that situation to be is perhaps the most telling indicator of a collective cognitive dissidence on part of the United States and its military services to recognize a war of rebellion, a people's war, even when they were fighting it. The messiness and slowness of these types of wars add to the organization's reluctance to think of these wars as wars, much less to affirm a role and mission in these wars.

However, I believe that organizational design flaws, namely in the institutionalization of modern-day doctrine development and operational planning as well as in the career development and professional military education (PME) of its officer corps, account for much of this difficulty in eating the proverbial soup with the proverbial knife.

As even our own civil-military history continues to reteach us, the U.S. Army can eat soup with a knife—it can achieve unparalleled success, tactically, in wars of rebellion, self-determination, and so on. Developing an operational acumen for waging war, holistic, from initiation of offensive operations, through transitions back and forth, through combatives and SSTR, and through or bypassing the rebellious episodes toward a legitimate lasting peace, requires a broader, operational, and full-spectrum concept of organizational self, purpose, role, and function.

There came a point during our yearlong stint of duty in Iraq back in 2003 and early 2004, before the return of "the War" as we have traditionally come to know war to be, when the growing sentiment throughout other military commands within the theater of operations was that the 101st Airborne, far off and away from the battles and engagements of the Sunni Triangle, was not even fighting a "War" in the north. The nightly MND Commander Conference Calls with the CJTF-7

Commander, General Sanchez, was perhaps one of the best examples of the different wars being waged within the different occupation zones. While the preponderance of reporting from other Division commanders made note of numbers of anti-insurgent operations conducted, number of insurgents and anticoalition forces captured or killed, and similar traditional combative indices, the 101st reports were a mixed review of anti-insurgent and counterinsurgent activities. The anti-insurgent portions of the situation report (SITREP) covered ongoing combat operations—close-with-to-capture-, close-with-to-defeat-, or close-with-to-destroy-operations. The counterinsurgency portions of the report covered preventive and preemptive operations and actions we were taking on behalf of stabilization and reconstruction operations. As time and our campaign plan progressed, the balance of our nightly reports to higher tilted more and more toward counterinsurgency reporting. As we became better counterinsurgents, the need for anti-insurgent TTPs lessened, or at least took a "follow and support" position in our overall war-waging repertoire. These reports were secure radio reports between each MND and CJTF-7—an open conference. The situation as time moved along became one of "one of us is not like the others." Something other than what was going on in other operational sectors was happening up in the north was the growing opinion. "They" were all surely fighting war. So, if what units such as the Marines, the 82nd Airborne (in the western regions), and the 4th Infantry Division (4ID) and the 1st Cavalry Division (1CAV) (north-central and south-central Iraq, respectively) were encountering and dealing with was "war" and "combat," then surely what the 101st had up north was something "other-than-war."

By October 2003, the CPA and CJTF-7 leadership was already beginning to direct individuals from other MND sectors up to the north to observe 101st operations and operational planning.[13] The first thing they would all come in contact with was our banner—*We're Fighting a War Too, We're Just Not Whining about It!* All in all, this introduction always seemed to set a progressive tone to the discussions that were to follow.

As more time and distance come between myself and Iraq—and my experiences there—this quotation takes on more and more of a substantive meaning for me. The fact that nonstandard approaches to the war-fight in Iraq was more susceptible to being evaluated more by its nonstandardness than by its achievements and success is a strong indicator of the paradox's prominence and influence. A reluctance to acknowledge what the 101st Airborne was doing in the north and how they were doing it as effective applications in the indirect method of war was more than a slight against the unit. It was indicative of a dominant cultural blindness to the potential effectiveness of nonstandard forms of war-waging. It was an indicator of our military's dogmatic fixation on the traditional, force-on-force combat offensive as *the* approved method of waging modern wars. A similar cult of the offensive drove the Great Powers of Europe in the early twentieth century to global cataclysm—the Great War (World War I). During the Interwar Years (1919–ca. 1939), France slowly fell into an organizational mindset favoring of doctrinal process-driven approach to war-fare, finally suffering from an ailment termed by military historians as "methodical battle." France lost not only its army but also its entire nation within just one month to the German Blitzkrieg, due to the bane of *methodical battle.*[14]

America is suffering from a form of *methodical battle syndrome.* Ours is unique to us and is a particularly virulent form of the sickness.

Part II

Lessons in Postmodern War: Civil-Military Operations in Northern Iraq

By most accounts to date, the experiences of the 101st Airborne Division (Air Assault), from Fort Campbell, Kentucky, stand out as one story of operational success in a building saga of stumbles and setbacks in the war in Iraq. The laudatory reports of the Division's actions during the major combat phases of the campaign by author Rick Atkinson in his 2003 book *In the Company of Soldiers*[1] affirms the idea that perhaps there was something to the 101st Division's way of war-fare worth bottling and distributing throughout other areas of operations in Iraq. The promotion of the Division's former commander Major General David H. Petraeus to lieutenant general (three-star rank), his selection to command of the Multinational Security Transition Command—Iraq,[2] and the delegation by the Bush administration of the enormous and enormously important task of the establishment and training of an effective Iraqi security apparatus are further confirmations that this military commander and the 101st Airborne did something "right," unlike anywhere else in the country to date.

Might the 101st Airborne's approach to civil-military operations in northern Iraq serve as a recipe for how to implement war, as policy, in the "postmodern age"? Might their approach remind us of the civil-military complexities of seventeenth-century Western war-fare (wars of position)—a complexity that once again, since the end of the interregnum of cold war bipolar stability, appears to describe the contemporary security and operating environment?

What follows is a narrative of operations and operational planning conducted by the 101st Airborne Division (Air Assault) during the strategic transition (pause) period of April 2003–ca. March 2004. The intent of the narrative is to evince the "war as policy" operational planning approach used by the 101st Airborne through illustration of some of the divisions' major plans and operations and to illustrate through anecdotal evidence the utility of some of the planning methods as a model for future postmodern civil-military operational planning.

Some of the observations and lessons gathered in civil-military operational planning in Northern Iraq discussed and evidenced through empirical results and illustrated through anecdotal evidence and vignettes in the section that follows include

- the development of a *divisional* campaign plan for northern Iraq as a near-first action taken after liberation and occupation of Mosul and the *viyalet of Mosul* in late April 2003;
- analysis and visualization of the "Battle space" and arrayal of "forces";
- early identification of the "compound threat"; subsequent identification of the operational, theater-strategic; and a reinterpretation (a planning ass umption) of the previously articulated strategic center of gravity (COG)—the critical capabilities feeding that COG and the resources (critical enabling strengths and debilitating weaknesses) that empower or weaken the COG.
- development of a systems and effects approach to operational planning;
- early embracing of local and regional tribal networks and incorporation of tribal engagement in the divisional campaign plan;
- early recognition of the shift (transition) of the contemporary operating environment in northern Iraq (and the rest of Iraq for that matter) to an environment of compound threats—insurgency, homegrown and transnational jihadist-based terrorism, unbounded criminal activity, and the degradation of the environment and essential services infrastructure that tended to feed these threats;
- the early development of a counterinsurgency (COIN) plan for operations in northern Iraq; and
- the development and implementation of tactics, techniques, and procedures (TTPs) designed to apply effective military power in a more nonlethal manner (i.e., "cordon and knocks" and demonstrations).

Chapter 5

The Liberation and Reconstruction of Northern Iraq

In mid-April 2003, the 101st Airborne received new mission orders from Combined Joint Task Force-7 (CJTF-7) in Baghdad: move to and occupy the three northern governorates of Iraq (Ninevah, Dahuk, Irbil, As Sulaymaniyah). It is important to note outright that prior to redeploying to northern Iraq for liberation and occupation of the northern provinces, the 101st Airborne had played a center stage role throughout major combat phases of the war, earning battle honors for three specific major battles (An Najaf, Al Hillah, Karbala Gap). This is an important point for two reasons. First, the 101st was not a force tailor-made for "other-than-war" operations. The 101st Airborne Division (Air Assault) is one of the nation's elite combat units, with possibly the richest battle lineage of all U.S. Army organizations. For those naysayers of traditional "combat units" ("war-fighting organizations") performing "other-than-war" functions and advocates of a removal of the Army from the sort of "low-intensity" operations typifying stability and support operations (SASO) and nation-building, the point that the 101st ably and effectively "transitioned" from major combatives to nation-building is an important counter. Second, the fact that the 101st was able to continue the "fight" into the transition and reconstruction phases without tiring and consequently becoming less precise and measured in its application of power is an important counter to the common idea that combat units require rotation following major combat operations and could not effectively transition in a full-spectrum war. To those who would use such an argument to either argue for limited 12-month-based unit rotations or against the application of any military combat force into an action for more than a short duration, the actions of the 101st is an important counterargument.

Contributing to the uniqueness of the northern Iraq approach to war was the emphasis placed on the assessment of the terrain itself. While other areas of operation in Iraq faced the challenges of Sunni-Shia divides, the north presented this and a myriad of other "human terrain" challenges. Arab-Kurd relations shape a very unique environment in the north. Complicating that landscape is the presence of Yezidi, Turkomans (with their ethnic ties to Turkey), and the "unofficial" presence of Turkish conventional and special operations forces throughout the region (see map 5.1).

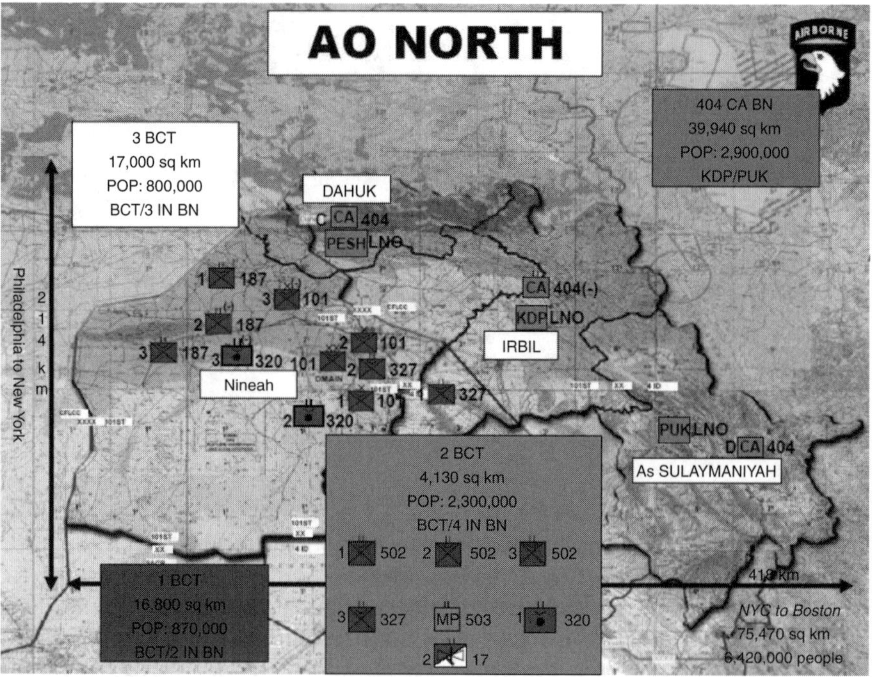

Map 5.1 Area of Operations North

Source: Official 101st Airborne Division planning briefings (unclassified versions and/or declassified materials), June 2003–May 2005.

Shifting to "occupation" came with an entirely different operational metric and operational approach. Part of knowing the enemy (including the landscape and the ethnoreligious and tribal array) included knowing one's own temporal and spatial place ("identity") in the area of operation. The temporal and spatial conditions throughout Iraq changed dramatically almost immediately after regime collapse.

Part of the ambiguity of the situation between the transition weeks of mid-May to mid-June was the result of a slowing of the tempo of operations (enemy, coalition forces, populace)—in part, a derivative of no operational plan for this transition period and the postoffensive phases that would follow. Military commanders and "operators," trained and experienced for rapid, fast-moving operations, almost immediately found themselves in a temporal quicksand. Time seemed to slow down; this was an indicator of a shift from major "force-on-force" linear operations to what 101st planners came to regard as *protracted steady-state SASO*. Occupation called for a positional war-fare approach to planning and operations, similar to seventeenth-century European wars of positioning and maneuver. Another peculiarity of the planning conditions for steady-state SASO that the Division discovered was that, unlike rapid maneuver offensive operations where the higher echelons had greater resolution on information and intelligence than tactical units (greater situational awareness), under steady-state SASO, the reverse was the case: higher fidelity on information and intelligence rested at the lowest echelons (brigade and below). The importance of "presence of place" (steady-state positioning) proved critical in future operational success. The Division dedicated a significant amount of time and effort in steady-state "positioning" to the operational problem in northern Iraq.

Amid the continuing pressures due to resource scarcity (not having enough "boots-on-the ground"), due in part to the absence of a full and comprehensive plan, the act of determining areas where risk could be taken and where it could not was not a choice but a vital necessity. The prime city of Mosul was determined as the theater-strategic center of gravity for the north (prior knowledge of the region's history helping in this quick assessment), and a preponderance of "available power" was allocated to this sector (the *viyalet*). The remainder of divisional combat power was allocated to the western sector (3rd Brigade Combat Team) and the southern sector (1st Brigade Combat Team). Partly due to prior knowledge of the history and politics of the region, partly due to a lack of resources and therefore few if any other options, the Division Commander Major General Petraeus accepted operational risk in the Kurdish-dominated provinces allocating a mere battalion of civil affairs soldiers to "cover" the three northern provinces of Dahuk, Irbil, and As Sulaymaniyah.

Compound Threat Assessment in Northern Iraq

Determining the composition of the compound threat challenging U.S. forces and the reconstruction process was seen as a critical step in effective condition-setting by the 101st planners and intelligence analysts. This analysis began in the traditional, doctrinal fashion of U.S. Army military decision-making process—intelligence preparation of the battlefield (IPB)—and the confirmation of remnant elements of the former Hussein state apparatus (identified as former regime loyalists/elements [FRL/E]) as the core element of the organic threat facing U.S. and coalition forces.

Moving the IPB process to the "advanced graduate level" allowed the division to expand its knowledge of the intricacies of what proved to be a complex, compound threat network. Again at the core were FRL/E. The northern region, Ninevah province in particular, was the traditional retirement homestead of former senior military leaders; it was natural that upon regime collapse, former senior-level (first- to fourth-level firqua Ba'athist) Sunni military leaders would migrate to this homestead. A large criminal population, compounded by Saddam's earlier release of over 6,000 hardened criminals, became a source pool of cheap hired guns for the former regime loyalists. Adding to this cheap lethal labor market was the growing number of unemployed male youths and recently unemployed soldiers, the former the result of the destruction of the employment sectors, and the latter, the result of Ambassador Bremer's blanket disbanding of the Iraqi Army. Completing what emerged as a triad of compound organic threats was the presence—small at first but growing—of an extremist (jihadist) element, in part homegrown and in part foreign-based and resourced (transnational). Identification of this threat was a critical first step; dissecting the goals, intentions, and methods of operation of each element of this triad was the more important second step.

"Attacking" the Causes, as Well as the Effects

A focus on "defeating" the organic threat could not be separated from the importance of defeating the inorganic one. The organic enemy was the stem of the problem; the environmental conditions in northern Iraq were the root. To "destroy" this enemy by stem and root required a stem-and-root operational plan and planning approach, an indirect approach to the war fight. Improving the environmental conditions was a means of "destroying" the enemy's support infrastructure. Civil reconstruction projects, directed broadly initially (a mass attack) to rapidly regain the initiative from the enemy, would later be applied more surgically and deliberately as a precision weapon against specific chronic problem areas and toward areas demonstrating positive trends (carrot and stick). Establishment of a civil works program, similar (not coincidentally) to the type of *get-back-to-work*, confidence-building projects initiated by the Franklin D. Roosevelt administration during America's depression years, would be used to employ the disenfranchised youth and soldiers and to rapidly inject the northern economy with capital.

These programs and projects would also provide the Division with an indirect weapon against the organic threat; it would serve as a means of disabling the threat at the root of both its justification for anti-U.S./coalition operations[1] and its means (resources) for combating U.S. forces. Getting some early wins and early control of the environmental situation in northern Iraq was a vital condition-setter and a key first step toward building a divisional campaign plan focused on the design of major operations (informational, diplomatic, governmental, economic, public administrative, cultural, religious, ethnic, etc.) that indirectly attacked to "isolate" and "destroy" organic threats by "seizing" and "securing" those civil functions essential to, first, the sustainment of basic life needs and, eventually, to the improvement of Iraqi quality of life.

"Early Wins" in the First 30 Days

The eerie silence and absence of U.S. military operational activity that defined the immediate weeks and months of transition between regime collapse and the final (reluctant) realization by the Coalition Provisional Authority (CPA) and U.S. military forces that the military mission would continue for at least another 12 months (late July 2003) in most parts of Iraq were not present in the northern provinces. There was no hiatus (no "cease-fire") in the north. The 101st Airborne conducted air assaults on Mosul, liberating the city on April 22, 2003 and immediately commenced with a full-spectrum implementation plan for occupation (duration still indeterminate and, as the Division considered at the time, largely irrelevant) that was admittedly still more an idea in the mind of the commander and leadership within the Division; it was a plan not yet fully formulated and legitimized (see figure 5.1).

As figure 5.1 shows, by May 25—a mere 30 days after initial occupation of Mosul—every critical public service sector was reestablished. A day after arrival, Major General Petraeus and a small action team met with community leaders (*mukhtars*), and in loose coordination with them, the 101st developed two ad hoc lines of operation to guide the initial 30–60 days of occupation and the reestablishment of civil and civic life within Mosul at first, then Ninevah province, and finally (rapidly) throughout northern Iraq. The first line of operation, *security/CPA tasks*, focused on the more traditional military functions: securing of the occupation base and expansion of that base (south to the Tigris River Valley, west to Rabia and the Syrian border regions, north-northeast to the Turkish and Iranian border regions),

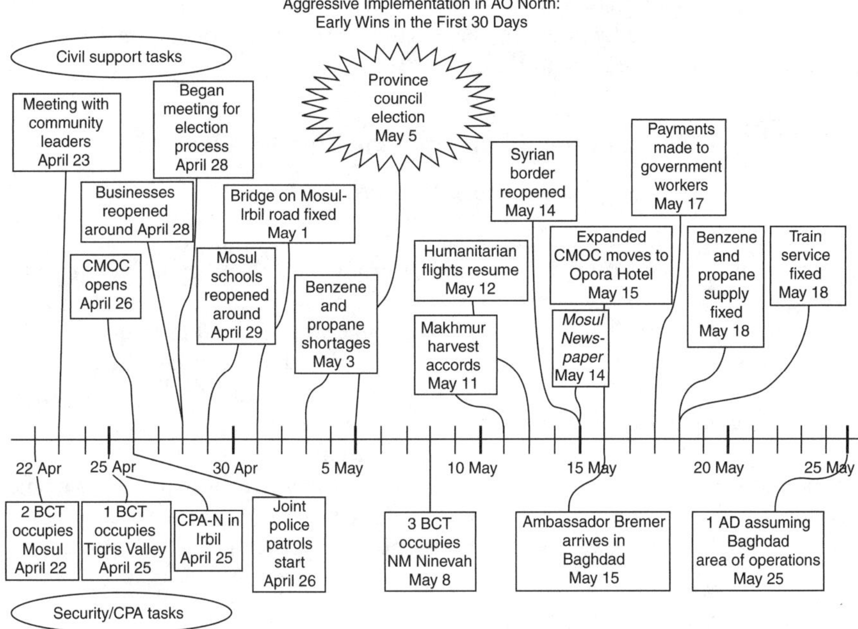

Figure 5.1 The First 30 Days

Source: Official 101st Airborne Division planning briefings (unclassified versions and/or declassified materials), June 2003–May 2005.

integration of military with ongoing police patrols (April 26), and the establishment of CPA North operations (key civil-military operations cell, established in Irbil on May 8). The second line of operation, *civil support tasks*, emphasized the application of available military combat capability to more nonstandard problems and in innovative ways. Key tasks in this regard included rapid selection of city and provincial leadership and leadership councils (government elections beginning with Ninevah province elections on May 5, 2003), the reopening of businesses (commerce) on April 28, the reopening of schools on April 29, the identification and assessment of key fuel shortages (benzene, propane, kerosene) on May 8 and the implementation of corresponding solution plans on May 18, the reopening of local print and radio media on May 14, and so on. Additionally, in this critical first 30 days, the baselines of several key political-economic policies were established, namely the reopening of the border with Syria (trade and cultural relations), the reestablishment of commerce via Turkish trade routes, the initiation of the Mahkmur Trade Accords,[2] and the establishment of a Veterans Employment Program.[3]

In hindsight, the avoidance of a temporal gap between the official cessation of major offensive operations and the initiation of postoffensive operations in northern Iraq was instrumental in the relative future successes enjoyed in the north as compared to other regions in the country in subsequent months. The 101st Airborne transitioned well, in part because the Division's leadership was able to think, act, then plan for further deliberate action, beyond the doctrinal (dogmatic) determinants of when certain war-activities are to begin and when other-than-war activities are to begin, and to begin by whom. In the north, there was no operational pause or culmination. This proved key to future progress.

Building the Campaign Plan That Was Not

Reconstructing Northern Iraq

By mid-July 2003, it was becoming clear that the war was not over, that the CPA and other civilian (governmental and nongovernmental) agencies on the ground—although well intentioned—were incapable of operationalizing an effective post-combat plan, and that the U.S. military would likely be retained in Iraq in order to secure and stabilize the situation.[4] Though still unstable, by mid-July, the 101st Airborne was working hand-in-hand with a shaky but present-for-duty and willing-to-learn provisional Iraqi regional government (see figure 5.2).

Building on the success of the two-pronged informal operational plan that spanned 30–60 days, Division planners began constructing a more formal campaign plan for Phase-IV operations. The original two lines of operation were expanded to four: security (LOO 1), essential services and civil society (LOO 2), governance

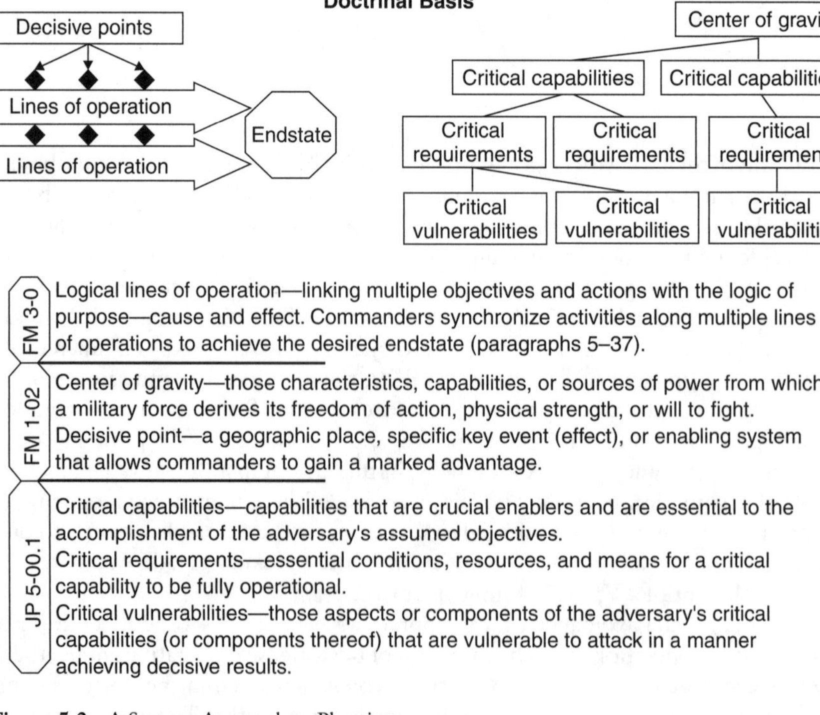

Figure 5.2 A Systems Approach to Planning

Source: Official 101st Airborne Division planning briefings (unclassified versions and/or declassified materials), June 2003–May 2005.

(LOO 3), and economy (LOO 4). Each line of operation was composed of key tasks—essential tasks by which success or failure could be determined/defined.[5] Defining these key tasks were a constantly evolving number of supporting tasks—tasks that defined each key task in terms of a quantitative and/or qualitative measure of effectiveness.[6] The importance of the supporting tasks was in their measurable characteristics. The setting of the measures of effectiveness for each supporting task was critical to assess the progress (or slippage) of the Division's tactical efforts along any given line of operation and, consequently, critical to period assessments of the overall campaign plan.

Key tasks for all lines of operation were further analyzed monthly, for achievement of an overall aggregate campaign assessment, by four components: *infrastructure, administration and training, production, and distribution.* Division planners saw these four components common to all functions, key tasks defining those functions, and the lines of operation those key tasks determined.

Security, essential services, economy, governance—each had their own form of infrastructure, administration, and training requirements/criteria. Each had their own form of "production," that is, each produced something. Each had a distribution function, that is, each distributed "something," be it a means of public voice, salary, or food stuff. Key and supporting tasks were organized in accordance with these four component areas, the analytical results of which were then recorded by way of the governorate to district, to subdistrict, to local community categories and levels of resolution. The methodology leveraged heavily on system theory and approached the entire northern area of operations as a *system of systems.*[7] All "systems"—from major cities to key infrastructure nodes, to the Mosul City Council, to Mosul University, to the three northern governorates, to the organic threat (anticoalition forces), and so on—were conceived of in terms of at least six components: input, transformation, output, feedback, information process, and control element. Major operations were planned and executed, therefore, to attack, to both "destroy" and to "restore," as well as to "compel," "influence," and so on. Thinking systematically allowed for a simplification of the problems at hand and consequently made for more successful operations (see map 5.2).

Map 5.2 shows the January 2003 assessment of Area of Operations North (AO North) by the 101st Airborne Division, just prior to transition of responsibilities to I Corps Headquarters and 3/2 Infantry (Stryker Brigade Combat Team). This methodology was the baseline of a broader Division-level Integrated Effects Working Group (IEWG) process, a modification of the doctrinal targeting process, where the Division "fire support" coordinator (DFSCOORD), in conjunction with the Division chief planner and analysis and control element (ACE) chief, led weekly working group sessions (Sunday evening "war councils")—collaborative planning and assessment working sessions with brigade-level subject matter experts and divisional unit representatives, covering functional areas across all campaign lines of operation.

These sessions proved critical for (1) synchronizing multiechelon plans and planning, and (2) vetting ideas and innovative approaches to upcoming or prevailing operational challenges. Ideas raised, discussed, argued, and that survived that process were then refined by small tailor-made operational planning groups (OPGs) or operational planning teams (OPTs),[8] facilitated by the chief of plans. Plans were then presented in weekly updates to the commanding general and Division leaders

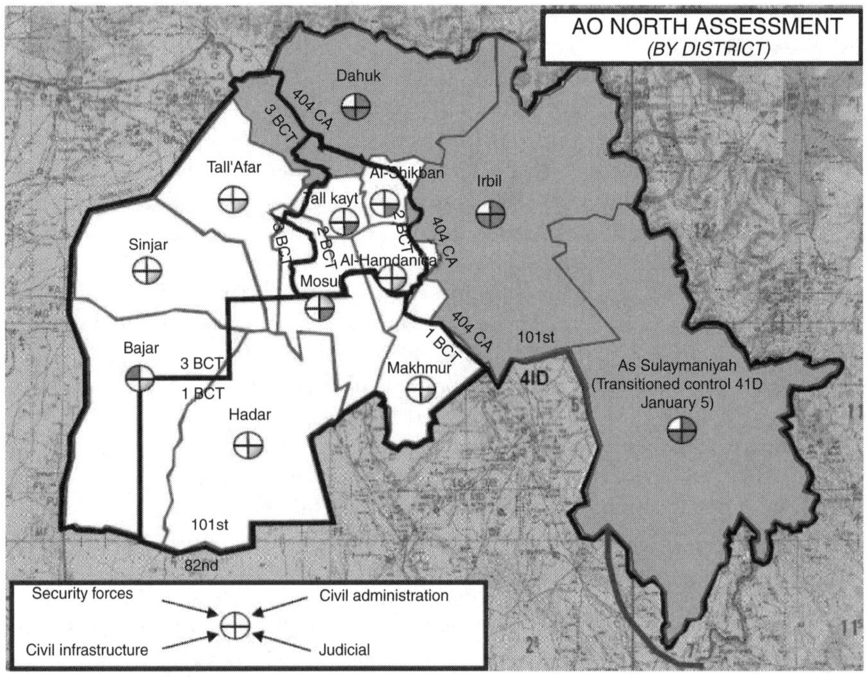

Map 5.2 Campaign Assessment AO North, by District

Source: Official 101st Airborne Division planning briefings (unclassified versions and/or declassified materials), June 2003–May 2005.

(staff and subordinate commanders) and/or as the situation dictated. Once formalized and refined, this IEWG plans update served as the venue and process for reviewing and formalizing all major operations (full-spectrum plan), to include weekly press releases and talking points for the Division leadership, the Mosul City mayor's office, governorate (provincial) councils, and so on.

In addition to the IEWG, predominately an "inside" (Division-internal) collaborative planning process, Division operational planners and intelligence analysts developed a companion integration-focused and information-/intelligence-sharing process: the Joint Interagency Task Force (JIATF) and the Coalition Information Sharing Task Force (see figure 5.3).

The JIATF was formally organized in late October 2003, although its functions had been implemented less formally and on an ad hoc basis since mid-summer. A handful of officers within the Division with prior experience with similar organizations in the Balkans and Kosovo saw the potential for application to the campaign plan in northern Iraq and brought the idea forward in a weekly IEWG. The overall purpose of the JIATF was to provide the Division commander with a mechanism for focusing the intelligence effort across an area of operation larger than the state of Maine (and exponentially more complex in terms of terrain, both human and environmental), to deconflict the intelligence efforts of the 101st and a myriad of other U.S. national assets, and to fuse that combined intelligence picture into a high-resolution common operating picture—all on behalf of facilitating more

Why AO North JIATF was established

- Needed a mechanism to focus our intelligence effort, coordinate/deconflict 101st Division and U.S. national assets, fuse intelligence, and coordinate coalition operations in order to facilitate joint targeting and, in so doing, create an environment inhospitable to terrorists.

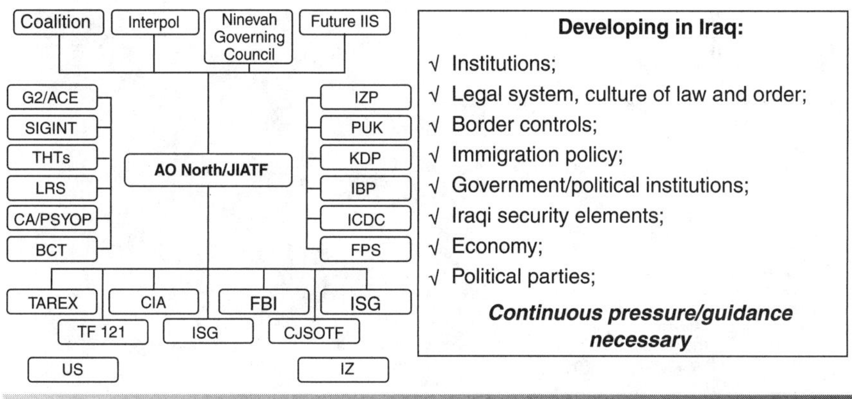

Figure 5.3 The Joint Interagency Task Force

Source: Official 101st Airborne Division planning briefings (unclassified versions and/or declassified materials), June 2003–May 2005.

effective and precise joint targeting. Division planners and intelligence analysts also maintained a more informal collaborative planning process with local Arab-Iraqi security forces, as well as with the major Kurdish-Iraqi *peshmerga* and other Kurdish security forces. This relationship was limited to information-sharing only, due to the delicate and sensitive ethnopolitical relationships and situation in the north. Information gathered from these weekly meetings proved invaluable for providing U.S. governmental and nongovernmental agencies effective *presence of place*—the next best level of indigenous information short of being native to the region.

Successful Postmodern Positional War-fare through Collaborative Planning

Collaborative, effects-focused planning contributed to the successful effects-based execution in full-spectrum operations for which the 101st eventually became renowned. The Division began to reap significant benefits from its relationship-building (engagement) plans after the first two months of regular and repetitive collaborative sessions. The information gathered through these tightly coupled relationships produced the type of actionable intelligence the Division required to execute anticoalition force operations preemptively, effectively, and in most cases bloodlessly (see figure 5.4).

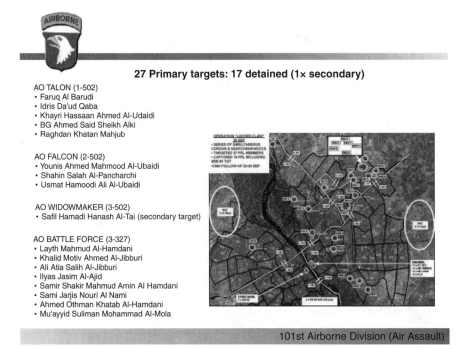

27 Primary targets: 17 detained (1× secondary)

AO TALON (1-502)
- Faruq Al Barudi
- Idris Da'ud Qaba
- Khayri Hassaan Ahmed Al-Udaidi
- BG Ahmed Said Sheikh Alki
- Raghdan Khatan Mahjub

AO FALCON (2-502)
- Younis Ahmed Mahmood Al-Ubaidi
- Shahin Salah Al-Pancharchi
- Usmat Hamoodi Ali Al-Ubaidi

AO WIDOWMAKER (3-502)
- Safil Hamadi Hanash Al-Tai (secondary target)

AO BATTLE FORCE (3-327)
- Layth Mahmud Al-Hamdani
- Khalid Motiv Ahmed Al-Jibburi
- Ali Atia Salih Al-Jibburi
- Ilyas Jasim Al-Ajid
- Samir Shakir Mahmud Amin Al Hamdani
- Sami Jarjis Nouri Al Nami
- Ahmed Othman Khatab Al-Hamdani
- Mu'ayyid Suliman Mohammad Al-Mola

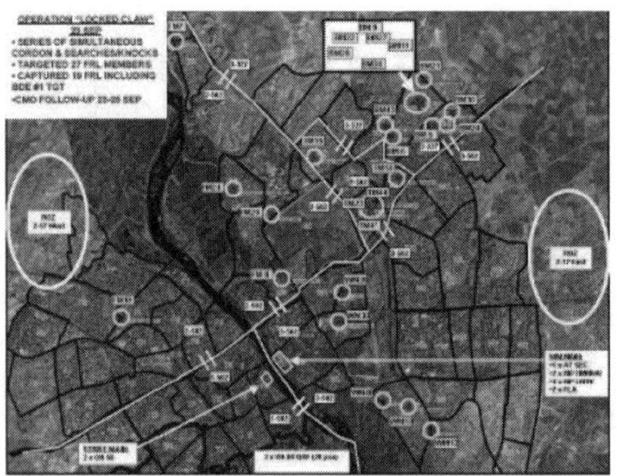

101st Airborne Division (Air Assault)

Figure 5.4 Vignette (Operation LOCKED CLAW) (Al Rifah Targets, Detained Mosul, September 23, 2003)

Source: Official 101st Airborne Division planning briefings (unclassified versions and/or declassified materials), June 2003–May 2005.

Operation LOCKED CLAW (September 23, 2003) is one case in point where the 101st, through the JIATF and IEWG processes, was able to develop a correct and common operating picture within the city of Mosul, identify key leaders and members of the Al Rifah Movement, and develop a major operational plan that facilitated the simultaneous seizure of 27 high-value targets (HVTs) scattered across the entire city of over 2.5 million people. The depth of presence of place (intimate knowledge of the area and confidence in the reliability of the intelligence at hand provided by multiple sources) enabled the Division to execute 27 separate combat operations simultaneously over a wide-expansive and complex area of operations. The 2nd Brigade Combat Team of the 101st Airborne Division, in concert with other governmental agencies (OGA), special operations forces, and local indigenous security forces, was able to detain 17 of 27 HVTs, within a 20-minute time period, with zero killed in action.

The Al Awda (Return) Party was an organization that 101st Division intelligence had identified as being composed of former senior Ba'athist Party members, formed on or around June 2003. The purpose of this group was disruption of U.S. and coalition progress in its SASO, with the intent of driving a wedge between coalition forces and the general Iraqi public. The Division operation to destroy the Al Awda Party as an organization began in earnest as a JIATF-based operation in July 2003

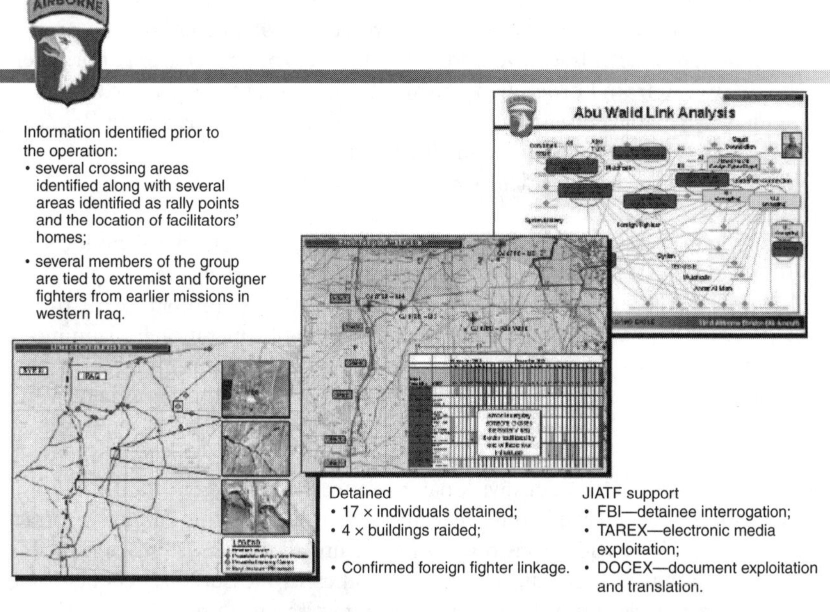

Figure 5.5 Vignette (Operation PREYING EAGLE)

Source: Official 101st Airborne Division planning briefings (unclassified versions and/or declassified materials), June 2003–May 2005.

and progressed through January 10, 2004, by which time, the Division with the assistance of OGA and continuous monitoring of party activities was able to effectively eliminate/delegitimize the Al Awda Party as a coherent anticoalition organization (see figure 5.5).

Operation PREYING EAGLE was another major divisional operation based on the IEWG and JIATF processes, and reminiscent of seventeenth-century style *positional* (full-spectrum) *war-fare.*

This operation focused on identification, isolation, and disruption/destruction of the Abu Walid Group, an Iraqi homegrown extremist (Wahhabist) organization, with foreign fighter support and ties to Al Qaeda. With information identified and obtained prior to initiation of the group's anticoalition operations, the 101st and supporting agencies were able to identify and surveil expected infiltration and exfiltration routes and safehouses used by group members. Perhaps, more importantly, by the time of this operation (December 2003–January 2004), the Division's operational and intelligence planning processes had evolved to such a degree and had developed such a deep and detailed repository of information and intelligence gathered from previous operations that detainees and the "pocket litter" collected from detainees could be rapidly compared with the resident database for potential linkage with other incidents and other anticoalition / antiprogress elements. In PREYING EAGLE, several detainees were linked to foreign fighter elements captured during earlier operations. This planning-execution approach provided the 101st with a limited degree of predictability of when and what type of a new threat organization was forming in northern Iraq, attempting to migrate from other areas of or entering into northern Iraq from bordering countries. In this case, the Division planners were able to identify what eventually was verified by CJTF-7 Headquarters in Baghdad as a new and emerging transnational, jihadist threat.

What these three vignettes demonstrate is the following:

1. The significant value of early and continuous engagement with the local community and local (indigenous) security forces during full-spectrum operations.
2. The importance of establishing steady-state, reliable (legitimate with the local populace) relationships and modes of operation and operational planning. The myriad of U.S. governmental and nongovernmental organizations and agencies in northern Iraq, working their own separate plans, could have easily proven the most effective threat to the coalition effort, had these agencies been permitted to conduct their own small wars in their own ways, rather than combining these efforts and expertise, under divisional guidance, in the larger "fight."
3. Establishing effective planning-execution battle rhythms under protracted steady-state SASO conditions takes time. Again, all of the systems and processes the 101st put into place did not yield significant, measurable benefits for two months after initial setup. Maintaining the tactical and operational patience to parent fledgling processes and systems to maturity is a daunting tasks, especially for military commanders and their staffs who have been trained and experienced in fast-paced, rapid-fire operations. Speed and tempo must be treated as an adjustable rheostat rather than a dogmatic accelerative concept. Speed saves lives and adds to tactical effectiveness under dynamic offensive operations, but speed can kill under steady-state SASO.

By January 2004, the CJTF-7 Headquarters in Baghdad was building its own IEWG and JIATF processes, using many aspects of the 101st as its model.

Essential Services and Civil Society

Combating the Environmental Threat and Managing Local Expectations

The compound threat of the SASO environment is always, in part, the condition of the environment itself. If and when that environment devolves into an environment of insurgency, winning the war over the environment is essential to beating the insurgent to the *hearts and minds* of the people.

While establishing a baseline of security, rebuilding the public services infrastructure in northern Iraq was an inextricably linked factor. There could be no modicum of security until the essential services and economic sectors could be stabilized. The enemy knew this early on to be the soft underbelly (critical vulnerability) of the coalition and therefore dedicated their meager resources primarily along that line of operation. The protection of critical "systems" became a major operation throughout Iraq but a peculiarly important mission in the north due to the already-tenuous relationships between Arab-Iraqis and Iraqi-Kurds, coupled with relations with

Syria, Iraq, and Turkey—all fragile relations based somewhat on fuel and water resources and the distribution systems relating to those resources.

The scarcity of available "combat power" (from infantry to "protect" to civil engineers to "construct and repair") greatly complicated the situation. Managing the growing and, in many ways, unrealistic expectations of the local population were complications as well. The people expected dramatic improvements to their quality of life conditions with the ending of the Hussein regime and the arrival of the United States; no excuses to why these dramatic improvements could not be attained in short order could easily alleviate these great expectations. The challenge, in addition to safeguarding the infrastructure as well as possible, was in *keeping the public informed.*

At first, information updates were only sent to the public when the Division could assure relative improvements. But at times, improvements were few and far between. By October 2003, Division planners conceived of a new way of approaching the problem. The Division would not abandon the deliberate work to repair and improve the infrastructure (oil, power, water, transportation [air/ground/rail/waterway], banking, etc.) but would reinforce this effort (and protect it) by attempting to provide the public with a reasonable schedule of when they could expect to be "without," the idea being that lending predictability and reliability to the bad situation was perhaps better than promising improvement and not being able to follow through. Planners knew that the power system would only support, initially, four to six hours of household power. By devoting capabilities and a plan to regularize the blackout periods and then advertising these blackout times in print, radio, and television media, the Division would at least appear "truthful and reliable," if only in reporting what it could not do in a reliable manner. Saying what you mean and meaning what you said goes a long distance in Arab society; this logic-defying and nonstandard approach paid significant dividends in the Division information operations campaign and facilitated trust between the unit and the local population.

As the 101st began to make strides forward in infrastructure improvement, the anticoalition forces began to focus their attacks on the interim and fledgling Iraqi civic leadership. CJTF-7 Headquarters had by September 2003 directed country-wide Operation POWER CRUDE, a major operation focused on infrastructure security (oil and electricity). The 101st planners expanded the premise of POWER CRUDE to include consideration of key civic leaders as "critical infrastructure" and therefore covered those committing attacks against power lines and pumping stations under the more robust rules of engagement (ROE) and stricter detainment and imprisonment conditions reserved. Other divisions adopted similar expansions of the infrastructure protection mission after seeing the success that the 101st was having with the operation.

Economy

"Money Is Our Ammunition!"

The security and economic lines of operation proved to be the two primary drivers of the successful SASO and reconstruction campaign waged by the 101st Airborne Division in northern Iraq (see figure 5.6).

Economy and Agriculture

- Makhmur agreement and payment scheme solved wheat crisis.
- Over $55 million was paid to farmers/mills.
- Over $2,000,000 in CERP projects and several other projects were supported by NGOs.
- Shifting focus to future needs of farmers for upcoming season; agricultural symposium was held on October 13.

Facility	Quantity of Class I Wheat Received	Quantity of Barley	Estimate of Amount Paid to Farmers
Mosul	19,873 MT	0	$5,200,000
Tal'A fer	12,564 MT	22,058 MT	$4,000,000
Al-Wa'ilia	6,576 MT	20,677 MT	$3,006,000
Rabi'a	9,600 MT	10,185 MT	$4,005,000
Al-Ba'aj	7,593 MT	18,494 MT	$4,480,000
Sinjar	26,000 MT	0	$0
Al-Shikhan	33,049 MT	9,107 MT	$3,200,000
Fayda	0	0	$0
Makhmur	64,394 MT	52,769 MT	$4,300,000
Al-Shurgat	24,779 MT	0	$6,300,000
As-Sulaymaniyah	8,000 MT	0	$1,133,000
Irbil	18,534 MT	0	$12,350,000
Zahko	14,954 MT	2,700 MT	$4,000,000
Ninevah Yards	0	35,296 MT	$3,350,000
Total	261,959 MT	201,979 MT	$55,750,000

Figure 5.6 Money Is Our Ammunition

Source: Official 101st Airborne Division planning briefings (unclassified versions and/or declassified materials), June 2003–May 2005.

Again, there could be no relative security without an acceptable and stable baseline of public service throughout northern Iraq. Areas and regions where essential services were of moderate reliability proved the more secure and procoalition. Solving the essential services and civil society challenge required economic investment. The motto *money is our ammunition!* soon covered the walls of all divisional units. From June 2003 to February 2004, the 101st Airborne invested more funds into their northern area of operations than any other multinational division within the theater of war (see map 5.3).

Using Iraqi funds that had been hoarded as personal booty by Saddam Hussein and his sons and later secured by U.S. forces, the Division commander used these discretionary funds[9] as tools for invigorating both the local communities and the economy as well as a forcing function for inspiring healthy competition among his brigade commanders; this competition resulted in more civil reconstruction projects being completed in a shorter time period (greater results, sooner than later, thereby better meeting public expectations).

The theater-strategic importance of the northern provinces not only to the country of Iraq but to the entire northern region as well cannot be overstated and

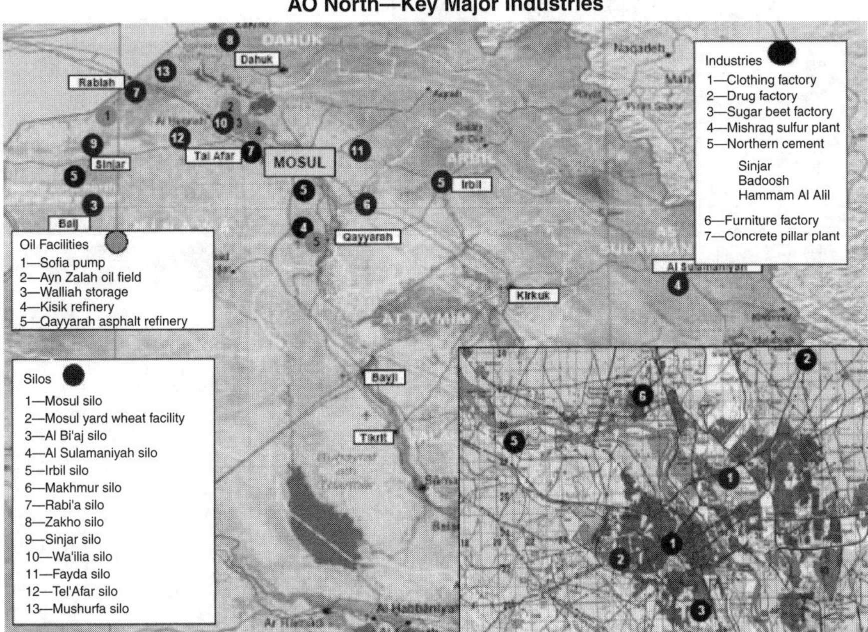

Map 5.3 Rebuilding the Economic Sector

Source: Official 101st Airborne Division planning briefings (unclassified versions and/or declassified materials), June 2003–May 2005.

should never be underestimated. Northern Iraq is a critical pivot region within the Middle East; it is a nexus between Iraq proper, Syria, Turkey, and Iran (see map 5.4).

Water and oil interests of all these countries (and beyond) are affected by the degree of stability and state of relations within northern Iraq. Complicating this resource situation is the cultural, religious, and ethnopolitical tectonics that reside within and around the northern Iraq region.

With the war in the north came devastation of the region's economic and industrial sectors. Regaining "stability" in the north directly impacted the security situation of all surrounding countries. The vital importance of stabilizing essential oil and power and water situations in and around the northern provinces led the 101st to implement some high-risk, high-payoff diplomatic and politicoeconomic ventures, the most significant being the oil for power trade agreements that Governor Al Basso of Ninevah province arranged with the assistance of the 101st. Though initially raising alarm bells with U.S. government officials and ridicule in the Western press, it was soon hard to find fault with the success of the trade agreement, both in terms of improved (stable) Iraqi-Syrian-Turkish relations and in terms of stabilizing the economic situation in this critical tristate region.

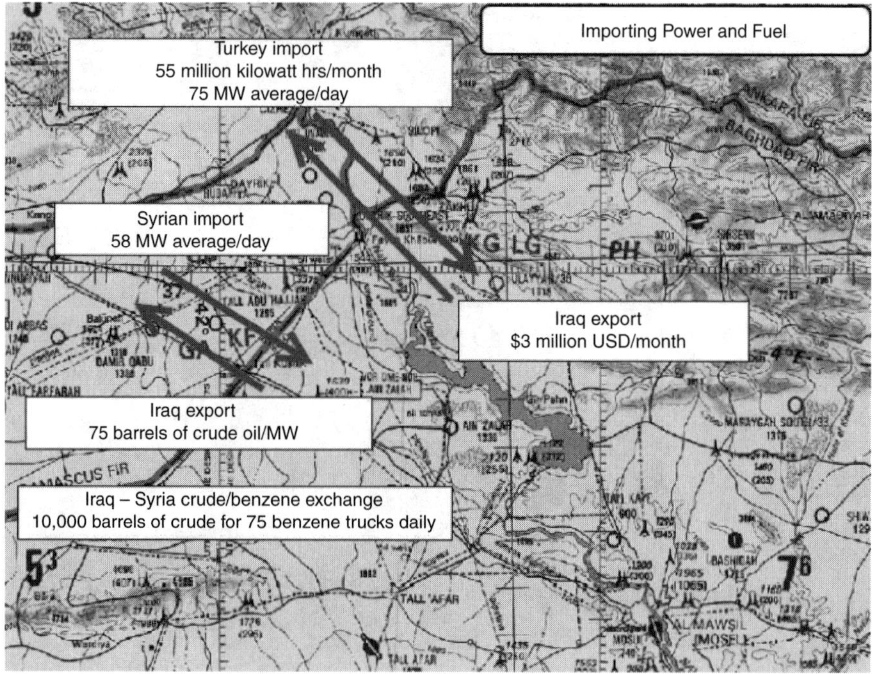

Map 5.4 Reestablishing Key Trade Sectors

Source: Official 101st Airborne Division planning briefings (unclassified versions and/or declassified materials), June 2003–May 2005.

Governance: "All Politics Is Local, and 'Local' Means 'Tribal'"

Developing the governance line of operation was recognized early on as the likely decisive LOO of the entire campaign plan, in the long run. However, in the near term (at least throughout the first year of occupation), security and economy ("guns and butter") would have to be the driving LOOs for the 101st campaign plan.

Within the first 30 days, the 101st had facilitated the election of an interim Mosul City/Ninevah Province Governing Council. The Division's planning for the selection and election of interim council members was a crucial means (a tool) of preventing and/or mitigating the possible ethnoreligious and tribal conflict that could have resulted from an "unequitable" and "unrepresentative" legislative body. Perhaps the most significant lesson gathered by the 101st Airborne regarding governance and the reestablishment of governance institutions and processes in northern Iraq was the importance of thinking beyond mere institution-building, thinking beyond American and Western *ideal types* of governance structures and regimes, and gaining, first, an understanding of the local ways of *public administration*, then gradually developing a skill at working within (and manipulating) those "local ways."

As former Speaker of the House Tip O'Neil famously stated, *all politics is local.* Thinking beyond traditional ideas of war-fighting and even beyond the prescriptive doctrine for nation-building enabled division planners and leadership to realize that same dictum holds true in SASO. In Iraq, and the Middle East in general, local public administration has always been, at its core, *tribal.*

Chapter 6

Patronage Politics in Northern Iraq: The Case of Tribal Engagement in Northern Iraq, June 2003–March 2004

In July 2003, shortly after my arrival in Mosul as the new Division chief of plans, the commanding general, then Major General David Petraeus, directed the Division planners, in addition to developing a formal campaign plan that could be subject to assessment, to determine how administration (how politics and policy occurred on a day-to-day basis) actually worked at the ground level in northern Iraq (see figure 6.1).

The answer to that question turned out to be, at least in part, what T. E. Lawrence and others had learned and told us decades before, from their own earlier experiences in Mesopotamia. Despite what "government" looked like on the outside, the functions of how things get done daily were based on family, tribal, and clan heritage. Understanding and respecting this, regardless of whether we as Westerners liked or approved of it, was essential to mastering the *art of the possible*—public policy and public administration—in Iraq.

Using the U.S. federalism model as an initial comparative tool helped planners to quickly obtain a rudimentary baseline understanding for the nature and function of the various systems (hierarchies) of tribal life in Iraq. Roughly, at the ground (base) level of the hierarchy, the Western "familial" political association structure marries with "family," subtribe, and clan. The progression moves through county government, labor union (Western)/tribe (Arab), through state government (Western)/ tribal confederation (Arab), to federal government (Western)/national tribal confederation (Arab). The entire tribal system and each subcategory within have its own peculiar tradition, heritage, notions of prestige and honor, just as each level of our own federal system has their own "rules" and "business practices." The comparison, for a base understanding of governing and administrative *function*, proved useful and reasonably accurate (see figure 6.2).

Knowing Iraqi tribalism was not good enough. The Division had to get beyond base knowledge and obtain an operational understanding of tribal life, specific to northern Iraq.[1] By late October, Division planners had developed a nuanced formal

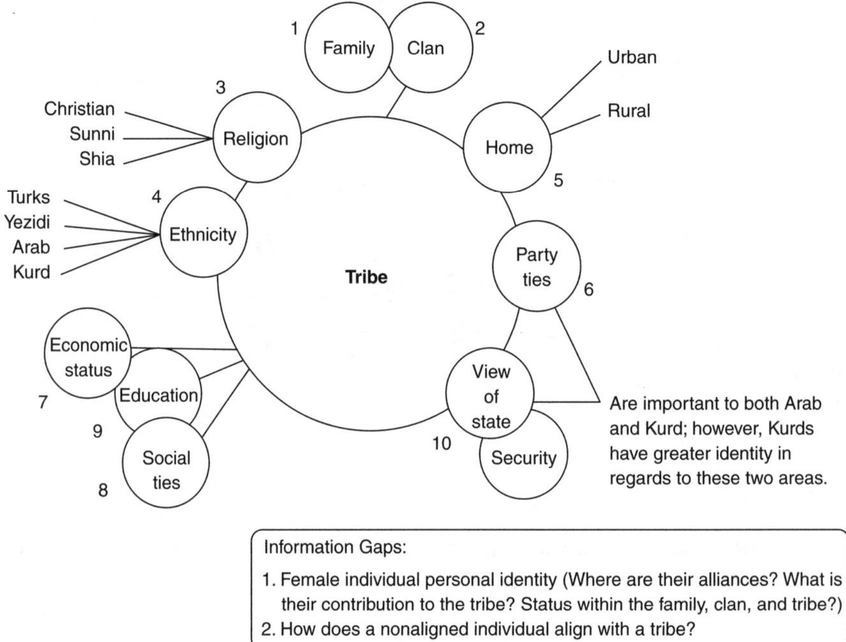

Figure 6.1 Sociology of the Tribe
Note: Allegiances and indentification may vary or shift depending on the gains perceived or real in any one of these areas.
Source: Official 101st Airborne Division planning briefings (unclassified versions and/or declassified materials), June 2003–May 2005.

tribal engagement plan and were employing it (operating within it) deliberately as a means of tracking anticoalition forces to their support bases and sanctuaries. The Division by this time, in cooperation with special operating forces, was also using the tribal system as a means of tracking Saddam Hussein (high-value target [HVT] #1) and other high-value targets in northern Iraq.

Improving Operationally through Acculturation

As the Division's understanding of the tribal ways of the north improved, so did the unit's operational effectiveness and its own force protection.[2] By November 2003, though not a formal member of any tribe (a Westerner could never achieve this status in true form), leaders within the 101st as well as the Division on a whole were considered as "friends" and *distant brothers* of the majority of the local tribes and confederations. This "inclusion" and specific labeling of the 101st as "distant family" was significant. There is an ancient Arabic adage, *me against my brother, my brother and I against my cousin, my brother, my cousin, and I against the world*. Being perceived as an invited guest or distant member of the local community would not

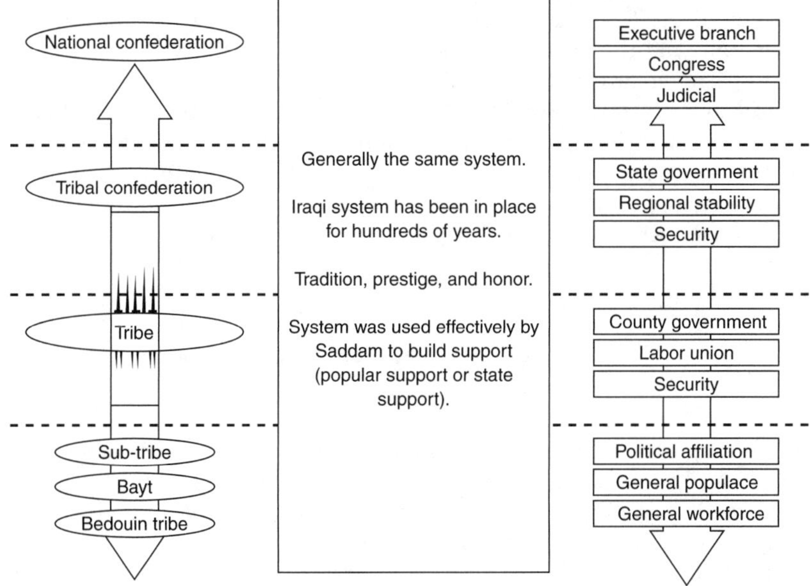

Figure 6.2 Tribal versus Patronage-Based Politics

Source: Official 101st Airborne Division planning briefings (unclassified versions and/or declassified materials), June 2003–May 2005.

confirm one's policy success or personal protection completely, but this status could and did prove very useful.

By this time, the 101st was also developing a detailed knowledge and understanding of the historical and political relationships between the various tribes and confederations. Tying the administrative tribal ways of each tribe to one another in the north painted a public administrative substructure to the entire region—literally revealing the informal trade, smuggling, and potential anticoalition infiltration and exfiltration routes that appeared to *work the seams* between the U.S. divisional battlefield architecture.

Combining our growing knowledge of these tribal byways (identified as *the ties that may bind*) with our expanding appreciation of the historic relevancy of these tribal byways to the former regime allowed Division planners to hypothesize about the whereabouts and "how-abouts" of senior high-level Ba'athist leaders (to include Saddam). Might they have reverted to their old tribal ways and locations after the collapse of the regime? *Might we find these elusive enemies along the very tribal routes and locations that enabled them to power in the early 1960s?*

On December 17, 2003, elements of the 4th Infantry Division (Mechanized) (4ID) in concert with special operations forces and other governmental agencies (OGA) discovered and captured HVT #1, Saddam Hussein, in a spider (hide) hole near his familial and tribal lands southeast of Tikrit. This location was on the southernmost edge of the tie that may bind tribal trails identified by the 101st tribal analysis process. This trail extended along an inner seam running along the Tigris River, from the Tikriti tribe, through the Jaburi and Al Tai confederations, to the tribal lands of the Shammar tribal confederation—the largest of the Iraqi tribal confederations and the most international in reach, with the Shammar lands and contacts extending into Syria.[3]

Understanding the tribal system in Arabia in general, more specifically in Iraq, and even more specifically in terms of how tribalism worked in northern Iraq provide the 101st Airborne Division with an intimate knowledge of how daily public policy "worked" within the region. This evolved aspect of the divisional campaign plan formed the bedrock of what grew into the Division's deliberate counterinsurgency program.

Tribes, the State, and Postmodern War

An Introduction

There has long been a *paradox of the American way of war*—a national propensity to "lose" small wars despite our unmatched prowess at "winning" all the battles and engagements in those wars. The reconsideration of the role of power, particularly military power, by the Bush administration as a principle tool of its democratization security strategy has set the United States on a potential collision course with its own history of losing small wars in spite of a national propensity of winning all the local engagements along the way. Finding a new means of waging war and peace—new way of intervening—is now a vital national security interest, not only for the fulfillment of the president's democratization vision but more importantly for the preservation of the nation's actual and perceived suasive power in intervention.

With the character of postmodern war-fare being more of the small genre, it is vital we find new methods of war-fare—*new stratagems of containment*—that allow us to achieve "big wins" in our "small wars" of the present and future. One alternative method may be found in the incorporation of local patronage-based, or "tribal," networks into our intervention policies and civil-military campaign plans. *All politics is local.* And that often means "tribal-," "clan-," or "kin-based" in a majority of the regions of the world where the United States is engaged today and will be engaged in war-fare and nation-building ("democratization") tomorrow. Such networks have persisted for over 6,000 years, serving as a sort of *public administration system.* Learning to understand, appreciate, work within, and manipulate these local patronage networks is a new and innovative approach to U.S. war-policy that has great promise as an effective strategy of democratization and containment.

This chapter is a preliminary exploration of the issue. It presents and examines one case study of effective tribal engagement war-planning in action in northern Iraq during the first year of the war as practical evidence of value of this operational method; it was a fully integrated method that was relatively successful in some regions of Iraq (the north and the south) but to lesser degrees in others. Where there was and has been success in Iraqi stabilization and reconstruction can be found an effective provisioning of local and regional essential public services through the incorporation of tribes and kin-based networks. Recent operational gains against Al Qaeda in Mesopotamia and toward stability-building in the western province of

An Anbar has been credited with a "bottom up reconciliation" based on partnership with local tribes. Incorporation of tribal engagement strategies into the current U.S. way of war-fare can provide new answers to age-old questions of why wars widen, how they widen, and how widening might be contained in the future.

Understanding Kin-Based Politics

Long before state structures emerged, societies where kinship divisions ran deep had nonstate institutions that governed the behavior of groups. Societies developed elaborate practices that would rein in future destabilizing forces before such forces could even have effect. These premodern, informal networks also served, during the genesis of the nation-state system, as necessary condition-setting processes enabling the slow and stable development and legitimization of more formal state governance institutions. Such networks served as incubators to the modern sociopolitical and economic institutions we are familiar with today.

Clan politics (kin-based, tribal) continue to influence power politics, in spite of modernity and the rise and dominance of the state and the nation-state system. And despite our particular "Western" (and even more particular "American") mythology about modern politics—that the modern state has cast all nonstate associative groupings to the dustbin of premodern history, that clan-based politics matter less and less in contemporary politics—the reality is clear: kin-based divisions and associations matter; they lie at the center of international, regional, and domestic politics.

In his seminal work, *Man the State, and War*, Kenneth N. Waltz helped to define international relations as a relationship between man (human behavior), the modern nation-state, and power politics ("War").[8] Waltz got the relationship right but not entirely. What his proposition left out of the political calculus and what realist theory negates (black boxes out of the discussion) or simply "assumes away" is the ways in which "man" associates and interacts within and with the state and the wider international community of nation-states. Man engages in day-to-day politics through *associations*. Alexander De Tocquiville told us so during his nine years of travels through the early American landscape.[9]

The realist or modern (i.e., largely Western) tradition still sees the political significance of clan-based politics as restricted in two significant ways: "spatially, to the remote margins of the state system where traditional and diffuse authority patterns prevail, and temporally, to historical periods before the emergence of modern state structures."[10] Neither restriction survives the test of empirical study nor practicality. The Western and American propensity to "wish away" the power of kin-based politics and the role it plays in a majority of world societal systems has defined and relegated modern politics to foci on issues of materiel-centric power and institutions (Weberian notions and architectures of politics) and to largely ignoring and underappreciating (undertheorizing) the power and role of ideas in politics. This bias against kin-based politics—ideational politics—is the result of many factors: our unique "Western experience," culture, geography, modernization profile, racial biases, and so on. This bias, ironically, persists in stark contrast to a full and realistic appreciation of our own American social-political ("democratization") experience—a nation of kin-based politics; in fact, the beacon on the hill of what positive results can come from a healthy marriage of kinship politics and the modern nation-state, if power is balanced well, legitimately, and therefore effectively.

Contemporary times are such that the proverbial "West" can no longer afford to render to its own dustbin of history the importance of kin-based politics. The so-called idiosyncratic and asymmetrical nature of international politics and its COE forbid ignoring the complexities of intrastate politics. If the nation-state system is to be preserved—if it is to survive—ironically as it may seem, then, scholars, policy makers, and practitioners must all get to know clan politics.

As Charles Lindblom notes,

> Kinship . . . . is not merely a logical apparatus consisting of complicated rules for terminology and marriage; it is instead a way of apprehending and ordering the world, replete with implications for the evolution and organization of political life.[11]

This alternative ordering principle is premodern, modern, and postmodern. And it is, as it has always been and always will be, an integral part of the American political system. This GWOT or war against global terrorism or, as most recently rendered, the *struggle against Islamic extremism*—whatever its label—is a political discourse rooted and premised in ideas and "tribal-isms" (some calling it, "The West against the Rest"). This ideational "war" is a nonlinear and noncontiguous one, with the nation-state ordering principle being made more and more "arbitrary" with globalization, every new evolution in information technology (IT), and the prevalence of kin-based diasporas within otherwise-regarded "homogenous" national states. Today's *transnationalization* of otherwise-"contained," intrastate clan-based politics (as witnessed in the American war-fights in Afghanistan and Iraq, the ethnic-based political unrest in France and Germany, and even in persistent racial and class-based conflicts within the United States) makes understanding kinship politics all the more relevant and critical. *Bringing the state back in* demands we appreciate those ties that have a substantial role in binding the nation-states together or ripping it apart into associations.[12]

Understanding "American" Kin-Based Politics

The U.S. strategy of democratization may be, from its inception, hobbled in its potential as an effective or promising security strategy mainly because of a faulty national conception of "good governance" and "democracy." This national preconception of "other" may find its roots in a misperception of "self." A more honest and historically correct interpretation of America's own modernization and democratization accepts the importance and significant impacts of the nation's tribal- and kin-based roots, as well as the continual and contemporary role patronage politics plays in American political life. James Madison, in at least two of his contributions to the federalist debate over the ratification of the U.S. Constitution, addressed the prominence of factions (associations, interest groups) in American political society and offered institutional and procedural ways and means of controlling the bane of factions.[13] George Washington in his presidential farewell address warned the young American nation of the bane of partisan-based (party) politics.[14] President Eisenhower in his 1961 presidential farewell speech warned of the rise of "unwanted and unwarranted" influences of a military-industrial complex.[15] The "melting pot" (or "marble cake") metaphor of the American polity is an appropriate one—the ingredients being one part kin, one part clan, and another part tribal. We are not so different from "other" as we might prefer to believe.

While serving as a war-planner in northern Iraq in 2003, I engaged in a policy dialogue with governance experts within the Coalition Provisional Authority (CPA) who were at that time leading the process of governance-building in Iraq.

Case 1a

"An Ill-Conceived Notion of Democratization in Iraq"

As the plans and concepts on how to democratize Iraq unfold, the choice of model upon which those plans were developed could prove telltale in terms of probability of success or failure. In short, basing the Iraqi governance process on our rosy view of our own constitutional history is not the best model upon which to build a new Iraqi state, particularly in the short run. In fact, accelerating the Iraqi democratization process along this line could result in the demise of democracy in Iraq in the long run.

Viewing Iraqi Democratization through the Right Lens

To state it baldly, viewing a future democratic Iraq through the lens of modern-day American and, to a tacit degree, British systems, institutions, practices, and expectations is compelling the CPA to press too hard and too fast in the democratization effort. What we fail to recognize is that the advanced form of American representative democracy is the result of over 230 years of slow, gradual and, at times, corrupt and bloody growth.

Architects of the new Iraq would be better served with a vision of a future democratic governing structure in Iraq that reflected the state of democratic governance in the United States at the turn of the nineteenth or twentieth century. Nineteenth-century democracy in America was enigmatic of all the positive themes and forms of free and democratic government that we hope to impart on the people of Iraq: representative government, liberty, rule of law, and so on.

However, it also had plenty of warts: monopolistic activities, limited suffrage, graft and corruption, riotous behavior, unbridled patronage, and so on. There is little logical reason to expect more from the Iraqis' progression through democratization. Yet, the November 15 Agreement and the accelerated plan for Iraqi sovereignty, elections, and constitution-building and ratification insinuate that the Iraqis can and must surpass the American experiment in terms of immediate progress and results. This is unrealistic and unfair to the Iraqi people.

What Our Own History Should Tell Us

A quick review of some of the realities of the early American experience in democratization is in order.

The debate overdrafting and ratification of the U.S. Constitution marked not the first but the second revolution in American democratization. For the first 12 years of the nation's history, the Articles of Confederation governed daily domestic and international political life. Passage through a period of confederation, in hindsight, was critical in the success of the later experiment—the move toward a national, constitutional form of government. The issue of "state's rights" was as volatile in our own experiment as debates over religious and ethnic rights promise to be in Iraq's steps toward democracy. For us, back then, confederation was the only viable (interim) solution to a semiunited government. Indeed, the Articles of Confederation may prove to be both the more realistic and the better governance model upon which to base Iraqi progress.

Meanwhile, the move toward a national, constitutional democracy in the United States was fraught with turmoil, argument, and infighting. We forget that our Constitution barely passed ratification—itself, a three-year process. That process forced compromise and deferment on many of the more contentious issues of the day—issues that forced the acceptance of a less-than-fully democratic democracy. Limited suffrage (the continuance of slavery for another 77 years after the signing of ratification of the U.S. Constitution in 1789) and the delicate and complex design of a national versus states balance-of-power architecture were the long-term costs for becoming a United States.

Turning to party-affiliated governance and day-to-day public administration, it will likely look less like the politics of modern-day New York City, but more like the "Gangs of New York" political style of the late 1800s or perhaps even the politics of 1920s Chicago. Expecting more, due in part to a desire of the administration to get Iraq democratic and self-ruling in short order, will actually do the Iraqis a disservice. It will deprive them of a longer, more evolutionary democratization process that is, in effect, the ugly (and sometimes bloody) tutor for a future legitimate democratic-like system of government, built and fought for by the Iraqi people, for the Iraqi people, and on the Iraqi people's own terms and experiences.

All Politics Is Local: So Deal with Local Reality

Iraq at its base is a tribal society. Despite recently coming to terms with this reality, there is still a lingering abhorrence of tribal ways of Iraqi governance within the CPA and higher policy-making circles that will continue to hinder the governance-building process. All politics is local, and the local level of Iraqi politics reflects its tribal system. Indeed, tribes have often served a public administration function in Arab society (to varying degrees). Building a new Iraqi governing structure without appreciating the part that the tribal system plays on a day-to-day basis will likely subvert the democratization process. America's own early experience with democratic forms had a vital "association" basis to its development. Iraq is no different, just that the associations are tribal. Recognizing Iraq's preexisting tribal affiliations is a healthy way of, first, understanding the relevance of tribal ways and their role in Iraqi society and, second, learning to assimilate these forms of societal interaction into perhaps more functional forms of governance.

Iraq is currently in the midst of insurgency, with the question of what type of governing society and national state Iraq will become hanging in the balance. The fact that we as a Western society and military think of this sort of war as a "small war" is unfortunately an indicator of the tragic flaw in U.S. (Western) ways of war, reconstruction, and peace. In reality, from inception this war has been a war of democratization. As such, if this process is to result in an effective and stable democracy of the Iraqi people, by the Iraqi people, and for the Iraqi people, then we will need rapidly to develop a more realistic and pragmatic approach to the governance reconstruction process in Iraq.

Understanding the Role of Kinship Politics in Iraq

There is a paradox in America's overall democratization strategy, but particularly as it has been applied thus far to Iraq. While U.S.-stated policy seeks a free and democratic Iraq, the process for "getting there" (democratization) seems to promote a very restricted (prescriptive) form of democratization—*American-style democracy.* "Stability" and "Western" governance forms and styles seem more characteristic of the policy being attempted through implementation in Iraq. The irony (and tragedy) of our current efforts in Iraq may be this: *we may be losing the democracy we hope to help the Iraqis build by how we are approaching democratization in Iraq. Can democratic governance be successfully mobilized in a new Iraq?* Perhaps so, but only if this "paradox" can be overcome.

In Iraq, the paradox is already threatening democracy and could soon reach a point of diminishing return for the United States, in terms of how legitimate its purpose and place in the country and the wider region are viewed by the Iraqi people. A change of course is needed, both in how we have set the democratization agenda for Iraq and how we implement democracy in Iraq. U.S. policy makers must offer the interim Iraqi leadership with a more pragmatic and historically honest vision of the (Western) model of democratization. Just like our own democratization experience, Iraq's process must be permitted to evolve through various stages, many of which will not be as stable or "ideal" as most U.S. policy makers and Western governance experts would prefer. *An interim stage of tribal democracy may be a necessary prestate for a future democratic Iraq.*

* * *

Net-Centric War-Fare

All politics is local, and that means "tribal" in a country such as Iraq. Tribal networks have persisted here for over 5,000 years, serving as a sort of "public administration" system. During the critical first year of the transition period between major combat operations and reconstruction (April 2003–June 2004), U.S. and British civilian policy makers and senior military leaders were reluctant and, in some cases, adamantly opposed to integrating local tribes and tribalism into ongoing reconstruction, which is countrywide reconstruction, national reconstruction, and all that it implies. Key to legitimizing any type of governance structure in Iraq, much less a democratic one, is a capability to provide for the essential demands of the populace—security and the day-to-day administering of public services being paramount.

While many academicians and even more military theorists posit that we are at the dawn (even past the dawn) of a new revolutionary epoch in modern military affairs –an information age of war-fare—most if not all of that new thinking has centered on the materiel (tech-based) aspects of this so-called information revolution.

Leveraging the power of information became one of the central tenets of the 1990's revolution in military affairs (RMA), the defense establishment's campaign to continue U.S. dominance in war-fare. What has so far resulted from this dedicated effort at rethinking modern U.S. military doctrine and force designs is known as Net-Centric War-fare (NSW). To NSW theorists, war-fare would no longer be about fighting for terrain or destroying forces but would instead be a fight for information. Whoever won the fight for information would not only win all the conflicts but the war and the peace to follow as well.[16]

But what does a net-centric evolution/revolution in sociopolitical and military affairs really mean? It is beyond this survey to address this question in detail, but for now it can simply and succinctly be said that a holistic revolution in information-age affairs (net-centric affairs) must be much more than merely a technological (IT) revolution. In fact, I posit that the true revolution lies in a new organizational and operational political-social command and control over patronage-based (kin-based) political networks.

Democratization is ultimately a process of identity politics. Key and critical to any identity-building democratization policy is understanding of the social networks that undergird preexisting subidentities, whether or not (and the degree to which) these subnetworks are deemed legitimate by the local populations, and, then, how these standing (yet flexible and transitory) networks can be either eliminated (if at all) or assimilated/incorporated for the production (reproduction) of a national (democratic) identity. The mechanisms of identity-building and reproduction must be understood and respected, if not completely accepted. Kinship networks are the de facto public administration systems existent within most societies. These networks are the connections between man, the state, and the day-to-day political discourse between man, nation, and the state. Understanding these networks—these connections—are crucial (critical capabilities)[17] connectors between those seeking access to a society (access seekers) and those seeking to provide essential services (i.e., nation-building, reconstructing, "democratizing") to national populations or associative subgroups.[18]

The promise of an effective, legitimate, and just U.S. democratization strategy lies in our knowledge of and incorporation of local and regional patronage-political networks into our *NSS* and *NMS*. The continued inability to do so will place current and future U.S. strategies of democratization on a path toward failure.

Managing Kin-Based Politics

Whether designed to address kin divisions or not, state institutions have an effect in making them a normal or abnormal part of political life; deliberately or not, states manage or mismanage clan affiliations.

To be effective in managing clan divisions, states must stitch new practices into the fabric of political life—practices that are tailored to and respectful of the peculiarities of kinship. Doing so may ultimately prove to be a more successful and enduring means of preserving stability, enhancing state performance, and ensuring representative government than attempts to undermine preexisting identity relationships.[19] "Modern" states typically take the opposite approach, viewing clans or tribes as a threat worth marginalizing or even eradicating.

Throughout 2003 and early 2004, prior to the transfer of sovereignty to the Interim Iraqi Government, the CPA was formulating policies for the direct elimination of all standing militias ("the militia threat") throughout Iraq, while senior military command in Iraq, Combined Joint Task Force-7 (CJTF-7), was beginning to develop operational and tactical plans for the same purpose. The following case (vignette) describes one multinational division (MND) headquarters' response (feedback)—an alternative strategy for the elimination of the militia threat consistent with a more indirect and a more positive and effective approach to assimilation (acculturation) of preexisting militias into the fabric of a new national Iraqi state.

Case 1b

An Alternative Strategy for Eliminating the Militia Threat

The continued existence of militias could in fact undermine the legitimacy and survivability of a future, democratic New Iraqi State (NIS). Arguably, however, the real threat lies in whether the interests and desires of the NIS continue to remain outside of the control of the emerging Iraqi state, to remain inconsistent with its goals, rather than the physical existence of the militia itself. What makes a militia a threat to an emerging or preexisting national state is the underlying intent, interests, and goals of the militia. In fact, if the interests of the emerging NIS are coincident with the interests of standing militias; the prevalence of such militias can actually prove beneficial to the legitimization of the new emerging state. In our own early trials with democratic forms of representative government, the United States embraced "militias." A more nuanced approach to the militia threat is critical in eliminating what is the real threat of militias without inadvertently destabilizing the effort to build a NIS.

As mentioned, the real threat of standing militias is not necessarily in their physical existence but rather may lie in the disharmony of interests between the militia and the NIS. Developing a federalism-based, representative NIS, which at least in part represents some of the interests of the militia forces, is a better way of eliminating the militia threat.

Even if a more direct, military offensive was the better strategy on elimination of militia, the CPA and coalition forces in Iraq do not have the requisite amount of combat power available to ensure the destruction of these forces, much less to ensure the impossibility of their resurgence in the long run. In addition to too few forces available, accelerated CPA timelines (for transfer of sovereignty by June 30, 2004) would preclude such an aggressive option. Conditions can be established—"a process can be set in train"—that can lead to resolution of the militia challenge in Iraq in short order (i.e., originally by June 30, 2004). However, the more effective approach—the approach with less probability of unintended blowback on the democratization process—is an indirect approach, one that eliminates the militia threat by assimilating the militia's political interests and policy agendas into the future governance plans in Iraq. If political entities that maintain standing militias have a stake in the NIS, then they are less likely to oppose the NIS; it is probable that they will even actively support the NIS. This is particularly true (probable) in the case of Iraqi-Kurd militia: the Kurdistan Democratic Party (KDP) and Patriotic Union of Kurdistan (PUK) *peshmerga*.

The *peshmerga* do not consider themselves militia and actually take an offense to this label that is justified in many respects. The *peshmerga* have evolved over time to reflect more of a paramilitary type force, in many respects, a professionalizing military, and in some respects, a useful and effective partner and ally—both in the past and potentially in the near future. The *peshmerga* have over the past five decades become more than just a military force; they have become the physical embodiment of Kurdish nationhood—a nation that still stands without a country. The democratization process underway in Iraq and about to pick up speed has great potential for providing the Kurdish nation a country: legitimate inclusion as Iraqis in the NIS. Any rapid and aggressive strategy against the KDP and PUK *peshmerga* has the potential of derailing the democratization effort in Iraq. It also has the potential of removing an effective combat and security capability from northern Iraq that has enhanced coalition force successes for the past year during Operation Iraqi Freedom-1 (OIF-1) and that may prove vitally important in coming months as the Central Command (CENTCOM) directs military actions against the Kurdistan Workers Party (PKK) terrorists in northern Iraq. This elimination strategy lies in direct contradiction to (1) the policy toward a federalism answer to the future of Iraqi governance; (2) past policy of working with *peshmerga* forces, indirectly, in seeking a safe and secure environment in northern Iraq; and (3) future requirements to work with these forces (as a "Northern Front"-type indigenous force) against terrorists in northern Iraq. Elimination strategies must be made coincident with these other policies.

Offer the militias something in the NIS, and there will be probable reason to witness an acceptance of the new government (an identification with the NIS) by these militias. It is not necessary that these militias shed their identification in order to don the identity of the NIS. In regards to the Kurdish militias, "once a *peshmerga*, always a *peshmerga*" is more than a credo: it is fact. However, the integration of the *peshmerga* into the Iraqi Civil Defense Corps (ICDC) in Area of Operations North (AO North) is ample testament to the ability of effectively incorporating "militia" into new Iraqi government institutions.

Assimilation of major militias (namely the *peshmerga*) into newly forming Iraqi security forces (e.g., ICDC) is a viable operational way ahead but only so long as the goal and endstate underpinning such an operational approach is rightly formulated. The *peshmerga* are likely to become members of the ICDC and NIA if these organizations reflect a new government that represents Iraqi-Kurdish rights as full citizens of the NIS. The Kurdish desire for "autonomy" and their willingness to settle for "semiautonomy" are compatible with the CPA desire for a federalist form of democratic government in Iraq. The situation is not, nor does it have to be, painted by current and future coalition and CPA policy as a situation of stark blacks and whites: "give me autonomy or give me death" has never been the situation with the Iraqi-Kurds in northern Iraq. Laying down the options to the *peshmerga* and the Iraqi-Kurds in such a stark manner is not productive.

Just as Americans have multiple identities (e.g., "I'm an American, but also a Texan") the KDP and PUK Kurds are capable of identifying as an Iraqi citizen as well as a Kurd and a *peshmerga*. Being *peshmerga* has always offered the Kurds continued voice, relevance, and survival. So long as the NIS has something to offer the Kurds, the likelihood of these militia serving the NIS (rather than opposing it) is high.

Dealing with the militias in Iraq is, at its base, a political issue. Politics is "the art of the possible." It is impossible to completely eliminate militia from Iraqi society (same holds true for tribes), particularly in the short run and/or through direct lethal methods. It is improbable that the threat of militia can be eradicated by any means other than a slow and progressive acculturation of these forces into the community of the NIS. This is the art of the possible that needs to drive future CPA approaches to militias. The 101st Airborne Division (Air Assault) in northern Iraq has been relatively successful in these sorts of nonaggressive transformation-type strategies, converting many standing *peshmerga* into members of the New Iraqi Security Forces (NISF).

The Kurdish militia (KDP and PUK *peshmerga*) are much more than mere armed militia—they are the embodiment of Iraqi-Kurdish nationalism. This nationalism is not necessarily incompatible or out of synch with a better future of Iraqi nationalism. Within the approach to federalism in the establishment of the NIS lies the effective answer to the "militia problem." So long as this new government reflects the minimum rights of Iraqi-Kurds as Iraqi citizens, it is highly likely that though these forces may not completely shed their *peshmerga* affiliations, those affiliations will become very compatible with the NIS.

This issue of militia is not a single issue and should not be addressed as such. The issue of militia, particularly the *peshmerga*, ties directly to the federalism question, and, therefore, the CPA strategy of transitional local sovereignty. It also ties directly to the issue of PKK terrorists in northern Iraq and pending operations dedicated to the elimination of the PKK terrorists' threat again, originally by June 30, 2004. Stated bluntly, the CPA/coalition understanding of and approach to militia stands in direct contradiction to what will be required, operationally, to eliminate the PKK terrorist presence in northern Iraq. The very forces that will likely form a psuedo-"Northern Front" partnering with U.S. and coalition forces against the PKK in coming months are the forces that are under scrutiny and potential attack by the CPA and the coalition. This incompatibility—this contradiction—has the potential of going well beyond the debate of policy; it could contribute to an increase in risk to U.S. and coalition forces in a counter-PKK operation.

An indirect (political) approach to the militia challenge through the democratization process (federalism) is a better policy approach than the strategy offered in this chapter; it is an approach that will have a better chance of success in the long run and one that has less of a chance of inadvertently subverting future military operations in northern Iraq

* * *

Twenty-First-Century Containment

Democratization through Tribal Engagement

To minimize the challenges that kin-rich societies play (including our own here in the United States!), the state must become more involved in managing these divisions by shaping their meaning, function, and role in contemporary political life. Students of political pluralism have long known that diversity presents challenges but also opportunities. Theories of political pluralism, therefore, have offered institutional and procedural solutions for managing cultural, religious, ethnic, and other pluralism. These scholars have also long told that distinctive divisions require distinctive approaches (one size does not fit all), that institutions must be crafted and tailored with an eye to the specific affiliations that require managing.[20]

What follows is a case that presents an alternative implementation strategy for civil-military reconstruction and nation-rebuilding operations that incorporate local tribal politics into stability operations and governance reconstruction efforts, a tribal engagement strategy that was a cornerstone to the 101st Airborne's campaign strategy during that unit's yearlong occupation of northern Iraq from April 2003 to March 2004, and a program in which I led the effort in designing and implementing while serving as the 101st Airborne Division's chief of plans. The relative success of the 101st Airborne in the northern provinces provides one example of the benefits that can be gained from an approach to democratization that incorporates local indigenous cultural, ethnic, religious, and, in this case, tribal ways.

Tribal Engagement in Northern Iraq

> *[S]ome Englishmen, of whom Kitchener was chief, believed that a rebellion of Arabs against Turks would enable England, while fighting Germany, simultaneously to defeat Turkey. . . . [T]heir knowledge of the nature and power and country of the Arabic-speaking peoples made them think that the issue of such a rebellion would be happy, and indicated its character and method. . . . [s]o they allowed it to begin.*
>
> T. E. Lawrence, "Introduction," *Seven Pillars of Wisdom*, 132

> *History hath builded her house, she hath hewn out her seven pillars.*
>
> Proverbs, 9:1

As the war in Iraq labors forward and the United States moves on in GWOT, questions, confusion, and arguments over the conduct of both campaigns dominate public, policy, and partisan-political debate. Less attention has been paid to gaining a better understanding for how the United States and its military have *waged* both wars.

Operations in both campaigns over the past year have taught planners (military, interagency, nongovernmental, etc.) a lot about what a full-spectrum, capabilities-based security strategy really means. Planners now better appreciate war-fare as a continuum of political activities that can range in time, space, and purpose, from benign policy and social debates, to humanitarian assistance, to conflict management, to full-scale military combatives. Operations in both Afghanistan and Iraq are illustrative of *compound campaigns* composed of dynamic combat operations, counterinsurgency and counterterrorism operations, and stability operations. The protracted nature of both war-campaigns all but proves the importance of operational patience, long-range planning and extended operational timelines, and robust logistical support.

Like Kitchener and the "English" before, the United States and its coalition perhaps were equally blinded by their "knowledge" of the nature and power and country of the Afghani and Iraqi people, a knowledge that reinforced a faulty hope and expectation of an "easier road ahead" in these operations, as reflected in the character and record of success (or lack thereof) of our military and civilian operations in Iraq.

A Lack of Wisdom in the Initial Operational Planning?

One of the more useful operational programs employed first in Iraq and more recently in the counterterrorism and counterinsurgency campaign in Afghanistan and western Pakistan is tribal engagement.

Stricken from the political lexicon of the Bush administration due to the affiliation of the term and operational concept to the Clinton administration, *engagement* at one time was a referent to the family of operational plans that employed nonlethal (low end of the spectrum) techniques in foreign interventions. Peace-time military engagement was the more explanatory term of those activities (diplomatic, economic, informational, and martial) our nation would take prior to, during, and after the initiation of combatives as part of a broad and comprehensive interventional policy and security strategy.

Despite its partisan past, engagement strategies are a necessary counterinsurgency and counterterrorism operational method. The following chapter was written in January 2004, during my tour of duty in Iraq. It describes in greater analytical detail the 101st Airborne's Tribal Engagement Plan—one form of engagement we adopted and implemented to positive effect, first in northern Iraq; this program eventually spread throughout Iraq and was finally implemented in Afghanistan and the tribal seams between Afghanistan and western Pakistan.

Iraq is a tribal society. Tribal norms, behaviors, rules, and rituals underlie all aspects of life in Iraq. The longest-lasting political landscape in Iraq, in fact, is tribal; it is as old as the land itself.

All efforts to reconstruct Iraqi sociopolitical life toward a more representative, free-market-based democratic construct must take this tribal landscape into account.

There has been a significant gap in the coalition's knowledge of and, consequently, its respect and regard for tribes and tribal society in Iraq. This lack of knowledge and understanding has prevailed to varying degrees at all levels (from the CPA to the MNDs). Part of this "knowledge gap" persists due to the complexity of the tribal system and its exclusivity to westerners. Part of this gap persists simply due to a lingering and limiting western cultural disdain for the existing tribal culture in and around Iraq. Such bias has hindered CPA policy and the policy-making process, eliminating tribal ways from the list of alternative mechanisms available for consideration in the redesign of future Iraqi governing and public administration systems.

Closing a Conceptual Seam

The persistence of a tribal knowledge gap can contribute to "operational gaps" at the national (CPA and CJTF-7) and regional/local (governate coordinator/multinational division commander [GC/MND CDR]) levels. Tribalism is a key component to what becomes and has always been, to varying degrees, the equivalent of a *public administration* system in Iraqi civil society. The way things get done on a day-to-day basis in Iraqi civil society—the way essential services are delivered to the local public daily—has throughout history been through tribal networks and relationships.

Ignoring or at least putting aside cultural judgments of Iraqi tribalism allows for the development of an understanding of the function and purpose of the Iraqi tribal system. This sort of understanding has proven essential at the divisional level in pressing forward a successful campaign plan for peace-making, peace-keeping, and nation-building in Iraq. The 101st Airborne Division (Air Assault) embraced this preexisting tribal landscape early in the development of and implementation of its campaign plan. Operations in northern Iraq have, consequently, reaped significant successes where success has been relatively fleeting in other MND areas of operation. In a war that has clearly evolved into a war of insurgency, developing and fighting a war-plan that is informed by the standing tribal ways and norms is essential to fighting and winning, as the counterinsurgent, the *hearts and minds* of the Iraqi people.

Local Politics = The Politics of Tribes

All politics is local. Political "experts" tout this saying as a given and develop political doctrine upon this notion as bedrock. Yet, the experts too often ignore the truths of this statement in day-to-day political interactions and in efforts at refreshing old and building new forms and functions of government. Understanding local politics in Iraq demands a detailed understanding of and respect for local tribalism. Gaining a better understanding and appreciation for tribalism does not necessarily have to equate to acceptance. Yet, understanding is vital for success, particularly for a hope of success in an Iraqi state reconstruction effort that is largely driven by "outsiders" to the local culture and societal ways and mores (see map 6.1).

It cannot be overstated: the historic and enduring tribal system in Iraq has always served as an informal "public administration" system. In the rural areas in particular, tribes provide daily sustenance and all essential services, employment, and security. Perhaps most important, tribes provide the people a sense of purpose, heritage, and reason for being. Tribes provide the "ties that bind" historically in Iraq. Under Saddam's rule and at periods of "low state-centric power," tribes served as a sort of indirect mechanism for rule, a secondary system of governance. Saddam on

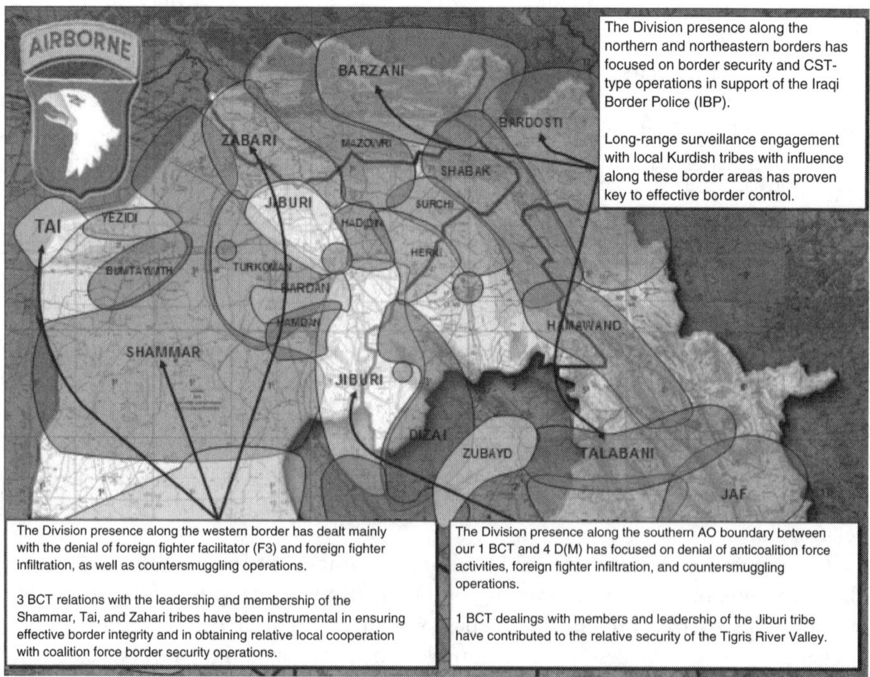

Map 6.1 The Local Politics of Tribes

Source: Official 101st Airborne Division planning briefings (unclassified versions and/or declassified materials), June 2003–May 2005.

several occasions made use of tribes to build and maintain his own legitimacy with the populace, to maintain relative internal stability and security, and to "administer" on a day-to-day basis. Getting government to work at the local level in the rural areas—and to a lesser but still relevant degree in the cities as well—will require a system of public administration that in part incorporates (assimilates) the tribes.

On Tribes: Tribal Norms, Rituals, and Mores—Lessons Gathered

This primer on tribal ways in Iraq cannot cover tribal lore in detail, nor should it attempt to do so. The history of Iraq and the Fertile Crescent in general is a history of tribalism—a recorded history of well over 5,000 years. The 101st Airborne Division (Air Assault) gleaned a great deal of knowledge about, and understanding and appreciation of, tribal ends, ways, and means (tribal strategy) 10 months after its occupation in northern Iraq. The remainder of this section will focus on these lessons gathered, lessons that can hopefully be learned by our Army and our nation, as an evolution of our doctrine toward counterinsurgency, nation-building, and engagement.

Saddam's Use of Tribes—What Should We Learn?

Saddam Hussein and his Ba'athist Party (the former regime) were experts in manipulating existing tribal networks, tribal lore, mythology, and practical processes throughout his 30-plus-year reign. The tribal system in Iraq proved essential to the rise to power (coup d'état) of Saddam and his Ba'athist Party. The tribal networks of northern Iraq proved particularly important to his rise to power during the 1960s. The international ties of the Shammar tribe provided a probable link (and transnational highway and transit line) between Syria and Iraq that could be exploited by Saddam and his loyalists in his first rise to power. Bedouin networks likely offered these Ba'athists roving sanctuary as well as a line of supply and communication.

During his reign of over 30 years, Saddam Hussein approached tribes in a *feast-or-famine* manner. During periods of strong national state power, Saddam divided to conquer the major tribes, as a way of *containing* their effects to internal infighting and blood feuds—coincidentally, providing a means of indirectly protecting his regime from internal threats and from potential overthrow. A purge of members of powerful, potentially threatening tribal confederations (Al Tai, Jiburi, etc.) from high-level military and Ba'athist ranks and positions was indicative of these periods of tightly coupled state power control. During periods of low state power, Saddam actually assimilated tribes as his indirect means of administering to the public. This technique offered a means of both maintaining his legitimacy with the Iraqi people (by being capable of still provisioning for the essential public service needs of the populace) and of shielding his regime from scrutiny at moments when that regime needed to reform and heal their institutional wounds.

The period immediately following the First Gulf War (1990–1991) is a case in point of how to make use of the tribes to reinforce legitimacy with and control over the local population during periods of "loosely coupled" national state power. It is likely that Saddam and many of his top loyalists went back to their old tribal ways, movement routes, and hiding holes that facilitated their rise to power 36 years ago

(November 1969) in the hope of surviving the attack of coalition forces and reestablishing a loosely coupled command and control network for an eventual return to power. The same tribal ways used in the 1960s had been used in 2003 by Saddam and former regime loyalists/elements as a mechanism for a growing insurgency throughout Iraq.

What can we learn from Saddam? What should we take away from his use of and maneuverings within tribal society?

Researching northern Iraqi tribalism from a historical context seems to have benefited the Division's typical and traditional intelligence lines of operation. A simple proposition drove the research: *IF Saddam and his Ba'athist supporters made effective use of certain tribes, certain tribal locations, certain tribal pathways, AND these tribal ways and means proved effective in the survival and eventual success of the Hussein regime rise to power, THEN in a natural (instinctive) response to regime collapse in May 2003, Saddam and his former regime elements (FRE) might have simply returned to these previous ways and methods; hide holes and exfiltration routes.* Charting this historical data, with the support of the Division analysis and control element (ACE) as well as the unit historian and Division planners, has, in hindsight, contributed to much of the success we enjoyed regarding the identification, targeting, tracking, capture, and killing of high-payoff targets—senior-level Ba'athist and FRE. The Division planners shaped operations in critical areas (nodes) along a templated line theoretically connecting these key tribal nodes. Planners referenced this as *the tie that may possibly bind.* The capture of Black List No. 1(BL #1) himself—Saddam Hussein—occurred in a spider hole along and at the southernmost extent of this hypothetical "tie that may bind." Analyzing the raid of July 17, 2003—the raid that resulted in the killing of HVTs #1 and #2, Uday and Qusay Hussein—reveals that the location of their final hiding place rested, again, along this line of probable operation (on the banks of the Tigris River, near the northern portion of the templated enemy line of operation).

The Division's successful decapitation and deconstruction of the Al Rafah movement in northern Iraq are in part attributable to the Division's tribal engagement program (resulting in valuable human intelligence) and tribal research (enhancing the location of probable hide sites and movement routes of key FRE).

The manner in which Saddam incorporated the tribes in his daily public administration offers coalition forces some lessons. The legitimacy of CPA/IGC (Iraq Governing Council) as a governing body is in a state of ambiguity, to say the least. It is safe to say that the status of governance in Iraq is a state of "loosely coupled" authority, a state quite similar to periods of low power during the Hussein regime. As argued earlier, indirect governance through the co-optation of tribes during periods of low state (centralized) power proved effective for Hussein and might prove effective for the CPA as it parents the IGC and Iraqi society on the whole through the upcoming democratization process.

Tribal Engagement in Northern Iraq

"It Is the Economy (and the Engagement), Stupid!"

In stability and support operations (SASO) and nation-building (reconstruction) efforts, *money is ammunition.* Simply stated, the key to establishing (and maintaining/

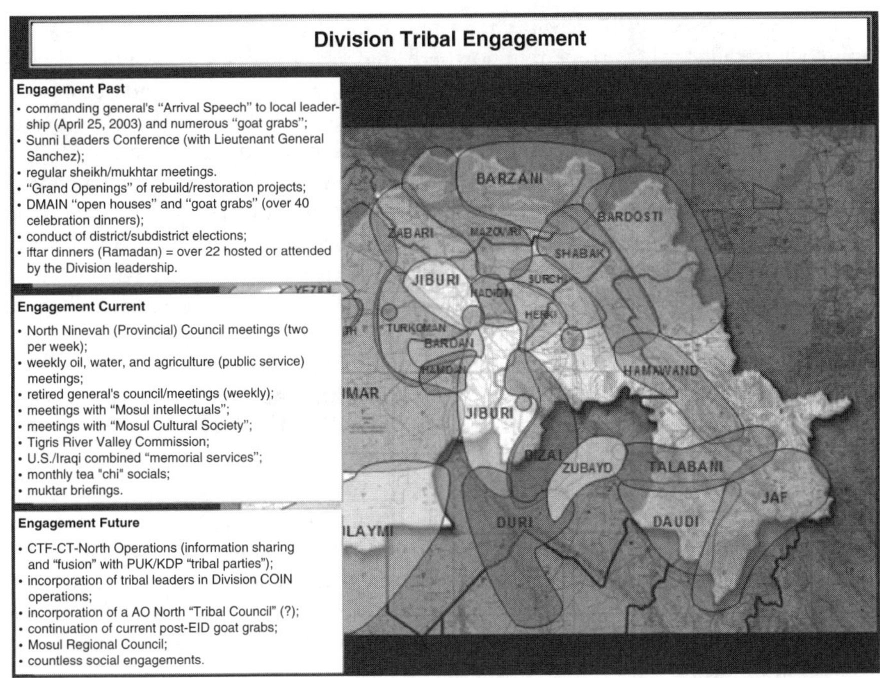

Map 6.2 Tribal Engagement in Northern Iraq, 2003–2004

Source: Official 101st Airborne Division planning briefings (unclassified versions and/or declassified materials), June 2003–May 2005.

retaining) a bridgehead within an insurgency campaign, as the counterinsurgent, is the ability to quickly restore minimum conditions of normalcy in all public service sectors (security, food and water, fuel and power, housing, employment, etc.). If money can be seen as the ammunition, then having an effective tribal strategy (engagement program) can be viewed as an available weapon for identifying areas of need and for delivering for effect. "Firing for effect" is greatly enhanced through a tribal engagement strategy (see map 6.2).

Division Tribal Engagement—An Overview

It should be noted and made clear from the start that the 101st Airborne Division (Air Assault) did not necessarily enter into SASO in northern Iraq explicitly planning to engage tribes and tribal networks. Some study and preconflict knowledge of the tribal landscape was evident; however, division leadership actually just determined to get to know the local environment and its people, its leaders (official and informal). Getting to know the locals ended up equating to getting to know tribes and tribal ways of doing business. Recognizing what was before us (a societal network steeped in tribalism) as we learned more about the local environment and its people required a historical and anthropological familiarity with the region. It also required a general agnostic respect for the tribal underpinnings of Iraqi lifestyle.

Reviewing the *Small Wars Manual* for hindsight's sake finds the 101st Airborne's approach to military government in northern Iraq near-textbook in its approach. On April 25, 2003, one day after initial air assault into the city of Mosul and occupation of northern Iraq, the Division commander, Major General Petraeus, delivered what we regarded then as an official "arrival speech"—what the Small Wars Manual (1940) (SWM) references as a *proclamation of military government*. Such a proclamation—a clear pronouncement to the local community of the tasks, purpose, and intent of the occupying force and the expectation of local obedience and hopeful, eventual allegiance—was proposed in military doctrine as a necessary condition for success in counterinsurgency; it proved vital in practical application. The first 30 days of occupation were a fury of pronouncement, promise, and delivery of local elected leadership; essential services; and establishment of rudimentary bureaucratic public access to the local civil-military government. The Division has ever since maintained a blistering pace, hand-in-hand with the local leadership, to win the hearts and minds (the respect) of the local people. Daily, intimate engagement has been the centerpiece to this counterinsurgency strategy. And again, at its root, all engagement in Iraq is tribal in fact, if not in actual form. Though coherent in terms of broad engagement method and intended endstate (become knowledgeable with local sheikhs and community leaders through daily interaction, build respectful relationships through demonstrated respectful behavior, and endeavor to gain the trust and respect of the locals), a decentralized approach to engagement has been a key to success in the north.

Each brigade combat team (BCT) area of operation (AO) shaped its own tribal engagement strategy; each was uniquely tailored to the unique tribal landscape of the regions under their control. Again, the SWM directs that the campaign plan be "tailored to the conditions of the local area and its people."[21]

Engaging the tribes did not always (or only) equate to the stereotypical Western recollections of the American Wild West and "powwows" with the natives, though similar types of native interactions and rituals did at times occur, particularly in the western areas of AO North. Tribal engagements differed from tribe to tribe and from AO to AO. In the urban centers, tribal engagement looked and felt more like the typical power politics we are most accustomed to in the United States. Yet, even in the cities the base behavior was tribal. North of the former Green Line, engagement with Kurdish tribes reflected political interactions more similar to Chicagoland party machine politics (Mafioso-style politics) of 1920's America. Though tribal at their roots, Kurdish tribes have transformed more toward partisan-political (ideologically based) factions than stereotypical tribes, although relations between Kurd tribes and families do revert to more traditional tribal norms and mores (i.e., blood feuds, rites of honor, etc.). The key to waging a successful tribal strategy was in approaching each region and its people in accordance with the norms and behavior patterns of different regions.

Tribes and Tribal Engagement in the West

If one was looking for an early American historical analogy by which to compare Iraqi tribal life in the western areas of northern Iraq, that example would be U.S. Army relations with the American Plains Indians at the close of the nineteenth century. The

Rakkasans of the 3rd Brigade Combat Team (3BCT) probably faced a tribal situation within their sector of control most similar to the traditional and stereotypical views most Westerners have of our own dealings with American Indians or perhaps, as a better comparative, the experiences of T. E. Lawrence in the early 1900s (as shown in the movie *Lawrence of Arabia*). The western zone of northern Iraq (AO North), though a collage of numerous tribes (traditional, political, fictive, religious, ethnic, etc.), is dominated by the Shammar Confederation—one of the two largest tribal confederations in Iraq and a tribe with international ties. The Shammar have both Syrian and Saudi Arabian links (Ba'athist Party links in the case of Syrian-Iraqi relations, royal links through marriage with the crown prince of Saudi Arabia). Under Saddam, the Shammar held high party and military positions. Because of its relative power (based on landholdings, international ties, and party affiliations), Saddam often found the need to purge the tribe from his governing ranks (from time to time) while also having to maintain tight bonds with the tribe in order to effectively administer. At one point, Hussein had even attempted to tie his own Tikriti tribe to the Shammar through a blood tie (marriage). The Shammar refused his offer, leading to a slight fall from regime grace just prior to the 2003 Iraq War (see map 6.3).

In addition to daily key leader engagements with local Shammar sheikhs and other tribal leaders, critical contracts were let between the 3BCT and the Shammar regarding security of oil and power infrastructure, occupation and surveillance of the Iraqi-Syrian border, and the protection of water wells and pump stations (i.e., Al Jazeera Pump Station). See map 6.4.

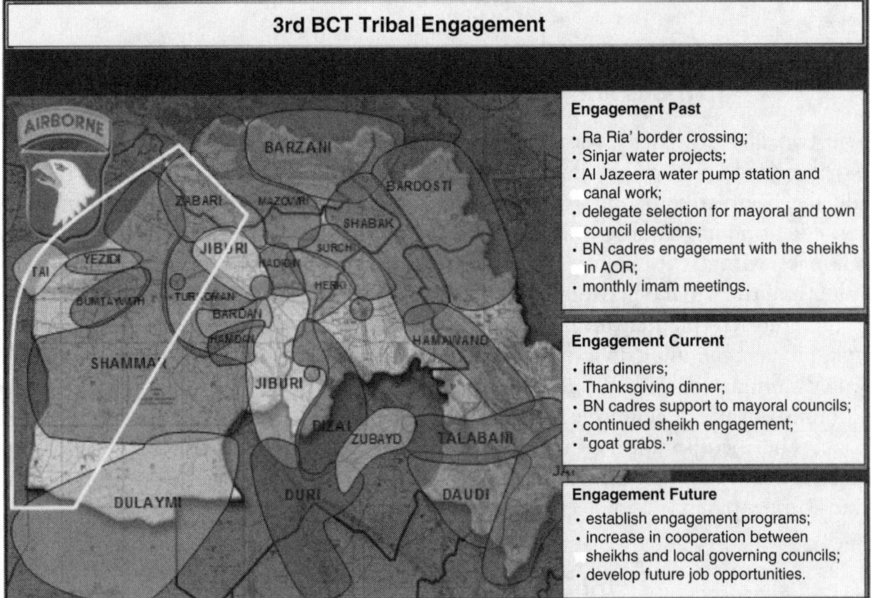

Map 6.3 Tribal Engagement, Western Sectors

Source: Official 101st Airborne Division planning briefings (unclassified versions and/or declassified materials), June 2003–May 2005.

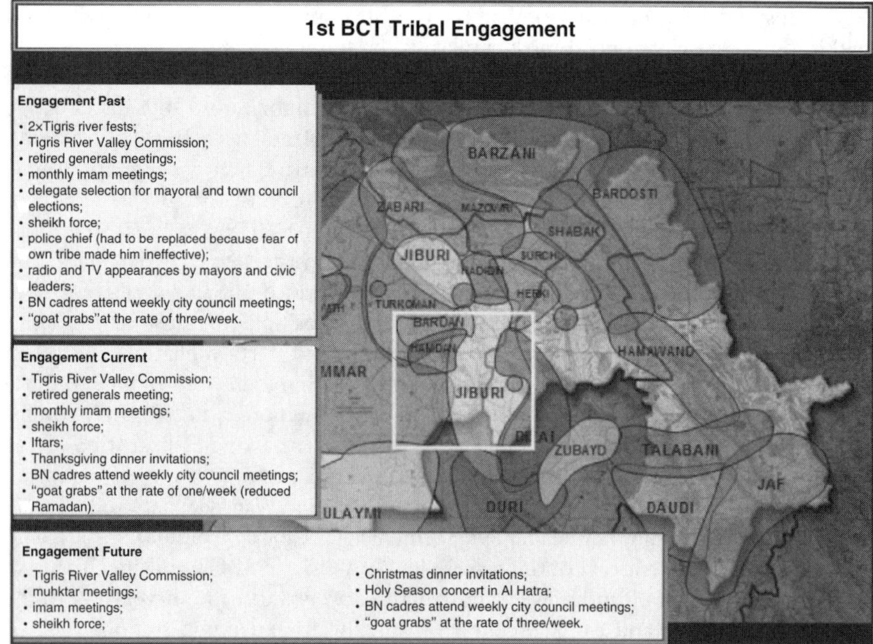
1st BCT Tribal Engagement
Engagement Past
• 2×Tigris river fests;
• Tigris River Valley Commission;
• retired generals meetings;
• monthly imam meetings;
• delegate selection for mayoral and town council elections;
• sheikh force;
• police chief (had to be replaced because fear of own tribe made him ineffective);
• radio and TV appearances by mayors and civic leaders;
• BN cadres attend weekly city council meetings;
• "goat grabs"at the rate of three/week.
Engagement Current
• Tigris River Valley Commission;
• retired generals meeting;
• monthly imam meetings;
• sheikh force;
• Iftars;
• Thanksgiving dinner invitations;
• BN cadres attend weekly city council meetings;
• "goat grabs" at the rate of one/week (reduced Ramadan).
Engagement Future
• Tigris River Valley Commission;
• muhktar meetings;
• imam meetings;
• sheikh force;
• Christmas dinner invitations;
• Holy Season concert in Al Hatra;
• BN cadres attend weekly city council meetings;
• "goat grabs" at the rate of three/week.
BARZANI
BARDOSTI
SHABAK
JIBURI
TURKOMAN
HERKI
HAMAWAND
JIBURI
ZUBAYD
TALABANI
JAF
DAUDI
DURI

Map 6.4 Tribal Engagement Southern Sectors

Source: Official 101st Airborne Division planning briefings (unclassified versions and/or declassified materials), June 2003–May 2005.

Tribes and Tribal Engagement in the South

The two largest "tribes" dominating the politics of the southern region of AO North ended up being the Bastogne Brigade of 1st Brigade Combat Team (1BCT) and the Jiburi tribe of the Tigris River Valley (map 6.4). The second largest tribal confederation in Iraq, the Jiburi, dominate the Tigris River Valley and hold a strong influence within the Greater Mosul area. Rich in alluvial fields, the Tigris River Valley and the tribal behavioralism within the valley reflected to the agrarian lifestyle of the Southern planter during the 1950s in the American Southern states. Planter-style life and the importance of oil and other mineral resources in the Tigris River Valley dominated U.S. tribal engagement in the south. The Tigris River Valley Commission was a centerpiece of the 1BCT engagement strategy in the southern zone. The incorporation of southern tribes (namely the Jiburi) as an indigenous security force (the "Sheikh Force") proved very effective in the protection of the Iraq-Turkey pipeline and electrical (power line).

Tribes and Tribal Engagement "North of the Green Line"

Unique to northern Iraq are the political-tribal peculiarities of Iraqi Kurdistan. Reminiscent of *The Godfather*-type relationships and interactions, tribal engagement

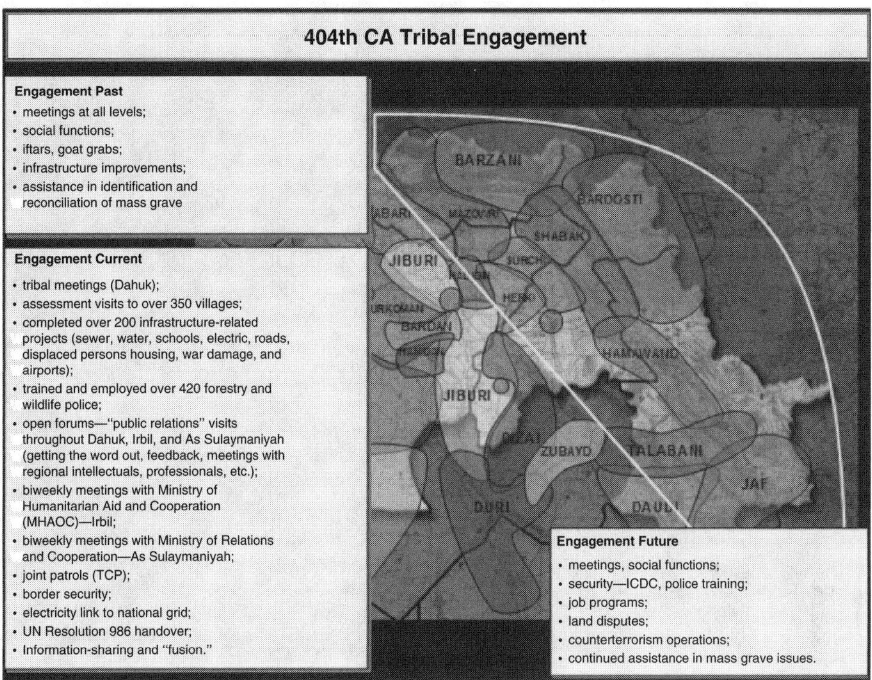
404th CA Tribal Engagement
Engagement Past
• meetings at all levels;
• social functions;
• iftars, goat grabs;
• infrastructure improvements;
• assistance in identification and reconciliation of mass grave
Engagement Current
• tribal meetings (Dahuk);
• assessment visits to over 350 villages;
• completed over 200 infrastructure-related projects (sewer, water, schools, electric, roads, displaced persons housing, war damage, and airports);
• trained and employed over 420 forestry and wildlife police;
• open forums—"public relations" visits throughout Dahuk, Irbil, and As Sulaymaniyah (getting the word out, feedback, meetings with regional intellectuals, professionals, etc.);
• biweekly meetings with Ministry of Humanitarian Aid and Cooperation (MHAOC)—Irbil;
• biweekly meetings with Ministry of Relations and Cooperation—As Sulaymaniyah;
• joint patrols (TCP);
• border security;
• electricity link to national grid;
• UN Resolution 986 handover;
• Information-sharing and "fusion."
BARZANI
SHABAK
JIBURI
HAMAWAND
JIBURI
ZUBAYD
TALABANI
JAF
DURI
Engagement Future
• meetings, social functions;
• security—ICDC, police training;
• job programs;
• land disputes;
• counterterrorism operations;
• continued assistance in mass grave issues.

Map 6.5 Tribal Engagement Northern and Eastern Sectors

Source: Official 101st Airborne Division planning briefings (unclassified versions and/or declassified materials), June 2003–May 2005.

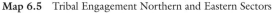

north of the former Green Line is more party machine-like than tribal engagement in a traditional sense. The 404th Civil Affairs Battalion maintained an economy of force presence in the Kurdish zone, engaging daily with a myriad of Kurdish tribes, but mainly with the two largest families: the Barzani tribe (KDP) and the Talabani tribe (PUK).

Engagement with the Iraqi-Kurds has ranged the full spectrum of the political, from combined intelligence-gathering operations to tea (*Chi*) sessions. Friendly relations with the Iraqi-Kurds empowered the 101st Airborne by reinforcing the Division's capacity to secure the northern and northeastern border regions. This ability to approach the northern provinces of Irbil and Dahuk and the eastern province of As Sulaymaniyah as economy-of-force regions freed resources for a focus on the center of gravity for northern Iraq (Mosul) and Ninevah province (see map 6.5).

Tribes and Tribal Engagement in the Urban Environment, Mosul

Though more political in form, engagement within the city of Mosul and other urban centers within northern Iraq, albeit to a lesser extent, was still tribal in behavior and function. Local civic leaders and politicians still abided by the rules of honor and tribal ties and obligations, although to a lesser degree within city politics (see map 6.6).

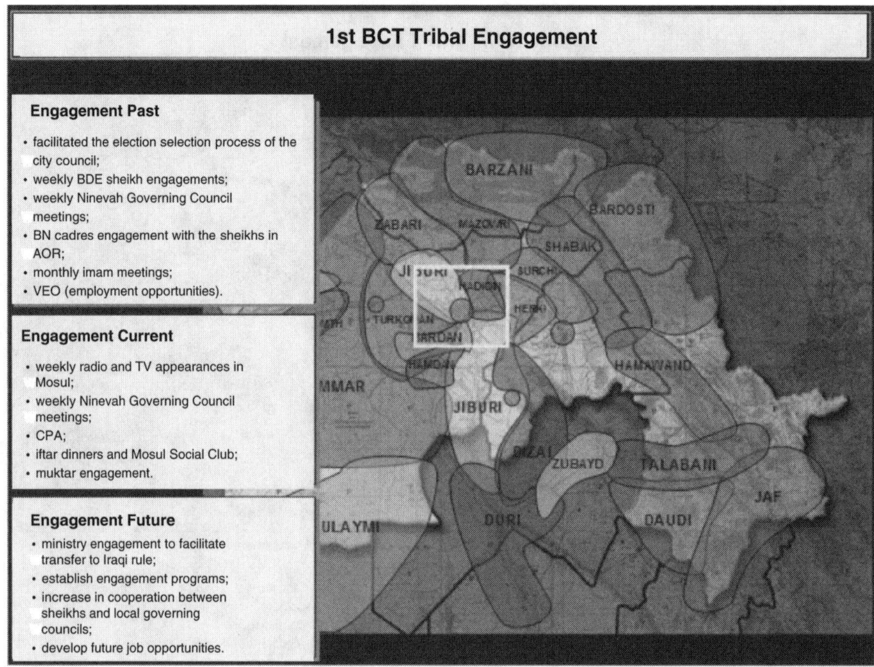

Map 6.6 Tribal Engagement North-Central Sectors

Source: Official 101st Airborne Division planning briefings (unclassified versions and/or declassified materials), June 2003–May 2005.

The "Right" Governance Mix

Key to getting the local urban politics for Mosul and Ninevah province right and balanced early on was to ensure as inclusive and well balanced a tribal representation in the council as possible. The Division succeeded (as much by luck as by providence and plan) in achieving a balanced and adequately representative city and provincial governing body. The interim government of Mosul and Ninevah province reflected Arab and Kurdish-Iraqis, Yezidis, Turkomans, Sunni, Shia, and Christians. The council also represents the tribes, with the initial oversight on the part of coalition forces of ensuring Shammar representation. Through happenstance, the Division promoted the election of Governor/Mayor Al Basso of the Al Hammadin tribe (a military tribe of lesser influence and regional power) over other larger and more powerful confederations. This act alone helped to stave off an imbalance between the Shammar, Al Tai, and the Jiburi confederations; election of a smaller tribal member as mayor/governor, therefore, did not equate to a zero-sum loss of honor and prestige on the part of any of the large and powerful tribes and therefore helped to prevent tribal blood feuds. Engagement has also incorporated efforts at extending suffrage and representation to women (four female council members have recently been added to the Ninevah Council). See figure 6.3.

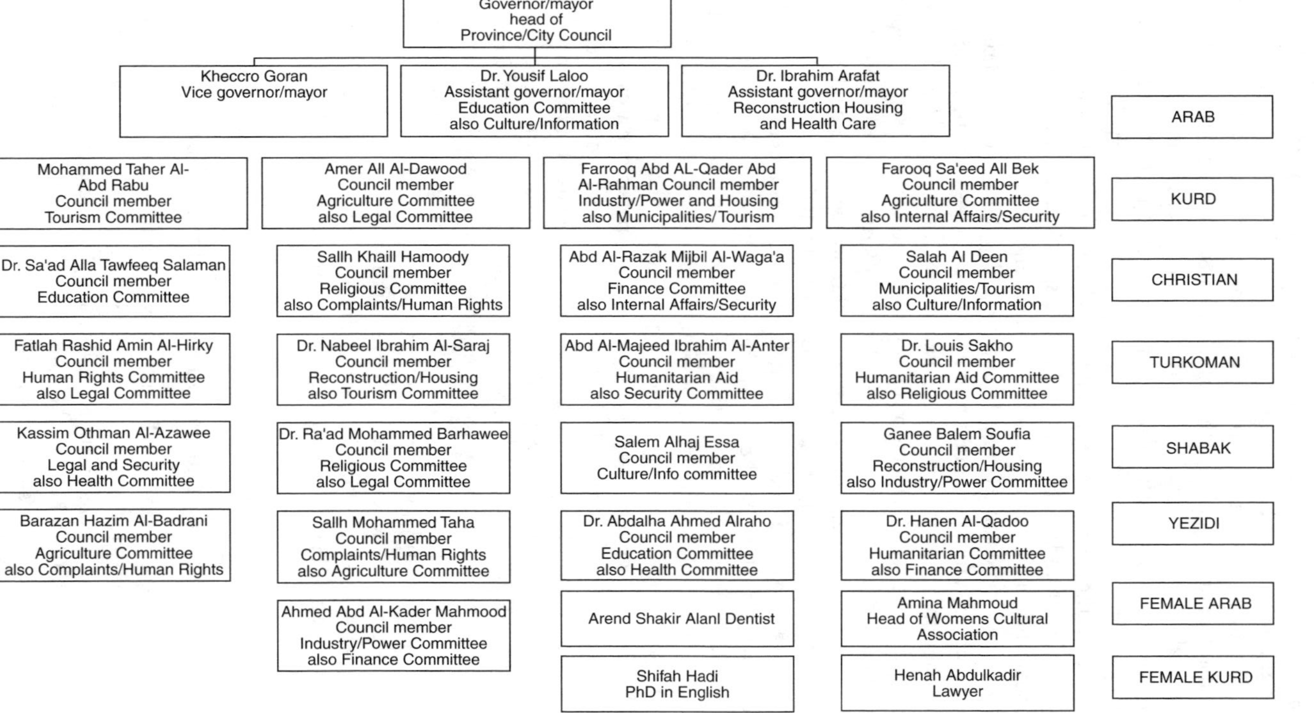

Figure 6.3 Ensuring Effective Sociological Representation in Iraqi Governance

Source: Official 101st Airborne Division planning briefings (unclassified versions and/or declassified materials), June 2003–May 2005.

The Use of Tribal Strategy in Northern Iraq

Knowing the tribes and their landscape and histories allows one to work within (if not among, due to an outsider status) and to exploit those tribal networks. Seams ("gaps") are areas in a military (or civil-military, for that matter) operation that remain outside of or beyond the effect and/or knowledge/understanding of a force. Due to several reasons, the least of which not being a persistent shortage of available resources, coalition forces were plagued through OIF-1 with the prevalence of gaps. Physical gaps within the northern area of operations (101st Airborne and 4ID zones) included the Sharqat salient (a divisional seam along the southern boundary between the 101st and 4ID) "ratlines" in the southwestern desert running somewhat parallel (north to south) to the Tigris River and the Iraqi-Syrian border area in vicinity of the Ra'bia customs point of entry. CJTF-7 Headquarters directed several major combat operations intended to cover these gaps—areas that due to minimal to zero coalition force presence were likely areas of sanctuary and exfiltration/infiltration for the enemy (Operations Longstreet and Chamberlain). Informational and intelligence gaps exacerbated physical gaps, offering the insurgent even greater advantage over the foreign counterinsurgent. Ignorance of regional tribal heritage, boundaries, histories, and tribal interplay contributed to a collective lack of situational awareness and understanding. The result was a degraded and less-than effective campaign plan. As the 101st Airborne Division (Air Assault) began to deliberately study tribal life in northern Iraq, Division planners and intelligence began to span some of the physical gaps within and beyond the area of operations by obtaining a better understanding of the tribal terrain. Tribal analysis began to reveal potential (albeit loosely correlated) patterns linking persistent areas of operational gaps and tribal boundary seams. Within the Sharqat salient (southern sector) lay the boundary between the Jiburi and the Duri tribes. A nexus of several tribes is found between Mosul and the northwest Badush area; the most prominent among these tribes are the Al Hammadin, Al Tai, Shammar, and Jiburi tribes. By simply overlaying operational maps on top of tribal maps showed a possible tie between tribal boundaries and operational gaps. This tie was also insinuated to a potential enemy line of operation, identifying potential tribal complicity. Again, although this tie that binds proposition was never fully proven, operations conducted along this enemy line of communication resulted in some of the major coalition force "wins" during OIF-1 (the killing of HVTs #2 and #3, the capture of Saddam Hussein, the capture of major FRE senior leadership, etc.).

Counterinsurgency Operations in Northern Iraq

In November 2003, CPA and CJTF-7 officially recognized and redefined the war for what it is: at least in part, a war of insurgency. CJTF-7 immediately issued an addendum to its standing campaign plan, formally incorporating concepts of counterinsurgency operations (COIN). Frankly, the name change was simply a matter of semantics in northern Iraq; COIN was inherent in the 101st Airborne Division's (Air Assault) campaign plan and daily approach to the war-effort from the beginning. Even during the major combat phase of the war (destruction of the regime phases), it was apparent to the Division commander that winning the hearts and minds of the Iraqi people would be the key to eventual victory. Destruction of the Hussein regime was merely a means to an end that would be based on reconstruction of a new regime, of, for, and by the people of Iraq. Understanding the human terrain would prove even more important than knowing the physical landscape. A knowledge of and familiarization with local tribal ways would be essential to a successful counterinsurgency campaign.

On Insurgency

Understanding one key and essential fact is critical to any hope for a successful counterinsurgency strategy: in insurgencies, the goal for both insurgent and counter-insurgent is to win and retain the support of the majority of the local population. Despite what may be a general Western society bias against tribal society, knowing the tribal system is critical to gaining and maintaining the support of the locals.

The following amendment to the Division commander intent reflects this inclusion of tribes into the Division plan for COIN:

> *Purpose*: To disorganize insurgent and anticoalition forces (ACFs), to organize and support local procoalition and/or "for-progress" Iraqi citizens in their reconstruction efforts, to co-opt local neutrals to the "for-progress" Iraq reconstruction effort.

According to the *Small Wars Manual*, a "campaign plan strategy must be adapted to the character of the people encountered . . . [a]daptation of methods to expedite mission accomplishment, while maintaining a high-moral plan."[22] The 101st Airborne Division's (Air Assault) campaign plan—its approach to combat and SASO in northern Iraq—shaped, as much as it was shaped by, the sociopolitical landscape of the people and terrain encountered. These encounters were daily, local, and tribal at their base.

Insurgency in Northern Iraq

The following words hung over the command center of the Screaming Eagle Division Headquarters' Battle Command Center (BCC) in Mosul, Iraq:

> We are in a fight to win the hearts and minds of the Iraqi people. What has your element done today to contribute to winning that fight?[23]

This has been the mantra of Major General David Petraeus, the commanding general of the 101st Airborne Division (Air Assault). These words strike very similar to advice given in the *Small Wars Manual* on how to wage a successful counterinsurgency:

> The initial problem is to restore peace . . . . peace and industry cannot be restored permanently without appropriate provisions for the economic welfare of the people . . . productive industry cannot be fully restored until there is peace.[24]

For the 101st, grassroots engagement was the key: engagements ranged from dismounted combat patrols to goat grabs with local sheikhs, to *Chi* (tea) sessions with local *mukhtars* (community leaders). These interactions were essential to developing the links to the local community (an awareness of the "terrain") that would eventually lead to indigenous human intelligence contacts. These contacts proved essential in securing a sustainable environment in and around the city of Mosul and throughout AO North. Until a semireliable stability could be restored in the area, essential services could not be reliably administered to the local public. A mix of *gloved fist with mailed fist* was crucial as a counterinsurgency strategy.

Counterinsurgency in Northern Iraq

Developing a close association with the local Iraqi people and gaining an in-depth knowledge of the human and physical terrain—embedding into the environment—was a key to the success of the 101st Airborne Division's (Air Assault) COIN operations. Knowledge of the local tribes was both a process for achieving this and a product of this engagement (see figure 6.4).

Knowledge of the local and regional tribal networks was a key enabler of the Division's intelligence-gathering system (a capabilities-based strategy).

The threat in northern Iraq is a complex collage of FRE, foreign fighters, and criminal elements. With over 1,500 square miles of porous border, with three strategic pivot states (Syria, Turkey, and Iran), the environment of AO North is a constantly fluctuating threat to contend with: Ansar Al Islam, Al Qaeda, mujahadeen fighters, jihadists, and so on. Leading the counterinsurgency as a Western outsider (and an infidel in the eyes of the virulent side of Islamic society) demanded an indirect approach to the counterinsurgency and counterterrorist fight through the building of relationships with local tribes and indigenous security forces (see figure 6.5).

In late August 2003, the Division ACE and Division planners began to formalize what had been up to that point a series of periodic and informal meetings between

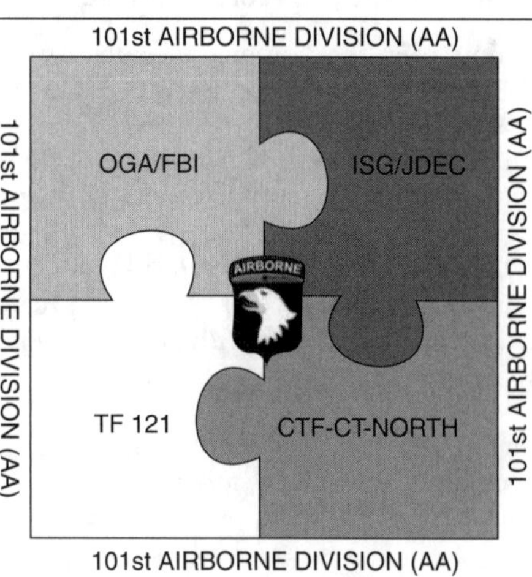

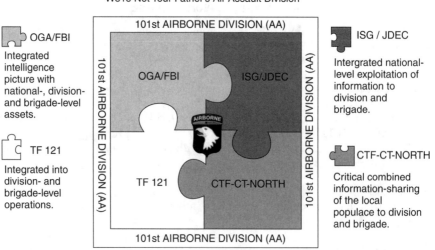

Figure 6.4 Reorganization for Effective Counterinsurgency

Source: Official 101st Airborne Division planning briefings (unclassified versions and/or declassified materials), June 2003–May 2005.

- Currently functioning within MND-N.
- **Purpose:** provide situational awareness on counterterrorism within AO North.
- **Method:** weekly coordination between coalition forces and indigenous forces in a meeting conducted to provide information-sharing on counterterrorism target groups and individuals within the area of operation. Information is then synthesized and back-checked by coalition forces to provide clarification on targetable information.
- **Endstate:** provide a venue to share information to indigenous forces and gain valuable information from indigenous forces.

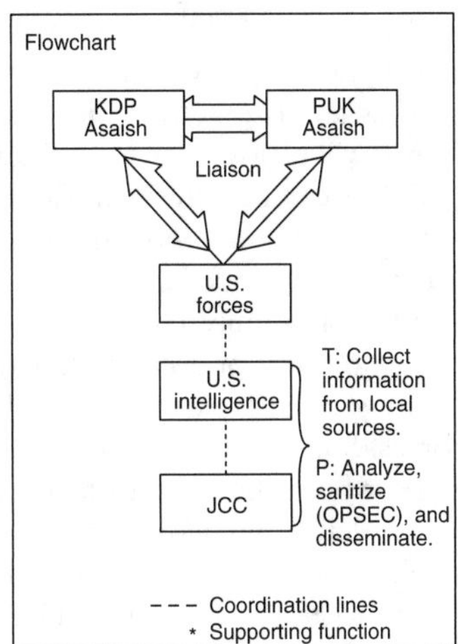

Figure 6.5 Combined Task Force Counterterrorism North
Note: "T" Stands for "task" and "P" stands for "purpose."
Source: Official 101st Airborne Division planning briefings (unclassified versions and/or declassified materials), June 2003–May 2005.

Division personnel and members of the local Iraqi-Kurd security forces (Asaish, *peshmerga*). Operation Informed Eagle was a deliberate effort to formalize these relationships, as a means toward the establishment of a dedicated information-sharing (intelligence fusion) medium. This has evolved into the establishment of Combined Task Force-Counterterrorism, North (CTF-CT-N), a formal collective security organization in northern Iraq where information of possible intelligence and operational value is shared between U.S. forces, KDP and PUK Iraqi-Kurds, and their *peshmerga* forces.

The Iraqi-Kurd Asaish (loose equivalent to the U.S. FBI) also attended these weekly meetings. Kurdish party and tribal contacts were vital in the capture of several high-value targets (e.g., CENTCOM #27) and served time and again as an essential capability for gaining and maintaining indirect contact with various enemy elements, from an intelligence, reconnaissance, and surveillance (ISR) standpoint.

Another key aspect of the 101st Airborne's (Air Assault) tribal engagement and COIN strategy was incorporating newly gained knowledge of tribal norms, ways, rituals, and so on into daily interactions, civil-military engagements, and combat operations. Honor and pride lie at the center of tribal society. Honor that is lost or taken must be returned by the offender through a ritualistic truce session, or else it will taken back through force of arms. This ritual is very similar to the tribal practices of certain American Indian warrior tribes (e.g., the Dakota Sioux) of the mid- to late 1800s. For the Sioux, "counting coup" (physical engagements with an enemy or rival, ranging from a simple physical close-combative nonlethal strike with a "coup stick" to lethal close-quartered fighting) was essential to the maintaining and gaining of honor for the family, for the clan, and for the tribe. Tribal blood feuds run long and deep, often due to imbalances in honor-based relationships between tribes or subtribes within confederations. Many of these feuds have persisted for centuries.

Intent is largely irrelevant in these honor rituals. Coalition forces inadvertently damaging property or injuring or killing a local citizen—a tribal member—can be seen as an affront to familial or tribal honor; as such, it must be avenged, or else honor will be lost. The loss of honor equates to a loss of power and status in the tribe. This loss can negatively impact the family in its share of tribal-provided essential services. Therefore, honor and survival are not far removed in these societies. What may seem an unintended infraction against a local Iraqi by a soldier could be viewed by the family, community, or tribe as a loss of honor. Nonsensically, this action could trigger a reaction days or even weeks later, in the form of a rocket-propelled grenade (RPG) or improvised explosive device (IED) attack or random drive-by shooting at coalition forces. Some of the attacks on coalition forces throughout the war theater are likely to have been the result of such tribal vendetta. It is important to note that in this sort of vendetta, often the act of taking a stand against the "subject of dishonor," is enough to restore honor to the family or tribe, and therefore the individual; whether the attacker is "successful" in injuring or killing is many times irrelevant, even unnecessary, and at times unintended. Like the Sioux, a simple nonlethal strike with a coup stick could return all the lost honor. Some of what has appeared to coalition force intelligence analysts as a "lack of training" or "targeting incompetence" of the enemy (their "inability" to hit their targets on a regular occasion) could be misread on our part. These "misses" could as easily be explained as the intended effort by some to regain lost honor through a demonstrated (and public-witnessed) strike that is short of injury or death against the oppressor.

Harsh treatment by coalition forces—the rough handling of detainees in public—can trigger familial/tribal vendetta. The innovation of the "cordon and knock" by the 101st Airborne Division (Air Assault) was a deliberate effort to maintain the combat effectiveness of a cordon and search operation but without unduly demeaning or disturbing local societal mores. When strong, violent, lethal-forced entry was required, Division soldiers executed such missions; these techniques, however, were not the only tools and approaches available to 101st soldiers. It is likely that soldiers in northern Iraq suffered less, relatively speaking, from vendetta-based assaults and attacks due to a better cultural understanding of tribal ways in Iraq.

Tribal Engagement Strategy in Practice—*The Case of HVT #27*

The key to success in a counterinsurgency is "powering down" to local leaders and commanders and facilitating a grassroots-level engagement strategy that incorporates tribes and tribal ways of interaction. The counterinsurgent recognizes growing success as the incidence of local cooperation increases and improves. So was the case in late July 2003, when a local Iraqi citizen approached a young sergeant serving with the 101st Airborne with information that led directly to the killing of Uday Hussein and Qusay Hussein. An advanced understanding of local and regional tribalism also contributed to one of the more innovative and "out-of-the-box" successes of the 101st Airborne's anti-FRE campaign.

Sultan Hashim Ahmed Al-Jabbur Al-Tai, the former Iraqi defense minister, and CENTCOM HVT #27, remained at-large. The sultan still was regarded as "one of Mosul's favorite sons"—a greatly respected military and tribal leader. He was also regarded countrywide, and beyond, as a true professional officer, with a nineteenth-century appreciation for the rules of honor and of law in war-fare. The Division intelligence community (led by the innovativeness of the Division G2) began as early as June 2003, in conjunction with OGA and Iraqi-Kurd intermediaries, to develop and maintain backdoor channels of dialogue between the Division and the family of Sultan Hashim. Rather than approaching the task of capturing or killing HVT #27 through direct lethal means, the 101st Airborne approached the challenge indirectly, working through the sultan's affinities for tribal and military sense of honor and respect, to compel his formal capitulation and surrender. An offer of conditions for surrender was drafted and transmitted to the sultan through third-party intermediaries. The letter itself was written in a manner reminiscent of tribal and nineteenth-century military tradition, stressing the importance of honor and the respect between warriors. Formal ritual, from the manner in which the memorandum read to the respectful manner in which the sultan was approached, detained, and transported, was a key to success not only in the bloodless capture of HVT #27 but perhaps more importantly in the message that was conveyed through good coalition force behavior to the Iraqi public: the coalition understood and respected honor and ritual and the coalition could be trusted at its word and actions.

The CPA and CJTF-7 are now debating the future disposition of HVT #27—whether to consider him for release (due to his cooperation with coalition forces and his reputation as a professional military officer) or to place him before trial either in Iraq or at the Hague. The respectful manner in which the 101st Airborne detained the sultan now presents a significant and unique opportunity. The sultan could be reinstated in northern Iraq as a supporter of the NIS and supporter of the coalition effort to reconstruct Iraqi civil society. No respect was taken from the sultan in his surrender by coalition force; in fact, it is likely that his stature has risen given the respect the coalition displayed toward him. Consequently, the sultan could serve as a pro-New Iraqi State/coalition forces (pro-NIS/CF) leader for northern Iraq—a candidate for sheikh of sheikhs in northern Iraq, and perhaps eventually for all tribes of Iraq. The opportunity is a real and viable one and is there for the taking and exploitation by the coalition.

Final Comments

Know your enemy and know yourself and you will find 1,000 victories in 1,000 battles. This advice was offered by the military strategist Sun Tzu over 2,500 years ago. It has, unfortunately, too often gone unheeded—often to the folly of the onetime victor who may win in the "war-fight" but lose all in the "peace" that follows. Part of the enemy in Iraq is the persistence of an ignorance of the local histories, culture, norms, and rituals of the people—the human terrain, an ignorance that comes from arrogance and prejudice against the local culture. Knowing your enemy is no longer enough for ultimate success. One must know the enemy, one must know the local population, and, most importantly, one must *respect* each. Respect does not necessarily mean acceptance or approval. There is much about Arab-Iraqi and Kurd-Iraqi culture and tribal society that is anathema to modern American norms. Acceptance of indigenous ways and mores does not have to be a prerequisite for acknowledging the practical relevance of local culture and making use of it for one's own strategic intent.

The 101st Airborne Division (Air Assault) made a conscious effort to know the full terrain of northern Iraq, so that it could truly be more than an occupier, so that it could be a member of the landscape and, as such, have a personal stake in the future stability and prosperity of northern Iraq. The Division learned the physical landscape—educated itself on the limits and opportunities this terrain offered. The Division equally became intimate with all aspects of the human terrain; we "lived" with the people of northern Iraq and, as such, became a distant "close friend" of the local and regional communities.

The Division indirectly acted as a "tribe" and interacted with other tribes in northern Iraq as the major tribe of the region. The commanding general was the de facto *sheikh of sheikhs*; each brigade commander was seen as the primal sheikh of their respective areas of operations. Deliberate effort was made, early on, to ensure that civil-military operational boundaries lied as coincident as possible with natural and long-standing tribal and physical boundaries and divisions.

Much of the "getting the boundaries right" was based on luck, initially. However, luck was reinforced by a deliberate and detailed study of the ground and its people, their history, and tribal pasts. For the most part, judgments were not passed on these societal ways but instead deciphered analytically and operationally for what they offered in terms of threat and opportunity. The success of the 101st Airborne Division (Air Assault) in northern Iraq must, to some degree, be attributed to the Division's knowledge and appreciation of Iraq's tribal society. Knowing and respecting this aspect of Iraq's past, present, and likely future has proven essential to fighting this war and hopefully setting a path toward an eventual victorious peace.

Conclusions

Thoughts on Kinship Politics as a Strategy of Containment and Democratization

Selective efforts should be made to embrace, rather than reject and/or stigmatize, kin divisions, since such networks and associations can be used for developmentally useful purposes. If the sayings hold true—that *all politics are local* and that *policy is the art of the possible*—then getting to know and learning to incorporate existing indigenous kin-based (patronage-)political networks is a necessary means to future democratic ends in our intervention policies and overall national security and military strategies. Just as in *Federalist No. 51* James Madison provided the American polity with a means of balancing and checking faction against faction and, in so doing, provided the young nation with a prescription for not only avoiding the fractionalizing effects of democratization but also turning the process (faction itself) into a necessary and sufficient ingredient for future democracy, so too may the United States learn to properly balance the existence of tribal networks with formal institution-building solutions to build effective and legitimate (in the hearts and minds of the locals) governance structures—stable, liberal democracies.

Reconsidering Lawrence's Way of "Containment"

A "peace map" was discovered in 2005 in the London archives outlining T. E. Lawrence's (Lawrence of Arabia) proposals for the reconstruction of the Middle East at the end of World War I. His proposals radically differed from what was eventually implemented by the victorious Allied powers. Lawrence's peace map illustrates the recommendations he made to the Eastern Committee of the War Cabinet in November 1918, demonstrating his opposition to the Allied agreement, which eventually determined the borders of modern-day Iraq. T. E. Lawrence's plan called for separate governments for the predominantly Kurdish and Arab areas in what is now Iraq. From 1916, he had heard the views from men across the Middle East during the Arab revolt against the Turks and was also in contact with other British experts on the region.

His plans, highly informed by years of direct observation of the "Arabian Way" and reflective of a knowledge of and respect for local tribal prerequisites, were strenuously opposed, however, by the British administration in Mesopotamia. The present-day state of affairs (illiberal and less-than legitimate governance structures) in Iraq is reflective of arbitrary post–World War I nation-building efforts. The United States is at present embroiled in a fierce democratization effort in Mesopotamia. The conditions America faces, and the strategic approach the United States has thus far adopted, are more reminiscent of the British and French approaches of 1921 than the geostrategic realities of 2005. A right, legitimate, and more effective approach to governance-building—democratization—this time around might be well informed and enabled by the incorporation of an indirect approach, one that makes use of and builds upon the foundational tribal networks that have underpinned this region of the world for the past 6,000 years. To best contain the potential ill effects (anti-Western, anti-American) of governance rebuilding in Iraq, a patronage-based strategy of democratization may be the better way toward lasting peace.

Part III

Lessons Gathered but Not Yet Learned

The chapters that follow are truly "beyond-war" chapters as well as *beyond-the-war* (the Iraq War) chapters.

Chapter 7 is a personal account, detailing my observations of *the Iraq War* since my return from the war. In a sense, these *post–my war* months serve as another case for study—the war that has come to follow our original ending of the 2003 Iraq War. This post-2003 observation raises a third partition in this latest war in Iraq, allowing us to view and judge the war in three parts: *the march up country* (March–May 2003), the *war of transition* (June–March 2004), and the *war of rebellion/revolt* (April 2004–present). The partitioning sets a stage for some intriguing and informative comparatives and reflections.

Chapter 8 tells the story of the decline and fall of Mosul and the demise of the stability and reconstruction victories achieved by the 101st Airborne in Northern Iraq during OIF-1. The story is, in part, tragic narrative. But more important, the story reveals a critical and potentially catastrophic flaw within the existing modern-age approach to U.S. military operational-level war-planning: flaws in our ways of *transition* and transition planning.

Chapter 7

My Iraq War: A Postscript

My personal war in Iraq ended on February 9, 2004. I was on board the final C-17 aircraft transporting remaining elements of the 101st Airborne Division from northern Iraq back to Fort Campbell, Kentucky. Our departure was bittersweet. We were all extremely excited about finally returning home and hoped and prayed that we would survive this flight out of Iraq. Yet, the feeling that we were leaving prematurely was palpable throughout the Division staff and Division Headquarters. I still remember boarding a UH-60 Blackhawk Helicopter a few days prior to our final transport out of the country—the last 101st Airborne helicopter taking the last members of the Division staff from the Eagle's Nest, our Division Headquarters in northern Mosul, to the Mosul airport. I was the second last to board the aircraft—our Division chief of staff was the last. As he finally boarded, he leaned over to me and, yelling over the roar of the engine and blade noise, said, "You know, we're leaving this place six months too early!" "You're right sir," I replied, as the UH-60 lifted and banked hard right to give us all one last look at what had been our home for the past 10 months.

A few days later, I was back home, but the war raged on. And for those of us just returning home, our own personal "postwar" had just begun.

Watching the war like a spectator since then has been hard. The soldier in me longs not for the sting of war but rather for the opportunity to share the misery with comrades in arms. As a soldier, it has also been very painful to sit and watch as the security situation in Iraq has degraded—degraded rapidly. Watching the withering of Mosul and northern Iraq has been particularly devastating to me as one who played an integral part in the planning to liberate, occupy, and restore civil society in the northern provinces. As a scholar, the experience of watching the localized "wins" whither and fall farther and farther from a theaterwide victory raised an intellectual curiosity within me. How could the situation throughout Iraq have turned so violent and unstable by April 2004—only three or four months after, by all accounts, the majority of the country had been successfully "pacified" and prepared for transfer of local control over to the Interim Iraqi Government? What had happened, and how did it happen so fast?

Tactical Victories, Strategic Defeat: A Chronology

The tale of Americas' Pyrrhic victories in Iraq since March 2004 is a tale of catastrophic successes and a return of "war" *as we have traditionally known it*. A brief chronology of major events since the end of the OIF-1 (Operation Iraqi Freedom) period tells the tale:

- *March 2004*: The first major troop rotation (OIF-1 to OIF-2) is complete.
- *April 2004*: There is a rise in rebellious activities, particularly from elements with relatively low representation within the Iraqi Provisional Authority (IPA).
  - Four U.S. civilian contractors from Blackwater Security (a private military contractor) are ambushed near Fallujah; their bodies are desecrated.
  - U.S. forces in concert with the IPA launch two major assaults: one on Fallujah, the center of the "Mohammed's Army of Al-Ansar," and another on Najaf, home of an important mosque, which had become the focal point for the Mahdi Army and its activities.
  - The April offensive ends in a truce-producing stalemate. U.S. Marines withdraw from Fallujah and Najaf.
- *June 28, 2004*: The United States transferred limited sovereignty to a caretaker government (Interim Iraqi Government).
  - Militia leader Muqtada al-Sadr openly takes control of Najaf.
- *November 8, 2004*: American and Iraqi forces invaded the militant stronghold of Fallujah in Operation al-Fajr, capturing or killing many insurgents.
- *December 2004*: Fourteen American soldiers were killed and over 100 injured when an explosion struck an open-tent mess hall in Mosul.
- *January 2005*: An election for a government to draft a permanent constitution took place. Although some violence and lack of widespread Sunni participation marred the event, most of the eligible Kurd and Shia populace participated.
- *February 2005*: Deputy Defense Secretary Paul Wolfowitz announces the withdrawal of 15,000 U.S. troops from Iraq as the expected start of a gradual transfer of the security situation to the Interim Iraqi Government and the Iraqi Security Forces (ISF).
- *April/May 2005*: Deadliest months for Iraqis and coalition forces since the inception of the war. There was a rise in suicide bombings.

May 2005: Launch of Operation MATADOR, an assault by around 1,000 Marines in the ungoverned region of western Iraq. Its goal was the closing of suspected insurgent supply routes of volunteers and materiel from Syria.

- *August 3, 2005*: Fourteen U.S. Marines were killed in two separate insurgent attacks; 11 were killed in one spectacular vehicle-borne, improvised explosive device (VBIED) attack that gave an indication of the insurgency's improved antiarmor capabilities.
- *August 5, 2005*: U.S. News-ABC Poll showed a drop in American public support for the way President Bush is handling the war in Iraq to 38 %—an all-time low.

The record of casualties in the war in Iraq adds to the tale (see table 7.1). All estimates are as of August 3, 2005 and include both the 2003 invasion of Iraq and the following postinvasion Iraq, 2003–2005.

The relaying of the story in the vernacular of casualty numbers—body count—is not meant as an advocacy of body count as an effective measure of "success" or "failure" (wins or losses) in war. The comparative numbers are important, however, as an illustration of the folly of our modern distinctions between war and "postwar." By the modern-age lexicon and measures, should we not expect to see more casualties

Table 7.1 Record of Casualties in the War in Iraq

	Estimate
Iraqis	Counts of civilian deaths specifically documented range from 23,209 to 26,264.[a] A study in the *Lancet* estimated 100,000 deaths[b] from all causes as of October 2004, with approximately three times as many injured. This has Been disputed.
U.S. armed forces	1,821 deaths, 13,657 combat wounded (6,568 evacuated) + unknown noncombat injuries
Armed forces of other coalition countries	194
Non-Iraqi civilians	From 254 to 434

Notes: [a] These refer only to deaths reported by two or more news organizations and include "all deaths which the Occupying Authority has a binding responsibility to prevent under the Geneva Conventions and Hague Conventions. This includes civilian deaths resulting from the breakdown in law and order, and deaths due to inadequate health care or sanitation." *Baruch Fischhoff Scott Atran Noam Fischhoff, Counting Casualties: A Framework for Respectful, useful Records*. Springer Science + Business Media, LLC 2007.

[b] The study's estimate of total deaths ranges from 8,000 to 194,000 at a 95 % confidence interval. This estimate was made in October 2004.

[c] For instance, a written Ministerial Statement (November 17, 2004) by the U.K. government.

Source: Randolph R. Rotte Jr., "Bearing the Burden of the Iraq War? An Analysis of the Demographics of Casualties in the Global War on Terrorism," online at http://www.jointcenter.org/publications1/Military%20Affairs/Bearing%20theBurden%20of%20the%20Iraq%20War%20.pdf (accessed March 22, 2005).

during the "war" and far less (and eventually zero) during the postwar? In fact, we see the opposite, dramatically so, in terms of soldiers and Iraqi civilians killed or injured prior to the May 1 declaration of mission accomplished and after that fateful announcement.

The mounting irony is stifling. The less-than 40 days of battle we comfortably called "the war" saw less than 200 combat-related soldier deaths, compared with the two years since—the "postwar" or the "nonwar"—accounts for the rest. We had robust strategic, operational, and tactical plans for what we called "the war" but nothing beyond high-level plans for the "postwar." More ironic anecdotes of the power and prevalence of the paradox.

American troops suffered heavy casualties in Iraq during the months of July and August 2005. On Wednesday, August 3, 2005, 14 Marines were killed in the Euphrates River Valley in the worst roadside bombing targeting Americans since the war began in March 2003. In a 10-day period (late July–early August), 27 U.S. soldiers were killed in Iraq—marking what some see (myself included) at the time of this writing to be developing as a new stage in the transnational-supported Iraqi insurgency. This marker, I predict, will also serve as time passes as a sad and significant note in the U.S. war-policy in Iraq. The measure is already boding poorly for the president and his administration, with early August 2005 polls showing a meager 38 % approval rating for the president in his handling of the war and a drop to 50 % in the public's trust in the president's honesty on Iraq and other policy issues.[1]

To add to the sad story, this chronology of a war-policy on the slide toward strategic defeat emerges in the face of unquestionable successes of soldiers and stability and reconstruction workers at local levels throughout the country. Anti-insurgency combat operations conducted by joint U.S. and ISF have been quite successful in capturing or killing insurgent and transnational terrorist forces. Equally admirable have been the localized efforts of humanitarian aid workers, civil engineers, and other "peace operators" to restore proper functioning within civic society in Iraq. The purity and nobility of all these security professionals will be sealed in whatever annals of history we write in the future with regards to the Iraq War. Yet, despite these local wins, we continue to question whether or not this war is "winnable."

The War since Late 2003: Observations

If we allowed the modern-age definitions of war and peace to continue to dominate our understanding and our reason, then it would be easy to consider what has developed in Iraq since late 2003 as a "New War." It would be all too easy, in part because of the lack of a comprehensive war-policy agenda since the war's inception. Prior to initiation of major combat operations (MCO), the stated goal of the war was to eliminate a grave and growing danger to U.S. security and the security of the Middle East region—a growing weapons of mass destruction (WMD) threat in Saddam Hussein's Iraq. The declaration of mission accomplished on May 1, 2003 was more accurate—and telltale—than anyone has given credit or notice to in all of the writings and punditry that has exploded since the war began. Based on that war-policy agenda, war conditions on the ground by May 1, 2003, did measure up to "mission accomplished"—Saddam and his formal state regime were no more; it was isolated by and then collapsed due to power and weight of the U.S. military and the coalition forces.

The conditions on the ground in Iraq by Spring 2004 certainly began to match with our modern mental picture of "war." By this time, a full guerrilla war was raging in Iraq, a four-alarm fire in some areas of the country (i.e., the Sunni Triangle, the Shia south), while still merely a spark of a blaze in others—like the north. As the situation in Iraq began to reemerge as a "battleground," and a return to MCO began to take form, we seemed to be returning to war—returning to war as we have traditionally come to known it, and honor it.

The Battle of Fallujah, April–November 2004

By November 2004, we were fully back on familiar—and comfortable—ground. U.S. Army soldiers and Marines launched a major "offensive" to pacify the city and environs of Fallujah on November 8, 2004. During Operation al-Fajr, despite arguments that a significant number of rebels had fled before the invasion, the operation was judged an overwhelming success. U.S.-backed figures put insurgency losses at over 2,000. Ruined homes across the city attested to a strategy of overwhelming force. As well, it was the bloodiest single battle for the United States in the war, with 51 Americans dead and several hundred wounded.[2]

U.S. Marine Corps commanders had reflected back on the lessons and tactics, techniques, and procedures used by the Corps during the Vietnam War. One particular operation during the 1965 Tet Offensive played an important role. The longest and bloodiest battle of the Tet Offensive occurred in Hue, the most venerated city in Vietnam. Located astride Highway 1 ten kilometers west of the coast and 100 kilometers south of the demilitarized zone (DMZ), Hue was the capital of Thua

Thien province and South Vietnam's third largest city, with a war-time population of 140,000. It was the old imperial capital and served as the cultural and intellectual center of Vietnam. The Battle of Hue ended, certainly, with the destruction of not only the Vietcong as a viable fighting force but also with the near-complete destruction of every standing structure within the city and with significant civilian and U.S. troop casualties. The Battle of Hue itself has become a modern-day exemplar of the paradox—the strategic tragedy of catastrophic success at local battles and engagements. That paradox—then and now—was sealed in the testament of one U.S. Marine Corps officer standing amid the ruins of Hue in Vietnam a generation ago. "In order to save the city," he declared, "we had to destroy it."

The Battle of Hue was recorded as a victory in terms of the tactical win over Vietcong and North Vietnamese regulars by U.S. Marines and their South Vietnamese partners. However, the victory at Hue proved irrelevant in the long run. Despite the overwhelming tactical victory achieved by the allies in the city and on the other battlefields throughout South Vietnam, the Tet Offensive proved to be a strategic defeat for the United States. U.S. public opinion, affected in large part by the media coverage of the early days of the offensive, began to shift away from support for the war.[3]

From Hue to Fallujah

Though it is far too early to draw any such conclusions or assessments of the Battle of Fallujah, the anecdotal parallels are curious and oddly coincidental, to say the least. Though there were no embarrassing proclamations to the fact, as in the case of Hue, the Battle of Fallujah, by the November 2004, resulted in the destruction of most of the city infrastructure. This battle did result in "freeing" the city of insurgents and terrorists but at a heavy cost. Similarly, the Battle of Fallujah seems to have become an event marking a shift in U.S. public opinion and support for the war-effort. Whether or not Fallujah will become the Iraq Wars' equivalent to the 1968 Tet Offensive remains to be seen. Nevertheless, the Battle of Fallujah does leave us in a quandary and with a sense of a Pyrrhic victory in the making. Our inability to convert our battle wins into systemic and wide-ranging victories has become increasingly apparent since the Battle of Fallujah. Some claim that the United States simply does not have enough forces to pacify the entire Sunni center of Iraq at once. As one officer interviewed soon after the battle concluded, "As soon as we press down hard in one place, they pop up somewhere else." These words were born out of a rash of small-scale attacks in places where U.S. troops had been thinned out for the assault on Fallujah.

Similar to Hue, Fallujah was a city that had unquestionably become a base for many of the car bombers and fighters who had staged attacks across central Iraq in the recent months. Similar to the situation leading up to the Battle of Hue, many believed that Fallujah's drift toward becoming an insurgency sanctuary was due to the resentment caused by previous attempts to win hearts and minds by military means—most notably the earlier botched U.S. assault in April. Like in the Battle of Hue, in military terms the Battle of Fallujah was successful, but politically it became just as disastrous as its predecessor, which fueled the present insurgency.

The comparative feeds an interesting "chicken or the egg" question—one that has persisted since the Vietnam War. Which came first: the insurgent safe haven or the anti-insurgent approach to the war that could have stoked the embers of insurgency? What factors added up and contributed to the necessity for a return to MCO in Fallujah? Was the city simply "bad" at its core—one of those unintended bypassed hot spots during the march-up-country phases of the war in 2003, which by late 2004 could be put off no longer? Or did the operational approach taken toward the pacification, stabilization, and reconstruction of the city—by military forces and humanitarian workers—contribute to the fall of the city to insurgents and transnational terrorists and finally to the firepower of the U.S. Marine Corps? The truth likely lies midway between these two questions. However, although there was likely nothing we could have ever done to correct for the former explanation (if the city was bad, it was destined to be bad despite our best efforts), there was and is much we can do to assure that in the future our operational approaches to implementing a war-policy do not unintentionally contribute to a worse outcome.

Fallujah is a city with a prewar population of about 350,000 inhabitants in the Iraqi province of Al Anbar, located roughly 69 kilometers (43 miles) west of Baghdad on the Euphrates. Within Iraq, it is known as the "city of mosques": there are 200 mosques found in the city and surrounding villages. It is one of the most important places for Sunni Islam in the region. Fallujah was one of the most peaceful areas of the country just after the fall of Saddam. There was very little looting and the new mayor of the city—Taha Bidawi Hamed, selected by local tribal leaders—was staunchly pro-American. When the U.S. Army entered the town in April 2003, they positioned themselves at the vacated Ba'athist Party Headquarters—an action that erased some goodwill, especially when many in the city had been hoping the U.S. Army would stay outside of the relatively calm city. A Fallujah Protection Force composed of local Iraqis was set up by the U.S.-led occupants to help fight the rising resistance.

Fallujah became one of the most dangerous areas for coalition military troops during the occupation of Iraq. Since the occupation began and up until early 2005, more than 200 Americans had died in the vicinity of Fallujah alone—more than any city except Baghdad. Following the November 2004 offensive, residents were allowed to return to the city in mid-December. About 7,000–10,000 of the roughly 50,000 buildings in the town are estimated to have been destroyed in the offensive and half to two-thirds of the buildings had suffered notable damage. Reconstruction had remained slow and mainly involved clearing rubble from heavily damaged areas and reestablishing basic utility services. This is also due to the fact that only 10 % of the preoffensive inhabitants had returned as of mid-January and only 30 % as of the end of March 2005. Over 150,000 individuals are still living in harsh conditions as "Iraqi Displaced Persons" (IDPs) within tent cities outside Fallujah or elsewhere in Iraq.

The Lessons of Fallujah

Fallujah may be well on its way to becoming the symbol of all that has been wrong with the United States' operational approach to the war, like Hue became a symbol of all that was at once possible and at the same time beyond our operational capacity in Vietnam. What lessons might we gather from these two incidents?

First, perhaps we should reflect on the conditionality of the city and its occupants back in April 2003, when U.S. military forces first entered the city. By most accounts, Fallujah was neutral to pro-American at the time. During my own travels through the city—and throughout the Sunni Triangle—between April and May 2003, the reception I and my traveling companions received was at worst lukewarm, and in most cases leaning toward pro-U.S. opinion. That is not enough to conclude confidently that our tide turned from better to worse in and around Fallujah due to what we had done—or failed to do—in the city. Nevertheless, it is important to understand what the state of affairs in the area was before the rise of the insurgency.

Second, it is important to understand the history of Fallujah, as a city and a cultural center within Iraq. In 1947, the town had only about 10,000 inhabitants. It grew rapidly into a city after Iraqi independence with the influx of oil wealth into the country. Its position near one of the main roads out of Baghdad made it of central importance. The city also has a storied record for rebellion under foreign occupation. In Spring 1920, the British, who had gained control of Iraq after the collapse of the Ottoman Empire, sent Lieutenant Colonel Gerald Leachman, a renowned explorer and a senior colonial officer, to quell a rebellion in Fallujah. Leachman was killed just south of the city in a fight with local leader Sheikh Dhari. The British sent an army to crush the rebellion, and the ensuing fight took the lives of more than 10,000 Iraqis and 1,000 British soldiers.[4] During the Gulf War of 1990–1991, Fallujah was one of the cities in Iraq with the most civilian casualties. Two separate failed bombing attempts on Fallujah's bridge across the Euphrates River hit crowded markets, killing an estimated 200 civilians and enraging city residents. Under Saddam Hussein, Fallujah came to be an important area of support for and a major industrial center for the regime, and along with the rest of the region it was labeled by the U.S. military as the Sunni Triangle. Many residents of the primarily Sunni city were employees and supporters of Saddam Hussein's government, and many senior Ba'athist Party officials were natives of the city.

With a preinvasion knowledge and appreciation for the geographic, contextual, and cultural history of the city and inhabitants of Fallujah, perhaps the U.S. war-effort could have progressed more effectively. Perhaps the necessity of destroying the city in November 2004 in order to pacify it could have been avoided or at least approached in a different way. With a preknowledge of the city's past dealings with liberators and wars of liberation, perhaps Fallujah should not have been one of those cities initially bypassed by coalition forces during the march-up-country phases of the war. Perhaps leading earlier with a carrot rather than much later with a big stick would have yielded a more positive outcome.

Learning from the Lessons "beyond" Fallujah

A more nuanced and integrative *stick-and-carrot campaign plan* approach to the entire war may have landed us—and the Iraqis—in a better situation in Iraq.

As I stated at the beginning of this chapter, not until Spring 2004 did U.S. military leaders—and the American nation for that matter—begin to view the war in Iraq as a "War" in Iraq and, at least in part, still "our war" in Iraq. Failing to "see" large periods of time and conditions within the country as part of a comprehensive "war" effort contributed to a disconnected war-policy in Iraq. This, in turn, contributed to the creation of gaps and "seams" within different operational and occupation sectors in the country, and in between, differing areas of operation within the wider theater of war. These seams provided opportunity for a homegrown insurgency to take root as created sanctuaries and safe havens within which a growing transnational jihadist movement could infiltrate, organize, and plan for attacks.

The degree of "stability" within these major occupation zones in Fall 2003 actually defies the usefulness of calling these zones "stabilization zones." Many have asked, *why was the north or the south not as hostile as central (the Sunni Triangle) Iraq?* At one political science conference in Fall 2004, the question was posed to me in a much more succinct and direct manner: *why was Mosul and the north not Fallujah?* The question is fair and important for several reasons, not the least of which being that it raises another relevant "chicken-egg" dilemma. Were the northern provinces and the southern provinces simply easier to "liberate," "occupy," "pacify/stabilize," and "rebuild" because of the "atmospherics" of the north and the south? Were the north and the south easier zones to occupy and govern due to "better genetics"?

Surely genetics mattered. Part of my answer to the question of why Mosul had not turned out like Fallujah at that conference was a simple statement of nature: Mosul was not Fallujah, and the north was not the Sunni Triangle. But my caveat was where all the relevant information lied. Yes, it was true that the Sunni Triangle, by its history, its culture, its nature was a harder nut to crack. The probability for rebellious activity was always high in the environs of the Sunni Triangle given the area's Saddamist affiliations and its history of antioccupation born of the Ottoman and British experiences. Much of the assumption-based planning during the preparation phases of the invasion took this history into account—early decisions to temporarily bypass many of the cities and villages within the Triangle during the initial march up country may have been based on the assumption that these areas were so pro-Saddam that early (and often) presence was likely to produce low yields. Hindsight now shows that this was probably not a good war-policy decision.

The argument that other areas of the country were "more benign" than the Sunni Triangle and therefore "easier" nuts to crack degraded into a growing dysfunctional sentiment within the theater of war that certain operational-level commands performing occupation duties in certain areas of the country were not even fighting a war. The southern stabilization zone under British operational command was considered as one of these "other-than-war" zones. The southern zone, under the "governorship" of the 101st Airborne Division (Air Assault), was another. This cultural bias within our own organizations added to the disjointedness of the overall theater plan and created an additional "operational seam" that the enemy was able to exploit and take advantage of.

What Kind of War?

In a published article written back in February 2005, I addressed this problem directly. In that essay titled "What Kind of War?" I offered that a major contributor to the impoverishment of the U.S. war-policy toward Iraq thus far has been a failure to properly scope and scale the theater of operations—a failure to define the type of war on which we departed on March 19, 2003. The father of modern Western military thought Carl von Clausewitz referred to this act as the first and supreme act of war-policy: *the first, the supreme act of judgment . . . is to decide the kind of war on which they are embarking.*[5] Judging all that was to occur after the collapse of the Hussein regime as "other-than-war" was our first and most tragic act of misjudgment.

This set the conditions for not one war in Iraq but many different and distinct wars within a wider war. Once it was clear that the war had in fact not ended on April 9, 2003, the second misjudgment was to allow to develop variations on what should have been a common theme of counterinsurgency and reconstruction throughout the country. The intervention needed one synchronized and integrated campaign plan but instead many separated, uncoordinated, and even countervailing plans emerged. Instead of one plan, we got as many and as varied operational approaches to the unstable and increasingly hostile situation in Iraq as there were operational-level commands. Each war-fighting division or separate/multinational brigade was compelled to create their own operational war-plans, based on their own interpretations of the war-policy goals and endstate. In many respects, separate interpretations were valuable—each division could assess the situation commensurate with the realities (geographic, ethnoreligious, ethnic, etc.) of their own area of influence. However, failing to link these separate interpretations together into one mutually supporting campaign plan that was directly supportive of the overall intent of the U.S. war-policy for Iraq set the conditions where, as time progressed, it would become nearly impossible (definitely improbable) for any localized actions to translate into theaterwide achievements. Furthermore, to allow sentiments to fester within the theater-command that supported notions that some areas of operations were "war-zones" while others were "something other" only made matters worse.

What follows is, in a way, my version of *revisionist history*. It is my offering of how we should have seen—and defined—the Iraq War from the beginning and how we still can and should view the war that remains.

The War in Iraq, March 2003–April 2003

It is essential that one gets away from the virulent partisan-political debates of the past few years—over the "goodness or badness" of the initiation of MCO in Iraq, March 19, 2003, in order to focus on a more important retrospective: *what kind of war were we really fighting during the MCO (Phases I–III) of Operation Iraqi Freedom?* Despite the rhetoric at that time, the war that actually waged from March to April 2003 was a classic preventive war; it was a conventional war executed through prosecution of MCO. It was a war focused operationally on the destruction of the Iraqi Army (the state's war-fighting capability) and the destruction of the Hussein state apparatus. OIF-1 was, in this sense, a continuation of the state versus state(s) war of Desert Shield/Storm, 1990–1991: an air-ground war between Saddam Hussein's Iraqi state and its military forces and the U.S. coalition and their military forces. OIF-1 was a classic external, interstate war of the Clausewitzian sense, whose purpose was the protection of the "center of gravity" (the source of all national power) of the United States and neighboring countries from the potential mass effects of a rogue Hussein state regime. This war was a preventive war initiated through preemptive military strike, justified at the time not only by the Bush administration but also by a joint resolution of Congress and the United Nations and by a presumed "grave and growing" danger posed by the Hussein regime. The rapid and decisive victory of MCO has already been cataloged in historical annals as an exemplar of the pure and noble courage of the American soldier and the tactical prowess of the U.S. military and the forces of its British and coalition partners.[6] This "certain victory" was perhaps more importantly a reflection of an effectively balanced war-plan and strategy (a balance between strategic ends and tactical means), an operational plan that ensured the intended strategic implication of the United States (a riddance of the Saddam threat) through our tactical actions. The initial three phases of Operation Iraqi Freedom are a good example of what can be achieved through thorough war-planning—what can be gained by clearly defining the war we are embarking upon.

The Forgotten War of Transition, May 2003–March 2004

The collapse of the Hussein regime on April 9, 2003 marked the culmination of the Phase I–III war-plan and the critical point in time where a redefinition of the war's purpose, method, endstate, and tactics was needed. I have labeled this war "the forgotten war of transition" simply because there was no deliberate rethinking of the war—what kind of war the "Phase-IV" period would be or needed to have been—after the collapse of the Hussein regime and the declaration of "mission accomplished" on May 1, 2003. Much has been written about the causes of this missed opportunity to redefine the war, but very little consideration has been given to the second-, third-, and "nth-" order effects. This failure to transition to a different kind of war, of *our choosing*, led to nothing short of an *operational culmination*. History may eventually show this year in the Iraqi saga as the year that gave birth to the Iraqi insurgency. This history is in part and sadly a history of our own making. As the United States and its coalition, including the membership of a fledgling pronational Iraqi interim government and security force, muddled through in its redefinition of its war-policy aims and its war-plan, the strategic ambiguity that ensued gave just the right amount of pause for an opposition force with its own counterculture and counterpurpose to organize.

The insurgency that year grew in full face of the massive efforts of the U.S. military, coalition partners, and State Department Foreign Service officials to restore civic society at the ground level in Iraq. Failing to define at the strategic levels, the kind of war we were actually fighting—civil-military battles being waged and "won" in various locales—unintentionally left many of those local efforts without a higher, guiding, and legitimizing purpose. Without that clarity of strategic purpose, these local efforts were left in an anemic state—"localized victories" in and of themselves but nevertheless tactical actions with an ambiguous strategic implication. Wars cannot be won by tactics and techniques alone, and in spite of the honest and valiant efforts of Coalition Provisional Authority (CPA) governing council officials and soldiers at the ground levels to restore essential services and a modicum of security and civic governance, without a clear war-aim—without a clearly defined "new" war-purpose—the strategic implications of our tactical actions were unintentionally left to broad interpretation. This "ends-means gap" allowed the opposition to begin to define the war on its own terms.

Counterinsurgency versus "Anti-Insurgency"

There has been and still is a gross lack of understanding of what constitutes an insurgency. Knowing what is an insurgency is an important first-order question that should be asked and answered before throwing the language of insurgency around the airwaves and into the hearts and minds of the local populaces—at home and abroad. Yet everyday, the U.S. war in Iraq is discussed and analyzed, debated and gossiped about, with most, I would offer, not really knowing exactly what they are speaking about.

This ignorance of the what and ways of insurgency has only been compounded in the punditries since early 2004 (when we officially acknowledged the insurgency in Iraq) through an equally consequential misunderstanding of the distinctions between *antiways of intervention* and *counterways of intervention*; in this case, between anti- and counterinsurgency operations. This second-order ignorance has plagued U.S. intervention policy and strategy over the past two years in Iraq, and if not resolved, it has promise of placing the United States on the losing approach to what may be emerging as a transnational (or global) insurgency against the Westphalian system of international politics.

What Is "an Insurgency"?

Volumes have been written on the subject of insurgency, and the art and science of insurgency is as old as the history of man and war-fare itself; it is the original sin of war, going back well beyond what we today regard as *conventional war-fare*. The Department of Defense (DOD) defines the term as "an organized movement aimed at the overthrow of a constituted government through use of subversion and armed conflict."[7] Bard O'Neill refines the definition further by emphasizing the factor of "an overtly political component" in his definition of insurgency:

> A struggle between a nonruling group and the ruling authorities in which the nonruling group consciously uses political resources (e.g., organizational expertise, propaganda, and demonstrations) and violence to destroy, reformulate, or sustain the basis of legitimacy of one or more aspects of politics.[8]

Thus, insurgencies combine violence with political programs in pursuit of revolutionary purposes. An insurgency is a struggle of legitimacy.

Knowing what constitutes insurgency is important. Knowing the ways of insurgency is equally important, as it is in the ways and means we develop and implement where we "do battle" against the causes and effects of insurgency; it is in our ways and methods where we either win the hearts and minds or fail to do so. Insurgent war-fare, or *guerrilla war-fare* as it has been popularized in the military lexicon, and our understanding of it suffers from both underdefinition and overprescription. Descriptions abound becoming over centuries the poor proxy for a complete and comprehensive definition of this peculiar form of war-fare. Most of those descriptions, though rich, are very particular to a given age, time, and context; they are case-specific and as such offer us poor substitutes for theoretical models on the subject and practice.

However, when one reviews the vast and voluminous annals of recorded history on the subject, the presence of some commonalities and trends can be seen and cataloged—this perhaps giving us a good starting point in the development of a theory of guerrilla war-fare (the art and science of insurgency) that transcends specific cases. Though a full telling of this rich history is well beyond the scope of this book, two specific historical vignettes are of particular interest here, given the anecdotal lessons they may offer for U.S. intervention policy toward future insurgency.

America's First Insurgency

The American Revolution—"Americans" as Insurgents

Even before Americans were "Americans," we were insurgents—guerrillas waging a guerrilla war against what was at that time the internationally recognized legitimate authority in the colonies of North America: Great Britain. Most of our own written (and popularly read) history of the American Revolution is focused on the conventional military victory over the British regulars. This half-history has fed the paradox, setting the conditions from the very beginning for Americans and the United States to define war and politics simply by the martial mechanics and moreover by the very specific martial functions of conventional force-on-force combatives. The more accurate history of the successful American Revolution acknowledges the victory as a political one, a compound victory the result of *compound war-fare*: a mix of conventional and unconventional war-fare with the proper politics (purposes), economics, diplomacy, and public discourse. The American Revolution was an insurgency and an insurgent's war; a struggle for the hearts and minds of the colonists—they themselves split between loyalty to the British regime and loyalty to independence from the British.

Partisan war-fare was an abundant aspect of both the northern and southern theater of the war of rebellion, but particularly so in the southern quarter where British loyalists (Tories) were more actively abundant. In his seminal work on the subject, author and professor John Shy offered the following observation:

> [I]n many respects, the outcome of the war in the South, to which the British switched their main effort in 1779–80, actually depended more on the irregular conflict at local level than on conventional battles between the British and Continental armies. . . . [N]either side could deploy sufficient regulars to protect its own supporters, hence the spread of uncontrolled guerrilla war through Georgia and the Carolinas. . . . [T]he American militias proved very difficult to eliminate, representing, "a great spongy, mass that could be pushed aside or maimed temporarily but that had no vital center and could not be destroyed."
>
> From the point of view of the American rebels, the militia was a vital coercive element, since Loyalism generally failed to flourish without a British regular presence. Neither British nor American generals entirely understood this.[9]

Insurgency against the Napoleonic Empire

Uprisings in the Tyrol, Calabria, and Spain in the Early 1800s

A brief and broad overview (review) of these insurrections is equally important to our own American story for the lessons it offers us at present as we struggle with insurgency, this time not from the side and romanticisms of the revolutionary but rather from role of occupier and imperial state (the hegemon).

All three of these uprisings against the Napoleonic Empire—Tyrol, Calabria, and Spain

- occurred in regions where there was already a tradition of banditry, local military organization (militia), and sociopolitical tensions;

- occurred where loyalty to the Catholic Church (the dominant religious authority in the region at that time) was strong;
- occurred in regions of endemic brigandage;
- occurred in regions of grinding poverty and near-feudalism regions;
- occurred in regions where despite localized rivalries and vendettas between local brigand groupings, all opposition groups shared a common hostility toward the centralizing influence of the French presence and activity.

The best known of these insurrections was that which occurred in Spain between 1808 and 1814. As Professor Ian Beckett summarizes the story,

> Taking advantage of deep internal divisions in Spanish politics, Napoleon moved to take over the country in February 1808 and forced the abdication of the Spanish king in May 1808, declaring his own brother, Joseph, King of Spain. The Spanish army was soon routed and a British army sent to help driven into the sea at Corunna in January 1809, Napoleon mistakenly declaring the "Spanish business" over.[10]

The lessons we can gather from these two stories illuminate several stark parallels—similar circumstances and conditionalities—that we see and face in Iraq. From our early experience as the insurgent, we can see how vitally important and providential to our eventual success in our uprising it was for us to wage a compound campaign premised on a political objective (independence from British rule), justified upon a grievance ("no taxation without equal representation"), and then legitimized through the prosecution of a war-fight that advantaged conventional and unconventional techniques, tactics, and procedures. We also prevailed as a factor of the British Empire's inability and/or unwillingness to muster the quantity of forces required to prosecute their war, to achieve the cause against the insurgents, and perhaps, most important, to protect their Tory supporters and their cause, within which the best long-lasting hopes of the British interests in America resided.

From the Napoleonic cases, we can perhaps see a possible, unwanted future of our own as we endeavor to sustain and maybe even extend our own "empire." The Napoleonic failure seems to be rooted in three causal groupings: failure to define the cause (the war) upon which they embarked, failure to know the "enemy" and the changing nature and aspect of the enemy over time, and failure to see the war beyond its conventional and martial aspects. These three "failings" bring us back to the teachings and warnings of both Clausewitz and Sun Tze before him—the failure to know of war beyond battle and the *military object*, the failure of *mad banditry* (a lack of understanding of one's own cause and effect).

Compounding the lack of understanding of insurgency war and war-fare is the confusion between anti-insurgency and counterinsurgency. The relevancy of the difference has been minimized in public debate and dialogue, either indirectly through the continued misrepresentation and misuse of the terms or directly in statements that relegate the distinction to a mere matter of wordplay: semantics.

Nothing less than the difference between winning and losing in an insurgent war lies in this so-called wordplay.

If it was not bad enough that the United States refused to recognize the war in Iraq as at least in part an insurgency until November 2003, then calling our overall campaign approach to fighting this insurgency a counterinsurgency only adds to the collective confusion and accelerates our strategy along a path of military misfortune and possible loss of the political war. What we have been waging in Iraq falls more under the doctrinal rubric of antioperations (close-with-to-destroy, lethal combative strike operations against enemy forces, be they conventional armies, insurgents, or terrorists) than counterinsurgent operations. To win in insurgency, one must wage a comprehensive counterinsurgent war-strategy, reflective of a comprehensive and legitimate political objective. A successful counterinsurgency campaign is a political enterprise—at least a five-pronged and integrated plan incorporating diplomacy, economic recovery and prosperity-building programs, public communications and relations programs, acculturation and socialization programs, civil governance-building and legitimizing programs, and military programs. A counterinsurgency campaign is holistic in its purposes, its methods, and its means. In a counterinsurgency campaign, the key to a lasting and legitimate peace (i.e., decisive) victory is not to be found in the military function (close-with-to-destroy, anti-insurgency) alone. In fact, such a one-pronged and obviously militaristic approach more often feeds and fuels an insurgency rather than quelling it. From a Western perspective, the British perhaps provide us with the best lessons to be learned. British manuals on colonial policing (as they called it during the eighteenth and nineteenth centuries) increasingly incorporated the introduction of more modern technology but also overemphasized the importance of political perception. British military historian Charles Gwynn's *Imperial Policing* (1934)[11] both laid down four principles of imperial policing that were proved at the time to be "sufficiently sound to be fundamental to the post-1945 British approach to more politically motivated insurgency":[12]

1. the primacy of the civil power;
2. the use of minimum force;
3. the need for firm and timely action; and
4. the need for cooperation between the civil and military authorities.

I offer that these four principles not only applied to the British in their post-1945 experiences but also serve as the right sort of mission statement to guide current and future U.S. counterinsurgency; these are lessons that we are still struggling to learn today in Iraq.

Back to Iraq, 2004–Present

By May 2003, the growing opposition was allowed to redefine the war, through its guerrilla-like and terrorist actions on the ground, as an insurgency—a crisis of political legitimacy. The "crisis of legitimacy" that began in mid-2003 and that progressively gained strength over the next few months could have been greatly stifled, even prevented outright, if U.S. and coalition forces had taken the time to reassess the situation and conditions of the war in Iraq and redefine the kind of war "required" at this stage in Iraq: a preventive war of counterinsurgency or rather a war focused on the removal of or avoidance of the potential rise of the causes of irregular, guerilla-style, insurgent war-fare through methods that we in the past have called peace-making, nation-building, "engagement," and most recently regard as stabilization and reconstruction operations.

Redefining the war as a war of "preventive counterinsurgency" in May 2003 would have required the commensurate redesign and reallocation of resources of the war-plan, from the MCO of Phases I–III to the theaterwide ("theater-strategic") civil-military campaign required of a countrywide counterinsurgency (e.g., the British "Malaysia Model" of the 1940s–1960s). This kind of counterinsurgency war might have more effectively focused and integrated the good civil-military stabilization and reconstruction works taking place at the local levels into a comprehensive and synchronized theaterwide campaign initiative with a purpose of setting the conditions for the beginning of a new Iraqi governance, *of the Iraqi people, by the people, and for the people.* Instead, all these good tactical actions lacked a clear and coherent strategic purpose and allowed a growing opposition to recast public perception of our collective activities as, at best, a muddling effort on the part of the U.S. coalition to assist the Iraqi people in their nation-rebuilding efforts or, at worst, as a deliberate decision by the coalition to undercommit to the Iraqi future while, instead, focusing on its own exit strategy.

Not until November 2003 did U.S. and coalition forces in Iraq begin to call and consider the war as a counterinsurgency. Even then, calling it a counterinsurgency was not good enough. Defining the war accurately was a necessary but not sufficient condition for success. Getting the number of forces right for an effective countrywide counterinsurgency campaign was essential. Directing new ways of applying military power on behalf of counterinsurgency efforts and ensuring a consistent application of counterinsurgent ways and means theaterwide was another necessary and essential requirement.

Counterinsurgency in Northern Iraq, May 2003–March 2004

Some U.S. military districts (multinational division areas of operation [MND-AOs]) constructed counterinsurgency operational plans and arrayed their battlefield geometry, reallocated and integrated available civil-military resources, and even modified their tactics, techniques, and procedures (TTPs) to execute a true-to-form counterinsurgency campaign. The actions and operations of the 101st Airborne Division (Air Assault) in northern Iraq are a case in point. From June 2003 to March 2004, northern Iraq was the symbol of what "right might look like" for a future pro-progress Iraq. The four northern provinces in Iraq were by December 2003 viewed by the CPA and more importantly by the Interim Iraqi Government itself as meeting conditions for transfer of "local control" to the Iraqis themselves. One of the main reasons why the north proved somewhat "exceptional" was, simply, the northern provinces were *not* the Sunni Triangle. Perhaps the north was already more benign and pacified than other areas of the country. This explanation cannot be denied, but it is suppositional. An opposite supposition can be posed: the theater-strategic conditions in the northern provinces (the challenges of keeping cries for Kurdish nationhood in check and keeping Syrian and Iranian "influences" out of the mix) that could place the potential threat of the north at parity with the Sunni Triangle.

The point here is not to engage in a "my war was tougher than your war" argument. Neither is the intent to say that one or a few units "did it better" than others. The point is to begin to get honest about the conditions of the war on the ground within the various MND-AOs and reassess and evaluate each of these areas of operation as the separate "wars" they have become due to a combination of factors: natural conditions, geography (and proximity/susceptibility to "external" influences), operational and tactical approaches to the conduct of the war-fight (anti-insurgency versus counterinsurgency), and so on. Plainly stated, the 101st Airborne waged a different war in the north than was waged in other parts. Winning the hearts and minds of the Iraqi people was the guiding purpose of all civil-military actions in the north—by definition, a counterinsurgency campaign in which the approach in other parts of the Iraqi theater of operations was at most "anti-insurgency" operations; they were activities that centered on the destruction through direct (and often lethal) means of the insurgent threat. Some areas merited and allowed more for a *counterinsurgency* approach, while others demanded a more heavy-handed *anti-insurgency* posture. The difference between a counterinsurgency and an anti-insurgency campaign is a vital one to understand. Equally important is for us to reevaluate the operational methods and tactical actions U.S. and coalition forces employed in various areas of operation over the past two years not just for the historians' interests but also to determine how much of the relative success or lack of success within particular areas of the country (the Arab-Kurd north, the Sunni center, the Shia south, etc.) was attributable to "how" war was defined, approached, and conducted in these different areas.

Reassessing our past performances in this manner is not meant to judge the pure and noble courage and dedication of all U.S., coalition, and Iraqi forces that did, and are still doing, the heavy lifting in Iraq but rather to triage our overall war-strategy for Iraq and to honestly determine the impacts and implications of our tactical actions. Did the ways in which we approached and executed the war in certain locales contribute unwittingly to the poor conditions in these areas? Only by discovering and accepting the impacts of our past actions (and inactions) can our nation and its military confidently readjust our war- and peace-winning strategies for a more positive result in the future of this ongoing war and the wars and interventions that may be waiting for us just around the corner.

The War of Revolution, April 2004–January 2005

The escalation of anticoalition force (ACF) attacks in April 2004 is, in hindsight, popularly regarded as the beginning of the war of insurgency in Iraq. The first Battle of Fallujah, and the subsequent withdrawal of U.S. forces from that city in May 2004, serves as a marker event for the rise of the insurgency. In fact, November 2003—"Black November"—is a more accurate marker for the beginning of the formal insurgents' war in Iraq. The months of December 2003 to March 2004 marked a theaterwide troop rotation period, with the largest troop rotation occurring during this period (over 120,000) since World War II. It was during this same time period when the theater-level command headquarters, Combined Joint Task Force-7 (CJTF-7), transitioned, transferring authority from V Corps to III Corps. It was actually during this time of operational transition when opposition forces consolidated and organized for a deliberate guerilla war. Delay on the part of U.S. and coalition forces to formally declare the war a counterinsurgency forestalled the recasting of available resources, civilian and military, to counterinsurgency (establishment of a "civil-military-police" triumvirate strategy) operations and activities theaterwide.

The war U.S. forces and its coalition and ISF has been fighting since March 2004 has been an *anti-insurgency war*—a war relegated to operations not designed to win "hearts and minds" (i.e., a counterinsurgency) but instead designed to kill guerillas.[13] Our allowance of the situation in Iraq to become limited in this way to the insurgents' agenda not only contributed to rising questions of the "winnability" of the war in Iraq but also fed a rising sense of illegitimacy of the U.S. cause and purpose in Iraq among Americans at home (in a sense, giving rise to a homegrown insurgency of our own over the issue of the war for Iraq) and a growing pessimism globally of the possibility of a positive future for Iraq. Commanders on the ground have become not only comfortable but also confident in their actions in the warfight as being no longer an effort at winning the hearts and minds of the Iraqi people but rather an effort to simply coax the people into participating in the January 2005 elections. This sort of message is an unfortunate sign of the real times in Iraq—an indication of the state of affairs of the war and an unfortunate indicator that we may still be overly focused on fighting and winning an anti-insurgency rather than setting conditions for Iraqi nationalism through conduct of a counterinsurgency campaign.

The War for an Iraqi Republic, January 2005–?

What kind of war will we face in the afterglow of a successful Iraqi election? Undoubtedly, it will be a war of our own choosing, whether it be by deliberate choice or the sort of choosing that comes from a missed opportunity to rethink, regroup, reconceive, and recast the war to our own purpose. To win, the kind of war we need to wage in Iraq is a war "for" Iraq; it should be a war of, for, and by the Iraqi people themselves. As Clausewitz said, "all wars are acts of force to compel the enemy to do our will . . . . continuations of policy by other means." All wars are political. The success of the Iraqi elections for a National Assembly on January 30, 2005 opens new opportunity for reframing the war. There is still a revolutionary war ongoing in Iraq (an internal political conflict for legitimacy within the country) that must be fought and won by pronationalist forces. But this revolutionary war must be a war with a broader purpose; this war must become a War for Iraqi Nationalism and republicanism (small "R") in order to fight and win the revolutionary war within. This War for Iraqi Nationalism must, first and foremost, be an Iraqi war for nationhood—one nation. American and other foreign forces cannot win this war for Iraq. But we can contribute to its loss if we "follow and support" our civil-military efforts in a manner that either indicates an intent to "cut and run" or that can be reinterpreted by insurgent forces (and misperceived by the Iraqi people) as a self-centered commitment to the war in Iraq only on behalf of U.S. geopolitical and geoeconomic interests. Labeling the U.S. commitment to the war in Iraq as a commitment to Iraqi *democratization* may play well in America and Western democracies, but in a country such as Iraq and a region such as the Middle East merely setting the agenda in "democratization" terms, despite the benevolence of our intentions, is widely susceptible to reinterpretation by those who oppose us and those who simply know no better, as a code for colonialization, exploitation, and Western imperialism.

The United States must legitimize its stated war ends in Iraq (to support the Iraqis in their struggle for liberty and a nationhood based on democratic ideals) in the ways in which it arrays its available power (military and beyond) in support of

Iraqi government objectives and how it resources those operational ways with the wide assortment of civil-military capabilities the United States' possesses. A mismatch between U.S. and coalition force ends, ways, and means in Iraq can undercut this War for Iraqi Nationalism and unintentionally feed a different war—a continuation of the revolutionary war in Iraq, the rise of a civil war for Iraq, or even a spillover conventional war throughout the region.

Conclusion: *This* Kind of War!

What kind of war needs to progress in Iraq at present, and what should America's role be in that war? The following is one offering of what such a War for Iraqi Nationalism should be, and what our role should be in support of it.

One grand strategy, simply and succinctly stated, could be to keep Iran and other external players *out*, keep the Shia and Kurd "majority" factions *down*, and bring the Sunnis *back in*.

Such a strategy, simple as it may sound, would actually be quite complex and demanding in its execution but could be an effective way of reframing the war in Iraq as a War for Iraqi Nationalism—a conflict of both an internal (revolutionary war, civil war) dimension and an external dimension, with the ever-present possibility of an external war of aggression (a territorial violation of Iraq's sovereignty by conventional or transnational insurgent and terrorist incursion) from a neighboring country.

Table 7.2 summarizes one possible war-policy for this new war for Iraq.

The concept of shifting from a posture of local control to regional presence to strategic overwatch is not a novel idea. The CPA strategic plan (dated January 2004) laid out this three-stage strategy. However, this strategic idea has suffered from a lack of theaterwide operationalization and reallocation and distribution of capabilities (civilian and military, diplomatic, informational, economic, military) commensurate with each progressive stage. Time-centric exit stratagems have filled the void left by there being no comprehensive, theaterwide conditions-based campaign plan driven and defined by endstate rather than enddates.

The "isolation" of Iraq from the unwanted and unwarranted influences of external forces (i.e., Iraq's state neighbors, transnational terrorists and insurgent operations, etc.) could become a key variable in the potential success of legitimate democratization in Iraq. The assurance of territorial sovereignty is an essential criteria for recognition of legitimate nation-state status and sovereignty in international law and convention. To say the least, Iraq's state of territorial sovereignty remains questionable. While the major official points of entry along its extensive border regions appear to be adequately and reliably secure, as indicated by Iraq's ability to control entry and exit during the recent national elections, the immaturity of ISF in terms of quantity available and the quality of training leaves the country susceptible to significant border incursions. Until Iraq can prove its capacity for stabilizing its territorial boundaries, questions over the legitimacy of the Iraqi nation will persist. The threat of external incursions by external forces directly threatens and compromises the internal war "for" Iraq—the democratization and nation-building process itself. One of the unique conditions benefiting America's own democratization process was insularity. The American experiment was relatively isolated by geography and distance from the unwarranted influences of "other" powers. America's

Table 7.2 Ends Related to Intentions, Objectives Related to Means

	Iraqi National Assembly	U.S. and Coalition Forces
Ends	• Establish/select a representative committee for drafting of a national constitution.	• Assure the U.S./intelligence "publics" of our commitment to a limited U.S. military "presence" in Iraq, in terms of scope and scale of mission.
	• Craft and "ratify" a national constitution.	• United States is committed to a civil-military presencewith a purpose of "following and supporting" Iraqinationhood and territorial sovereignty of Iraq.
	• Set conditions for a late 2005/ early 2006 "free" national election.	• U.S. definition of its "democratization" strategy in Iraq is to set conditions for Iraqi legitimization of a freely elected Iraqi our commitment to end to military presence "republic" and reinforce once these minimum conditions are set.
	• Formally reconsider scope and scale of continued U.S./foreign military presence and support in Iraq.	• "Contain" the democratization process within Iraq and secure it from unwarranted outside influences.
Ways	• Ensure equitable representation of majority/ minority factions on all select committees.	• Establishment of a deliberate, conditions-based (not time-based) plan for rearrayal of forces from a local control to regional presence to strategic overwatch posture (inside to outside presence and posture).
	• Incorporate a "bicameral-like" check and balance structure, integrating tribal affiliations (a "Tribal Council" as an combined auxiliary parliamentary chamber for assurance of representation).	• Conditions-based refocus of civil-military operations from internal security to external security mission focus (endstate posture may resemble a small civil-military advisory group presence and role for assistance to the Iraqis in internal security combined with a military presence on Iraq's borders for assurance military presence on through "armed suasion").
	• Set a post-2006 election summit date for reconsideration of future foreign presence policy.	
Means	• Continue to organize, recruit, and train all types of Iraqi Security Forces.	• *Near-term objectives*: Condition-based, stay the course on military presence (allow a small "token" redeployment of some U.S. forces as a confidence builder for Iraq and U.S. public opinion), begin toorganize and deploy civil-military advisory teams with Iraqi Security Force units and local/regional governing councils.
	• Develop a Professional Military and Civil Service Education Program that includes a robust	• *Short-term objectives*: Shift military presence from local control to regional presence posture. • *Long-term objectives*: Shift military presence to "strategic overwatch" posture; forward presence

Continued

Table 7.2 Continued

	Iraqi National Assembly	U.S. and Coalition Forces
	schooling- abroad program with the intent of growing Iraq's future leader pool (civil-military).	on Iraq's borders for assurance of regional friends and armed suasion against potential interlopers. • "Civil-military" assistance and "maneuver enhancement" become key counterinsurgency supporting tasks for U.S. and coalition ground forces; U.S. and coalition combat and multiagency forces (OGA) continue to follow and support Iraqi government and security forces in anti-insurgent and antiterrorist activities.

Source: Major Isaiah Wilson, III, February 2005.

island-nation condition was instrumental in its democratization, setting conditions where Americans were permitted to struggle among themselves on behalf of their future as a nation-state. Iraq, geographically, does not benefit from this special providence. However, one legitimate role for U.S. and coalition military forces in Iraq over the long run could be in establishing conditions similar to geographic insularity, by posting U.S. forces along the territorial borders and around key and vital infrastructure nodes within the country, in order to directly enhance external security (and promote territorial sovereignty) and in doing so enhance Iraq's internal security situation, indirectly. In this way, U.S. forces could be used, at the request of the Iraqi government and the endorsement of the American public, to "isolate" the democratization process—protecting the internal political discourse from external threats as well as taking certain ethnoreligious issues (key and contentious terrain) off of the table, setting the best conditions possible for a successful and legitimate democratization experience in Iraq.

A new logic and rationality can be given to some of the U.S. military activities taking place on the ground in Iraq (i.e., the establishment of semipermanent fixed bases, the retention of a large complement of U.S. military force in and around Iraq, etc.) by taking the time and making the effort to redefine the kind of war the United States now "sees" in Iraq and is now dedicated and recommitted to supporting. The Iraqi people and their newly elected leadership can be reassured of America's commitment of friendship to Iraq and of its commitment to supporting the rise of an Iraqi representative republican nation-state for Iraq, not for the United States, through a clear and open redefinition of the war. The international community can be reassured of America's return to status as a *reluctant* belligerent, a promoter of liberty and self-determination, and a nation with no imperial interests in territorial acquisition.

Finally, the American public can be reassured of America's commitment to the ideals of self-determination and global freedom, and not American empire-building. We can all be reassured that the terrible sacrifices our nation has suffered in 2003–2005 in Iraq are serving a higher and moral purpose that goes far beyond the immediacies of partisan politics—that the dictum "I am my brother's keeper" is much more for Americans and America than a trite slogan and perhaps, most importantly, that the blood we have shed on behalf of a better future for the Iraqi people is a truer indicator than any other that "brother" goes well beyond our water's edge. Our next supreme act of judgment must be in clearly and candidly redeciding what kind of war "our" war in Iraq is to be. The outcome of this calculus will not only shape the next decade of America's foreign policy but will also be telltale for the world community—and for ourselves—of what kind of nation America is to be in this millennium.

Chapter 8

Whither Mosul? The Story of Transition Failure and the Rise and Fall of Northern Iraq

In December 2004, 14 American soldiers were killed and over a hundred injured when an explosion struck an open-tent mess hall in Mosul, the prime city of Iraq's northern provinces and third largest city in the country. The attack, believed to have come from a suicide bomber working from *inside-the-wire* information, was still by the time of this writing one of the most costly attacks on U.S. troops during the war. This assault was one of a string of attacks centered in and around the *viyalet* (state) of Mosul and part of a growing instability throughout the northern provinces. The mess hall attack in Mosul came on the immediate heels of the November 2004 Battle of Fallujah (Operation Phantom Fury)—a major U.S. Marine Corps and Iraqi Security Forces (ISF) combined anti-insurgency operation. While it was presumed, and to a large degree true, that the growing instability in Mosul was the consequence of the "squeezing" of Fallujah and the consequent flight of insurgents and transnational jihadists from that city to the north, instability had begun to return at a moderate pace to the north as early as Spring 2004. For the previous year, Mosul and the four northern provinces (Ninevah, Dahuk, Irbil, As Sulaymaniyah) had been the near-picture-perfect examples of all that was going well with the U.S. war-policy and the Coalition Provisional Authority's (CPA) and Interim Iraqi Government's civil reconstruction agendas. The war had by all accounts been working in the north. So much confidence there was that the north was a story of a successful liberation, occupation, and stabilization that CPA—and the Iraqis themselves—had collectively determined by December 2003 to select the northern provinces as the first provinces for transfer of stabilization and reconstruction authority to local control. How could the situation in the north have degraded so completely and so rapidly?

This was the question that began to haunt me soon after my return stateside in February 2004 as I watched, first, the fall of Tall Afar, a major border city in northwestern Iraq, and, finally, the compromise of Mosul itself. This was also the question I began receiving from academics and journalists in Fall and Winter 2004 and particularly after the Mosul mess hall bombing. The answer is complicated, and for most who had posed the question to me they lacked the time—or frankly the interest or patience—to take in a full explanation. As such, I never gave any sort of answer—not wanting to add to the cavalcade of misconceptions and misrepresentations of the truths to the happenings and going-ons in Iraq at the time—and since.

The Fall of the North—A Relevant Case Study

The peculiarity of northern Iraq's relative "rise" as a pacified and stabilized (recovering) region during the first year of the war in/for Iraq (2003) as well as its subsequent "fall" into instability and insurgency since 2004 is a relevant case for study.

The Popular Explanations

There have been many "he said, she said," second-, third-, and nth-hand accounts of why the situation in Mosul and the northern provinces degraded as and when it did. These explanations range from the pure naturalist (evolution) interpretations (i.e., the decline was a natural occurrence arriving with the countrywide advancement of the insurgency) to full "creationism" explanations (i.e., the decline of the north was due to an intelligent design of our own making). A healthy selection of these latter explanations attempted to level culpability directly on the 101st Airborne Division and the shoulders of the unit's commanding general, Major General David Petraeus.[1] Some high-ranking officials within the CPA and the U.S. Department of State began around Fall 2004 to rumor that the state of stability in northern Iraq under the watch of the 101st Airborne had been overoptimistic and more rhetoric than substance. Some went further, positing theories that the leadership of the 101st had been duped by local and regional Iraqi leaders—that the Iraqis had feigned support and "friendship" to the Division in order to suck reconstruction dollars from the United States. A few even went as far as to indirectly accuse the war-approach of the 101st Airborne of strengthening the insurgency.

In this chapter, I will try to overcome my own bias and address these explanations. I will also offer my own explanation from the perspective of someone who was on the ground in the north and had a direct hand in its rise and perhaps an indirect hand in its decline.

On Transitioning

Not a lot has been written on transitions in war-fare. The historical literature on modern, Western military operations offers scant anecdotal insights on transition operations in past wars and armed interventions. Historical records provide brief snapshots of how forces were initially mobilized and how those forces were initially deployed into a theater of operations. Very few, if any, observations have been annotated for official records on the redeployment of forces from a theater of operations at the completion of a campaign. Standing doctrinal records do better but not well enough. The U.S. military maintains an adequate body of knowledge—approved ways of doing business—on the mobilization of armed forces, the deployment of those forces into a theater of war, the reception, onward movement into theater, and integration of those forces into tactical war-fighting force packages (reception, staging, onward movement, and integration [RSO&I]). On the conduct of military, civil-military, and peace operations once battles have been engaged, the U.S.

military maintains a robust and effective body of doctrine. If someone is looking for the definitive word on how to get a combat force (martial or nonmartial) into a theater of operation or how to fight that force in a series of battles and engagements, then U.S. military doctrine is the right source.

However, if that same someone were to cull through existing doctrinal manuals for insights and methods and operational ways of transitioning from one particular category of operations to another within a long and protracted campaign, that someone would be left wanting.

Wars may be fought battle by battle, but they are eventually won, lost, or left unfinished by how coherent day-to-day engagements are tied together in time, space, and common purpose. Achievement of a decisive campaign (theaterwide) victory is a result of the comprehensiveness of the campaign plan. This, in turn, depends on how well one anticipates and adjusts for changes in the nature of the intervention. A campaign (civil, military, or both) can be regarded as the tying together and sequencing of a series of battles and engagements (tactical-level activities) in a common time and space, all derived from a common strategic purpose. Campaigns are composed of major operations; operations are composed of battles and engagements. Operational planners typically and traditionally have developed plans for campaigns and major operations by sequencing—or phasing—civil and military (martial and extramartial) activities based upon a particular temporal and spatial construct. The end of one operational phase is normally easy to predetermine and is most often defined, at least in the military vernacular, as an operational objective. Similarly, the beginning of subsequent operational phases is often as easily surmised, if for no other reason than the inherent ability of the offensive opponent (the aggressor) to set new conditions through gaining and maintaining the operational and tactical initiative. Having the raw capacity to do something—anything—during a fast-paced and ambiguous civil-military engagement or operation can be a determining capability of short-term success in a major operation or campaign. And again, the United States has a preponderant amount of this sort of raw tactical capacity, a literal get-out-of-jail free card, an ace in the hole.

Rarely is much thought or planning effort given to that period of time and space lying *between* the end of one operational phase and the initiation of a subsequent one. It is in this domain where the challenges of *transition* lie.

The challenges of transition lie at the policy-setting level of campaign planning. A change in policy intent is perhaps the clearest defining variable of a policy-level transition. A change in intent most often equates to, or initiates, a change in mission purpose. Failure to make such policy shifts clear to civil-military planners can promote an "out-of-phase" misalignment between the policy goals originally guiding operations and the operations themselves.

Transition challenges exist at the operational (formulation and legitimization) level of the campaign—that level of planning where the purpose of the campaign is transformed ("operationalized") into a legitimate or, rather, into an executable plan. This is the rubber-meets-the-road dimension of the campaign plan where transition is most susceptible to failure. Making a plan executable relies on how well the plan can be manned, equipped, and sustained logistically and from a command and control aspect.

There is a cause and effect dimension to the challenges of transition at the tactical level of the campaign plan—where the plan actually gets put into play or implemented. A failure to properly or adequately compose and field a force package (a capability package) for the conduct of a battle or series of battles or similar activities, either due to a failure on the part of the tactical or operational "command(er)" to request and array forces or on the part of the policy decision makers and policy makers to appropriate the right type and quantity of capabilities in the first place, can be the cause of significant ends-means misalignments or the result of the same.

Operation Iraqi Freedom: A Story of Flawed Transitioning

It is difficult to pinpoint the beginning of the story of transition failure. However, several recent popular writings on the war have intimated an important marker event in that story in their discussions on the lack of a postwar plan for Iraq and, more specifically, the immaturity of the organization originally designed for leading the postwar-effort in Iraq—the Office for Reconstruction and Humanitarian Assistance (ORHA).[2]

While these accounts make note of ORHA's anemic organizational structure and operational capacity, few offer answers to why the organization was seemingly destined to fail. *Why was General Garner's team, individually some of the most experienced and brightest of experts in reconstruction and humanitarian assistance operations, as a collective entity too little and too late for the mission of rebuilding Iraq?* Much of the failure lies not in "who" was ORHA but rather in "what" ORHA was seen as being (or rather what it was not seen as being) and *how* and *when* it was integrated into the operational plan.

In *Squandered Victory*, Larry Diamond provides a relatively detailed account of the rise and fall of ORHA. As he tells it, the ineffectiveness of the organization was apparent from the very beginning of prewar deliberations—bitter, relentless infighting—between U.S. government agencies over who should govern in "postwar" Iraq. In an interview that Diamond conducted with an Iraqi American who had participated in these interagency discussions, the following was said:

> There was never any discussion of *how* the Pentagon would implement their plan, or anybody else's. There was never any dialogue on it. Each group had its own plan, but nothing ever got done or decided because of the infighting.[3]

The problems continued to mount when President Bush appointed the Department of Defense (DOD) as lead agency in charge of "postwar" Iraq. Many have argued that this was—and is—the primal cause for the bungled stabilization and reconstruction effort in Iraq.[4] I disagree. That is not to say that the failure of the administration, after appointing the Pentagon as lead agency, to supervise and ensure an effective incorporation of other governmental (i.e., state) and nongovernmental organizations with long histories and experiences in reconstruction operations as supporting arms of the military effort had no negative impact on policy outcome. It surely had a significant impact. The bald reality of the Iraq War is this: the situation on the ground has never been "stable and secure." As the *New York Times* expressed it, "[I]t was the first time since World War II that the State Department would not take charge of a post-conflict situation."[5] But the situation in Iraq—the conditions on the ground—never measured up to what could be logically labeled as a "postconflict" environment. As a war-zone, Pentagon was probably the correct organization for the postmajor combat operations phases of the war. However, this appointment of the DOD as lead should never have been interpreted by DOD—nor allowed to be interpreted in this manner by the president—as a Pentagon monopoly over the war-policy.

I believe that the really significant—and telling—failings were (1) the administration failing to ensure a cooperative planning and execution symbiosis between the lead agency (Pentagon) and all other "supporting organizations"; and (2) the failure of this "collective" to properly scope and scale the "War," prior to the initiation of it, to the fullest extent of its nature. The Pentagon's de facto monopoly over the war-planning unintentionally condemned us all to an inability to see the war beyond the combatives and limited our functions in the war to tactical actions. We had no operational plan for the "whole war," and without such a comprehensive ("holistic") campaign plan, we have been limited to waging the war piecemeal—battle by battle, whether those "battles" be anti-insurgent or pro-reconstruction.

Once assigned as lead agency (or in the military/joint vernacular—"Supported Command"), Secretary Rumsfeld appointed General (Ret.) Jay M. Garner to head ORHA. Garner was selected based on his successful command of the 1991 Operation Provide Comfort—the mission to assist the Kurds at the end of the First Gulf War. The effort was not only woefully too late (Garner was appointed on January 20, 2003—less than two months prior to initiation of the war) but also wrongly conceived as merely a struggle to overthrow the preexisting regime rather than the larger affair the mission was by its nature preordained to be: a mission to support the building of a new regime once the old Hussein regime was ousted. The Pentagon's "vision" of the "postwar" as a humanitarian aid effort reflected in the appointment of a personality such as General (Ret.) Garner—a "military someone" with recent "humanitarian assistance" in Iraq—and fatally flawed the entire scoping and scaling (i.e., timing, resourcing, purposing) of the war. State Department experts in civil administration and reconstruction activities as well as similar experts from other governmental and nongovernmental agencies were to varying degrees discounted; too few made the late-in-coming ORHA team, exacerbating the already-doomed venture even more with a lack of the right mix of civil-military experts—folks who perhaps could have overcome the late start and successfully accelerated the efforts to come up with an executable plan to "win the peace." Some accounts have said that this dismissing of relevant expertise from the ranks of ORHA was partisan-politically driven.[6] Though possibly true, I believe the dismissal was more a *sin of omission*—Rumsfeld and the Pentagon failed to see the need for certain beyond-the-military experts because of the way the Pentagon was (and is!) *designed* (organizationally and culturally) to see the situation in Iraq at the time—a postwar and humanitarian-based operational set. How the relevant players at the strategic levels saw Iraq determined how we organized for the fight at the operational level of the war-policy. How we organized for the "fight" unfortunately did not adequately incorporate the majority of the "War-fight": the "beyond-war" (stabilization and reconstruction) activities. This operational-level flaw has condemned our tactical "wins" on the ground in Iraq (the noble actions of the soldiers and humanitarian workers) to just that—tactical wins. We have been unable to effectively convert ("Transition") tactical wins into strategic victories, unlike our adversary, who has been relatively successful in commanding and controlling the *strategic implications of their tactical actions.* In 2004, I wrote that the United States lacked an operational plan for Phase IV (Transition), that because we lacked the plan we came to an operational pause in our war-activities—between April and July 2003—a pause the enemy was able to take advantage of. I also wrote that the consequence of that failure to plan for the whole war has caused us to play a catch-up game ever since.[7] I hold to that same opinion today, an opinion increasingly supported by emerging evidence.

Assessing Transition

Northern Iraq Goes to "Local Control"

What began with the deployment of the 3rd Brigade, 2nd Infantry Division (3/2 IN—Stryker Brigade) into Iraq in November 2003 by the end of May 2004 became the largest troop rotation since World War II, with the replacement of over 130,000 U.S. soldiers completing one-year tours of duty with approximately 120,000 new troops. As complex as these large numbers paint the rotation and transition process to be, the movement of large combat divisions—the people, the combat materiel, and the support equipment—is only one small part of what is a larger, beyond-the-martial process of transitioning in a holistic war-campaign.

To state it bluntly, the first troop rotation (OIF-1 to OIF-2) was a hurried affair indicative of a flawed concept of "Transition" that began with the too little, too late transition of ORHA into the theater of war, that progressed through the ineffective integration of ORHA and its postwar reconstruction efforts into the Combined Forces Land Component Command (CFLCC) and Combined Joint Task Force-7 (CJTF-7) command structures, and that culminated in an anemic transfer of occupation authority and responsibilities throughout the country during the 2003–2004 period. The story of the withering of our war-effort in and around the city and state (*viyalet*) of Mosul is an important vignette in the larger story of our transition failures in Iraq.

Redeployment planning for the northern Iraqi area of operations began as early as July 2003. Keep in mind, in July 2003, the 101st Airborne Division was the major command over all northern provinces. They had been in occupation of the north for three months, and the word from higher headquarters at that time was that the Division would be back home no later than September. I assumed my duties as chief of plans for the Division in early July 2003 and anticipated that my major duty would be in leading the planning effort for our redeployment stateside. As we began to plan, I found it curious—and troubling from a redeployment standpoint—that our Division had not been given any official word on our replacement unit. The operational question of the day was *who would we be handing the battle over to?* No word came initially, but later the words that we did not want to hear came—all OIF-1 units would be continuing mission in Iraq indefinitely but expectedly extended duty for the full year. The news, though not surprising, was nevertheless a shock. All redeployment plans were shelved as I redirected the plans staff toward the development of a post–Phase-IV (Transition) campaign plan for northern Iraq and toward the planning of major combat, stability, reconstruction, and counterinsurgency operations.

It takes time to facilitate the effective transfer of authority (TOA) of an occupied territory over to another occupying force and to redeploy a 16,000-soldier combat

Division out of a combat zone and back to the United States. In fact, it takes months to properly plan for an effective transition. The 101st Airborne, which had arrived (with lead elements) in the theater of war in February 2003, was scheduled for a redeployment back to Fort Campbell, Kentucky, no later than March 2004.[8] By late September, the Division's campaign plan was effectively in play and the plans shop formed a small team to return a focused attention on the redeployment task. As the small operational planning group (OPG) focused on the operational- and tactical-level planning, I worked with higher headquarters in Baghdad (CJTF-7) on unit replacement options (courses of action) and TOA concept plans. Determining who should replace the 101st Airborne and when they should arrive in country to begin to facilitate an effective rotation was key and essential. A major determinant in that calculus had to be measuring and evaluating the preparedness of the northern provinces for the transfer.

Transitioning on Enddates Rather than Endstates

The calculus was an exercise in *bad math* from the very beginning. In early, August all operational units (divisions and separate brigades) received written notice of extension of duties in Iraq. All units would hold in place and should be prepared to remain in Iraq based on a deployment timeline that would retain each unit up to, *but not to exceed*, 12 months from first boots-on-the-ground (BOG) in the theater of operations.[9] How did "higher" arrive at this 12-month timetable? Why a 12-month clock? This simple memorandum and the rally-the-troops letter all units in country received a few weeks later from the Office of the Secretary of Defense (OSD) that expressed gratitude for the soldier's determination and strength to stay the fight set the entire theater of war—the entire war-plan—on a time-based troop rotation cycle, informed more by the politics of the day back in the United States and on Title 10 laws regulating lengths of active duty rotations of National Guard and Reserve units than by the state of conditions on the ground in Iraq. By late summer 2003, a clock was set to guide the U.S. war-approach when, instead, a comprehensive plan should have done so.

What ensued from this time-based transition plan was the setting of a new context to the U.S. approach to occupation, reconstruction, and combat operations in Iraq. Combat divisions—the governing and administrative authorities over Iraq's 18 governorates or provinces—were immediately set on a redeployment timetable, but whether or not this theaterwide timetable synched with the conditionality of each governorate was undetermined at the time the redeployment schedule was set. Division deployment enddates were arbitrarily determined prior to governorate endstates, placing the proverbial *cart before the horse*. Of course, it is true that no plan is perfect (in fact, a perfect plan is often the enemy of a good-enough plan) and that no plan survives first contact. However, what was driving the trains (literally) was a wrongly conceived and wrongly calculated unit rotation plan. *Timing is everything*, but the "everything" must first be determined before a timeline is put to the task. By September 2003, the 101st Airborne was the elder of all operational units still in Iraq since the Spring 2003 march up country. The last elements of the 3rd Infantry Division were already teaming back to the United States. That meant (dictated) that the 101st was the next to return home, the next to hand over its authority and responsibilities to the northern governorates. But did this make sense? Was the north prepared to be next for TOA? Whether or not the 101st was ready to go did not necessarily mean that the north was ready to see the unit go. Moreover, who would replace the 101st? Since it was September 2003—and by timeline the last boots-on-the-ground of the 101st had to be out of Iraq no later than March 2004—was there enough time to prepare the north for the transition, to receive a replacement unit, to educate and orient that replacement to the "ground" in the northern provinces, and to build confidence between our replacement and the northern Iraqis? These were the second-order questions facing the Division and its planners in Fall 2003. They should have been the first-order questions determining the transition plan, but they were not. Instead, our prime set of questions became *how do we get this done to a "good-enough" measure of effectiveness in only five months' time?*

Who Is Our Replacement? Where the Hell Are They?

Though difficult if not impossible to support with empirical data, anecdotal evidence does reinforce the questioning of whether or not the transition (unit rotation) timelines that were set in 2003—12-month unit-based rotation cycles—negatively impacted the effectiveness of stabilization and reconstruction operations in Iraq. It is hard to argue against the realities of planning pressures this timeline placed on operational divisions. With a 12-month mission profile, each major command once entering the theater of war and completing their TOA (Battle Handover and Relief-In-Place in the military vernacular) had only about two to three months (max) of focused efforts toward the stabilization and reconstruction mission—the war-fight—before a significant portion of the unit's planning resources had to be turned toward the unit's impending redeployment operation—a major combat operation in its own right. Similar to a congressperson's lifecycle—a two-year term of office that, because of the importance of campaigning requirements (fundraising, etc.), leaves only about 6 months of effective time for legislating—once a 12-month unit-based schedule was mandated, operational commands were destined to spending more time on getting into the fight and leaving the fight than on the war-fight itself.

Gathering specific and committed information on our replacing unit was *the* important variable in our early mission analysis for redeployment. The answer to this question was as much a political issue as it was an operational one. The operational dilemma was clear enough—we had to know who was replacing us on the ground at the earliest, else we would not have enough time to integrate the replacement unit into the area of operations in time for our own redeployment or in a manner commensurate with a steady and stable—and legitimate—transfer of the Iraqis' future over to a "newcomer" or "foreigner." But the politics of the issue clouded operations and pushed operational concerns somewhat to a side argument, and the politics were severe. A combat force from Turkey was an early option. At least two major political constraints contributed to the derailing of this option. First, wounds were still raw at the national levels over Turkey's refusal earlier in the year to allow U.S. combat forces a northern avenue of advance into Iraq. The refusal was a blow to U.S.-Turkey relations, but there were more relevant operational implications. Turkey's refusal robbed the U.S. military war-plan of its vitally important northern route—a route that would have opened a second front against Saddam's forces, a front that would have allowed the U.S. military to apply increased combat pressure and destruction on Saddam's regime, simultaneously, from opposite directions.

Many have reflected since 2004 of what might have been, had we had the northern front at the start of the war. Many argue that the Turkey refusal allowed many of Saddam's most elite fighting forces—and maybe his weapons of mass destruction (WMD) capacity as well—to fade away, to dissolve, and to slip out of the country and the grasps of U.S. and coalition forces. Many blame the Turkey refusal, at least in part, for unintentionally setting the conditions for the rise of the current transnational insurgency in Iraq.

Turkey's refusal delayed the arrival and operational placement of the 4th Infantry Division—it raised the operational risk of the march-up-country phases of the war (the 4th Infantry Division [4ID] spent the major combat phases of the war on board ships offshore, awaiting permission to enter through Turkey—that offer never came, causing a diversion of the Division to the south for a southern entry). This delay added to the already "too little, too late" campaign approach to the "postwar" mission.

The second political nail that closed the coffin on the Turkey replacement option was related to Turkish-Iraqi-Kurd histories and relations. Turkey's strategic position as a pivot state in the region has served the United States and our European NATO allies well over the past 60-plus years. But the one negative implication of that long-standing relationship has always the cleavage issue of Turkey and the Kurds. Suffice it to say, given that history, Turkey was never a plausible option as a replacement force, at least not for the immediate northern zones. But even still, much time—too much time—was expended on "exploring the option."

The months of September and early October saw planners within the Division and CJTF-7 Headquarters in Baghdad "exploring" a plethora of replacement unit options. These options ranged from Indian units to a Korean replacement.[10] Each possibility led to a planning "spin cycle," where substantial resources (time and planning expertise) had to be devoted toward mission analysis—planning to determine the feasibility, acceptability, and suitability of each option as an effective replacement course of action.

The Stryker Option

As early as August 2003, I and the plans staff had been intrigued by the possibility of the integration of one of the Army's new Stryker Brigades into the fight in northern Iraq. Of the many positive factors supporting the incorporation of the new Stryker capability into northern Iraq, the organizational composition and capability of the unit was determinative.[11] The new Stryker Brigades brought to the fight a mix of combat infantry (riflemen, BOG) capability with state-of-the-art intelligence, surveillance, and reconnaissance (ISR) capability—all packaged in a highly mobile, fleet, lethal, light-armored and light-wheeled vehicle configuration. Stryker also brought a robust and integrated combat support (supply and logistics) capacity, an unmanned aerial vehicle (UAV) capability, and a civilian augmentation force (CAF) family-of-capabilities that gave the organization an effective extended operational reach (i.e., a capacity to physically reach a wide-expansive battle area) and capacity for effective operations of depth ("deep operations" in the sense of informational and cultural depth of operations).[12] Stryker, like all combat configurations, also had its limitations. The Stryker Brigade was just one brigade of combat capabilities. It was configured and organized to meet a wide range of threat scenarios—to provide the U.S. Army with a "middleweight" force that would help bridge the operational gap between the Army's "light forces" and its heavy, mechanized forces. But there was no magical genie in that bottle—Stryker was not the end-all solution. It was a simple *economy-of-scales* issue—by size alone, Stryker on its own could only effectively "cover" a certain amount of operational "terrain" (geographic and human). *Size does matter* when it comes to properly balancing an operational force to the ground situation.

In late August 2003, the idea of a Stryker Brigade deployment to the north—and to Iraq for that matter—was still a novel idea. The idea was at the most a back-burner, low-probability, albeit thought-provoking, option. Planners in Baghdad who were listening and considering our proposal for Stryker in addition to their own concept plans were reluctant to even present a Stryker-to-the-north option. The reasons were many, but included in those rationales were long-standing branch parochial arguments against the deployment of these new mechanized infantry capabilities into operational environments that were under the operational control of other-than-mech or armor Division command. There were some logical and substantive operational justifications for not assigning a mech-infantry unit to a "light"-infantry command: the complexities of logistically sustaining a mech-infantry organization with the supply and support capabilities organic to a light-infantry organization. Augmentation of the 101st Airborne's logistical tail would be required to adequately support this type of operational addition—something that was completely within the feasibility of the course of action. Other less tangible factors still made the option unacceptable to communities within the U.S. military and beyond. The politics behind Stryker were virulent. This deployment option would be the first operational deployment of this new organizational set—in "combat." The politics that could potentially come out of this deployment—for whatever unit and branch of service in operational command and control of Stryker—would have a substantial branch parochial impact (positive and/or negative). Assignment of Stryker to a mech-armor Division made logistical good sense, but it also offered great potential benefits (depending on the success or failure of the Stryker Brigades) to the Armor Branch. Conversely, assignment of the brigades to a "light-infantry" division might send the wrong message to DOD program authorizers—or defense appropriators on Capitol Hill. Beyond this, there was also great "glory" (or infamy) to be had by becoming the first to command a Stryker Brigade in combat. Just because these factors were "political" did not make them irrelevant for planning consideration. Nevertheless, such factors did complicate the operational planning for transition.

By early October 2003, the improving situation in northern Iraq was becoming evident throughout the theater of war and back in Washington. From our vantage point on the ground in northern Iraq, our campaign plan was finally beginning to bear visible fruit; our localized wins in our stabilization and reconstruction efforts were becoming more and more measurable and reportable. By October, the strategic situation was changing as well. Ambassador Bremer had replaced General Garner a few months prior, and the mission had changed its colors from a humanitarian and reconstruction operation to a full-born occupation and administration mission, under the CPA. The CPA agenda called for a rapid stabilization of the security-political-economic situation in Iraq so as to facilitate a quicker TOA *of postwar Iraq* to an Iraqi authority. The whole idea and context of transition changed with this changing of the American guard in Iraq in late Summer 2003. That change of context did not marry well with the unit rotation schedule already set in motion. The November 15 Agreement of 2003 determined a full TOA over Iraq to an Interim Iraqi Authority *no later than* June 30, 2004. The trickle-down impacts of this grand strategic-level decision on operational-level unit rotation and transfer of local and regional authority planning were substantial. The operational problem was now much more than just a battle handover between one combat organization and another—it was also a transfer of the "War" over to the Iraqis, with U.S. and coalition forces relegating themselves to a "smaller footprint" and a footprint in Iraq that would be *one step behind and to the left* of the Iraqi's lead. The timing was bad enough when the planning problem was a redeployment problem; it became enormously complex now that the problem was one of preparing for a troop rotation *and* ensuring that the situation in northern Iraq was stable and that the Iraqis themselves were adequately prepared to take control of their destinies.

Preparing the North for Local and Regional Control

As luck would have it—as well as effective campaign planning—the northern provinces were, like the southern provinces under the British authorities, the provinces most prepared for transition to *local and regional control.*[13] The Division's campaign plan, tribal engagement plans, and its indirect and holistic approach to the northern war-fight were all working. Daily commander's reports showed a steady and marked improvement along all lines of operation in northern Iraq.[14] Relative to the situation in other regions in Iraq, the north was a success story. For Ambassador Bremer and the CPA, the north soon became the ideal for driving forward on its plan for an earlier-than-originally-scheduled transfer of sovereignty.

The 101st Airborne, along with all other multinational division (MND) commands throughout the theater of war, prepared reports with complete and comprehensive assessments of the state of their region's progress toward local, then regional, and finally strategic overmatch control. Our Division's December 2003 and January 2004 reports reflected the northern provinces in an overall local control state of readiness. Though the three Iraqi-Kurdish provinces of Dahuk, Irbil, and As Sulaymaniyah were judged an overall "Green" status (i.e., ready for local control transfer), we reconsidered that evaluation by assessing the security sector as "amber."

For Ninevah province, particularly the far western regions, the entire region received an "Amber" rating, with the security sector ranging and fluctuating back and forth between "amber" and "red" (i.e., not ready for transfer to local Iraqi control). The assessment was an honest one—conditions had improved significantly in the north, but the stability attained was extremely tenuous (see map 5.2). The rotation of the 101st out of Iraq soon to be followed by an overall transfer of sovereignty of Iraq to the Iraqis was going to take place all at too soon, all within a three to four-month period and at the same time of the overall theaterwide OIF-1 to OIF-2 unit rotation. It was a train wreck in the making.

Preparing for Battle Handover

By mid-October, the 101st finally received notification of its replacement force. The news was bittersweet. On the positive side, we finally had a replacement unit, which meant that we could finally progress our planning from concept development to an operational plan—putting specific units and troops to specific replacement timelines and oriented toward particular transfers of troops to requirements and tasks.[15] The worrisome news was that our replacement unit was to be the 3rd Brigade, 2nd Infantry Division (3/2 IN—Stryker Brigade) augmented by a small ad hoc command and control headquarters out of I Corps Headquarters in Fort Lewis, Washington. My first impression upon receiving this information was that this would be the lead element of what would obviously be a larger contingent of forces to replace us and continue to administer the campaign plan in the north and parent the transfer to local Iraqi control through Spring 2004. That impression was hopeful but wrong. The Stryker Brigade and the I Corps contingent (later known as Task Force Olympia (TFO), in recognition of the organization's Washington State origins) was as good as it was going to get.

Working to Make the Relief-in-Place Work

November 2003 was known as "Black November." Until the April 2004 insurgency explosion, November 2003 was the most deadly month for U.S. and coalition forces. In hindsight, the month-long religious holiday of Ramadan had been used (abused) by anticoalition forces—the fledgling insurgency—as a rallying event for its cause. Our planners had predicted and forewarned of this potentiality, but in spite of the warnings, Black November still arrived. November 2003 found our Division—and the entire theater—back at "War." It also found the 101st in full redeployment and TOA planning and execution mode. Time was fleeting, and oddly, so it seemed that the fragile stability in the north was too. This made our concerns with battle handover to a mere brigade-sized and capable organization more than just a concern—the plan was turning into a high-risk venture, perhaps even a gamble. Our daily and weekly theater assessments and commander's reports reflected a change in the "mood" in northern Iraq—at first a slow degrading of the situation. Yet, trains were already in motion. Even a change in the speed of one moving train (e.g., an acceleration or slowing of a deployment) would have dramatic theater-strategic implications. Outflow and inflow of forces were forced to funnel through one air and sea ports of embarkation and debarkation (aerial port of embarkation/debarkation [APOE/D])—Kuwait. This funnel was fatal and final in it directives for deployment and redeployment; one way in and the same way out meant that our war-plan had to become a slave to a draconian timetable. There was little to no room for modifications, no matter how operationally relevant the rationale for a change to timetable and "plan" may have been.

To add to the complexity—and potential tragedy in the making—we learned in early November of the delay of 3/2 Infantry's arrival for transition and TOA in the north by 30 days.[16] The cause of delay was due to a last-minute request from the 4th Infantry Division (Mechanized)—the MND to our immediate south. The 4ID(M) had argued convincingly to higher headquarters (V Corps/CJTF-7 in Baghdad) that they needed the capabilities of Stryker for a major combat operation directed against a rising transnational terrorists infiltration from the western border areas. The mission was a relevant one and justified the delay and diversion of Stryker. That said, the delay and diversion of 3/2 Infantry would have a lasting impact on the northern TOA and on post-101st approaches to northern operations.

The original plan anticipated a two-and-a-half to a full three-month TOA and battle handover to TFO and Stryker Brigade. This would have seen the arrival of the replacement forces beginning in mid- to late November. Lead battalions from the Arrowhead Brigade (Stryker) did not arrive ("close") in AO North until the end of December 2003 (see map 8.1).

This left only the month of January 2004 for completion of the TOA[17]—30 days to prepare ourselves for redeployment (and to redeploy!), receive a new combat organization into the northern area of operations (under fire), receive and help form a new ad hoc command and control element/headquarters in the north, orient all new elements to the enormous complexity of missions and activities that made up the 101st campaign plan for northern Iraq, and, finally, introduce our replacements to the Iraqis and facilitate a level of comfort and confidence (trust) among them for the incoming "occupiers"—and trust in the new U.S. force in the local Iraqis—that would keep *the genie in the bottle* in northern Iraq. By January, the timing and conditions were not on our side.

The TOA was a major combat operation (MCO) of substantial complexity and risk. Reception and staging of the incoming relieving forces were the first components of TOA. The question of how and where to literally "fit" the arrival of nearly 10,000 troops and their complementary equipment was a driving factor and constraint to this stage of planning and execution. The second major component of the TOA was integration of the newly arriving forces physically into their occupation and operational zones as well as functionally and psychologically into the missions and activities within their areas of influence. This integration stage in military doctrine is regarded as *relief-in-place* and *passage-of-lines* operations (see map 8.2).[18]

Next would come the actual formal TOA—a relatively short but critical array of tasks and functions conducted jointly between the outgoing command teams, incoming command teams, and the local Iraqi leadership. TOA ceremonies were essential tasks in that they helped to legitimize the transition with the local population. Following TOA would come the onward movement of 101st Airborne elements out of country, by combinations of air movement and ground movement south, and sea departures—the actual redeployment itself. All of these activities, combined, made up the Transition Operation in northern Iraq. The execution was part sequential, with the actioning of some activities dependent on the actioning of one or a series of priors, and part simultaneous. Also, there was not only one large TOA but actually at least nine separate "mini-TOAs" ongoing semisimultaneously within the broad overall AO North Transition Operation. While the Division headquarters facilitated the overall transition, it was also executing its own TOA operation with TFO (TOAs 1 and 2). Each of our brigade combat teams (BCTs), commanding and controlling the three major areas of operation within AO North—with our 1BCT controlling our southern sector, 2BCT controlling Mosul proper, and our 3BCT controlling our western sectors (TOAs 3–5). The three northern Iraqi-Kurd governorates of Dahuk, Irbil, and As Sulaymaniyah were under the command and control of our 406th Civil Affairs Battalion (CAB)—these areas of operation were TOAed with special operating forces (SOF) and a myriad of other civil affairs and nongovernmental organizations (TOAs 6–8).[19] Lastly, there was the TOA over logistical (services and supply) operations in AO North. Logistics operations for AO North were commanded and controlled by the 101st Corps Support Group (101 CSG) and the Division's organic Division Support Command

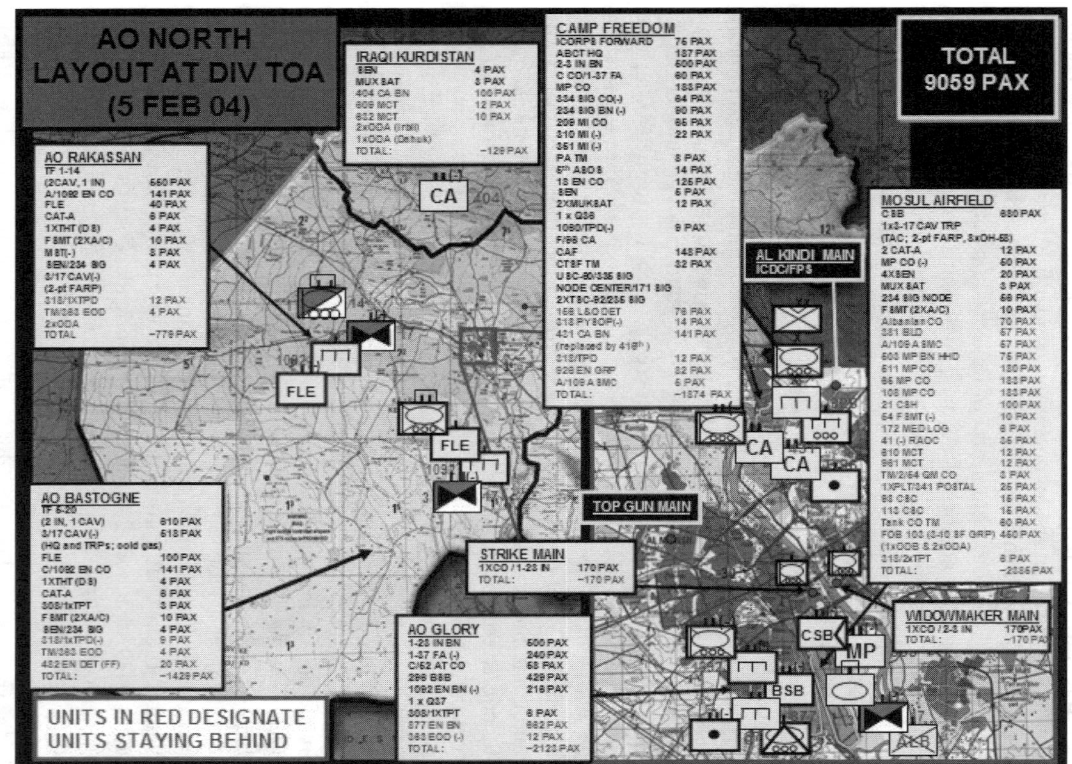

Map 8.1 AO North Layout, February 2004

Source: Official 101st Airborne Division planning briefings (unclassified versions and/or declassified materials), June 2003–May 2005.

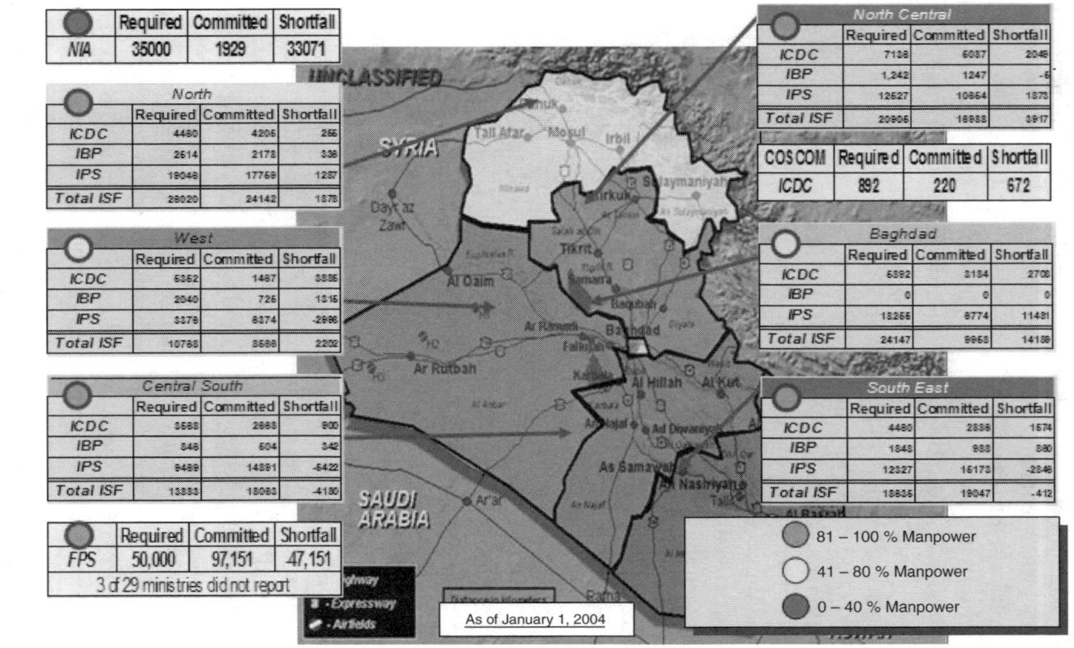

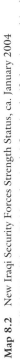

Map 8.2 New Iraqi Security Forces Strength Status, ca. January 2004

Source: Official 101st Airborne Division planning briefings (unclassified versions and/or declassified materials), June 2003–May 2005.

(DISCOM) and would be transferred over to an equivalent logistical organization provided by 3/2 Infantry, albeit at a much smaller organizational size and functional capacity (TOA 9). Within each brigade-level TOA, the process was repeated as many times as there were levels of organizations—brigade to battalions; battalions to companies; companies down to platoons and sections (see figure 8.1).

That was TOA. Redeployment operations rounded out the transition. Figure 8.1 shows the scheme of maneuver for the 101st redeployment and its linkage to transfer-of-authority operations and the relief-in-place. The physical dimensions of the transition were daunting, entailing the ordered removal of the 101st Airborne Division—a complement of over 22,000 troops, over 280 helicopters, over 700 ground vehicles, assorted mission support equipment,[20] and the replacement of this force with a much smaller and more austere incapability force—a force of less than 10,000 soldiers.

Just the right placement of TFO and Stryker Brigade capabilities was the key to making the most effective use of a much smaller and lower-capacity replacement force. The operational task was simple in concept but extremely difficult in implementation: stretch the assets of a less-than 9,000-person force to cover the "ground" and the missions previously covered by an over 22,000-person combat Division with operational reach capacities able to extend throughout an area of operation greater than the size and geographic complexities comparable to the state of Maine. The differential between raw BOG numbers was obvious. But compounding the forces available problem was a capability shortfall—even if forces available were adequate, 3/2 Infantry and TFO, by their organizational designs, did not provide the type and quantity of capabilities (i.e., light-wheeled vehicles, armed and transport helicopter assets, etc.) required and demanded by the environment and operational profile of the northern area of operations. To mitigate this capability gap, Division and TFO planners stretched the 12-month BOG constraint to its limits and were able to extend the operational capacity of our replacement units for an additional 30–40 days by calculating to the day each of our unit's 12-month BOG time. This detailed planning provided a package of stay-behind units and capabilities that we would leave in the north to augment TFO and Stryker—units that had served as part of the 101st deployment but that had arrived in country later than the Division and therefore had weeks to months of additional "BOG time" remaining. This "stay-behind" package was composed mainly of National Guard and Reserve units with engineering (construction) and civil affairs capabilities—capabilities that we deemed essential enablers to the ongoing stabilization and reconstruction missions in the north. The avoidance of an unintended operational pause (or worse, a culmination) in the stabilization and reconstruction program was key to maintaining stability and security in northern Iraq. The spring months were pivotal in the grand scheme of the war, with the complete transfer of Iraqi sovereignty planned for late June.

Any additional forces we could scrounge up to augment the TFO/Stryker contingent—if even for a few weeks or a month—would be key. Even with our stay-behind augmentation, the maximum troop size of the TFO/Stryker contingent was just over a 9,000-person force, with only about 3,000–4,000 of that force being combat riflemen and the rest combat support (i.e., engineers, military police, etc.) and combat service support (i.e., quartermaster and supply, transportation, etc.) soldiers and civilian augmentees.

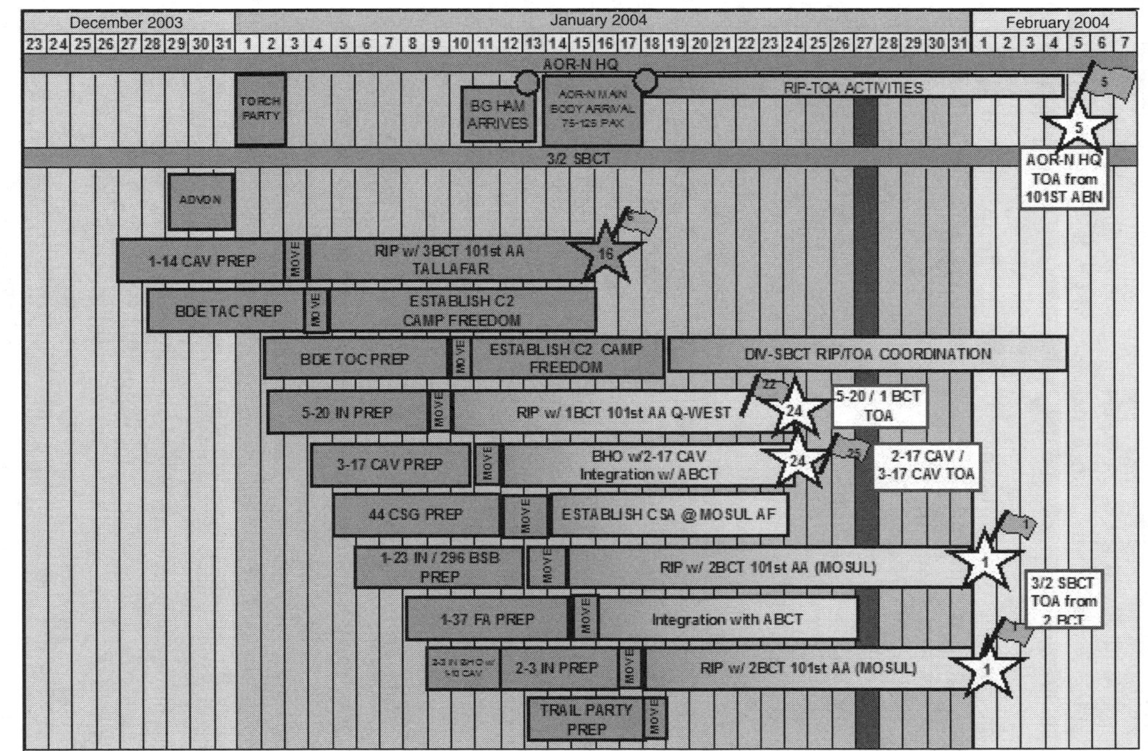

Figure 8.1 Absorption of Task Force Olympia into AO North, Late December 2003–Early February 2004

Source: Official 101st Airborne Division planning briefings (unclassified versions and/or declassified materials), June 2003–May 2005.

By March 1, 2004, that 9,000-person force would decrease by approximately 600 persons. March would see the redeployment of elements of the 956 Combat Engineer Group, an active duty reserve vertical construction unit and an integral asset in the AO North reconstruction and force protection program. March would also witness the redeployment of critical civil affairs capabilities. By our April 1 planning projections, the force numbers would drop substantially, by about another 1,000 troops. April would see the complete rotation of the 956 Engineer Group (956 EN GRP), the 418 Civil Affairs Battalion (418 CA BN), and numerous other small but critical capabilities (i.e., military police assets, air ambulance assets) back stateside.

What has not been mentioned—or added to the correlation of forces calculations—up to this point has been the availability of ISF in AO North. By December 2003, the 101st Airborne had trained and established a robust complement of ISF—Force Protection Services (fixed-site security), Iraqi Civil Defense Corps (ICDC) forces (rough equivalent to an Iraqi National Guard), border security forces, Iraqi Police Services (IPS), and New Iraqi Army (NIA) units. By the time of TOA and transition, the 101st had been operating jointly on patrols and major operations with these ISF capabilities. Adding these ISF to the organic numbers and capabilities of the 101st Airborne Division ballooned the Division from its natural fighting weight of 16,500 soldiers to around 30,000 available troops.[21]

So it was conceivable that TFO/Stryker numbers, added in a similar fashion with available ISF, would increase the forces available in AO North from approximately 7,800 to nearly 16,000–17,000 available troops. The validity of this planning assumption depended on three factors: the continued availability of the ISF in the numbers anticipated, the training effectiveness of ISF, and the trustworthiness of ISF and the degree to which TFO and Stryker Brigade were comfortable with integrating these forces into day-to-day operations. These assumptions would prove invalid, contributing to the decline of the north beginning in Spring 2004.

Streamlining AO North for Post-101st Operations

Another key aspect of transition operations in northern Iraq in 2003–early 2004 was the "rightsizing" of the battlefield geometry of the Division AO and subsequent brigade, battalion, and company areas of operation. While proper deliberate planning approaches would have found us scaling the replacement forces to meet the environmental (i.e., geographic, threat condition, cultural) conditions, what we as planners were forced to do was the opposite—scale the environment as best we could to the incoming forces, identify the "gaps" and "seams," and, once identified, convince the senior leadership of our Division and that of TFO (Brigadier General Hamm and staff) of the shortfalls and of their need to submit request for additional forces to higher authorities.

Again, like the TOA and relief-in-place, this aspect of transition had both physical and functional dimensions. One major example of the physical dimension was in the reallocation of existing base camps and the overall arrayal of forces throughout AO North.

The basing array reflected an effective "operational set"—the right stationing of available forces given the "atmospherics" of the area of operation. The determination on the number, type, and location of base camps were the metrics for the macro-battlefield arrayal of forces. The micro level (inner-city) of analysis saw, for example, the decision to station elements of our 2BCT (Strike) in small company and platoon-sized camps within the city of Mosul, in support of providing ourselves and the local Iraqis a cop-on-the-beat security as well as to reinforce the impression among the Iraqis that we were living like them and with them and working in partnership to stabilize and reconstruct "our" neighborhoods.

The availability of forces made the critical difference in terms of effective operational stationing options available. With a complement of over 22,000 available troops, organized in three brigade combat teams that provided robust command and control capacities and an ability to decentralize operations, the 101st could literally afford to approach the operational situation in northern Iraq from an "all politics is local" position and profile. The limited number of troops and capabilities available, and the peculiar organizational design of those assets within Stryker Brigade, made a local approach nearly impossible. Additionally, the ad hoc and austere composition of the TFO Command Headquarters and its limited staff and planning capacity further denied our replacements with the option to approach the mission from a local cop-on-the-beat operational approach.

The operational planning problem, when it came to downsizing the base camp profile in AO North and the redrawing of brigade, battalion, and company operating jurisdictions, was figuring out how we could simplify the redistricting in a way that could provide operational sectors to the smaller Stryker units without lowering effectiveness within those sectors and figuring out which base camps could be maintained and which could not. Redrawing the operational sectors was itself problematic. The 101st had since April 2003 tweaked the alignment of our operational sectors (brigade down to platoon sectors) to marry with the preexisting political districts and subdistricts as well as with the dominant tribal jurisdictions. These terrain-based atmospherics were determinative—the ground array was the ground array; it demanded a particular arrayal of forces that could not be adjusted in any major way without risk of compromising the war-policy relationships that had been formulated for over 10 months and legitimized over that time period. There was little we felt we "should" do to shrink existing operational sectors. Our only other option was to modify the organizational designs and compositions of Stryker Brigade's tactical (implementation) units to provide them an effective means of function to the full expanse and context of their particular sectors of responsibility. Planners briefed a plan to Major General Petraeus and Brigadier General Hamm that called for the force tailoring of the Stryker Brigade into balanced-mixed task forces. Reorganizing Stryker into these task forces allowed us to take what were organically (i.e., by original design) separate pure-in-capability units (i.e., 1–14 Cavalry "versus" 5–20 Infantry) into multicompositional packaged mixes of both "cavalry-type" capabilities and "infantry-type" functions. Two task forces were organized. Task Force 1–14 was a heavy cavalry mix (2 cavalry troops and 1 infantry company) and was assigned the western sector of AO North. The western sector was a wide and expansive area of operation of mainly open desert; it was also the western border region—between Iraq and Jordan and Syria. The conditionality of the western sector called for the allocation of a unit with a physical means of reaching all areas of the zone and also ISR capabilities for the border guard mission. A heavy cavalry mix was the right choice for the west. The second task force was TF 5–20—a heavy-infantry task force (2 infantry companies and 1 cavalry troop). The conditionality of the southern sector called for a more robust "close-with-to-destroy" (hold-ground) type of force capability. The southern sector abutted against the northern sector of the 4ID(M) area of operation. The 4ID(M) is an armor-mechanized infantry organization assigning an infantry heavy force to our southern sectors made good operational sense, give the number of joint mech-infantry operations the 101st and 4ID had conducted across this operational seam for the past year. Both operational commands agreed that this set was *as good as it gets.*

A Base Camp Has to Go!

Deciding on what base camps had to go was a related transition challenge. The original 101st base camp plan was designed with an eventual transition (relief-in-place, TOA) in mind. However, what dominated the early decisions on base camping—and rightly so—was the mission at hand: station our forces and capabilities based on the operational situation, mission requirements, and in a way that facilitated the most effective means of implementing the campaign plan. At the time of this initial planning, our Division still did not know for sure what military force would be taking our place in AO North. Rumors at that time were calling for an expansion of the 4ID(M) area of operation to incorporate the 101st area of operation—creating a "super AO" in the north under a reinforced 4ID(M).[22] We had also considered in late Summer 2003 the eventual turnover of authority to the Iraqis themselves. If the campaign plan was working, then this would be the goal—the endstate for the AO North campaign plan, and so our AO North "enduring" base camp plans project a future infrastructure that would effectively support future troop presence as well as a future under Iraqi sovereignty—a future we all hoped would come sooner than later for the Iraqis and for ourselves.

The 101st base camp plan called for four *enduring base camps*, two *temporary camps*, and a number of *initial standard camps* to facilitate effective operations in AO North.

The second phase of this two-phased plan would see the eventual transition of base camps to full Iraqi sovereignty and civil-military use—a gradual evolution through a series of transition stages. The size and capacity challenges that came with TFO and Stryker Brigade as the replacement force caused us to consider some accelerations of the turnover and conversion plans. It was easily determined by both planning staffs that at least one enduring camp would have to be eliminated from the TFO/Stryker layout. Determining which enduring camp to eliminate was more complicated. One option was to eliminate the Mosul Palace base camp and to headquarter the Task Force Headquarters in Camp Freedom (vicinity of Mosul Airport) instead of stationing at the Mosul Palace. Colocating the operational headquartering functions of TFO with the logistics functions made good sense. However, 101st planners made it clear that choosing to base all TFO functions out of the airfield would probably force the task force to also retain the adjacent AO Glory, due to the dominance of this piece of terrain over the airfield. Failing to occupy and secure AO Glory terrain could place all operations on AO Freedom in force-protection jeopardy, since the high ground of AO glory could provide potential overwatch and covered and concealed attack positions to threat forces seeking to attack coalition operations at the airfield. AO Freedom and AO Glory were a package deal according to the 101st Airborne.

The decision made by TFO—to return Mosul Palace and AO Glory to local Iraqi control and to subsequently base all major operations out of the airfield—proved tragic for the contingent in late 2004 when over 20 TFO soldiers and civilians were killed by an insurgent bombing assault on a task force mess hall. Video later obtained by U.S. media showed that the enemy had surveiled and coordinated the attack from locations in the vicinity of the old designated AO Glory. TFO also made the decision to abandon most of the company- and platoon-sized camps inside the city of Mosul. Their lack of BOG made the decision to abandon these sites a logical and necessary one. However, by not basing in and among the local populations, TFO and Stryker Brigade unintentionally traded away one of its most valuable and effective operational tools and methods—day-to-day knowledge of local activities and the trusting relationship with the locals that can only come form being a *cop-on-the-beat.* The diminished BOG, organizational design, and overall capabilities available limited TFO and Stryker to a reactive and defensive posture in AO North. A rising insurgency and transnational threat would soon begin to exploit this situation to their own advantages.

Size (and Shape) Matters!

The size of the force available and the way its resident capabilities are organized for the mission matters significantly and can become a key determinant of operational success or failure. What makes the tragedy of failing at grand strategic levels of the war-policy-making process prior to the war were the errors in resourcing (trooping-to-tasks) that inadvertently resulted from the failure to properly scope and define the war to its full dimensions and to then resource accordingly/appropriately. Getting the scale and nature of the war wrong from the start set the United States on a resourcing plan that would prove too little, too late, not enough, and of the wrong type; it was a flawed resourcing of the war, *by design.* Flaws at the strategic levels cascaded down to the tactical levels in their implications. By the time the planning errors reached northern Iraq in Winter 2003, operational commanders and their planners were facing a daunting and dramatic paradox—a big operational problem to solve over a wide and complex mass of terrain (human and physical) but with a very small and inappropriately configured force to work the problem. We were essentially given the huge task of building a new house but only provided a hammer to build it. A hammer is a handy tool and a primary one in house-building. But used alone, it cannot complete the build, and, in fact, can lead to more damage than good during the construction.

The Stryker Brigade unit design, as discussed earlier, brought many positive capabilities to the stabilization and reconstruction mission in northern Iraq. However, the size of the force—a brigade of about 5,000 soldiers—was not anywhere near the number for troops demanded by the conditionality of the area of operations. The size problem negated in too may ways the value of having Stryker as the replacement force for the 101st Airborne Division. Perhaps three to four Stryker Brigades in the north, instead of one, would have made the capabilities of the Stryker concept more effective. Yet, there were other shortfalls and limitations inherent in the Stryker Brigade design itself that made for a bad "fit" within particular areas and mission profiles in northern Iraq. The Stryker vehicle itself—the light-armored vehicle (LAV) at the center of the Stryker Brigade concept and organizational design—was, in some significant areas of the operation profile of the north and the Iraq War itself, the problem. A mounted force approached missions and the overall operational problem from a different vantage point, different perspective, and different context than would, say, a dismounted, light-infantry force. A light and dismounted force, such as the 101st Airborne, due to its lack of ground troop mobility (lack of trucks) was forced to approach operations more as a cop-on-the-beat. Foot-patrolling and daily living with and among the local population came with that type of design. The urbanized areas of operations throughout Iraq called for this type of approach and these types of forces to carry them out effectively. Moreover, stabilization and reconstruction operations, by their nature and purpose, likely called for more of a dismounted patrolling approach, with all politics being local. The political objective, for both the insurgent (the enemy in this case) and the counterinsurgent (us in this case) is the people—winning their support, trust, and legitimacy. Reaching this political objective and sustaining that relationship demanded a local, direct, and day-to-day approach. Relegated primarily to mounted operations, 3/2 Infantry Brigade could not physically reach many neighborhoods within major cities due to the massiveness of the Stryker vehicles. In November 2003, I directed that an engineering route and area reconnaissance and survey be done throughout the city of Mosul in order to identify the areas that would hinder or outright prohibit Stryker presence due to street widths and other factors. The survey results revealed a substantial number of severely restrictive areas within Mosul—areas where the 101st plans shop recommended Stryker employ dismounted patrolling techniques or, in some less restrictive areas, light-wheeled vehicle (Humvee or SUV) operations. There was a theaterwide shortage of light-wheeled vehicles, such as the Humvees, limiting the operational risk mitigation potential of that course of action. When it came to dismounting from the LAVs, politics came back into the mix. Remember that this deployment was the Army's first operational employment of the Stryker concept and organization. All eyes of the program authorizers and funding appropriators were on this employment. What kind of strategic signal would it send back stateside, when the nightly news would show LAVs abandoned on the side of the road, with the infantrymen walking a beat? Many, including the plans staff of TFO and Stryker Brigade thought that this would send an unacceptable message—many of the staff openly stated that as much had been directed to them from "higher channels" prior to their deployment to Iraq. The Stryker vehicles were to be used, period—in spite of what the operational requirements and conditions called for. But it must also be noted that simply dismounting from the Strykers would not have been adequate. As a mechanized infantry force, Stryker Brigades are composed of fewer number of BOG than a light dismounted brigade. Mechanized units are designed for a mechanized fight—a machine war. Light units are designed for a bare-knuckled street fight. If in combination, both can provide an operational commander one hell of a middleweight punching and counterpunching capability. This was why our early request for the deployment of Stryker to AO North was intended as initially an augmentation of our own air assault configuration and combat capabilities and later as one part of a larger and multicompositional replacement force package. We never achieved our intended goal in this regard, and consequently AO North was, again, unintentionally robbed of a more stable and secure future.

Lost in Translation and Transition

The force at hand[23] and the posture of that force[24] have a direct and immediate impact on the degree of armed suasion that force holds. How the force itself translates to the local population (the political objective of an insurgency/counterinsurgency) and to the enemy is a determinative factor in war-fare. Chance, as much as deliberate planning, had an impact on the positive reputation the 101st Airborne Division (Air Assault) enjoyed with friend and foe during its first year in Iraq. The Division's reputation as a fair-handed but lethal fighting force, earned through its battles and engagements during the march-up-country phases of the war, preceded its arrival in northern Iraq. The 101st benefited from a modicum of legitimacy gained from the stories that had traveled to the northern provinces ahead of time. Local Iraqi leaders and citizens gave the 101st at least some benefit of doubt during those first few days and weeks that I believe provided the Division just enough breathing room to get its feet under itself and to get the planning right for the conditions at hand. Other intangible benefits came from our unit design. Our air assault (helicopter-borne) configuration added to the mystic of the Division, adding to the suasive power of our organization design and force composition. The fact that our lineage was that of the Screaming Eagles and that our unit patch and organizational mascot was the Bald Eagle paid unexpected benefits to us and our operations. The eagle was a respected symbol of the professional Iraqi military and most Iraqis even during Saddam's reign. As a little bit of fate, coupled with "no place else to go" would have it, the Division Headquarters would end up occupying Saddam's Eagle Palace in northern Mosul, covering it into the epicenter of 101st Airborne's presence and operations in northern Iraq.

The 101st Airborne Division (Air Assault) out of Fort Campbell, Kentucky, also arrived in northern Iraq with an international reputation for excellence and professionalism dating back to World War II and the D-Day Invasion. The battle lineage of the Division transmitted far and wide throughout AO North and throughout the local population that made up a region of the country known for its military heritage. The composition and capabilities of the Division were not only legendary but also highly effective. The airmobile and air assault capacity of the organization gave us the ability to reach all parts of the wide AO North in a timely and effective manner. A community's confidence in its "policing force" improves when that force can consistently respond to the 911 (emergency) calls in a timely and effective manner. When no one comes—consistently—when you make that emergency call, eventually you stop calling altogether. The ground assault capabilities (troop and logistical transport) capacity of the Division, similar to its airmobile capability, added confidence and therefore legitimacy to the operation. They also provided critical capabilities that could be used in direct support of reconstruction efforts and the delivery of essential services to the locals. These capabilities gave the Division a valuable and respected public administration capacity, allowing them to administer to the day-to-day needs of the local Iraqis and live up to the adage *all politics is local.*

The Stryker Brigade had an effective complement and mix of capabilities; there simply were not enough of it to meet the demands of the area of operations. Stryker did not have enough combat capability resident in its organizational structure to hold the line established by the larger and more robust 101st Airborne and definitely not enough to advance the campaign plan. It was a simple case of the math not adding up—a Division-"plus-" sized and shaped organization being replaced by a brigade-"plus-" sized and shaped organization should have never been judged as a *feasible, acceptable, or suitable* course of action. The conditions in and around northern Iraq would have had to have been stable and secure—to the extreme—to pull off an effective division-to-brigade downsize. Even then, downsizing to a brigade presence in the northern sectors while the situation in adjoining areas of operation still called for a larger and more robust presence would have created a seam, or gap, in the theater array of forces—a seam that enemy forces could exploit. My assessments of the post–Battle of Fallujah (November 2004) show that insurgents and terrorists who escaped the ring of death around the city of Fallujah naturally migrated to the north. A factor contributing to this migration was the thin line of resistance that existed in the north. In many respects, the United States, by failing to provide an "active defense" capability in the northern provinces after the departure of the 101st Airborne, actually contributed to the exfiltration of threat elements through the north and the fall of Mosul city and Ninevah province.

The size and shaping shortfall also affected the tactical and operational approach that was adopted in AO North after the TOA. Simply stated, the larger 101st Airborne Division could "afford" to address the stabilization, reconstruction, and remaining combat operations in northern Iraq in a more nuanced and indirect way. A lack of force capability left Stryker Brigade and the TFO Headquarters with fewer tactical and operational options. One example is a comparison of patrolling techniques undertaken by the two organizations. Having more BOG available for patrolling facilitated more daily—and nightly—patrols. Being a dismounted infantry division allowed for more cop-on-the-beat-style patrolling. At the height of the Division's operations in AO North, the Division was conducting over 350 patrols—jointly with ISF—on a daily basis in Mosul alone. The 3/2 Infantry Brigade simply did not have the capacities or the right organizational design to approach the operational problem in the same way. From the Iraqi-on-the-ground perspective, no longer seeing (literally) the U.S. presence in their locales—no longer seeing the U.S. forces as neighbors living in their locales—must have had a devastating negative impact on the public psychology and its levels of trust and confidence in coalition forces. TFO Headquarters—only 78-person "strong" by the time of the 101st departure and ad hoc in organization—simply did not have enough staff or the resident expertise to manage, command, and control the holistic campaign plan left by the 101st, a plan that was "working" and a plan that, in the eyes of the Iraqis, was legitimate.[25]

During the TOA, 101st and TFO planners recognized this gap in functionality and administrative command and controllability and briefed our respective senior leaders. While we were successful in convincing our commanders of their need to request for additional capabilities from their higher-level commanders, there was a limit to "extra" capabilities within the theater—and stateside. Any additional forces coming from the United States would, first of all, take too much time to cycle into theater. Second, the resourcing game had turned into a zero-sum game—there were no more "uncommitted" capabilities to fulfill the request for forces. Any accommodation of a request for forces (RFF) from theater would directly impact (lessen) the combat capacities of stateside units, already tagged for deployment either to Iraq or Afghanistan. *Getting it while the getting is good* was true to the word. If you did not have it with the force that arrived to replace you, you probably were not going to see it for your tour of duty.

A Catastrophic Success?

A Failure in Effective Transitioning

What lessons should we gather from the story of decline in northern Iraq and the fall of Mosul? In his memoir, General Tommy Franks, former commander of U.S. Central Command and the theater-strategic-level commander in charge of the "early" phases of the war in Iraq, wrote about something he called "catastrophic success," as he reflected on the paradox of the American war.

While describing the paradox, quite accurately, as this "catastrophic success," Franks, and no one else to date, has adequately addressed the phenomenon. What is catastrophic success? What contributes to it—what might its causal mechanism be? Catastrophic success is a useful way of characterizing a potential negative outcome of a critical but all-too-often unconsidered war-planning mechanism: transition operations or, as is more often termed, *transitioning*.

In the specific case of northern Iraq, it was not the relatively successful implementation of the 101st Airborne's campaign plan that led to the decline and the fall of the stability attained in the northern provinces during the first year of the war *but the failure to reinforce the successes achieved by the 101st with the assignment of a relieving force similar in organizational makeup and functional expertise.* The decline of the north is a case study in the violation of several *principles of war* and *elements of operational art*—bedrock tenets of the U.S. military modern war-fighting doctrine.[26]

The principle of war (operations)—*mass* (effects)—is defined in the contemporary military lexicon as "the concentration of combat power."[27] In simple terms, the United States failed to adequately mass the right concentration of the right forces for the war-fight that would continue in northern Iraq well beyond the redeployment of the 101st Airborne. This failure led to failures of *massed effects*—the failure to "mass the effects of military power in a decisive manner in time and space"—then to failures of *Maneuver*[28]—"the capacity to place the enemy in a position of disadvantage through the flexible application of military power (dynamic shifting of military power, forces and effects)." These "failings" all derived from a broader failure—born during the predawn stages of the war itself—of objective: the United States' failure to define the war-aim fully and appropriately and, hence, the failure to then direct every military (and "civilian") operation toward a clearly defined, decisive, and attainable goal. At its root, this was a failure of strategic leadership and strategic vision—a failure of not having a clear vision of what the world should look like following operations.[29] These roots bore poor fruit at the operational art level of the war-plan, contributing to weak tactical "stems."

At the level of operations, we emphasize the power of planning. Plans reflect (at least they should) a fundamental operation design—a linkage of ends, ways, and means. Two large and systemic failures at this operational level bear specific mention here: *setting conditions* and *maintaining momentum.*

Failure to Set the Right Conditions for Transition

By all recorded and oral history accounts, the operational and tactical approaches taken by the 101st Airborne in northern Iraq reflected a successful blending of combatives with restorative, nation-(re)building tactics, techniques, procedures, and philosophies. The 101st campaign plan was an exemplar of effective holistic war-planning and war-execution. In this regard, the Division did a commendable job of setting the right conditions for an eventual effective transition. These conditions, however, were derailed and compromised (squandered) by a wrongly timed and inadequately resourced relief-in-place and transfer-of-military authority during the phase shift from OIF-1 to OIF-2. This mismatch converted—spoiled—what was a conditionality of success into an environment ripe for catastrophic failure. Failing to reinforce our success turned our local and regional victories into *a Pyrrhic victory*—a *catastrophic success.*

Failure to Maintain the Momentum

"If not of the context of conflict, then seizing the initiative during execution would be enough. However, in a conflict [a War], forces compete for the initiative with a living, thinking adversary. Given the time and opportunity, he will adapt. Presented with a consistent pattern of activity, he will devise a countermeasure. Given an enemy's determination to frustrate a forces plans, the initial benefits that accrue from seizing the initiative have a short life span."[30] Momentum is the favorable shift in a situation or in the terms of battle and the overall operational war-plan. The overall paradox of the Iraq War is a failure of maintaining momentum—of failing to develop and resource operational plans that sequeled and went beyond—during the initial *march-up-country* battle victories. This loss of theater-strategic momentum led the U.S. war-plan to an unplanned and unwarranted operational pause (between April and August 2003) that drove U.S. operations toward a culmination point near Spring 2004—the point where the United States and the Iraqis returned to a state of traditional war-fighting, by the actions and adaptiveness of an able insurgent- and jihadist-based enemy force. This cascaded down to the operational and tactical levels of the war-fight, and it is here where we suffer from the paucity of planning for the troop rotation, the TOA and sovereignty over MND areas of operation, and the overall failings of *transition.*

Transition operations and transitioning as a domain of war-policy planning have long become a lost and forgotten art and science. It is unfortunate for those suffering the consequences of the Iraq War that the war has become the last case in point. For the American way of war, the loss of this art and science is particularly critical and worrisome. In a global contemporary operating environment that finds the United States projecting a full-spectrum array of force capabilities rapidly and continuously and sustaining these capabilities abroad for a protracted amount of time, becoming experts (again) at effective transition operations will prove essential, perhaps even necessary, and sufficient for finishing well and winning the postmodern wars that are soon and sure to follow the Iraq War.

Part IV

Past as Prologue

The chapters of this final section speak to two issues that will in the long run prove determinative of whether America succeeds in recognizing the need to change its conceptions and ways of war and peace (how it intervenes) in light of postmodernity and whether America succeeds or fails to make these necessary changes. The first issue is reformation in how the nation plans and develops (designs) its forces for intervention. The second focuses on how America develops and prepares its future interveners—its security professionals, its holistic, postmodern warriors.

Chapter 9 bridges the conceptual and structural gap between strategy and force planning and tells a story of the impacts and unintended consequences of war on force design, and vice versa. It examines the complex relationships between the politics of war (the determinants and determinations of allocations of scarce resources) and the effective practice of war-fare (the interrelationship and intended balance between war-policy *ends, ways, and means*). Specifically, this chapter narrates the impact of Army Transformation to the Modular Force on the war-waging effectiveness of the fielded force.

The final chapter, chapter 10, considers the need for a *revolution in educational affairs* (the manner in which we create, educate, train, and inspire our warrior castes) that reinforces the *(r)evolution in military affairs* (RMA) many believe to be underway. The chapter proposes that one major solution to the paradox of the American way of war can be found in a complete bottom-up and top-down overhaul of the modern career development and education systems of the military services, as well as all other foreign and domestic security professions and organizations. The creation of a whole new caste of holistic warriors—full spectrum of war policy experts—has the greatest potential for long-term systemic relief from the paradox. Both chapters are to varying degrees reprints of previously written essays on the subjects of military force planning and innovation and professional military education.

Chapter 9

Fighting to Change, Changing to Fight: The Lessons of Iraq on Army Transformation, *Under Construction*

The Dogmas of the quiet past are inadequate to the stormy present. The occasion is piled high with difficulty, and we must rise—with the occasion. As our case is new, so we must think anew, and act anew. We must disenthrall ourselves, and then we shall save our country.

President Abraham Lincoln, Annual Address to Congress, December 1, 1862

This address not only accurately described the daunting challenges facing America in the throes of Civil War but is also an appropriate description of the daunting challenges facing the U.S. Army as it attempts to evolve, perhaps even revolutionize, to remain relevant and effective in the present and future geostrategic environment.

The United States has adopted an offensive, preventive, and openly preemptive grand security strategy. This strategy has been a work in progress; it is a development in the aftermath of the terror attacks of September 11, 2001, a reaction to an emerging global war on terrorism, and a response to growing national responsibilities and national interests. Over the past four years, this strategy has become codified in the Bush Doctrine, the 2005 *NSS*, and the administration's democratization agenda. America is *on the march*, and democracy is following her! Whether this new U.S. grand strategy will yield the intended outcome (i.e., more democracies and therefore less global wars) or some unintended future (i.e., more rather than less stability, failing states, and, therefore, more global wars) will largely hinge on the mechanisms of Americas' democratization strategy; it will likely depend on how our nation reconfigures its instruments of power for this new age of war and peace.

Military transformation and its "U.S. Army" derivative are the most recent attempts to "disenthrall ourselves" of the old ways of war; they are the latest attempts at adaptation—a reshaping and reorienting of our military to better deal with a new security environment. Thinking anew is enough of a challenge, but acting anew (Army Transformation) is the key. The two are essentially interconnected. The former begets the latter. At least that is how we have always been taught adaptation, innovation, and reform are supposed to work. Like any policy, the ends of transformation (the intended goals or requirements) are expected to determine the ways and the means of transformation. In other words, the causes (the why) of change are intended to drive the effect (the how) of change.

Might The Iraq War Be a Useful *Measure of Effectiveness* for Transformation?

There is an old adage—actually a warning—that goes like this: *be wary of refighting the last war when planning for the next.* Though this is good advice, it would be our folly if we were to take the adage too far. The lessons of our recent military history—as well as the history in the making of ongoing wars—do have something important to tell us as we prepare for future wars. These lessons are integral to effective change: adaptation and innovation. If not so, the voice and experiences of the war-fighter on the ground would have little to no impact. That seems silly in an academic sense and critically flawed from a practical perspective.

So, in this chapter we will examine the Army's latest endeavor in the evolution of *Transformation*—the reorganization of the Army Force[1] from the Army of Excellence (AOE) design to the Modular Force configuration under the plan of the Army Chief of Staff General Peter Schoomaker. This examination will be largely based on my firsthand experiences in this transformation initiative, gained from two years of duty as the chief of planning and operations for the 101st Airborne Division (Air Assault) Transformation Initiative and will include a preliminary assessment (evaluation) of the degree-of-fit of this ongoing force design reform for the operational challenges, requirements, and opportunities of this new-age contemporary operating environment (COE), as evidenced in the war in Iraq. Although this phase of *Army Transformation* has already revealed some very promising improvements to how we fight and organize for war-fare, this chapter also serves as a cautionary tale, highlighting some aspects of this reorganization scheme that instead of providing us with a better way of organizing capabilities for a war-fight might actually be lowering our overall capacities in war-fare and, hence, perpetuating the paradox of the American way of war and peace.

The "Why" of Transformation

Why transform? What are the *causes* behind Army Transformation, "causes" in the sense of the purposes and goals behind the change as well as the atmospherics affecting the environment for change? "Transformation" has been a Pentagon and OSD watchword since the mid-1990s. However, like any policy, the term represents various meanings and serves different means, sometimes and in some ways coincident but in other respects potentially counterproductive. As a very peculiar type of policy—a national security and defense policy—transformation can and does refer to various things: adapting the military to a fundamentally new security environment, infrastructure, and management reform, with an aim of streamlining the military and reducing overhead costs; integrating new information technology and, in accord with this, restructuring the armed forces to increase their effectiveness, efficiency, and flexibility.[2]

The "Why" of Army Transformation refers to the strategy behind the change initiative: the strategic relationship between all causes that build a logical case for the need to adapt, innovate, and change from old business practices to new ones. "Why transform" intimates or insinuates that some sort of change takes place in the character of war-fare, perhaps in the very nature of war itself, and that those changes in some way have or will affect our national purposes in war. Wars can be won or lost, even before they are fought, if the policy calculus of military reform is errant. Thinking and then acting to produce a balanced cost-benefit or "cost-effective" solution are the ultimate goals of any military adaptation; it involves fashioning a change to force design, tactics-techniques-procedures, materiel solutions, and so on, that meets and overmatches the threats of the contemporary operating environment (COE), at an acceptable cost (an *effective cost*) and within the time available. It is offered here that this should be the approved measure of effectiveness (the certification of a "good" reform policy) for Army Transformation, whether the product effectively solves for the operational challenge. Testing against the current fight, then, is a healthy test, if taken and approached with moderation.

The "How" of Transformation

How do we fight at present, and how should we fight in the future? Military doctrine, tactics, techniques, and procedures (TTPs) of war-fighting, and the resources and capabilities of war-fighting (the "wares" of war-fare) define the *how of transformation*. This domain of questioning relates to the capabilities-based aspects of our *National Military Strategy* (*NMS*) and to the *correlation of forces and means* (COFM)—the calculus of war-fare. How we fight as a nation and its army speaks to tactics and the tactical level of war. Questions of tactics, techniques, and procedures are natural and healthy occurrences within a military profession for it reflects a military organization and professional culture that is aware of the ebb and flow of continuity and change within the policy domain of war and that is willing to adapt to the establishment of a new state of equilibrium. The scope and scale and nature of change in military affairs have differed, and still differ, dramatically throughout the recorded history of modern war-fare. While some epochs have brought forward evolutionary innovations, others have heralded revolutionary adaptations. The characterization of such changes as evolutionary or revolutionary is important. It can indicate a period of adaptation that by the environmental and atmospheric conditions of the time calls for changes in tactics, techniques and procedures, doctrine, and related military affairs of a degree and nature that does not reflect a dramatic change in the "why" of war but merely an advancement in war's prosecution, or it can be indicative of a dramatic shift in the nature of war itself (the timing, spatial-societal relations, and purposes of war). The former are examples of evolutionary change, and the latter are examples of revolutionary change. Technological and tactical developments can be mistaken as the signals of evolutions or revolutions in military affairs in and of themselves. Academic and theoretical debates rage to this day over past periods of technical and tactical ("techniques") change: *was this period or that period an example of evolutionary or revolutionary change in military affairs?* The contemporary debate over Army Transformation is greatly impacted by the rapid and vast technological changes that have occurred since the end of the cold war. The quantity of these "technical" changes is potentially deceiving and creates conditions for military leaders and decision makers to miscalculate in their adaptation strategies, driving forward with wholesale revolutionary changes to current business practices when the environmental and atmospheric conditions may be only calling for relatively minor evolutionary adjustments to how we fight. Such miscalculations can unintentionally set the conditions for a misaligned national security strategy itself, one that is determined as much (or more) by *the means available* than *the ends those means are to serve* (ends justifying the means).

What Gets Transformed?

What is transformation? What does it look like? What does it reflect and represent? These questions represent the organizational and operational "ways" of war. This conceptualization is consistent with the theoretical traditions of J. F. C. Fuller[3] and his privileging of organization and operations as the seedbed and source pool of effective military change. Fuller's argument during the early years of the twentieth century and its episode of innovation argued that the fighting power of an army lies in its organization.[4] Colonel Douglas MacGregor, a founding father behind this energy for affecting change, argues in a similar manner that the most crucial aspect of transformation is organizational, personnel, and conceptual (doctrinal) change.[5] Where the final verdict on Army Transformation stands will depend on where and in what configurations our military capabilities lie within organizations and operational designs. *What is Transformation* will be determined in the organizations we build, what capabilities we place inside these organizations, how we place them there, and how we plan to operate in these organizations. Those organizations and those operational ways (business practices) will reflect a particular and identifiable *American way of war—a personification of who we are and what we stand for as a society at war—why we fight—by how we fight.*

That way of war now has a physical form and an emerging operational and organizational (O&O) concept, one that can be examined, at least in a preliminary sense. Does that organization and the operational concept undergirding it "measure up" to the needs and wants of the nation and the challenges of the contemporary operating environment (COE) that the nation must face and overcome? Additionally, does it also marry with and reflect who we are as a nation—is our Army a reflection of the *soldier and the state*[6] relationship we intend? It is here where the long-running debates of military revolutions and the revolution in military affairs find their true relevancy. Do environmental changes in the geostrategic environment and atmospheric changes within the United States and its alliance and partnership networks reflect merely evolutionary changes in our nation's approach toward and conduct in postmodern war? Or are we part of a tidal change in world politics and witnesses and participants in the promotion of revolution in military affairs (RMA) indicative of a revolutionary change in the *American way of war*?

Army Transformation—Under Construction, Under Fire

This chapter evaluates Army Transformation primarily from an implementation vantage point, but it does so in a dynamic sense, by looking at how the changing context (causes) defining the reasons for transforming the force may have impacted, positively and negatively, the outcomes we are beginning to see and are soon to employ in the war-fight at the tactical level. This story of implementing Army

Transformation is told and examined from a single case study perspective, focusing on the conversion and reorganization of the 101st Airborne Division (Air Assault) into a "Modular Force," September 2003–March 2005. The conversion, reorganization, and Transformation of the 101st Airborne Division (Air Assault) have been the Army's first full implementation[7] of Army Chief of Staff General Pete Schoomaker's Transformation Initiative. The 101st received its mission orders to transform no later than March 2005, back in early September 2003, while the unit was still war-fighting in Iraq. The 101st Airborne Division at the time of this writing was preparing for its second tour of duty in Iraq. It is my hope that through the telling of one story of transformation, "under construction" and "under fire," our collective understanding of the challenges, pitfalls, and opportunities of military reform can be improved.

America's History of *First Battles*—A Cautionary Tale

John Shy,[8] in his retrospective on America's "First Battles," found that the peculiarity of this nation's experiences in first battle (a propensity to lose the first battle of its wars) lies mainly in "the lack of recent, relevant combat experience by forces engaged."[9] Testimony of senior military leaders regarding their first contact with postmodern war-fare in the early 1990s spoke directly to a "lack of knowing" and understanding of the new ways and meanings of war.[10] War as they once knew it had changed; these leaders had to relearn war, or at least some aspects of it, "on the fly." Shy also noted that political circumstances still appeared to have two major effects on first battle experiences: "politics limits the military possibilities to certain resources and locations, and pushes strategy in certain directions at certain times."[11] Understanding, appreciating, and then learning to wield these "political limitations" as an effective war tool seems to be an important element of success in future war.

As Shy notes, "[W]hen doctrine lacks clarity or credibility, soldiers at every level will fall back on other notions of warfare, whatever their source—prior experience, film images, even childish fantasies. . . . [d]octrine, whether explicit or implicit, is never absent; defined simply, it is the general consensus among military leaders on how to wage war."[12] The Army will "fight" based on the latest rendering of doctrinal ways and means it has been educated to employ. That doctrinal baseline should reflect all aspects of postmodern war-fare in an adequate fashion. The blending of the "domestic battlefield" with the foreign one—the broadening of the idea of national security to the point where it now encompasses any and all other policy contexts—compels the U.S. Army to rethink its role and function in future wars. Homeland security and defense redefine war-fare and the U.S. Army's role in it in radical ways. Learning to be an effective "supporting component" in these new wars—and a member of a broader holistic security profession—demands that the Army broadens its understandings of what war is and its acceptance of what constitutes a capability of or action in postmodern war.

The question of whether the United States has already faced or is yet to face its first battle of the postmodern age needs to be addressed. This book has already offered an answer—yes, America has faced first battle in this new age of war, and even further, America may now have a sixth[13] addition to its record of first battle losses. Our failings to see and prevent the 9/11 attacks could be termed another American First Battle. Even before 9/11, our intervention in Somalia and our non-intervention in Rwanda could be seen in hindsight as two prior *First Battle* episodes. So, perhaps we are well beyond John Shy's modern count of five.

How might the United States fare in its upcoming *First Battle* as a transformed force? Will our reorganization and reformation efforts contribute to a win or another loss in Iraq—our current case? The history behind this story is still in the making. Nevertheless, there is enough data mounting to allow us to explore these questions, and there may still be time to make some corrections improve the chances for the achievement of a win in this *First Battle* for *Army Transformation*.

The History behind the Theory of "Transformation"

The collapse of the Soviet Union and the end of the cold war gave rise to a national debate over the scope, scale, and nature of change taking place—or perhaps more accurately said, needing to take place—within the U.S. military in the face of revolutionary changes in the global security environment, military technology, and the traditional concepts of how the United States (the West) employs military forces.[14] That debate continues today. It persisted long prior to the cold war; it is a debate that derives from the questions of change and continuity that have informed military thought since the dawn of the age of modern military history.

Studying the impacts of societal changes on land war-fare is a vital endeavor. During any given societal epoch, capturing, categorizing, and characterizing domains of change versus domains of continuity are essential for ensuring a right and balanced path for military adaptations and innovations. Misinterpreting what has changed from what has remained the same in war (war-fare, military formations, organizations, tactics-techniques-procedures, doctrine, etc.) can lead to drastic and catastrophic miscalculations in a nation's way of war. Twentieth-century history provides some examples: the "offensive bias" among the Great Powers of early twentieth-century Europe that led to the cataclysm of World War I; the "defensive bias" and adherence to "methodical battle" by France that contributed to its rapid and decisive defeat at the hands of the Germans in 1940 and the U.S. Army's initial experiences in Korea in 1950 (Task Force Smith).

In fact, some have argued convincingly that the United States has a historical propensity for getting the calculus of change and continuity wrong (America's "First Battles" phenomenon).[15] The present, like the past, is a time of both continuity and change and must be understood as such. The military theorist and historian A. T. Mahan described the relationship between continuity and change:

> While many of the conditions of war vary from age to age with the progress of weapons, there are certain teachings in the school of history which remain constant . . . [I]t is wise to observe things that are alike, it is also wise to look for things that differ.[16]

So it is in the school of war. Distinguishing between true and justified rationales for affecting change in a society's military affairs from "false labors" and determining in this fashion what demands adaptation and what things remain constant and deserve preservation are perhaps the key determinants in the success or failure of any military transformation. This is also the case of our war in Iraq. By looking at *Army Transformation* holistically, from the historical trends that drove the new concepts and theories of transformation to the current construction of the Modular Force underway throughout the U.S. Army, this chapter sheds light on causes and effects of Army Transformation in a way that helps defense planners, military strategists, decision makers, and the public to evaluate (judge) the course line and destination of this dramatic reform initiative, to determine whether this evolution—or perhaps revolution—in military affairs is necessary and sufficient for meeting and over-matching the security dilemmas challenging America's ideals and interests in the twenty-first century.

Fighting to Change

The modern history of the U.S. Army's efforts at military adaptation is a history of fitful struggle against the political and organizational *laws* regarding change. At the national strategic level, those laws stipulate that there must be a clear and present danger facing the status quo and threatening to alter that equilibrium to such a degree such as to risk the survival of the national life and interests. This law commands that the military change-agent articulates the cause for change in such a way and with such a tenor that it gains the full support and consent of the people and the nation's political leaders. At the operational and organizational levels within the U.S. Army itself, these laws command that *if it ain't broke, don't fix it!* Here, change agents must compel those within the profession to alter the way they think about their traditional roles, branch missions, and loyalties; they must prove the case to their own brethren of the need to allow organizational entropy to take hold of their organization and their personal places of security within that organization. The service itself must be convinced of the longer-term benefits of short-term self-imposed *disorder.* At the tactical and implementation level, the "laws" command that the changes offered must pass the test of implementation, in this case, capability to over-match contenders on the "fields of unfriendly strife" and to effectively *fight and win America's wars.*

Historians and theorists, Elliot Cohen and John Gooch note in their work *Military Misfortunes* the record of military failures to successfully anticipate, learn, and adapt to changes in the nature and conduct of war-fare.[17] These mis-fortunes are the result of failures to build a right and accurate case argument (cause, or in keeping with the legal analogy, *motive, opportunity, and method*) and convincingly win the argument itself. Ensuring the argument remains true to the full case file for military change throughout the trial. The closing argu-ment must be convincing to win, it is true. The argument by itself is necessary but insufficient; winning the right argument in the trial of military adaptation is the only argument worthy of winning. The causes must be reflected in the effect for the change to be both necessary and sufficient and for the laws of change to be satisfied.

The Army is constantly evolving. Since the late 1980s, the U.S. Army has been on a path of "major" change. Three Army chiefs of staff—Sullivan, Reimer, and Shinseki—have each in succession strived to marshal forward comprehensive and wide-sweeping change to how the Army mans, trains, stations, deploys, and fights.

The experiments of FORCE XXI, the OBJECTIVE FORCE, and the Modular Force (Transformation) are testaments to decades of thought on the need, causes, and challenges to change and to a full decade of action toward making those changes. The first two of these initiatives were born from a time regarded as post–cold war and "peace-time." This latest manifestation reflects a variant from the peace-time models but a model informed by causes and "realities" more after the attacks of 9/11 than before. The "under peace-time conditions" models of the Sullivan era and Reimer era benefited from a luxury of "controls"—these experiments were able to be conducted in a relative vacuum of peace and with time available to conduct a deliberate and graduated modernization. These models suffered from a lack of a war-context. The fog of being unable to clarify the future enemy (the COE) for the public, decision makers, appropriators, and members within the service itself created its own unique frictions. Although there was time available to test and modify force designs and other military affairs (training, PME, doctrine, etc.), funds were scarce, the result of both a lack of available funds during the 1990s and a failure of the Army to be able to clearly articulate a threat justification for bankrolling the changes. Time to experiment and the space to do so but no clear purpose driving those ideas for change defines the operational conditions surrounding and impacting these early military change initiatives. As theoretical and conceptual models, they could be classified as models demonstrating more parsimony (simplicity) than explanatory power.

Shinseki's Cause and Rationale for "Transformation"

Shinseki's Objective Force model was born of this same time of "relative peace" and was initially subject to the same operational constraints and conditions as FORCE XXI and the EXFOR experimentations. However, being third in the succession, Army Chief of Staff General Eric Shinseki was able to recognize the fog of peace that invited the frictions that always tend to slow change to a slow crawl. Through this recognition, he was able to incorporate into his case file a clearer operational purpose for his change effort. Shinseki's Army Transformation conceived of an operational purpose upon which a case for change and the resourcing of that change (dollars, professional and service clout, public will) could be argued and won. Although Shinseki's model lacked parsimony, it gained ground in explanatory power: the launching of an Army Transformation toward an Objective Force realized by roughly 2020 would be built and justified upon two pictures of the "threat," one from the recent past and one from the near-distant future.

The future threat or better and more fully said—the COE—was similar to that upon which the Sullivan and Reimer models had been based, a future environment that recognized the end of "symmetrical wars" and the containment of war as a national state enterprise with the end of "modernity" and the cold war age and the rise of a postmodern age of war-fare, asymmetrical and an open bidders' market where the nation-state and the traditional war stakes of nation-state war-fare were now only one aspect of the COE. The Objective Force was conceived of this postmodern alternative future and was centered around a conceptual core future combat system (FCS) force design.

Every goal or quest for reform is born of some shock to the present-day "ways that it is," either from the survival of a shock or, preferably, from prior recognition of an impending shock. As goes the popular saying, necessity is the mother of invention, so it goes for innovation and adaptation as well. Shinseki's "shock" turned out to be a threefold potential crisis: a capability gap between the "light" and the "heavy" force; a legacy Army Force born of cold war conventional symmetry that would eventually become outdated in an emerging contemporary operating environment of asymmetry, digitization, and information dominance (net-centric war-fare); and a large and bulky force and strategic deployment system that was proving itself too slow to effect the operational effects required by the regional combatant commanders at a time and place of their choosing.

Shinseki Says "Never Again"

The "threat" upon which General Shinseki built his case for his "Interim Force" stemmed from the desert floor of northern Saudi Arabia from August 1990 to January 1991. The military operation was DESERT SHIELD, and the historic vignette was one of potential catastrophic failure—the destruction of the light-infantry 82nd Airborne Division by Saddam Hussein's Republican Guard heavy-armored forces—and the nonoccurrence of this military disaster, not at the capacity or choice of the U.S. Army to prevent it but rather due to the irrational and inexplicable decision of Saddam Hussein to choose not to destroy the vulnerable U.S. Division. The inability of the U.S. Army to immediately correct this mismatch of forces for several months due to the unwieldiness of the force and the delays in deployment this "obesity" caused provided all the short-term "crisis" needed to argue and win authorization for the Interim Force, appropriation of funds, public support for the adaptation, and enough service will to execute the change in rapid fashion that the chief needed.

General Shinseki announced the "Army Vision" in his keynote address at the AUSA Annual Meeting's Eisenhower luncheon in 1999. He outlined a three-pronged approach designed to keep the force ready to confront present security challenges and concurrently shape its long-term future.

This three-pronged operational scheme was modeled to retain the theory of the earlier experiments (the causes) and move those forward through an interim operational mechanism (causal mechanism) to obtain an alternative force design—an entirely revolutionized Army—in the future (an Objective Force as intended effect). The Shinseki model sought a balance between parsimony and explanatory power. His "Transformation Campaign Plan" was intended as an operational map for setting a course line to transform the Army into the Objective Force while recognizing and negotiating with the shoals that lay along the way of that long-term expedition—affecting change toward and for the future while still maintaining a war-fighting and war-winning capability of the past and present through the "interim period."

- *The LEGACY FORCE*: To guarantee near-term war-fighting readiness, selected heavy force formations from the Active Component (AC) and Reserve Component (RC) and key combat and aviation systems would be upgraded with digital technology in order to enhance the lethality and survivability of our light forces. The chief's intent was to enhance current capabilities by recapitalizing the right equipment to ensure the force remained trained and ready until transformed to the Objective Force.

- *The OBJECTIVE FORCE*: The chief of staff waged what George C. Wilson considered, the war that "really matters"[18]—the war for appropriations and authorizations on Capital Hill—to increase investment in science and technology to accelerate R&D and rapid development of the *future combat systems* (FCS). The Objective Force prong of the strategy focused efforts to support a FY03 Technology Readiness Decision to build prototype system demonstrators in FY04–05. The idea or vision was that once the technology was mature and production lines were readied, the Army would field the Objective Force in unit sets—of at least brigade size. These organizations would be complete suites of new integrated combat systems achieving the capabilities outlined in the Army Vision—*responsive, deployable, agile, versatile, lethal, survivable, sustainable.*
- *The INTERIM FORCE*: Shinseki viewed the Interim Force as an essential "operational requirement," borne of over 10 years of a shortchanging of the lighter half of the Army arsenal with much-needed mobile, maneuver, and force survival capabilities. The idea of an "interim force"—a motorized and light-armored, middleweight force—was intended to bridge a past and persistent operational gap within the Army as well as to form an interim bridge (conceptual and practical) connecting the force of the present with the Objective Force of the future. Shinseki fought for and won funding for six interim brigade combat teams (IBCTs), which included one RC brigade. These IBCTs would be off the shelf (government and civilian) equipped with a then yet-to-be-selected Interim-Armored Vehicle (IAV). The Interim Force was not to be viewed as an experimental force to be tested for development. According to General Shinseki, the requirement was well known for a long time—the need for a mediumweight force capable of rapid strategic power projection with a landed combat and survivability capability of overmatching a full-spectrum threat. Shinseki saw the Army in need of this operational and war-fighting capability in the now and determined to as quickly as possible, make the brigade combat teams ready to respond to immediate operational requirements, providing the National Command Authority enhanced strategic options.

Changing to Fight

The attacks on the American homeland on September 11, 2001 altered the dynamics of Army Transformation. A nation at global war changed the cause-effect rationale of transformation. The threat was more present and clearer than it had been only a day before. The modus operandi of this transformation would be less a fight to change the force in the face of an emerging but still only looming foe but more a change to fight the present foe, with a notion that the current threat was a sentry of the foe we were to face in the future.

The Changing of the Guard

General Peter J. Schoomaker became the thirty-fifth chief, U.S. Army, on August 1, 2003 and with his arrival came a new *Army Transformation.*

This transformation, like all of the others, stayed true to the Mahan maxim of military continuity and change; it did not affect a complete break with the past nor did it discard the Shinseki model and operational approach outright. It did change the operationalization and the intent: transformation would have to focus on the present while keeping an eye on the future.

Transformation "under fire" was a different operational problem, with its own timing and spatial requisites. The present practical aspects of the Shinseki vision, those that "fit" with the current challenges, would be retained. That meant a continuation of the "Interim Force" force design, the STRYKER mediumweight force. All six brigade-sized programs were continued under the watch of General Schoomaker. The future combat system (FCS) would remain a concept and on the authorizations and high-tech R&D appropriations books, but operational funding would all shift to modernizing the "Current Force"—no longer to be considered as an antiquated legacy of the past but rather as the current force that proved its war-fighting worth during the First Gulf War of 1990–1991 and, by August 2003, proved effective in what was seemingly a rapid and decisive victory over Saddam Hussein's state apparatus in Iraq and a successful mission accomplishment of the Second Gulf War of 2003.

At the October 8, 2003 AUSA Annual Conference, General Schoomaker unveiled his vision and intent for Army Transformation. This plan within this declaration, though informed from decades of military thinking and theorizing,[19] was also highly informed by the operations against the Taliban and Al Qaeda in Afghanistan and major combat operations (MCO) in Operation Iraqi Freedom (OIF). Due to the foresight and great efforts of the former chief of staff, the lessons-learned processes for both OEF and OIF (Phases I–III) had been accelerated—launched as operations commenced—in an attempt to gather practical tactical and operational lessons for a rapid injection into the Army Strategic Planning Board (ASPB) and budgeting processes and to effect needed changes to the force at a time acceptable to the regional combatant commanders (RCC) fighting the war-fight. Some old legacy (Shinseki's negative connotation) systems and new systems still born of an old "modern" mindset that were surviving reform for service parochial reasons deserved "killing." These lessons learned and history writing projects also had an ulterior mission to identify wastage or systems that simply failed to work in the field of battle and to eventual cut these from authorizations and appropriations bills. The Joint-Modular-Expeditionary (JEM) Army Force Model that General Schoomaker unveiled at AUSA reflected some of those lessons gathered from the "fields" of Iraq and Afghanistan as well as concepts and theories offered by defense and force planners over the past—true to their original form and intent. Other "lessons" reflected the chief's own ideas and concepts, the internal bureaucratic and budgetary frictions of the day, and interpretations of the lessons gathered from the ongoing war-fights. All these variables affected the Modular Force designs that define Army Transformation at present, that are still "under construction," and that will be committed to war. Whether the balance of this force and the new way of military affairs that come with it and in support of it prove effective from an operational point of view is *the* essential question of this, any, and all military adaptations.

This contemporary Army Transformation is the latest in a long chronology of change—a "variation on a theme." A major part of that "theme" has obviously been about doing better in the war-fights of the day—the making of tactical adjustments to how our forces *fight*. How we have traditionally defined the fight is a key theme of this book and is a key to the reform of our ways and organizations for war.

What is most peculiar is that in each of these major "transformations" what changed were mainly the structures of the war-fighting designs and the types of equipment and other wares of war-fighting (capabilities), while what remained the same was *the nature of the war-fighting formations and their organic capabilities.* What did not transform was our approved and accepted conception of what constitutes a war-fighting organization and war-fighting wares. This book has argued and presented a strong case for a systemic reform of our war and war-fighting concept, method, and overall doctrine in a way and on a scale of change that revolutionizes our very ideas of what constitutes war and the war-fight. The present war-environment sees less and less distinction between the warriors and the nonwarriors. The asymmetrical nature of the postmodern battlefield has a much more limited acknowledgment of who merits the status of a protected person as against who does not, despite what modern international humanitarian law and the law of land warfare may still dictate. These new "conditions" may be calling for a reform of our war-waging organizations and processes that is far beyond the scope, scale, and nature of the change initiative our military has already embarked upon. The postmodern times may be signaling for an entirely new organizational and operational approach to war-fare—an approach that merges the martial with the nonmartial acts and methodologies of waging war and peace. The following discussion on the theories behind Transformation reinforces this idea. What follows this brief interlude into theory will be a discussion of the practical realities of transformation—what our recent experiences in postmodern war-fare may be trying to tell us, a message that may be falling on deaf ears.

The Theories behind the History of *Army Transformation*

In 1999, General Eric Shinseki, then chief of staff of the U.S. Army posed an essential point to the members of his organization: "[I]f you don't like change, you're going to like irrelevancy a lot less." With those words, the Army was pressed forward in full-scale organizational reform, not the first of its kind—for the Army like any adaptive organization is ever-changing—but what was believed to be then, and has proven thus far to be, the single most extensive and ambitious change initiatives in the Army's 230 plus year history.

The Dialectic of Military Change

Ensuring long-future relevancy as a service and continual readiness as a war-fighting force defines the two contentious but mutually reliant halves of the dialectic of military change.

The Army has been "rolling along" ever since in an effort to "transform the ponderous cold war force that stared down the Soviets for half a century into something more useful in the disordered new millennium."[20] The U.S. Army has since been determined in its intent and efforts to reshape itself based on new capabilities. Defense planners and theorists alike have been fascinated by the concept of an imminent revolution in military affairs (RMA). This revolution, according to the experts, involves changes in technology, organization, and operations intended to achieve orders-of-magnitude improvements in military performance and combat power.[21]

The Army considers this "Transformation" its revolution in military affairs. Every revolution must have a goal. In this case General Shinseki set the truly ambitious goal of achieving a transformation into a new kind of fighting force by 2010, declaring that "heavy forces must be more strategically deployable and more agile, with a smaller logistical footprint, and light forces must be more lethal, survivable and tactically mobile."[22]

The RMA approach takes a holistic approach in the study of modern war-fare and military innovation, accounting for *more than mere technological advancements* in the tactics, techniques, and procedures of war (battles and engagements). This holistic approach rightly accounts for (considers) the geopolitical, geoeconomic, societal, operational, and strategic factors that contribute critical pieces to the puzzle of modern war-fare.

Modern RMA theorists seem to agree on the following definition offered by Andrew Krepinevich:

> [RMA] occurs when applications of new technologies into a significant number of military systems *combines with innovative operational concepts and organizational adaptation* in a way that *fundamentally alters the character of conflict.* It does so by *an order of magnitude or greater*—in the combat potential and military effectiveness of armed forces.[23]

The origins of modern armies drew upon larger, nonmilitary developments in European societies. The following Michael Howard quotation succinctly describes this seventeenth- and eighteenth-century "RMA" reinforcing the arguments made by Krepinevich that emphasized the criticality of integrating new capabilities into new operational concepts and organizations:

> The growing capacity of European governments to control, or at least tap, the wealth of the community, and from it to create the mechanisms—bureaucracies, fiscal systems, armed forces—which enable them yet further to extend their control over the community, is one of the central developments in the historical era which, opening in the latter part of the seventeenth century, has continued to our time. In the eighteenth century, this process was to gather increasing momentum, but until then it was a very halting affair. Its progress can be traced as clearly as anywhere else in the gradual acquisition of state control over the means of making war—over that violent element in European society which . . . had in the early seventeenth century virtually escaped from control and was feeding itself, so that the historian has to speak not so much of "war" of "wars" as of . . . a melee.[24]

Howard's recipe for the makings of a RMA emphasized the importance of capturing the change within the state's controls over the means of making war, so as to avoid the degradation of war-fare into violent chaotic melees of limited or no directed and controllable purposes—*melees for the sake of melee.* The question of the day—our times—is whether or not this transformation is on a path that will take the nation and its fighting forces where they need to go and how they need to go?

A Looming Trial by Fire

Shifting to contemporary times, one of our military's more outspoken and heretical theorists and historians, Lieutenant General (Ret.) Paul Van Riper provided his own assessment of and opinions on the current state of Army Transformation during an interview for *PBS's Frontline*:

> I have no truck with those who talk about terms like *transformation*. It clearly indicates they don't know what they're doing. All it is a slogan rather than getting to the hard problems. . . . *These ideas have never truly been vetted*, and yet they're being sold to our headquarters, our services, as the way we want to fight in the future. This intellectual renaissance that I've referred to repeatedly that occurred after Vietnam has not been revived. *Rather than trying to think our way through the problem, we're trying to buy our way*. So we had to buy our way in terms of technology; we buy our way in terms of some of these ideas without the underpinnings of real bases that you can fight on. . . . I see a very close parallel to what happened after the end of the Second World War. At the end of the Second World War, the focus was on atomic weapons, the technology. Today, the analogous idea is on information technology. We believe that's the cure-all for everything. *There's an art and science to war. The science is in support of the art. The science gives you the weapons systems; it allows you to have the communications; it allows you to have all the things that support the actual conduct of war. War, as it is fought, is an art. It's not a science. If you try to make it a science, you're bound to be disappointed. The saving grace at this point, here in the middle of 2004, is the fact that none of these things have found their way to the operating forces to any great degree.* So the operating forces are still using tried-and-true methods of operations that they feel very comfortable with. It's only a matter of time, however, before those ideas are pushed down and this very rich body of doctrine that came out of the post-Vietnam era, proved in two large operations, is swept aside and we find difficulty. (Emphasis mine)

Lieutenant General Van Riper, as well as other senior-level leaders have questioned the latest rounds in Army Transformation,[25] primarily in the raising of questions with regard to the overall strategic approach to the reform. Van Riper and others are asking the right question, albeit perhaps late in the game. Arguments against the sort of "cart-before-the-horse" approaches to national and military strategy agenda-setting and force-planning that move directly toward the building of new tech solutions and the integration of those "solutions" into old but modified organizational designs without a comprehensive review of contemporary operating environmental conditions, changes to the national interests, or doctrine have been made since the early 1990s and the end of the cold war.[26] Unfortunately, these earlier warnings were made in the backdrop of "the 1990s era of peace," in the context of armed interventions that were regarded as "other-than-wars" and as such were not seen as relevant examples supporting those cries for a comprehensive, purpose-driven reform of our nation's war-fighting ways. Since 9/11, there exists a "War-context" that we recognize and acknowledge as relevant for promotion and guidance of Army Transformation. *But are we reading all of these tea leaves?* Have we seen all that there is to see to rightly inform this current transformation? What does the war-fighter in the postmodern fight have to tell the change makers, and have they listened intently enough?

The Modular Force

On October 8, 2003, the 101st Airborne Division received what would be its first formal hint in writing that it would be one of two of the Army's combat divisions to lead the way in implementing General Schoomaker's transformation to *the Modular*

Force. The Division by this time was eight months into its yearlong tour of combat duty in Iraq. The Division was one of the three original major U.S. combat organizations that had been deployed to Iraq in early February to prepare for and wage major combat operations against the Saddam Hussein state apparatus. The Division had distinguished itself during the march-up-country phases of the war (March–April 2003) in its manner of conduct in battle (*jus in bello*) and its overall approach to and concept of the. The battles of Karbala, Najaf, and Al Hillah are the most well-known testaments to these claims. In late April 2003, the 101st Airborne was diverted from its missions in and around Baghdad and the Sunni Triangle and remissioned for the duty of liberation of the city and state (*viyalet*) of Mosul and the four northern provinces. By October 2003, the Division had already established a reputation within the departments of Defense and State and more importantly with the Iraqi people and their leadership (formal and informal) as an effective and professional occupying (*jus post bellum*) force. The 101st Airborne was a right choice for the shared lead in this transformation experiment, given its experiences in all aspects of the war in Iraq as well as in all dimensions of this new age of war.[27] The other Division slated to implement was the 3rd Infantry Division (Mechanized). The 3ID(M) had waged and "won" the major war-fights of the initial march-up-country phases. The Division had distinguished itself in these battles and in doing so had not only brought a swift end to the formal regime of Saddam Hussein but had also revalidated the pure and noble courage and capabilities of the American soldier and the continued relevance of the Army's so-called legacy forces—the Army's Big Five: the Abrams Tank, the Patriot Missile System, the Bradley Fighting Vehicle, the Apache Helicopter, and the UH-60 Blackhawk Helicopter.[28] The 3ID's entire experience in Iraq had been during the early stages of the war—"war-fighting" phases of OIF-1. The 3ID had been *first to fight* in Iraq and was back in the United States by October 2003, the *first to transform*.

General Schoomaker had conceived a two-pronged approach to kick off this round of Army Transformation—an approach he hoped would perform a deliberate and thoughtful conceptual development for transformation but one that would also accelerate that process to produce new organizations and technologies that could be sent to the front to provide the war-fighters with more effective fighting capability. At the strategic level, General Schoomaker created Task Force Modularity—an organization of 11 subject-area specific working groups composed of uniformed and DOD-civilian experts and focused on the study, analysis, and development of modularity concepts and organizational designs. These subject areas ranged from working groups focused on new war-fighting unit designs (UEx, UEy, and Unit of Action development) to personnel and manning system redesigns. Task Force Modularity was tasked with the development of Objective Table of Organization and Equipment (OTOE) concepts—alternative future concepts. The chief of staff's second arm of the transformation experiment was set at the war-fighting level—divisions and brigades. The 101st Airborne and 3ID were ordered to develop their own operational and organizational concepts for how their organizations and their war-waging capabilities should be transformed (converted and reorganized). It was from these war-fighter designs that the chief hoped to get his real-world common sense check on the transformation agenda, since it was expected that the design concepts offered by Division and Brigade leadership would reflect the practical realities of new-age war from the ground experience.

It was believed that by combining these top-down, bottom-up experiments what would emerge would be a cost-effective solution—the design of a new joint, modular, and expeditionary (JEM) force capable of fighting, winning, and surviving in the postmodern environment, all at an acceptable cost of production given the investment in improvements in Army combat capability and effectiveness. The concept was and is a logical approach to reform, so long as the bidirection feedback mechanisms remain open and unhindered. This would prove not to be the case.

The CSA mandated that the Army reorganize and redesign into a new form of force, joint capable (i.e., able to "plug-and-play" with sister services), modular (i.e., configured in scalable units of action and units of employment, better organized for a full spectrum of conflicts), expeditionary (i.e., lighter organizations for combat, more capable of rapid strategic deployments); it also mandated that these new forces be created at the earliest in order to positively impact the ongoing fights in Iraq, Afghanistan, and across the spectrum of conflicts making up the global war on terrorism (GWOT).

The designs and concepts developed by Task Force Modularity were true to the CSA's specific taskings. There was operational value to be found in the concept as well. The Army had long been plagued by its girth and perplexed by its dialectical need for speed and lethality as compared to its equally important requirement for survivability on the battlefield. Smaller, lighter but more lethal, survivable, and deployable was what was needed, but this is a tall order indeed. The Army's legacy system for planning, organizing, and implementing the movement of large land combat forces—the TPFDD process—had its problems and contributed to the Army's problem of "getting there in time." Commanders in the fight and requesting to higher headquarters for additional combat capabilities of a specific type and quantity were forced to receive an entire war-fighting organization, due to how our war-fighting capabilities were organized and how the TPFDD process organized for deployment of capabilities—by Force (unit-based) Modules.

That commander might only need two battalions of infantry, a company of troop helicopter transport, and some military police and combat engineers for the mission at hand but what he would get would have to be an entire brigade of division where those necessary capabilities were resident by organization design. The wastage of time and resource is evident. Changing the ordering principle of the Army—from set-piece, division-centric organizations into brigade-based modular organizations of a multicompositional design, could better serve the war-fighter, providing him with the type of capabilities he really needed, when he needed it, where he needed it, and without overburdening him with the care and sustainment of "additional capabilities" (excess capacities) that he did not need. There was great hope in this new ordering and operating principle for effective cost savings and operational solutions it might bring to war-fighting. According to the TF Modularity Organizational and Operational (O&O) Concept, these new multicompositional, multifunctional, JEM-based plug-and-playable organizations, the Total Army Force would be better organized to effectively cover the entire spectrum of conflict, closing gaps that had long existed under previous organizational designs (large and cumbersome Division-based designs) that had unintentionally created capability gaps between different types of Division war-fighting organizations—between the light versus heavy division organizational set. This new ordering would provide the Arym with a middleweight war-fighting capacity, better able to fight and win in what was reconceived as three mission categories.

The O&O concept was solid and logical and was a natural evolution of the concepts and justifications for change offered by previous Army chiefs of staff. What was missing, however, was a measuring of these new conceptual organizations and rudimentary constructs for how these organizations "should fight" against the barefaced realities of the current and recent history of war-fare the Army has been facing and waging since 9/11, perhaps as long ago as the interventions of the 1990s. Without a healthy dose of reality from the operational and tactical war-fighters, the TF Modularity O&O might prove to be no more than a *paper tiger*.

The two experimental organizations—the 3ID(M) and 101st Airborne divisions—had been on the tip of the nation's spear ever since the attacks of 9/11. By Fall 2003, both divisions had several "field" lessons and advice to share with the designers within Task Force Modularity on how to redesign and reorganize the force for the twenty-first-century fight. Much of the 3ID story from Operation Iraqi Freedom had already been recorded, told, and infused into the transformation initiative. The major combat operations phases of the war had provided many lessons for further assessment, not the least of which being the following: the quality of the American soldier, the relevancy of the heavy force (M1 Abrams and M2 Bradley Fighting Vehicle and the power and survivability that comes from speed and audacious offensive combat operations). These lessons had already been gathered and rapidly infused in the 2003–2004 ASPB process, and their influence on the TF Modularity *Unit of Action* designs was apparent. The rapid and decisive, heavy-armored, shock-and-awe march up country of OIF-1 flavored army transformation with a mech-centric organizational design and rapid offensives-based operational philosophy. The lessons of the effectiveness of rapid and decisive operations (RDO) through the use of heavy mechanized forces using speed and audacity, leveraged by smart weapons and real-time intelligence-gathering capabilities were evidenced in the early actions of units such as the 3ID(M). The war our policy makers and our military leaders wanted to remember—and rebuild the Army upon—was the "War" that was "won" by units like the 3ID(M). The new Armored Brigade Combat Team (Unit of Action) OTOE design retained the heavy armor and infantry mix that had helped achieve "mission accomplishment" by May 1, 2003, but it also added additional infantry (boots-on-the-ground ["BOG"]) capability to the brigade construct as well as light-armed helicopters and other "enablers"—capabilities that the lessons-learned team, Shinseki's OIF Study Group, had captured as missing but necessary during that earlier war-fight.

But were these the only lessons to be gathered, learned, and incorporated into the transformation experiment? There was a war that commenced beyond the march-up-country phases of OIF-1 and lessons that went beyond the 100-hour victories of the First Gulf War and beyond the traditional set-piece battles of our honored military pasts that deserved attention. Without the context of the "rest of this war" and others like it from the recent and distant past transformations' transition to the Modular Force would be lopsided and incomplete.

The Other Side of the Mountain—Lessons Gathered by the 101st Airborne

The Division plans shop added Transformation to the family of war-plans that were already being developed for the ongoing fight in northern Iraq. The Division already was behind the power curve in terms of meeting the timelines directed by the CSA—and we were not even home yet! Deliberate and detailed planning had to commence immediately, in hopes of submitting our design concepts up-channels to TF Modularity and meeting deadlines.[29] By October 17, 2003, I and the plans shop were briefing the Division commander and primary staff on our concept designs for 101st Airborne Division reorganization and transformation. Over the next few weeks numerous variants were developed from the original Division concept.

The overall concept for the new modular Air Assault Division was not only true to the CSA's intent but was also true to the war-fighting realities the Division was currently facing and those that it had faced throughout its history as one of the nation's premier war-fighting divisions. The 101st had more than proven its abilities to fight and win and innovate in a war-fight since its first Rendezvous with Destiny during World War II. The major macro changes were a complete light-armored and light-wheeled capability to the organization, the addition of one infantry brigade combat team (IBCT), and a mulitcompo, multifunctional redesign of the BCTs.

The Division had always operated in accordance with the "brigade combat team" concept—the habitual integration of various supported and supporting combat, combat support, and combat service support arms under the operational control of a single, infantry brigade commander. The habitual relationship these informal operations ties formed created a lethal and effective bond. The habitual teaming concept of the 101st was a heavy influence on the CSA in its decision to make the BCT concept formal and organic to all brigade formations across the Army. In this respect, moving to a formal BCT structure was nothing new to the 101st.

The incorporation of an armored and wheeled configuration was new. The full-spectrum and "holistic" nature of the post-9/11 operating environment had already taught the soldiers and leaders of the 101st some hard lessons. First, mobility was key to survival and success. The new adversary operated within the geographic and procedural gaps our traditional organizational and operational set afforded to him to exploit. The enemy operated in complex, compound terrain (the mountains, the cities, the remote desserts, underground, etc.) largely because that is where we failed to station ourselves.

A long-standing and systemic limitation of "light forces" such as the 101st Airborne had always been the lack of ground tactical mobility. The Division's aerial transport helped to mitigate this capability gap, but it did not completely solve it. The lessons of Afghanistan and Iraq alone retaught the old lessons: the unit needed to have the option of going totally mobile under certain circumstances. Having a mobile capability at hand did not necessarily mean that the 101st was advocating the end of light infantry and the dawn of the "Mobile Infantry." Instead, what we were advocating was the utility of all light-infantry organizations to be equipped with a fleet of light-armored, highly durable and mobile wheeled vehicles to accommodate certain mission profiles. This capability could be maintained in a sort of "arms-room concept," where the capability could be keep in a closet—ready for wear at the choosing of the command, depending on the atmospheric condition of the day, the hour, the minute.

The planning approach of the 101st Airborne had an important impact on the planning outcomes—a factor that would later prove critical and telling. The Division commander's guidance was clear and succinct, providing the planners with just enough guidance to ensure mission completion but flexible enough to allow the planners to think outside of the box.

The key was to create four war-fighting brigades that retained the strengths of the Army of Excellence (AOE) design air assault division, while adding an additional capacity for *semi-independent operations of prolonged duration at theater-strategic operational distances and context.* Resource savings mandated by the CSA were to come from the identification of resident capabilities that past experiences had proven to no longer be essential, and to use those excesses as bill payers for new capabilities the contemporary operating environment proved we now needed.

TF Modularity "Versus" the War-fighters

Establishing contact with the designers within TF Modularity was nearly impossible, due to the sheer distance between us in Iraq and the designers backing the States. But a lack of connectivity was only part of the problem. Word had arrived at our headquarters in Mosul by November 2003 that designers within TF Modularity had been forbidden to directly contact or coordinate with any of the operational planners within the two experimental divisions.[30] This restriction made it impossible to balance the concept designs TF Modularity was creating against the COE-informed design recommendations and lessons gathered by the operational planners and tactical operators. This prohibition derailed a vitally important check-and-balance subsystem in the transformation process. Without the authorization to coordinate ideas and efforts, the two prongs of the CSA's Transformation experiment were left to their own interpretations—leaving TF Modularity susceptible to being biased in their analysis due to their distance form the realities of the postmodern war-fight, and the war-fighting divisions potentially biased in their analysis by being too close to the subject.

Not until mid-February 2004, two weeks after the redeployment of the 101st Airborne Division to Fort Campbell, Kentucky, three months after the 101st Airborne's submission of its O&O concepts to TF Modularity, and over six months after the return the 3ID(M) and the start of its reorganization, did planners receive DIRLAUTH. And by mid-February, it was too late. The CSA, on February 16, 2003 had already approved the TF Modularity designs, with minimal to zero appreciation of the requirements and design concepts offered by the war-fighting divisions. When XVIII Ariborne Corps representatives arrived at Fort Campbell in late February to update the Division leadership and planners on the transformation processes, we were informed that further debate over organizational designs was futile—the word to the divisions that would have to live with these designs was simply to focus its planning and operational efforts on making the new designs work.[31] Implement what we had was the mission we received. The 101st set about the task of making it work, as 3ID(M) was already struggling to do.

Lessons Gathered but Not Learned

Assessing the Preliminary Impacts of Transformation

The flaws inherent in the current O&O concepts and designs are significant both in their immaturity and absence accountability with the practical realities of recent and ongoing war-fights and in their potential impact of the future war-fighting and war-winning capacity of our force designs. The flaws are also important in a procedural sense. The two ways in which we have approached transformation—top-down and bottom-up—resulted in two distinct answers to the transformation challenge; one of those answers now dominates the entire process of change. Study and consideration of both these flaws are important to the future effectiveness of Americas' Way of War. Let us begin a discussion of the latter.

"Leaping Before Looking"—Flaws in the Planning Approach

There was an essential difference between the concept development approach of the war-fighting divisions and that of TRADOC, FORSCOM, and TF Modularity—a difference that manifested by the time its influences reached the implementation levels in negative impacts on operational and tactical effectiveness of some of the modular organizations.

Transforming from the top-down inlaid certain assumptions and premises into the planning problem, which actually defined a problem substantially different from the planning problem, as conceived from the tactical and operational level upward. That is not to say that the TF Modularity designers were not concerned with producing a more effective fighting and winning solution. There were no sinister plots to undermine the war-winning capacity of Americas' fighting forces. That said, the top end of the initiative was simply closer to the realities of the defense policy process and the bureaucratic business end of the profession of war. Effectiveness? Yes. But in the end, this effectiveness had to make sense—*dollars and cents.* The TF Modularity designers were closer to the political end of transformation than they were to the working end of the initiative, and this great distance from the ground influenced their planning approach and their planning products.

As Lieutenant General Van Riper noted, much of the top-end approaches to the reorganization and transformation effort reflect an attempt to "buy our way in terms of some of these ideas without the underpinnings of real bases that you can fight on." That is to say, in the absence of a thorough and detailed reassessment of our traditional and long-standing war doctrine measured against an equally robust and comprehensive evaluation of the change (nature, scope, scale) to the contemporary operating environment (COE) as the leading force and driver for reform, what we see instead has been a reformation of America's ways and of war that has been informed perhaps more so by the wares of war than the new emergent nature and purpose of war. Task Force Modularity unit designs appeared far too long before the first drafts of new operational concepts. The O&Os were very late in development and even later in delivery to the war-fighting levels. When the draft (interim) operational concepts finally did arrive at division and brigade levels—around September 2004—the 101st Airborne was already one full year along on its own concept development and a full three to four months into execution. If there were no O&Os to guide and direct the TF Modularity concept designs, then what could possibly be informing the changes that were being recommended to—and approved by—the CSA? With no regular or permissible collaboration between the theorist and strategist, the operational commanders and their planners, and the tactical-level implementers, what was driving this train toward change, and where was the train heading? The top-end approach to concept development was critically flawed in its distancing from the geographic, temporal, spatial, and ideological realities of the postmodern war-waging environment. The concepts themselves were informed by a sound conceptualization of a new operating environment—a conceptual future that was articulated in the U.S. Army's 2001 edition of *FM 3–0, Operations*, the foundation of all other U.S. Army operational doctrine and tactics, techniques, and procedures. The development of *FM 3–0* had been at least a five-year reconception process. This document was bold—perhaps even revolutionary—in its conceptual departures from past versions of the manual and past doctrinal principles. In fact, the concept developers intended this edition to be more of a conceptual blueprint for future joint war-fare and combine-force-enabled land war-fare rather than a recipe for action that past versions had been. One of the more dramatic and noteworthy offerings of the 2001 edition was the articulation of a new battlefield ordering model—one that while acknowledging the relevancy of wars natural linear geometry made note of a new algebraic form of war brought on by the revolution in technological affairs (RTA). Advances in technological innovations, and more notably information technology, were having (had had) a revolutionary impact on the modern battlefield—a transformative impact that changed what had long been a linear battlefield to a noncontiguous, nonlinear battlespace. That battlespace was extended as well as emptied by the powers of IT. The information technology revolution had introduced the warrior to a new stage. The concept developers of *FM 3–0* did well to acknowledge that new stage. Learning to act on it was the next important and difficult step. Hearing back form the actors themselves, after acting on the stage for much more than three plays, much less three acts of one play was vitally important if we were to take what *FM 3–0* had presented us in concept back in 2001 forward into the further development of practical war-fighting ways and means. An effective transformation depended as much on feedback from the actors as it did on the directors.

The new battlespace concept articulated in *FM 3–0* married well with the new operational design constructs—the *Unit of Action* (UA). The wonders of information superiority through superior IT would allow land forces to transcend the linear confines of traditional land-based war-fare. Unbound, land forces were free and able to operate as smaller wholes, operating semi-independently at wildly extended operational distances form command and control and logistics nodes—nodes that could, again, because of advancements in IT, effectively support from faraway sanctuary bases. Just-in-time logistics, real-time intelligence, and rapid-decisive operations were all possible. The concept read well. But the realities of the postmodern warfight told a slightly different story.

The Iraq War Meets the Modular Force Concept

The approach taken by the 101st Airborne Division began with a reassessment of our resident capabilities to wage effective full-spectrum war-fare under the conditions of the COE, as evidenced through and informed by our long past history as a war-fighting organization and our recent practices in postmodern war-fare in Afghanistan and Iraq.

Our approach followed with a determination of the operational problem—why build it?—and then progressed to the conduct of a comprehensive capability-gap analysis of the modern, AOE-designed Air Assault Division. Again, our commander had provided the plans team with clear-enough guidance that had set the balance for how far the planning could proceed in the incorporation of last-war lessons gathered into this operational problem.

History would inform our reform but only up to and not beyond the point where those past experiences and their contextual uniqueness made them suspect. In this way, we could avoid the pitfalls of refighting the last war in our preparations for the next, which the CSA had already warned would be in less than 365 days.

Then Major General David Petraeus conformed and approved our proposed commander's intent for our redesign of the Division and its resident war-fighting brigades during our Receipt of Mission brief to him on September 17, 2003. A look—relook—at our *capabilities* was paramount and our operational driver. Our assessment of these capabilities—what worked and what failed to work as advertised—against recent past experiences went back well beyond the current fights, reflecting back across the Army's and this Division's experiences throughout the period of time that I will call the *Forgotten Nonwars of the 1990s.* One of the reluctances that OSD and DOD had about allowing the war-fighting divisions to have a heavy hand and a loud voice in this transformation redesign was a concern that the war-fighters would, first, be too close to the issue (and therefore susceptible to observer bias) and, second, that the war-fighting organizations, designed along branch-specific lines, would become parochial in their planning. The fear was that the ever-present branch "tribalism" within the Army would set transformation into a quagmire of branch civil war. These concerns were valid and supportable from past experiences. The 101st recognized the realities, operational and, in this case, political, and set about to ensure as best we could that parochialism would take a backseat to effectiveness—even if that meant the end of the Air Assault Division as we had come to know and love it.

Division planners incorporated an innovative variation of traditional center of gravity analysis planning methodologies—the Critical Capability, Critical Resources, Critical Vulnerabilities (CC-CR-CV) Analysis Model—as our analytical methodology.

The model had been developed by Dr. Joe Strange of the Marine Corps War College and provided a useful model for categorizing and characterizing Division capabilities as well as a rigorous "degree-of-fit" method for analyzing and evaluating those capabilities. This capability-gap analytical framework also incorporated a deliberate consideration of the Air Assault capability in total and in terms of what benefits it had provided to the overall combat capability of the United States in the past, and whether the current and future times would still find the need for this peculiar type of organized capability. The 101st Airborne Division (Air Assault) is the only combat organization of its kind and configuration in the world. Its habitual approach to cross-leveled war-fighting (the BCT concept) coupled with its heavy BOG capacity and its heavy complement of utility, transport, and attack helicopters provide the Army and the nation with a true middleweight force—and one that can extend the effective reach of the operational commander out to extreme theater-strategic distances. Experiences in Afghanistan, particularly during Operation Anaconda (Tora Bora) demonstrated the agility, flexibility, and extended reach capacity of the air assault capability. The assets that came as capabilities organic to the TF Rakkassan contingent in Afghanistan (Gator[32] light ground mobility vehicles, attack and air assault helicopters, light-infantry and complex terrain-experienced BOG) proved instrumental in the Battle of Tora Bora.[33]

OIF was also demonstrating the unique qualities of the air assault capability and the 101st Airborne Division—Air Assault—in particular. The multicompositional and multifunctional makeup of the Division provided an operational-level commander with a buffet of capabilities for his use in the war-fight. The choice to shift the placement of the 101st Airborne from central Iraq to northern Iraq was a fortuitous decision in hindsight but one that at the time probably lessened the capacity of the CJTF-7 commander in a substantial way. The north needed the capability of the 101st, given the complexity of its human and geographic terrain. However, by correctly answering the operational needs of the north, the CJTF-7 commander diminished his options and capacity for reaching the full extent of his theater-strategic area of interest (AI) with forces under his direct command. In short, the CJTF-7 commander lost his theater-strategic reserve capability by missioning the 101st to the north. The decision was the right decision to make—actually the only one to make, given that there were no other units available in theater in Spring 2003 when the placement of forces decision had to be made. This was another unintended consequence of having far too few in-country capabilities to facilitate a smooth and seamless transition from MCO to stability and reconstruction (S&R) operations. To compensate, the 101st was missioned on four separate occasions during 2003–2004 by the CJTF-7 commander to execute major combat operations (antiterrorism and counterinsurgency operations) in the western An Anbar provinces and in vicinity of the Sunni Triangle (Fallujah and its environs), from its base in northern Iraq. These theater-strategic (intratheater) employments were necessary due to the inability of General Richardo Sanchez to effect the far reaches of these sectors of the country with the forces within those sectors. These operations found the 101st Airborne Division extending beyond its own AO to distances of well over 400 kilometers and sustaining those operations logistically for extended periods. Figuring ways to retain this Army capability (and convincing upper echelon leaders of the value of the air assault capability) was integral to the 101st approach to transformation as well.

Missed Opportunities

The fact that higher-level force designers were forbidden from collaboration with mid- and lower-level planners set the implementation of transformation on a path that was rocky and perhaps moving in an errant direction. The absence of cross-talk and cross-fertilization of ideas and concepts set in motion a process of *sinning by omission* at the FORSCOM levels and higher. However, not knowing what we did not know was, as SECDEF Rumsfeld might term it, a *known unknown*. Much of what senior-level designers are now claiming to not have known as they developed their OTOEs back in 2003 and 2004—the need for more BOG in the BCTs, the need for an armored and ground tactical mobility capability within all UAs just to name three of the major capability gaps—could have been known as early as Winter 2003, if the voices of the two divisions, undergoing and implementing transformation, would have been heard. They were not. And so, as of Summer 2005, transformation had taken on a reorganize-on-the-fly aspect, with much of the reorganized units being reorganized and reinforced as best as possible within Kuwaiti staging areas just prior to these units crossing the berm and rejoining the war-fight in Iraq.

This just-in-time transformation robs the operational and tactical units of critical and valuable time and opportunities to integrate new equipment fieldings, reconfigure the logistical support processes for sustaining these new fieldings, and training personnel on the uses of these new fieldings. The 30–40 days that units may receive, in country, to force integrate and train is, in my opinion, not good enough. Time will tell.

Conclusion: Looking to the Future

In July 2004, Colonel (Ret.) Douglas MacGregor testified before the House Armed Services Committee (HASC) on the stare of Army Transformation. During that testimony, Colonel MacGregor said the following:

> Current Army transformation programs are not informed by the realities of modern combat or rigorous testing and experimentation. While it is gratifying to see interest in the concepts of rotational readiness and unit cohesion, the disastrous decision to keep American soldiers and units in Iraq for 12 months at a time reinforces my broader reservations about Army transformation. Today, our ground force is apparently exhausted and incapable of securing the stretch of road from downtown Baghdad to Iraq's international airport. Thus, my greatest concern is that the current thrust of Army transformation may actually reduce the Army's fighting power and operational flexibility just as the international environment is placing greater demands on our ground forces.[34]

My personal experience with this latest round in Army Transformation supports the offering by Colonel MacGregor. What is most interesting about this testimony, however, is that it comes from an officer who has been, since the 1980s, one of the military's strongest, most capable, and dedicated theorists and strategists in U.S. Army and military reform. Moreover, during the early 2000s, and up until Summer 2004—just prior to this HASC testimony—Colonel (Ret.) MacGregor had served with the Center for Technology and National Security at the National Defense University, and his most recent book on the subject of transformation, *Transformation under Fire*, was endorsed by the Office of the Secretary of Defense (OSD). The fact that up to early 2004 MacGregor had been a close ally to the OSD and DOD transformation upper echelons but by mid-Summer 2004 had become one of its most voiceful critics indicated the positive attributes of OSD as an organization willing to allow and accept dissenting opinions from its members. But still, it was curious to see such a dramatic turn of opinion from one of transformation's godfathers.

Colonel MacGregor's 1997 book, *Breaking the Phalanx*, became the seminal work for this most current variant of Army Transformation and a source manual for the design of *the Modular Force*. His second book, written under the aegis of the OSD, *Transformation under Fire*, advertised the current transformation approach—an approach that was favored by the Bush administration. To hear the 2004 testimony indicated that something had been lost perhaps in the translations and transitions of the transformation concept (from OSD) to the transformation designs and plans beginning to come out of DOD.

Who knows? But to be sure, there has been a turn, possibly toward the worst of consequences, in the current reorganization effort, and the critiques and concerns are mounting. Colonel MacGregor cited three major concerns with the current reorganization, which I have summarized as follows:

1. The light-infantry BCTs are *too light.*
2. The Stryker Brigades are *a poor man's substitute for a combat arms brigade.*
3. The BCT design is too thin on ISR, armed reconnaissance, helicopter, and battle command capabilities.

Our experiences at the division and brigade level confirmed these absences, again, as early as Fall 2003—if heard and heeded, then there would have been more time available to effect changes to the design and resourcing plans for 3ID, who is currently fighting some of the modular units, and definitely for the 101st Airborne, which by 2005 became the first of the U.S. Army's fully modularized divisions. The organization that returned to Iraq in 2005–2006 was not the same organization that fought for and achieved relative success in northern Iraq back in 2003–2004. In many respects, it was a better force—more net-centric, and complemented with a core of seasoned combat veterans. But in many respects, the organizations proved to be worse (less capable) than its predecessor Air Assault Division. Though the Modular 101st returned to Iraq with an additional brigade combat team, each BCT was approximately 300–400 "BOG" lighter than its AOE-101st predecessor. The Modular 101st returned to Iraq with less helicopter assets, albeit the assets available will likely prove better organized from a logistical support standpoint than its predecessor. Within each modular BCT, there was one less battalion of infantry resident—each with a new capability, a Recon Squadron, but that squadron will not be capable of fighting for intelligence or fighting to close with and destroy enemy forces or hold ground. The Division headquartering and command and control element of this new modular form (the Unit of Employment-Xray) was and is smaller and less robust in capabilities than its AOE predecessor. This difference alone may have proven to be a critical loss to the OIF-5 mission profile, given the likely nature of the war-situation over the next two years—the requirement for U.S. organizations to be capable of waging full-bore anti-insurgency operations and counterinsurgency support operations, while also playing a key role in theater-strategic public diplomacy. The modular designs, from my planning perspectives, simply do not have the right capabilities—in the right types and quantities—to effectively cover these mission requirements.

Nor did we get it right and complete at the war-fighting end of the planning. The Army is in fact a learning organization, and there has been a lot of learning going on over the past three years. From my own standpoint and ideas—ideas that I have already expressed and tried to justify in the chapters of this book—as absent of the right types and numbers of military force capabilities the new Modular Force designs may prove to be, they are even less capable and prepared, by design, to fight and win in the postmodern environment due to their lack of stability and reconstruction capabilities. Army Transformation, so far, has only considered the martial side of the force redesign COIN. There is much rethinking and redesigning to be done so as to create new war-forms that are holistic in their designs and their resident capabilities.

As a preliminary and very rudimentary exercise, I put forth the following capabilities that should be considered for direct incorporation into military war-fighting organizations:

- more civil affairs planners and operators (UEx and UA, down to company levels);
- more media and "public information and diplomacy" capabilities (down to company);
- FEMA-educated and trained personnel;
- customs- and treasury-educated and trained personnel;
- FBI and municipal police-educated and trained personnel;
- government and public/international finance-educated and trained personnel; and
- civil reconstruction expertise (engineers, architects, sociologists, anthropologists).

This is just a short list of some of the "other-than-war" capabilities that might be needed at the war-waging levels and within our war-fighting organizations. A mix of military and civilian experts, cross-training and cross-educated on one another's expert knowledge, would be an effective ordering principle upon which to rebuild not only our military war-waging forms, but all of our preexisting "other-than-war" organizations. Each of us as postmodern warriors, be we civilian or soldier, must be allowed to become semiexperts in the other's fields of knowledge and must allowed to reside within one another's jurisdictions.

Again, a return to Colonel MacGregor's testimony to the HASC is appropriate. And an appropriate closing of my own thoughts, experiences, and opinions on Army Transformation:

> Today's senior leaders, dealing as they do with life and death should be as utterly realistic and ruthless in discarding the old for the new, as General Marshall from the time he was elevated from one star to four stars in June 1939. But the historical record makes clear that senior officers are not always realistic. Comfort with the status quo breeds distrust of change. Victory over weak, incompetent adversaries creates the illusion of strength and capability when the reality may be quite different. Ultimately, new fighting forces with new ideas and new capabilities emerge as the result of political interest and private sector pressure. In the 1930s for instance, the Germans got tanks and the French got forts. In the United States where there was no interest in the Army at all, there was no pressure to make substantive change and the Army's generals were given tacit leave to romanticize warfare in the form of horse cavalry.

Today, the United States and its military services are assuredly facing pressures to make substantive changes in organization for war—pressures brought further to bear given the challenges the United States now faces in places such as Afghanistan and Iraq. The U.S. military has made some noteworthy reforms (the latest U.S. Army-U.S. Marine Corps joint counterinsurgency manual, Department of Defense (DOD) Directive 3000.05, "Military Support for Stability, Security, Transition, and Reconstruction (SSTR) Operations," November 28, 2005, etc.) in the past four years. Yet, despite indications such as these that show the nation now having a greater appreciation for the need for change in how the nation prepares for and conducts war-fare and peace operations, there remains an inability or unwillingness (or a combination of the two) to affect the necessary changes—to make new exceptions to old rules of doing the business of war and peace the new ways and rules. While no "tacit leave" has been given to our armed services to romanticize war-fare in its traditional modern-era mechanized forms, current tides in military transformation do still seem to flow in directions that "romanticize" old ways and forms that are increasingly proving antiquated by the character of the new global security environment. Thinking anew while necessary is woefully insufficient as a transformative way ahead for our nation and the community of Western nation-states. The West writ-large must now begin to act anew in hopes of saving the "Westphalian" system in the long run.

Chapter 10

Educating Holistic Warriors

How the U.S. Army is designed to educate its officers in strategy and planning will determine success or failure in its efforts to produce and sustain strategic planners. The security challenges that face the next generation of military leaders demand that action be taken ahead of time to reassess and redesign the ways in which the Army educates and develops uniformed professionals, experts in advice-giving on matters related to national policy and national strategy, and experienced individuals in the operational planning and tactical execution of martial actions intended to translate strategic goals into tangible effects. This new information age of war-fare reflects a uniquely complex strategic environment. It reveals a graying of the distinctions between the strategic and the tactical levels of war and a growing similarity between the martial and extramartial aspects of war. Perhaps at no other time in modern history has the notion of war as a continuation of politics and policy by other means been closer to reality. The professional officer education system needs to accurately and effectively reflect and affect the prevailing epoch of war-fare. There are indications (empirical and anecdotal) that the U.S. Army education system needs to be updated; the system is more an example of the past ("modern") strategic environment than the present and future ("postmodern") strategic environment. The modern professional military education (PME), a derivative of the mechanized age of war-fare, is typified by separate approaches to strategic-level education, operational-level education, and tactical-level education; differentiated (partitioned) career paths for officers trained in strategy versus operations and tactics; a seniority-based approach to the education and experiential learning of officers in national and grand strategy; a service-based centricity in its pedagogy; and a military-centric approach to war-policymaking and the development of future roles, functions, and missions for military strategic planners. The 2003 complex strategic environment called for the synthesis of expertise in the three domains of war into one entity: the uniformed strategic planner. To meet this educational end, the present educational ways and means must be assessed and evaluated. Weak spots and points of failure must be identified—all on behalf of retooling the system in ways that facilitate the development of Army experts in national strategic planning. This chapter offers specific structural and procedural treatments to an education system "flawed by design" and therefore ill equipped to consistently produce the quality and quantity of strategic planning experts demanded by the security challenges that face the Army, the military services, and the entire nation. This chapter proposes the following key changes:

- Remove arbitrary branch qualification requirements for O-4/Major and above, particularly for those officers identified early as potential future strategists and develop a more flexible professional qualification model that places "leadership" on par with "commandership."
- Formalize an advanced military studies education experience in the PME of all officers designated as future "strategic plans and policy planners"; expand opportunity for Advanced Civil Schooling (ACS) beyond the strategic core for a wider number of operational track officers.
- Dual-track uniformed strategic planner education, incorporating civilian and interagency academic and experience-based education into the pedagogy.
- Make the education of the uniformed strategic planner truly "joint" and introduce this joint system into the career development of the designated strategist early on. This could call for the creation of a Joint Services Academy at the undergraduate/precommissioning level of professional education and the merger of separate-service mid-career programs (command and general staff colleges [CGSCs]) into one Joint Command and General Staff College, similar to the 2000 British reform.
- Expand the military services' advanced military studies programs (School of Advanced Military Studies [SAMS], School of Advanced Warfighting [SAW], School of Advanced Strategic Studies [SAAS]); expand each individual program's curricula to incorporate political-economic-cultural studies (a war-policy and planning curriculum) and include more than token interagency and domestic security profession/organization representation; extend these programs across the interagency and domestic homeland security organizational network and into the educational programs of our domestic war-fare agencies in order to foster comprehensive and best practice-based theater operational planning methodologies and practices.

Considering a Revolution in Educational Affairs

Professional attainment, based upon prolonged study, and collective study at colleges, rank by rank, and age by age . . . those are the title reeds of the commanders of the future armies, and the secret of future victories.

Winston Churchill, U.S. Congress, House Armed Services Committee, Panel on Military Education Report. Report to the Committee on Armed Services House of Representative, 101st Congress, 1st Session, April 21, 1989

The secret of future victory in future war-fare will, as Churchill cautioned, depend largely on how military leaders are educated in war. Reviewing the current status of the U.S. Army's "prolonged collective study" of war is an important contributor to an effective transformation to twenty-first century war-fare—the dawn of an era that brings war closer to its Clausewitzian ideal, as a "continuation of politics by other means."[1] The challenge to military theorists, scholars, and decision makers—governors and their generals—has always been to rationalize the theory, the history, and the doctrinal practices of war, as policy, during any period or epoch of war-fare, in order to effectively prosecute war-policy and win in war, whenever and wherever war might come. As the purposes of war change over time, political leaders and their military lieutenants must relearn war. Well-educated martial experts are the key to success in future war.

Theorist and scholars alike have recognized throughout history occurrences of "profound, discontinuous changes in the conduct—sometimes even the nature—of warfare." Such "Revolutions in Military Affairs"[2] (RMAs) fundamentally alter the character and the conduct of military operations.[3] So state the theorists.[4] Recent intellectual effort has focused on the potential emergence of a new, post–cold war ("postmodern") RMA, heralded by, or at least most easily identified to date by, the rising importance of information-based systems and digitization—technological revolutions that, like the armored tank of its day, once operationalized into military and war-policy doctrine, changed war-fare itself. Experts on the subject see the potential for a new way of war-fare—full-spectrum operations—deriving from this latest evolution in technological affairs. Indeed, the most recent U.S. national security and military strategies,[5] the most recently revised Joint Vision statements,[6] and the most current service transformation initiatives[7] all reference to and ground themselves in the idea that an information-age RMA is at hand.

As War-Fare Changes, Education of the Militarist Must Change

The growing lethality of war-fare, brought about by technological advances and innovative operational ways of employment, has made the "effects" of a war-policy instrument as important a factor (perhaps more so) as the instrument (capability) or the threat wielding that capability.

A genuine revolution in international politics is underway, promising changes like those seen following the French Revolution, in 1815 with the Concert of Europe, in 1870 after the unification of Germany, in 1919 with the end of World War I, and in 1945 with the end of World War II and the creation of the United Nations. The common, vexing characteristics of all such international politicomilitary transformations are uncertainty, vulnerability, ambiguity, complexity, and change.[8]

As the world changes, the fundamental purposes of military organizations may change. Indeed, U.S. military experiences during the 1990s, with the partial exception of the Gulf War, have witnessed a changed realization of war-fare and war's nature. The PME debates of the late 1980s and 1990s took place amid this environment of "limited" wars of self-determination, ethnic cleansing, environmental degradation, forced population displacements, narco-terrorism, and so on.[9] In fact, the debates and the policy reforms that have commenced since the late 1980s found their genesis in the recognized shortcomings of the United States and its military services to effectively meet the security challenges of the times.

The Goldwater-Nichols Department of Defense Reorganization Act of 1986 (GNA '86) was the seminal legislative-led reform; it was largely the response to the lackluster performance of U.S. armed forces during the Iran hostage rescue attempt

(Desert One) and the Grenada invasion.[10] On the heels of the GNA '86 was the Panel on Military Education of the House Armed Services Committee in 1987 and its review of joint (multiservice) education at the command and general staff colleges of the four services.[11] The lack of a multiservice, operational focus in the PME was found, back then, to be the clear shortfall[12] to the effectiveness of U.S. military forces in future wars.[13]

Purpose of This Chapter

While Congressman Ike Skelton, in a lead article for the May 1992 edition of *Military Review*, asked, "JPME . . . are we there yet?" this chapter asks *mastery in operational and theater-strategic art and planning, are we there yet?* More directly, this chapter ponders over whether the modern JPME system is joint-based, civilian-based, and operationally focused enough to adequately meet the demands of information-age (postmodern) war-policy and war-fare. While anti-intellectualism[14] still haunts the culture of the U.S. military to a significant degree, the complexities of the postmodern international politicomilitary environment have awakened the U.S. military to the broader context of war-fighting, and have opened military minds to the notion that expending time, effort, money, and other resources on the education of officers in the widening domain of functions and fields of study that increasingly fall within the context of "war" is not only worthwhile, but it is also a necessary area of competency that must be incorporated into the PME system if the U.S. military is to dominate in future war.[15] War-fights in Afghanistan and Iraq as part of the global war on terrorism reinforce the need for a complete redesign of the way our nation educates[16] its future holistic warriors, who are a composition of the traditional warrior caste (the military soldier) and the myriad of emerging peace and security professionals, including experts in war-fighting as well as peace-winning operations.

The military services have over a long period achieved great success in joint-effects-based operations, with those successes tested and largely proven through real battle and campaign experiments in the deserts of the Middle East (the Gulf War, 1990–1991) and in the jungles and urban terrain of Panama (Operation Just Cause, 1989). Yet, the times have changed since the Gulf War and the Panama invasion. The U.S. experience with war during the 1990s did not manifest the "decisive" victories of the type that the Gulf and the Panamanian experiences did. There were successes during the 1990s but failures as well; however, "decisions" on these post-modern "battlefields" were political and strategic, coming about only as an indirect result of direct military actions on the battlefield. In Somalia, the U.S. military destroyed an enemy—its traditional mission and mandate—but in this instance, the enemy to initially be "destroyed" was less a physical threat than an ephemeral one: the idea of denying food to a starving people as a weapon of domination and coercion.[17] Such alterations in the scope, scale, and perhaps even the nature of war have raised the issue of the need for a new round of GNA-type defense reviews.[18]

Why Does It Matter?

Tracing America's experiences in "major wars" since, and including, the American revolutionary war, the historical record leaves the nation with a foreboding reality: many of America's innovations in both its capacity to make war and its capacity to understand and accommodate the changing nature of war has come late in the day, after the "loss" of the "first battle."[19] Armies generally fight along lines of how they were prepared.[20] Therefore, it is important to examine how the U.S. Army has developed its organizations, equipment, war-planning, training, and rules—its battle doctrine. It is argued here that transforming the educational system is the key and essential foundation of any true future revolution in military affairs.

From the Need for Joint Specialty Officers to the Call for "Uniformed Strategists"

In 1989, General (Ret.) John R. Galvin[21] added a critical literary piece to a then growing body of literature that recognized and debated over an evident shortfall in the knowledge and understanding of strategic affairs within the armed services; it was a shortcoming somewhat similar to Congressman Skelton's recognized gap in joint-specialized war experts. General (Ret.) Galvin wrote the following:

> The strategist in uniform provides advice to political authority in the development of national policy (what is to be achieved) and national strategy (how to achieve it). He has a role in forming national strategy and policy by explaining capabilities, the limitations of armed force, and how military power can be used as an element of national power.[22]

The very title of General (Ret.) Galvin's *Parameters* article, "What's the Matter with Being a Strategist?" spoke volumes to the prevailing skepticism of anything "political" and, therefore, "strategic" within the military culture of the 1970s and 1980s.[23] General (Ret.) Galvin recognized the prevalence of a systemic gap between national strategic aims in war-policy, the capacity of the military experts to effectively translate those often ambiguous ends into tangible military objectives, and the ability (and willingness) of senior military leaders to advise political authorities on the policy-setting, planning, and execution of war-policy.[24] Earlier in 1984, Theodore J. Crackel had alluded to where the gap between the capability to understand the national strategic aims of war and the capacity to translate strategy into tactics might reside:

> American military education has at its heart two crucial processes—the making of lieutenants and the making of colonels. How we prepare young men [and women] to lead others into battle, and how we ensure that those who assume the highest commands are well-qualified, are issues that must be addressed with utmost seriousness, because failure here can have the gravest consequences.[25]

The two processes—the making of lieutenants and the making of colonels—continue to define, albeit in broad terms, the current (modern) professional military education system of the U.S. armed forces in general and, for sake of emphasis in this chapter, the U.S. Army more specifically.

From an organizational perspective,[26] the division of educational labor, authority, and responsibility within the U.S. Army[27] seems to affect the operationalization and integration of tactical, operational, and strategic education, and, therefore, effects in war-policy implementation. There are three distinct levels of war, each overlapping the other and arrayed in a hierarchical manner: tactical, operational, and strategic. The primary responsibilities for education and training within the tactical band lies with the Army's "basic" and "advanced courses." This tactical band emphasizes platoon through division "battles and engagements."[28] At the higher end of the tactical band and overlapping with the operational level is the Command Arms Services Staff School. At this level, corps-level battles and "operations" are the primary educational and training focus.[29] The seam between the operational and the lower-end strategic band falls within the educational and training responsibility of the CGSC. The CGSC focuses on "subordinate campaign plans, and joint, services and combined operations."[30] The U.S. Army War College (AWC) is the primary institution for strategic-level education (theater strategy and campaign plans).

One expert and faculty member at the AWC makes the point succinctly when he states,

> [T]he "compartmentalization of skills" so typical of earlier training and education (civilian as well as military) is less and less adequate for the roles and responsibilities today's security practitioners and certainly senior military leaders must assume.[31]

Experts seem to be coming to the same conclusions: what is needed for success in the twenty-first-century security environment are practitioners with the adequate skills, knowledge, and capabilities that enable them to effectively practice the strategic art *at all levels of war-policy*. Scholars and practitioners agree that to practice this "strategic art"[32] successfully requires the *integration* of three related roles: strategic theorist, strategic leader, and strategic practitioner[33] or, rather, the useful merging of leadership, management, and action.

The word strategy is one of the most ill-defined and errantly used terms in the military lexicon. The term has had a different context during different time periods in military history; what was once termed "strategic" today refers to a whole other domain of war-fare—the operational. Strategy, today as always, is about both product and process.[34]

Earlier Recognition of a "Civilian" and "Operational" Shortfall in JPME

The experts are noticing that there is a need for strategic leaders who can coordinate ends, ways, and means; strategic practitioners who can apply ends, ways, and means (and translate non- or extramartial objectives into military objectives that are feasible, acceptable, and suitable); and strategic theorists who can formulate ends, ways, and means, all on behalf of fulfilling U.S. national security interests.[35] What is desired and demanded is the creation of "complete strategists"[36]—the human embodiment of the integration and combination of the strategic leader, strategic practitioner, and strategic theorist. What is desired and demanded are military strategists who are

> officers, all up and down the line, because it takes a junior strategist to implement what the senior strategist wants done, and it (usually) takes the input of juniors to help a senior strategist arrive at his [or her] conclusions.[37]

What is called for is a professional military education system designed to identify officers with natural propensity for study and practice of the "strategic art" early on in their careers (Lieutenants and junior captains) and to provide these officers with a continual dose of martial and extramartial knowledge, skill, and experience commensurate with twenty-first-century strategic planning. What the experts argue for is the production of the postmodern strategists (who I term the "holistic warrior" or "strategic planner"), yet, what persists is a "modern" PME system that is possibly producing something less than what is called for (as visioned by Galvin and others) and demanded by the new security environment.

Morris Janowitz posited that military professionals had to be given "a candid and realistic education about political matters and follow career patterns that sensitize them to political and social consequences of military action."[38] In his assessment, the U.S. Army needed to foster the development of what he termed "warrior-scholars"[39] at every chain-of-command level.[40] This chapter joins these debates and speaks to the educational impacts on the operational effectiveness of martial activities related to postmodern war- policymaking.

Edward Luttwak, arguably one of the preeminent experts of modern military strategic thought, found in his long years of study a paradox in the logic of strategy.[41] As in "normal" politics and policy, there is a horizontal and a vertical dimension to strategy making. In the horizontal dimension, one finds war and strategy's true nature—policy and plans, the result of contention between adversaries "who seek to oppose, deflect, and reverse each other's moves" in war.[42] In the vertical dimension, one sees the multidimensional nature of strategic policymaking—the vital interplay between the different levels of conflict—the tactical, technical, and operational. Like in policymaking, there is no natural harmony betwixt and between these aspects of strategy. The paradox that defines the overall process of strategy is only rationalized as policy is rationalized—through the operationalization of strategic aims and visions into tangible and executable plans and policies.[43] The operational domain facilitates the effective dialogue between strategy and tactics; it permits the dialectic to take place in a functional and effective way.

Of "Prophets" and "Leaders" of Military Strategy and War

In his study of strategy, operations, and tactics, B. H. Liddell Hart noted the following:[44]

> History bears witness to the vital part that the "prophets" have played in human progress—which is evidence of the ultimate practical value of expressing unreservedly the truth as one sees it. Yet it also becomes clear that the acceptance and spreading of their vision has always depended on another class of men—"leaders" who had to be philosophical strategists, striking a compromise between truth and men's reactivity to it.[45]

What Liddell Hart reveals are the core elements to war itself: war as theory, war as history, and war as it is practiced at any given time and under any given condition. He acknowledges the need for both prophets and leaders in war-policymaking—those able to understand war in the broad and the abstract and those capable of putting war's plans into action.[46] The education of future uniformed "prophet leaders"—strategic planners and holistic warriors—specialized in the full domain of war-policy is a growing necessity.[47] Understanding the changing characteristics and lexicon of war is a useful starting point in this exploration of a common understanding of both domains in relation to one another.

To understand the evolutionary development of the strategy-operations-tactics lexicon, four critical points are emphasized:

1. The evolution from eighteenth to twentieth century witnesses a shift from the agenda-setting, policy formulation, and execution of war-policy being vested in one or a small body of ruler-generals (soldier-kings) to a growing separation of war and war-fighting into separate entities—the setting of war-policy into the hands of the ruler and the power of execution of war-plans (tactics and techniques) into the hands of the general.[48] By the turn of the twentieth century, the compartmentalization and separation of the domains of war expand even further: academics who theorize over issues of strategy, civilian leaders who handle policymaking, and uniformed experts who execute war-policy.
2. There is the emergence of a formally recognized "operational" domain of war, first, defined simply in terms of logistical lines of communication (supply) but eventually expanding to include the command and control of forces within particular geographic theaters of war/operation and the array of forces in time, space, and purpose for realization of the higher war (grand strategic) aims.
3. There is the shift from tactical-driven (execution-based) stratagems to capabilities-driven strategizing (planning). One sees the rise of force development and modernization (research and development, programming and budgeting, acquisition and procurement) of weapons systems and related technologies, normally specific to a particular military arm or service.
4. There is the expansion of the military lexicon, by the twentieth century, to include and distinguish between grand strategy (multinational, extranational, and extragovernmental) and national strategy, from national strategy to the military strategy toward theater-specific campaign strategies and the development and husbanding of service-specific, force-based stratagems advocating particular operational methodologies and tactical techniques and procedures.

The evolution of the lexicon, particularly in Western political-military society, and the ensuing complication of the issue of strategy, operations, and tactics derived logically from the growing complexity of war-policy itself. What could once be studied, written about, understood, taught, planned, put into practice, and more often than not won through a single decisive battle or engagement by single individuals (soldier-rulers)[49] evolved into a complex policy issue that expanded well beyond the power and capacity of a single person—or nation—and, equally, could not be determined through just one battle. By the mid-twentieth century, it had become all too clear that war-policy could rarely be determined even through a series of battles and engagements (operations and campaigns).

Understanding this progression is important. The growing complexity of war-policy altered the civil-military relationship defining war making.[50] The challenge of the twenty-first century is to develop an educational system that can produce in one expert or a small body of experts all the skills and attributes endemic to the planning and execution of war-policy, while maintaining the delicate civil-military balance vital to American republican, representative democracy.

The "Modern" Education System

The modern, U.S. military education system is emblematic and symptomatic of the American and Western societal approach to war and war-policy. The civil aspects of war-policy are considered, even structured, separate from the martial aspects of war. The PME system reflects this separation in its design to a significant degree (see figure 10.1).

Senior military leaders (the generals) are formally educated in the martial arts and sciences, in a bottom-up, and slow progressive manner. Education and training begins in the tactical and technical sciences of war. The art of command and leadership in war is fostered through further advanced military schooling through the company grades. Early field grade education comes in the form of more military schooling and focuses on staff-planning. It is typical that only near the end of the standard military career (between the fifteenth and twentieth year of service) that some officers are provided the opportunity to study those aspects of war that lie outside the martial realm and experience. It is rarer that these officers are afforded the opportunity to study the other-than-martial sides of war-policy in institutions *outside the martial realm* (advanced civilian education and internships/fellowships). Granted, self-study in the liberal arts is ever-present and greatly supplements the education and experience of officers in the full spectrum of war-policy. However, to say that this and other exceptional, stopgap fixes to the education gap in modern soldier-scholars are adequate solutions would be overoptimistic.

Exacerbating the education gap even further is the division within the military profession between senior ranks, field grade ranks, and company grade ranks, and how the educational and experience-based learning process has been stovepiped along these rank-based lines to the detriment of the development of multidimensional uniformed experts in war-policy. Company grade officers are typically relegated to tactics and techniques of war-fighting. Field grade officers are nominally educated and developed in operational-level and, to a lesser degree, theater-strategic planning. The study and practice of strategy (national and grand) fall to the purview of the senior leadership (colonels and generals).

This hierarchy of educational and experience opportunities is tied to the seniority-based promotion and assignments processes. Such a system takes egalitarianism and fairness into account and adds a much-required efficiency to the system, vital for the effective administration of a large military force (a large army). Officers are typically not endorsed or resourced for the attainment of operational- or strategic-level education until a certain point in their careers. Even then, few are selected for such opportunities, and of these, few are able to remain competitive in the normal, progressive command track upon their return from these extraordinary education- and experience-based learning opportunities.[51]

Grade	Cadet/Midn	WO-Captain	Major	Lieutenant Colonel–Colonel	General
PME Level	Precommissioning	Primary/Career	Intermediate	Senior	General/Flag
PME Programs and Schools	• Service academies; • OCS; • ROTC units.	• TBS/AWS • CommO courses C&C system courses; • Other service basis and advanced war-fare specialty courses; • War-fighting skills MCI; • Nonresident AWS MCI.	• MC C&SC; • MC School of Advanced war-fighting; • Air C&SC; • Army Command and general staff; • College of Naval C&S; • Equivalent intelligence/ civilian programs; • Nonresident command and staff MCI.	• MC art of war; • Air War College; • Army War College; • College of Naval War-fare; • NWC; • ICAF; • Equivalent intelligence/ civilian programs.	• Capstone; • Seminars and courses; • JFOWS.
			Armed Forces Staff College		
Level of War	Tactical		Operational		Strategic
Education Focus	Introduction to service missions	Military Specialty • Service doctrine; • Service values; • Leadership; • Staff skills.	• Theater-level operational art; • Combined arms war-fare; • Introduction to national military and security strategy.	• Service school: National military strategy; • Joint school: National security strategy.	• Theater-level joint/combined operations; • Synthesis of national military strategy with national security strategy; • Synthesis of national security strategy with national policy-making requirements.
Joint Emphasis	Joint Introduction • History; • Purpose; • Overview.	Joint Awareness • Organizations; • Missions; • Interservice relationships.	• Joint forces and the operational level of war; • Organization and command relationships; • Joint C3/intelligence; • Defense planning systems.	• National capabilities Command service; • Joint doctrine; • Joint planning; • Intrala joint/ combined operations; • Compaign planning; • Joint/combined war-fare (theater context).	

Figure 10.1 The Modern-Era PME Career Progression

Note: Programs and courses listed above indicate the PME Marines in that grade complete in order to be qualified for promotion to the next higher rank.

Source: Official 101st Airborne Division planning briefings (unclassified versions and/or declassified materials), June 2003–May 2005.

Toward a "Postmodern" Education System

President John F. Kennedy, in his words that follow, correctly captured the signs of the security times of his generation—a security environment that has only become more complex since, demanding even more that the military to adjust its ways of educating its officers in the strategy, operations, and tactics of war:

> You [military professionals] must know something about strategy and tactics and logistics, but also economics and politics and diplomacy and history. You must know everything you can about military power, and you must also understand the limits of military power. You must understand that few of the problems of our time have . . . been solved by military power alone.[52]

A time when politics and war—the foreign and the domestic—were less recognized seems to have returned. Ironically, it is at this very point in time that the U.S. military and the U.S. Army in particular seem intent on compartmentalizing war into separate domains in the education of its future war experts. In these times of strategic ambiguity, the United States needs officers who are both prophets of strategy and the theorizing of war and practitioners (leaders) of war-policy.[53] The twenty-first century demands a return to a time when much of the policy, planning, and execution of war-policy was vested in one or a small body of experts. It is time to educate and develop future uniformed strategic planners—the nation's holistic warrior caste.

Conclusions, Current Trends, and Recommendations

The gap between the strategic aspects of war and the tactical actions in war and war-planning has been well documented.[54] Reviews of the 1980s called for a reform of the existing PME to facilitate more joint expertise within the armed forces. One of the answers, then, was the mandating of JSO development within the PME. This latest period of reform, review, and transformation may be indicative of a similar shortcoming in the prevailing PME, this time indicating an anemia with regards to advanced civilian, graduate-level study in international affairs and operational planning.

A Gap in Civilian-Based Education?

Changes in the security dynamics of the postmodern international environment should have a significant vote in the election to round out the educational experience of Army strategists with more civilian academic and operational planning expertise or to remain focused on the martial, tactical-level of war-fighting. New trends have already influenced the redirection of U.S. foreign and security policy and the rules and practices governing the interaction of nations, businesses, individuals, and transnational groups and organizations.[55]

"Academia" Has Started to Adapt and Innovate

The information revolution has clouded what was at one time a clearer divide between those issues domestic and those of a foreign policy nature; the digital era has grayed the distinction between the military aspects of war and the nonmilitary.

Civilian graduate programs have adjusted accordingly:[56]

> At Georgetown University, the National Security Studies of the Edmund A. Walsh School of Foreign Service has added courses on low-intensity conflict, conflict resolution and peacekeeping, transnational relations, and economic aspects of national security to the standard fare on defense and military policy. International communication and environmental policy are among the concentrations offered by the School of International Service at American University and the School of International and Public Affairs at Columbia University. [S]ome programs, such as George Washington University's Elliot School of International Affairs and Johns Hopkins' Paul H. Nitze School of Advanced International Studies offer executive versions of their programs for working and/or mid-career professionals.[57]

The military's inextricable relationship with politics and policymaking is not a contemporary phenomenon; there have rarely been military actions without political ramifications.[58] Morris Janowitz parrots the positive and necessary requirements of an advanced civilianized conception of war-policy for the future martial expert, noting that

> the contemporary officer must relate national policy to the military organization, . . . [t]o assume international policing and peacekeeping (PK) responsibilities, the postwar officer needs an understanding of national policy and objectives, which demands a broader scope of "citizen attachment"—that is, closer ties to society and state.[59]

Authors and national security experts John W. Masland and Lawrence I. Radway identified three categories of qualifications[60] that all officers should meet:[61]

- Professional Military Qualifications, consisting of military competency, the representation of the national security viewpoint in a democratic society and knowing the problems of enlisted personnel;
- General Executive Qualifications, including the evaluation of people and information, effective communications and the efficient and economic conduct of affairs; the ability of officers to grasp large and complicated situations; the ability of the military officer to see the "big picture"—making cognitive connections among, and balancing, war's diverse components;
- Military Executive versus Combat Leader, being less distinguishable in this new age of warfare, calling for a good military education system, as well as [an assignments] rotation system designed to enhance military officer adaptability amongst the civil-military aspects of warfare.

How the Army develops its war experts—its strategic planners—has promise of being one of the more effective treatments for curing the strategic planning anemia afflicting the service. Experiences seal and confirm (or deny) learning. If war is not only about war-fighting but a whole lot more, then the Army must do better at aligning the experiences of its officers with the full domain of war-fare.

Looking to the Future

What postmodern war-fare and the threats that help to define it demand in terms of competencies to deal effectively in the new environment should determine the

Core Competencies of the "Strategic Planner"	Measures of Effectiveness
• Tactically and technically proficient and confident in tactical-level leadership and implementation of martial tasks. • A thinking-doer, educated early and often (continually) in the multifaceted aspects of "holistic" war-fare. • Expert in the theory, history, doctrine, operational art and science of the U.S. military and familiar with same competencies for multinational military forces. • Competent in the combatant command and management roles and functions of the Total Army force, competent in joint force integration. • Expert in comparative politics and international affairs, competent in U.S. domestic politics and policy-making processes. • Experienced in the interagency processes, familiarized in PVO/NGO/corporate operations.	• Branch-qualified (traditional system) as a company grade officer, emphasis on platoon and company leader time, with less time allocated to staff familiarization. • Advanced civilian-based graduate study (minimum of 18 months in a prestigious program), attainment of masters-level degree, PhD preferable –> attain between fifth and eighth years of service. • Teaching, internship, fellowship, and/or training-with-industry experience as senior captain/junior major (postgraduate reinforcement). • CGSC-SAMS (or equivalent) graduate (Captain/Major). • JPME II and JAWS-type program graduate (Major/Lieutenant Colonel). • CTC OC experience (preferable). • Joint staff experience (either resident or through formal outreach learning). • Continual outreach learning throughout career lifecycle (tracked and validated by PERSCOM/JCS).

Figure 10.2 Core Competencies and Measures of Effectiveness

Source: Official 101st Airborne Division planning briefings (unclassified versions and/or declassified materials), June 2003–May 2005.

Army's next moves in transformation. This includes the next steps the Army takes toward the education of the officer corps in general but specifically in terms of how the Army will produce and husband its core body of strategic planning experts. The experts allude to what collectively forms the core competencies and measures of effectiveness (see figure 10.2).

The need for a greater "international practitioner" competency in the generalist officer population but particularly within the Army's strategic experts is acknowledged and emphasized. A "beyond-the-martial" educational experience is explicit in the writings of theorists, scholars, and practitioners alike and is implicit in the nature of the postmodern security environment. With the dwindling distinction between domestic and foreign security policy issues, the future Army strategists must be more than familiarized with both domains; they must be competent in both policy domains, a competency that can only be obtained and sustained through frequent and continued (periodic) academic study and experience-based learning in both domains.

A fourfold approach to an educational reform geared toward the creation and fostering of a small, manageable body of strategic planners in the U.S. Army is one way of conceptualizing policy treatments and recommendations. What follows is an offering of one approach and one possibility (see figure 10.3).

Advanced Civilian Education

Detection and designation of future strategic planners much earlier than the current system are admittedly difficult if not impossible to achieve; it is particularly true if no

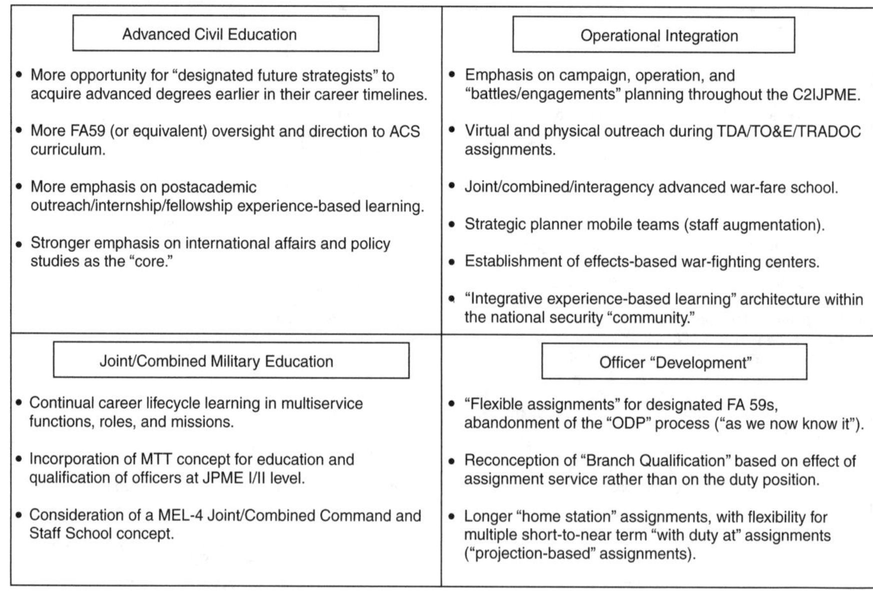

Advanced Civil Education
• More opportunity for "designated future strategists" to acquire advanced degrees earlier in their career timelines.
• More FA59 (or equivalent) oversight and direction to ACS curriculum.
• More emphasis on postacademic outreach/internship/fellowship experience-based learning.
• Stronger emphasis on international affairs and policy studies as the "core."
Operational Integration
• Emphasis on campaign, operation, and "battles/engagements" planning throughout the C2IJPME.
• Virtual and physical outreach during TDA/TO&E/TRADOC assignments.
• Joint/combined/interagency advanced war-fare school.
• Strategic planner mobile teams (staff augmentation).
• Establishment of effects-based war-fighting centers.
• "Integrative experience-based learning" architecture within the national security "community."
Joint/Combined Military Education
• Continual career lifecycle learning in multiservice functions, roles, and missions.
• Incorporation of MTT concept for education and qualification of officers at JPME I/II level.
• Consideration of a MEL-4 Joint/Combined Command and Staff School concept.
Officer "Development"
• "Flexible assignments" for designated FA 59s, abandonment of the "ODP" process ("as we now know it").
• Reconception of "Branch Qualification" based on effect of assignment service rather than on the duty position.
• Longer "home station" assignments, with flexibility for multiple short-to-near term "with duty at" assignments ("projection-based" assignments).

Figure 10.3 A Four-Stage Model of Reform

Source: Official 101st Airborne Division planning briefings (unclassified versions and/or declassified materials), June 2003–May 2005.

significant trade-off in military tactical and technical learning is desirable. One way of overcoming the loss of an earlier civilian-academic learning experience is to maximize the opportunities after postgraduation and to reinforce and add to that learning and knowledge through civilian and governmental (private, public, and international) experience-based and research-based outreach. Participation in Department of the Army, Department of Defense/Office of the Secretary of Defense (DOD/OSD) research is conceivably possible during normal assignment cycles—even during operational assignments. The challenge is to integrate such activities into the guiding mission essential tasks of the parent unit, so as not to detract from daily unit requirements.

This sort of challenge is not insurmountable; in fact, such opportunities can add relevancy to some traditional unit-based educational programs, such as unit professional reading programs and leader development programs, which often receive scant emphasis. Infusing more firsthand experience with the extramartial worlds of war-policy into the traditional career lifecycle of the Army officer (future strategists), either through more formally supported and resourced academic learning and/or through postgraduate outreach, internship, and fellowships could prove an effective innovation in the civilian-combined-interagency, joint professional military education (C2IJPME) system of the twenty-first century.

As noted earlier, civilian-based academic institutions have outpaced the military in many respects in identifying the new challenges and nuances of the twenty-first-century security environment and have made significant movement toward improving their curricula and programs to accommodate the postmodern war-environment.

Part of these civilian-based institutional and philosophical reforms has been a reconceptualization of the value of having mid-career military officers as part of their student bodies. Civil-military relations can be greatly enhanced through military officers' attendance in in-residence ACS. Civilian educational institutions and the U.S. Army (U.S. military) must work together and collaborate in order to make these educational experiences more affordable and beneficial to both domains of war-policy development. Positive trends already abound. The national service academies as part of their processes and programs for acquiring high-quality company grade officers from the fielded force for ACS and instructor/teaching assignments have found ways, in coordination with civilian-academic institutions, of offering officers high-cost, prestigious education at affordable rates through mid- to low-cost programs.[62] The seeds of greater civil-military cooperation on the education issue have been laid for some time now. The Army needs to become more effective and efficient at reaping what has already been sown.

Joint/Combined Military Education

If career timelines and OPTEMPO rob officers of the time and opportunity to go to the resident courses, then perhaps bringing the course to the officer is the next best option. A combination of virtual (distance-learning-based) and physical (educational management teams concept, similar to the MMT design) remote learning alternatives could enhance the building of joint culture and joint capability within the Total Army Force. Reaching a higher level of joint cognition is one step closer to a more holistic strategic conception of war-policy and the strategic planners' future role in it.

Operational Integration

Of the treatments offered in figure 10.3 above, the establishment of a joint/combined, and interagency advanced war-fighting course (similar to SAMS, SASS, and SAWS) and the move toward mobile strategic planner staff augmentee teams (MSPSAs) are two innovations that have some degree of empirical support through contemporary practical experimentation. The mobile strategic planner team concept has some recent operational reinforcement, from experiences, with the addition of ad hoc, modular staff to the 10th Mountain Division during Operation Enduring Freedom in Afghanistan.

Officer Development (Assignments)

Experience is the best teacher. This popular statement does not consider enough the fact that experience, if left to its own ends, can teach the wrong lessons as much as well-balanced experience can reinforce success. A purpose-based or "effects-based" approach to branch qualification should be considered as the new measure of educational and experience-based learning success. Seniority, rank, and position may be adequate measures of success and effectiveness for some traditional branches but should not be standard for all branches and specialties. New ideas on old negative notions of officer "homesteading" need to be reconceived. Longer tours at a particular station or post could add the degree of officer stability needed from which short- and near-term "with assignment at" opportunities can blossom. The secretary of defense has been considering ways of stabilizing the force (particularly O-4/Major) for efficiency and quality-of-life reasons. Stabilization can also be a ways toward increasing the experience-based learning of officers in holistic war-policy. Innovation in strategic planner education can only progress as far as the assignments process will allow. Fixing the latter is a prerequisite to fixing the rest.

In Conclusion

The military experiences of U.S. Army senior leaders during the 1990s revealed—by their own recollections and their own testimonies—that though Army education was good throughout their careers, this education proved less effective in the light of the new war-fare, perhaps even irrelevant in certain respects. Future success will depend on educating future strategic planners adequately, appropriately, and holistically for the challenges of the twenty-first century.

War-fare during this new age has already, in many ways and on many instances, been as much about the political, economic, cultural, ethnoreligious factors of war as it is about the traditional martial aspects of war and war-fighting. Future war experts must be educated, trained, and should have gained experience early and often (continually) in all these aspects. Revising the PME for a body of war-policy "translators" for civilian policy makers and the generalist military population could greatly enhance future civil-military operations but only if the education of this small cohort is holistic. It may serve as a useful interim corrective to the problems in the generalist PME system that we know exist but is beyond fixing in the immediate.

Policy Treatments: New Conceptualizations of War-Policy Education

What follows is an offering of some new ways of thinking about how the U.S. Army educates for production of the complete strategist: the strategic planner. Although most of the programs and programmatic ways presented here are not new in and of themselves, where innovation can be found is in the manner of redesign proffered.

Formal Academic Learning: The "West Point Core" as the Baseline

Inculcating future strategic planners in the holistic nature of war-policy needs to begin at the precommissioning and undergraduate education stages of officer development. One of the arguments made in this chapter is that while some familiarization with the various martial and nonmartial aspects of war as policy is provided to the generalist population, the Army as an institution is remiss in developing core competencies by which to guide future and continuing (career lifecycle) officer education. The United States Military Academy (USMA) at West Point has traditionally maintained a core academic and experience-based curriculum derived from, and in support of, the U.S. Army vision and mission. The USMA is presently experimenting with a new curriculum, commensurate with the changed national security environment of the post–cold war era and coincident with the Army's concept of information-age war-fare and full-spectrum operations. The "West Point Core" may serve as a useful guide for all officer accession and undergraduate learning institutions.

The USMA has departed significantly but not completely from its engineer-heavy and physical sciences traditions to better accommodate the peculiar needs of warfare and nation-based politics of the twenty-first century. Stronger emphasis is given throughout a cadet's four-year experience, in this newly proposed curriculum, to issues of comparative politics, culture-based studies, information management and infotech studies, history, and international relations. Of particular note, the new approach recognizes the importance of operational integration as a tool of success for future Army officers and strategists. Referenced as the "Integrative Experience," the curriculum change currently under consideration cordons off time, space, and resources within the four-year program dedicated to teaching the cadets how to "integrate" all that they have learned and experienced. This multidisciplinary, multifunctional operational planning experience could serve as the bedrock upon which an operational planning learning experience could be built, inculcating every stage of an officer's broad education experience.

The formal curriculum is only part of what could be a universal precommissioning PME for all Army officers, regardless of whether they access from the USMA, Reserve Officer Training Corps (ROTC), or Officer Candidate School (OCS). Infusing experience-based learning into the undergraduate education experience is vitally important to the education of future holistic war-policy experts. Having the opportunity to intern as cadets within the U.S. interagency process with nongovernmental and private organizations and having the opportunity to learn about the joint service community would contribute immensely to the familiarization of war's full and true nature to these young leaders, early on. Laying this seed of understanding early can bud into an officer corps with a better appreciation for all aspects, functions, and elements of war as policy.

Formal Academic Learning: Advanced Civilian Schooling

Though the experts all seem to agree that at least theoretically or idealistically it would be of some benefit to afford all officers earmarked early on as future strategists with a prestigious advanced graduate learning experience, two issues continue to stymie making this a reality: cost in dollars and cost in time available in the present career developmental lifecycle.

The dollar cost will continue to inhibit the process of achieving the goal of better education for future war experts; no solution can be offered. However, one thing is sure: if concerns with future effectiveness in war's prosecution demands that war's experts are better educated in war's multidimensional character and purpose, then the U.S. Army will need to recalculate the cost benefits in providing high-quality academic education to its core war-strategists. Again, the USMA has been experimenting with innovative public-private cooperative initiatives with prestigious academic institutions and civilian-based foundations to find cost-effective ways of making graduate-level study available and affordable to Army officers.

The challenge of available time is more an Army self-imposition. The "arbitrariness of branch qualification" mentioned earlier greatly prohibits not so much the opportunities available to the officer in advanced civil studies but rather the opportunity the officer has in taking advantage of these learning opportunities. If an Army officer wishes for a successful long-term career in the service, then the officer cannot "afford" to deviate too far or too often from the command track, a track that has been shown to provide few opportunities for civilian graduate study. Distanced-learning and co-op educational programs may prove the only feasible, suitable, and acceptable means for providing young company grade officers advanced civilian learning experiences. It would be difficult, and potentially damaging to the tactical and technical training of officers in their core war-fighting and leadership roles and functions, to offer much less mandate in-resident civilian study any earlier than the Army does now. However, the Army does need to consider whether or not it is maximizing the potential of the company grade years of a typical officer. Many young officers, after completing the vital duty assignment of platoon leader or company executive officer, move on to serve for two more years as assistant staff officers. Might some of that time, after platoon leadership training but before branch-qualifying company command, be used to provide these young officers with an advanced civilian-academic learning experience? Again, if the need is recognized, then ways must be found to accommodate the need.

Experience-Based Learning: The Postgraduate Fellowship/Internship

The shortfalls identified in this evaluation regarding postgraduate academic and research ("outreach") opportunities are not that there are too few opportunities available. On the contrary, the opportunities abound in terms of military-based, civilian-/governmental-based, civilian-/corporate-/private-based, and international-based internships and fellowships for U.S. Army officers and particularly designated "strategists" to take advantage of. The shortfall is in time available in an already-saturated "normal" career progression. Not a whole lot of time can be allocated to such extratactical endeavors without taking valuable time away from the technical and tactical training for war-fare. Time "away from troops" is also perceived as time that could be "better spent" within the dominant U.S. Army culture. An officer can unintentionally take on the brand of "the intellectual" rather than be recognized as "the warrior" if too much time is spent thinking about war. Though uncomfortable to hear, these cultural biases and the arbitrary administrative restrictions that largely derive from them are well documented by senior military leaders, scholars, and practitioners.

One possible way of rethinking of postgraduate outreach experience as an enhancing aspect of war preparation could start with a reconsideration of officer education as a nonstop progression. There is absolutely no reason why a Table of Organization and Equipment (TO&E) duty assignment or a Training and Doctrine Command (TRADOC) course should mean the end to outreach opportunity. In fact, outreach—relevant research opportunities for DOD, the services, and so on—should be integrated into the JPME, at a minimum, and even infused into the daily activities of "field forces."

While assigned as an assistant professor with the Department of Social Sciences, USMA, West Point, I took part in numerous real-world, relevant DOD-directed research projects. Attendance at and participation in civilian-based international affairs conferences were encouraged during this particular duty assignment. These activities were "extra" activities from a formal duty assignment perspective, yet they were a vitally rewarding and educational experience both for the individual officer and the Department of Social Sciences program and the U.S. Army in general. While in attendance in the Command and General Staff Officers Course (CGSC), I continued research-based outreach activities; once the administrative barriers were breached (typically, issues relating to lack of funds), such opportunities were encouraged by the staff, faculty, and command group. The Office of Homeland Security even "unofficially" solicited a small group of CGSC officers for six months of out-of-the-beltway research and analysis regarding the preparation of the nation for the new homeland security function.[63]

Fellowship, internships, and training-with-industry opportunities—typically one-year assignments—often interfere with the standard two-, three-, and four-year officer assignments. The fact that such opportunities are recognized, all too narrowly, as "extra" relegate them to perceived time away from more legitimate duties. Consideration of fellowship- or internship-based assignments as branch-service-enhancing, or even branch-qualifying (particularly for FA59 officers) could help to overcome the perceptual barriers. To date, such assignments are still seen as "great, but a threat to needed branch qualifying time." Receipt of an "academic evaluation report" (AER) rather than the "officer evaluation report" (OER) relegates such outreach opportunities as less career-enhancing and therefore less career-relevant. Giving branch-qualifying credit to such assignments (granting the OER rather than the "letter of appreciation" or AER) should be determined based on the relevancy of the job itself, rather than on whether the duty position is "owned and operated" by the U.S. Army, or an officially recognized officer development position (ODP) assignment. The complexities defining this new information-age war-fare actually make some of these fellowship- and internship-based opportunities "more" relevant to future martial expertise than some of the traditional experiences that have long defined career success in the U.S. Army. If the Federal Emergency Management Agency (FEMA) has assumed a lead-agency role in most future homeland security operations and if the U.S. Army is going to service as a supporting command in such missions, then facilitating the education of U.S. Army strategists (at a minimum) in FEMA-based operations is an important core competency to resource and recognize as "branch-qualifying."

Incorporating outreach opportunity for officers assigned to "fighting MACOMs" is a tougher challenge to overcome, but the problem is not insurmountable. All divisional units and those below maintain "professional reading programs." It would not be all that difficult to infuse some real-world relevancy to such programs by integrating them into some ongoing TRADOC and/or DA/DOD research project. Integration of outreach opportunities into traditional intelligence preparation of the battlefield (IPB) activities could greatly enhance the IPB process itself, again, adding relevancy and adding a means of educating the force on the new way of war-fare.

Time and resources available are the standard excuses given to such ideas and, unfortunately, effective excuses for ending the discussions prematurely. Time is a relative thing and is as much of a constraint as planners and decision makers want it to be. Why does an officer need to stabilize in a duty assignment for a minimum of two years (with the exception of overseas short tours) to get "credit" for the work done, much less to get credit for the educational benefit of the experience? The requirement is arbitrary and is limiting the educational opportunity of future Army strategic planners to attain the requisite experiences and knowledge they will need to be effective and relevant as master strategists in the postmodern war era.

Experience-Based Learning: Postgraduate Studies in "Operations"

Learning how to operationalize strategic challenges into tactical or implementation-level plans and actions is perhaps the most important factor to consider in redesigning the U.S. Army educational approach to strategists development. When one thinks of operations in its effects-based context of "integration," the importance of operations-based education becomes even more evident.

Despite accomplishments by the Army and the other armed services in this area over the years (and with the helpful nudge of Congress in 1986), there remain problems in both how the Army conceives of "operations" and how the Army therefore prepares its officers for integration.

There is a prevailing notion within the U.S. Army that the "operational level of war" and to some degree the notion of "operations" itself are martial constructs and are relevant only to the martial domain of war-policy. It is doubtful, though possible, that the former contention is a correct one; the latter contention is wholly inaccurate and limiting in its perspective, given the realities of postmodern policy in general, much less war-fare. While the official U.S. Army, U.S. Marine Corps, and even the joint doctrinal definitions of "operations, et al." qualify the integration of force in "military" terms, all other renderings avoid the martial qualifier. Although the operationalization of "operations" as a formal domain or level of war during the eighteenth century did in fact take on a unique characteristic to the martial science and art, that particular operationalization, martial as it was, was of a particular time period and strategic-environmental context. This in no way means that "operations" were to be defined forever in the linear, mass-oriented military tactics, techniques, and procedures of that time, nor did it relegate operational science and artistry to merely the martial realm.

Appreciating the larger-than military context of force and power integration—operations—demands a larger-than martial education for the martial expert. FEMA has its own integration process and artistry, as does NASA, the FBI, and the INS. Foreign countries have their own unique ways and means for integrating strategic aims with resources available for operational effects. Tomorrow's uniformed strategic planner must be familiar with, if not expert in, all these various operational methodologies and more. Operational expertise must begin with formal academic learning and must be reinforced by training and experience-based learning opportunities throughout the career lifecycle.

Learning from the Lessons of the 1986–1989 Joint Officer Reforms

The Skelton Panel was the first official governmental review of jointness in DOD; it was the first formal review to identify systemic shortfalls and the first statutory attempt to rectify some of those shortfalls. The current Joint Staff transformation initiatives in JPME continue to find shortcomings and continue to strive toward possible solutions. One of the JCS' latest reviews find an educational (academic, training, experiential learning) gap between the captain and lieutenant colonel ranks in joint integration.

The junior grade—middle ranks gap in joint integration education has been substantiated in a recent Boos-Allen study, conducted under contract by the JCS.[64] While the civilian-contracted study found an absence in joint integration education at the company grade levels, the reviewers acknowledged the continuing importance of focusing the majority of company grade training and academic study on service core competencies—developing and reinforcing service expertise prior to joint education. However, the study did emphasize the need for improved joint education and familiarization earlier in the officer career development timeline. The solution mentioned is becoming a popular panacea for the education dilemma: distanced learning.

The pros and cons of distanced learning are beyond the scope of this book. However, self-study, no matter how enhanced through improved information technology and digitization, should not be considered as the cure-all for joint officer education. The same holds true for solving the strategist education gap. One remedy initiated in November 2002 by the Department of the Army for Army Strategist (FA 59) education is the establishment of a distanced learning correspondence program: the Defense National Security Studies Program (DNSSP). So far still a voluntary self-study program, the DNSSP is a useful supplement to what should be a broad, wide-ranging curriculum for the education of Army strategic planners. Valuating the program as more than a supplement may be a programmatic misstep toward a better more holistic educational system.

Advanced "War" Studies Programs: Infusing More Joint, Civil, and Strategic Insights

History will confirm the year 1982 as a watershed in U.S. Army PME. Due to a recognized gap within the preexisting PME of their time in operational art and science, a handful of senior Army leaders dedicated efforts to the establishment of a postgraduate program—a second-year follow-on to MEL-4 graduate study at CGSC—focused on in-depth study of the advanced theory, history, and doctrinal development of military art and science and the near-term production of officers who are experts in operations and campaign planning. Since the founding of the U.S. Army School of Advanced Military Studies (SAMS) at fort Leavenworth, Kansas, the U.S. Air Force and U.S. Marine Corps have developed comparable programs of their own (the School of Advanced Strategic Studies [SASS] and the School of Advanced Warfighting [SAWS], respectively). As best that could be determined by me, there are no comparable operation-focused programs neither within the U.S. military nor in the governmental or private sectors. Yet, as this study and others reveal, knowledge of, expertise, and confidence in the art and science of operational integration (agenda-setting, planning, and execution) are perhaps the necessary and sufficient core competencies for success in war-policy.

Despite the best efforts and outputs of SAMS, SASS, and SAWS, there remains a crucial shortage in operational integration expertise—both within the military domain and within the civilian sectors. The merging of the domestic with the foreign aspects of security policy and the corresponding rise of homeland security issues make the absence of a cross-cutting, civil-military operational integration education system all the more substantial and foreboding. Attaining full joint integration between SAMS, SASS, and SAWS remains a challenge; infusing full-combined (multinational) and full-interagency integration via some formalized educational system and/or institution remains an even more distant endeavor. The call for a joint advanced studies program is not new. Yet, there is a new initiative underway within the J-7 of the Joint Staff to realize a joint equivalent to SAMS and the other service-based advanced war-fighting programs. Labeled the Joint Advanced Warfighting School (JAWS), this program supplements (not replaces) the one-year service-based advanced studies programs, focusing academic, training, and experiential learning on joint operational integration—the development of theater-strategic plans.

The same thought and effort need to be committed to the establishment of strategic integration education, though it is a program similar to the proposed JAWS initiative. Or better still, the JAWS concept could be reconceived and redesigned even before its development and implementation (implemented as of Fall 2003) to go beyond the joint integration competencies, incorporating full-spectrum integration education (civilian, interagency, corporate, multinational, etc.). A broadened conception of the joint operating concepts (JOCs)—one that incorporates martial and extramartial capabilities and competencies within the scenarios—could serve as the baseline for the course curriculum and andragogy. Piggybacking on the positive movements toward better joint education may be the best means of bettering the educational opportunities of future strategic planners.

Merging the Learning: "Flexible Assignments"

This is not the first study to pinpoint major shortcomings in effective officer development to the officer personnel management system. It will surely not be the last. Without elaborating the point, "flexibility" in officer assignments, promotion selection, branch qualification crediting, and career development is an important factor in future educational success of war-policy experts. The "command track" pathway to officer success needs to be relooked, reconceived, and redesigned so that it accommodates the acquisition of core competencies and expertise that are now redefining success in the postmodern age of war-fare. The Army's notion of "command" itself is perhaps ready for a review. This latter point remains more of a philosophical discussion, but practical evidence is beginning to mount, supporting at least the plausible idea that notions of command in the past no longer fits nicely with the command needs of this new age of war-fare. The U.S. Army, though successfully evolving its tactics, techniques, and procedures to postmodern war-fare, is already experiencing cognitive dissidence in transforming fully and confidently to the new emergent ways and purposes of war-policy. Under such transitory conditions, the need for a small but capable body of strategic planning experts to serve as "translators" and mediators between the traditional Army and the emergent one—between the martial and the extramartial halves of the war-policy COIN—is perhaps more important than ever before.

The U.S. Army must rethink what it values as "relevant assignments" versus less relevant assignments. Three-year assignments in staff and command positions are important for the achievement of "mastery-level" experience, confidence in operation integration, and execution of plans and orders. However, there is no reason that three years spent in a particular duty assignment—to a particular unit of action—should relegate experience to the confines of the particular unit of assignment. Outreach opportunities should be incorporated into standard unit operations. Three-month, six-month, and one-year internships/fellowship experiences should be infused in TDA and TO&E assignments and seen for their staff and for planning relevancy. Perhaps longer stabilizing timelines are the solution, with the caveat that officers are parceled out to various outreach opportunities during perhaps a four- to six-year duty assignment, in a "with-duty-at" or "with-duty-with" status. This sort of recommendation would require innovations in the overall assignments philosophy and processes. Yet, if the nature of postmodern war calls for such innovation and adaptation, then innovation of existing educational and assignments-based processes must be given credence and consideration.

Some Final Thoughts on the *RME*

The U.S. armed services have suffered a trend of anti-intellectualism for a long part of its modern-day history. The degree of that anti-intellectualism has varied with the cultural proclivities of the services and the evolving nature of each service's roles and functions in war-fare. Our more technical services have perhaps been more rapid in the expansion of the breadth and scope of their PME programs. As the technical complexity of our Naval service functions grew, so also did the need to expand the breath and composition of the Naval PME system. Necessity is truly the mother of innovation in how we educate our warriors. The dawn of manned flight brought about one of the most revolutionary explosions in military affairs and educational affairs. The addition of this radical innovation in war-fighting capability heralded a dramatic modification of U.S. Naval war-fare—the birth of Naval aviation and the rise of the carrier-based fleet operational approach to Naval war-fare. Its impact on the U.S. Army was even more dramatic, for it eventually harkened the rebellion of the Army Air Corps and the formation of an entirely new arm of service: the Air Force.

Was the need for a more broad, comprehensive, and advanced civilian (graduate-level and technical) educational program to support these innovations in military affairs a partial cause of these organizational breaks with tradition? I have been unsuccessful in finding any such study in the existing literature. But the proposition is intriguing, one that instinctively and anecdotally seems to make logical sense.

Perhaps one reason for the Army's lag in PME modernization is because of the stable and steady-state nature of land war-fare, relatively speaking, as compared with the other services. Maybe the Army has had less necessity to change how it thinks about the role of education and how it has gone about educating its officer corps? And perhaps this is a cause of the Army's relative orphaned status—no "mother for the innovation," or at least not a very attentive mother. In the Army's defense, when we think of the revolution in educational affairs question in this light, we can begin to understand at least some aspect of the service's rational for allowing an anti-intellectualism to fester in its ranks. Time in classrooms is time away from the battle. There would have to be a clear and strong reason to convince the Army's senior leadership that the investment in education—much less a radical and revolutionary reformation of its education system—was worth the cost imposed on troops available for the daily performance of the service's core functions. When a service is at war, the cost-benefit calculus is even more stark.

The need for change has to be clearly visible to the service leadership. Perhaps this is why the majority of our nation's military educational innovations has come in the aftermath of evolutions and revolutions in technological affairs. This *military-technological* driver for our service adaptations has lead to our traditional (modern) *materiel-centric capabilities-based approaches* to force development and strategy. It is much harder when the changes to the contemporary operating environment (COE) are as much human-based as they are tech-centric. It is nearly impossible to see and appreciate when the changing nature of war-fare is predominantly a cultural and ideological change. The U.S. Army has always prided itself as the service that privileges people over machinery—*People First, and Always!* has been a long-standing Army slogan and a core part of its professional ethos. Yet, having people as your base standard of measure as a service can be problematic, particularly when it comes to the politics of war-policy. It is easier to justify to Congress the need for a bigger slice of the defense budget when you can show where the money is going—materiel wares, such as F-22 Striker Aircraft or Submarines, are tangible benefit-to-cost measures. To ask for and convince the appropriators for the allocation of billions of dollars over a multiyear plan for a comprehensive overhaul of the Army education system is a hard sell. What does this sort of investment buy us? When can we see the benefits? These are hard and fair questions to ask and most difficult ones to answer.

At present, we owe a debt of thanks to our enemies, for they have accomplished for us what we could never have on our own. The enemy, particularly since the 9/11 attacks, has given us clearer measures for demonstrating the significant need for reform of our PME system. The adversary has marketed this new postmodern COE in clear and stark terms—a "hard sell" but an effective one. Because of the threat, we are better able to see what our PME and overall way of war have long been missing. The enemy has demonstrated the Clausewitzian theory of war, proving that it is true that war is simply a continuation of politics by other means. The enemy is helping us to realize that *it is all war*!—that there is no clean line dividing domestic war-fare from foreign war-fare, civil action in war from martial action in war. Thanks to the enemy, we can hopefully now begin the revolution—the radical redesign of our PME to form a new system that goes well beyond the "Professional" in PME, well beyond the "Joint" in JPME. The enemy will hopefully prove to be our mother of innovation, an innovation that will lead us toward the creation of a new education system for the creation of *holistic warriors*.

Epilogue: No More Iraqs?

Writers of history have warned time and time again of the dangers of attempting to chronicle a happening too soon or too close to the occurrence. The annals of our own histories record a repeat violation of this warning. I am not writing this as much as a historian as I am as a political scientist.[1] That is not to say that I am not a student of history, nor that this book is not an endeavor in histiography of the Iraq War specifically and war in general. Yet, this particular history is a history with a political purpose—that purpose being an effort to gain a relevant and timely understanding of this particular war, our collective march into it in March 2003 in the broader historical context of previous marches to war, in hopes of a discovery: why we fell into this war when we did, the way we did, and how this fall might relate to previous "falls" showing us new ways of not falling in the future, a quest for new balance in our ways of war and peace. While it will probably be at least another 20 to 30 years until we receive the full history of this war in Iraq, I offer that we can certainly not afford to wait that long in our effort to find answers to the questions that linger today (e.g., how did we get here and why?), questions that if left unasked and unanswered will find us stumbling toward another failing intervention.

Summoning New Trumpeters

General (Ret.) David R. Palmer, soldier and scholar—military historian—faced down those challenging his own efforts to better understand the war of his own age (Vietnam) so soon after the event.[2] Palmer's answer to those admonitions was straight and direct: "But we live now. And we may be compelled to wage another war before those volumes [the definitive version of the Vietnam War] become available." And he went even further to state,

> History, if it is to have any real purpose, tells us where we have been and where we are, thus helping to point out the best avenue into the future.[3]

Palmer was absolutely right in his political purposing of his early chronicling of the Vietnam War. In 1996, nearly a full 20 years after Palmer's early history and a full two decades after the end of America's war in Vietnam, then Major H. R. McMaster wrote and published what has become one of those "definitive versions" of the Vietnam War. His book *Dereliction of Duty* has become the definitive word on the political failures behind the U.S. intervention failure in Vietnam.[4] Albeit more definitive than earlier works, McMaster's political history came far too late in the day and, as such, with far too little to offer by way of lessons gathered that could have at a time closer to the events leading to America's war-loss in Vietnam perhaps aided in the avoidance of that loss (or at least mitigated the degree of loss) and offered lessons learned for the avoidance of similar failings—and similar derelictions of duty—that would come to haunt U.S. interventions for the subsequent decade up until this very day.

I originally began writing this book in early 2004 in the immediate wake of my own experiences as an official historian of the ground campaign of Operation Iraqi Freedom and later as a civil-military planner for one of the United States' major combat divisions (the 101st Airborne Division) conducting liberation and occupation duties in Iraq that initial year of the war. In the original preface to the book that follows this addendum, I stated that mine would be a story of war and peace and specifically of how America intervenes. I wrote that early on in the project, completing the manuscript in Summer 2005. Why did we fail to see the unavoidable requirements of a postwar Iraq that would undoubtedly fall to those with a hand in the war—the need to reconstruct that which we had a hand in deconstructing? How could we as the United States, the greatest (most materially powerful) of all great powers, now be finding ourselves on the losing end of a military intervention against what by all established metrics would be a weaker and lesser adversary? How could we once again be finding ourselves bogged down in another insurgent quagmire even after declaring definitively that there would be no more of these kinds of wars in America's future—*no more Vietnams?*

Most important for me, and I would strongly contend—for all of us—were those questions that lie beyond this war in Iraq (albeit reflected in it) and all those similar interventions before it, namely, are the reasons for this repeat of failure in our counterinsurgency interventions to be found in the actual derelictions of duty on the part of intervention policy decision makers, policy planners, and implementers, or in those factors that shape and direct and constrain the duties of those individuals in ways that make their doings derelict? Might we be suffering the unintended consequences of flaws in how we are designed for intervention and therefore how we approach problems of intervention? At a time (2004–2005) of caustic partisan divisiveness in American and international politics, much of that discussion centered around the questions of justness and rightness of the Iraq War. It was my thought and hope that a different angle of focus on the problem—one looking for explanations for our persistent failure to "secure the peace" in spite of our ability to "win all the wars" along the way—might at least help to elevate the political discourse over the war in this country (and beyond). Moreover, this kind of focus might just reveal to us all a major source of a paradox that has plagued us for decades—a cause that, if in fact of a structure and organizational sort, can be resolved.

In this sense, this book by its completion in mid-2005 was in its own right a new summons of new trumpeters not only of what went wrong in the U.S. intervention in Iraq but also a summons for new ideas for curing those ills in an effort to avoid future failures to win.

Since 2005 . . .

When I completed the manuscript in Summer 2005, I knew at that moment that the book was already, in some places, an outdated record. Since then, two years of war have raged in Iraq and Afghanistan. I did not stop thinking on war (and beyond war) with the completion of the manuscript. Nor did others stop thinking and writing on the subject of the Iraq War, what brought us their and to this point (at the make or break point), and what has kept us there up to this point. Many new voices have joined the debate and the search for explanations and new solutions since those earlier years of the war, where many if not most were either firmly "for" the war or equally firmly "against it" and not much inclined to parsing between those two positions in the search for common answers, much less common solutions.

Rereading my original work now, I have found myself feeling both vindicated in some of my original arguments, offerings, and propositions by the investigative reportings, analyses, and publishings of others, yet at the same time saddened by that vindication, particularly when if heard and heeded earlier some of the warnings I and others had offered might have saved lives and/or helped to avoid the disaster that seems to have befallen us of late. At other times, I am left more hopeful particularly when looking at some of the inroads we have made with regard to identifying and making efforts at resolving some of the organizational flaws inherent in our prevailing systems and approaches to intervention policy. Overall, I am left as wanting for a final favorable solution to our intervention puzzle in Iraq (and our puzzle of how, when, where, and why America should intervene in the future, writ-large) as everyone else.

In 2005, I concluded my commentary with some warnings of what might come to pass if some of the problems (flaws) inherent and embedded in our very national ways of war and peace were not recognized, addressed, and resolved. Unfortunately, some of those warnings have already come to fruition. The spread of insurgent and transnational jihadi-based terrorism has become a wider and more virulent contagion since 2005. The latest U.S. National Intelligence Report released in January 2007 describes the insurgency in Iraq as a growing hydra-headed composite of homegrown antigovernment elements (former regime loyalists), bona fide foreign fighters, and criminal elements. What I offered as still only a possibility back in 2005—a metastasis of insurgency into sectarian-based civil war-fare has by 2007 all but officially been declared as such.[5]

We have witnessed somewhat of an insurgency of our own here in the United States, cousin to the one broiling in Iraq over the war-policy toward Iraq and more broadly, the track the American nation now seems committed to traveling along regarding the future of its intervention policy. The mid-term elections in November 2006 resulted in a regime change, a partial one at any rate in American politics, with the Democrats overthrowing 16 years of Republican majority rule in Congress—both chambers of Congress going to the Democrats by a majority consent of the governed. The message sent, despite those who would be forever committed to denying no matter how strong the supporting evidence, was one of a "lack of confidence" in the previous regime's ability to govern, particularly with regard to governing toward an acceptable solution in Iraq. The war policy for Iraq has since 2005 become a referendum on American governance as much as it has been one on the future of governance for Iraq; quid pro quo regime change for regime change. The U.S. intervention in Iraq brought about the premature ending of Donald Rumsfeld's tenure as secretary of defense as well as a purge of two of the senior military architects of the military campaign for Iraq stability and reconstruction, generals John Abizaid and William Casey.

All of this change was perhaps part of the wake left by the release of the Iraq Study Group Report in late 2006 (December). A highly respected group of former (and future[6]) senior governmental officials, headed by two seasoned senior statesmen—James A. Baker III and Lee H. Hamilton—the Iraq Study Group recasted the die on Iraq, calling the situation in Iraq as "grave and deteriorating" while at the same time offering a prescription of actions (79 recommendations to be exact) for the immediate taking, that if taken, might be capable of improving the situation and protecting American interests in Iraq and the wider region.[7]

The year 2007 marks a new watershed in U.S. intervention policy toward Iraq. And well beyond, as the situation has now become one of as the U.S. policy toward Iraq goes, so may go the suasive powers of U.S. intervention policy in the wider Middle East region and beyond. Again, the dire situation in Iraq has metastasized aggressively since the U.S. invasion in early 2003. By Summer 2003, the absence of WMD validated the previous arguments of many—that there was no link between Saddam's Iraq and bin Laden's al Qaeda and the latter's attacks on the U.S. homeland in 2001. By 2004, the question of whether there was or was not a clear and present dangerous linkage between the war in Iraq and the wider global war on terror was a partisan political football being kicked back and forth between Republican advocates of the war and those in opposition to the war effort, largely Democratic Party voices. By 2005 and time of my completion of this book, the story of linkage was still partisan-soaked but also one increasingly becoming an empirical reality—the metastasis was happening but perhaps still treatable.

Today, at the time I write this epilogue, the metastasis is chronic, perhaps even terminal. Where there was once no evident link between al Qaeda and the situation in Iraq, today, it is extremely difficult to find a difference between the two diseases, their causes, or their symptoms; there is less and less reason to even attempt the differentiation. Where the situation in Iraq may have been controllable, confinable—containable—to the geographic and geopolitical/geoeconomic terrain of Iraq at one time, today, it is hard to speak of a U.S. war in Iraq that is logically definable to the confines of "Iraq." The Baker-Hamilton Report reveals and validated as much, calling for a dramatic shift in U.S. policy toward Iraq and the wider region by offering the need to enjoin the neighborhood surrounding Iraq into the political discussions over what to do about Iraq, in its entirety, to include opening discourse with two members of our declared "axis of evil"—Iran and Syria. The Baker-Hamilton Report of late 2006 only recorded what the situation on the ground in and around Iraq by 2007 bears witness to—a war that has widened well beyond Iraq that demands a treatment regimen that is at least as regional in scope as is the contagion, and perhaps even calling for a fuller international long-term rehabilitation.

The 2007 State of the Union Address delivered by President George W. Bush, which preceded days earlier by an address to the American—and Iraqi—people, defied what the realities of the ground situation in and around Iraq were already telling, and still telling now: the need for a new comprehensive policy and "grand" strategy[8] toward the situation in and around Iraq rather than simply another programmatic change to the conduct of the war in Iraq. The president in his address to the American people in early January 2007 offered what he and the administration touted as a "New Strategy" for Iraq—the latest in a series of such "new strategies" offered for Iraq by the administration since 2005. This "newer" strategy—or at least the discussion surrounding it—has to date centered around (and not gone anywhere beyond) the subjects of new operational leadership over the U.S. campaign plan in Iraq (i.e., the elevation of Lieutenant General Dave Petraeus to the four-star rank of general and his placement in command over Multinational Force-Iraq), the addition of another 21,500 U.S. troops into Iraq (i.e., the so-called surge), a new approach to the campaign approach itself (i.e., a turn to/return to "counter" insurgency), and a refocus on the administration's Clear-Hold-Build strategy, first introduced on the ground in Iraq in early 2005—a refocus necessarily beginning with a reclearing of Baghdad proper. The year 2007 finds all hope resting on the four pillars of this so-called New Strategy. Where all hope of success lies in the strength of all four pillars being brought to bear, a failure in any one now appears to promise doom to the entire enterprise of turning the situation in Iraq around for the better. Where the strength of all four pillars is a necessary condition for any probable success, failure of any one seems sufficient to doom the entire enterprise.

Still Failing to Think (and Act) "Beyond," Despite Some Important Lessons Gathered

All four pillars of this New Strategy seem to speak less toward a new policy and grand strategy for Iraq and the internationalized internal conflict we face there and more toward another set of programmatic changes at the margins of the original policy and strategy, anemic from its very formation back in 2001–2002. Four plus years after the initiation of major combat operations in Iraq, we still seem trapped and "locked in" to ways of intervening that deny us complete finishes and comprehensive victories. This lock-in seems pervasive, particularly when we consider and briefly review some of the insights we have gained—lessons we have in fact gathered—that reflect a better appreciation for some of the systemic flaws in our organizational approaches to war-policy that we have gained since 2005.

Lessons Gathered at the Strategic and Operational Levels of Intervention

Several important lessons have been gathered from the Iraq War experience to-date, lessons that today identify critical flaws in how our nation thinks about intervention, is organized for carrying out interventions, and approached intervention.

The most likely conflicts of the next 50 years or more will be wars of insurgency bringing with them irregular war-fare tactics and techniques all within an expansive "arc of instability" that currently encompasses much of the greater Middle East, parts of Africa, and Central and South Asia.[9] Iraq is one node in this wider global insurgency, albeit now a centrally important one. To wage war-fare to a sustainable win in these kinds of wars demands more than a military approach and more than a martial solution and definition of "victory." A counterinsurgency way of intervention—one that focuses on closing with those to be governed (the local populations) in ways that restore trust and confidence in those populations and rebuilds legitimacy between the government and the governed rather than merely on "close-with-to-destroy" tactics and techniques—is the key to success.

Final victory in these kinds of interventions lies in the legitimacy of ideas that are brought to a negotiation more so than the material power that can be brought to bear to a fight by a government in-residence, a foreign nation, or community of foreign nations taking part in the intervention.

The U.S. Interagency Process—that process that serves to get various U.S. government agencies to pursue common and coherent policies, both laterally across different agencies at varied levels of government but also vertically through different echelons of government (federal, state, local, city, community, etc.)—is broken. President George W. Bush's February 2005 executive directive to Department of Defense armed services and activities ordering a renewed emphasis in their preparations for stability and reconstruction (nation-rebuilding) operations to parity with their core traditional major combat operations (MCO) functions and responsibilities. While reflecting an effort to move the nation's understanding, appreciation, and concept of the challenges of a twenty-first-century security environment, the nation still struggles to take steps toward the kinds and degree of institutional, organizational, and operational reforms necessary for realizing more effective outcomes from America's interventions. In short, formulating new ways of war and peace are still lagging terrible so behind new policy agenda-setting as well as the new innovations and adaptations in tactics and techniques taking place at implementation level.

America's military, particularly its landwar services (i.e., the army and marine corps), are nearing a breaking point under the strains of ongoing interventions and the policy preventive war underpinning these interventions. In a widely distributed public after-action report from his 2007 visit to the open theaters of war in Iraq and Afghanistan and tour of the wider Middle East region, General (Ret.) Barry R. McCaffrey offered 11 "observations on Iraq." Of those 11 observations, two focused specifically on negative consequences of the Iraq War on U.S. combat forces and consequently long-term U.S. national security and defense capacity. According to General McCaffrey, by early 2007 we are already witnessing a need for the United States to reduce its military footprint in Iraq to get down to ten combat brigades by December 2007, with a further commitment at current much less higher troop and equipment numbers leading to the breaking the U.S. Army and perhaps the Marine Corps as well.[10] In two other related observations, General McCaffrey offered two pictures—snapshots of a U.S. National Guard and Reserve Force (army and marine corps) already broken (upwards of 40% of the equipment of the USNG and Reserves nonmission capable due to the stress of near-continuous combat tour rotations) and of America's other "longer" (the GWOT), increasingly becoming the impoverished and ignored "middle child" of America' foreign and domestic security and intervention policies.[11]

On the U.S. domestic home front, the stresses and strains coming directly from our nation's interventions and indirectly from the ambiguities of this new security environment are already showing in ways making America worse for all the wear and tear. And there signs of tears within the political-civil societal relationships that define our representative democratic republic and within the relationship between American society and its military (what we refer to as "American Civ-Mil Relations"). Public trust in the Iraq War policy and strategy is at an all-time low (ABC News Poll, June 1, 2007, showing 68% of the public lacking faith in the viability of the current U.S. strategy). This downturn in faith behind our Iraq War policy and strategy is increasingly reflecting a downturn in American's trust, faith, and confidence in its governing institutions, its elected leaders (and in those policymaking officials appointed by those they have elected), and perhaps most worrisomely in their nation's ability to solve problems and achieve goals, both at home and abroad.

At the end of the 1970s, many (namely Republic Party pundits and campaign strategists) said that the Carter administration had left America with a *malaise* and at no worse time—at a height of U.S.-Soviet confrontation. Today, while there is not the same kind of malaise, there could be a much more worrisome American character developing of this G. W. Bush (and soon to be post-Bush) era—*a state of fear and denial.* It is within this state of denial and fear that the paradox gains its strength and resiliency.

The attacks on the American homeland, September 11, 2001, marked a watershed in U.S. history. America's response has become a watershed in world affairs. Nearly 60 years before 9/11, there was 12/7—the Japanese surprise attack on the American homeland at Pearl Harbor. Pearl Harbor was a watershed event for America. And then like now, the U.S. response proved a watershed for the post–World War II world. As almost predicting the darkening of already darkened days for Americans in the grips of a great globalwide depression, President Franklin Delano Roosevelt calmed, collected, and redirected the American polity with the following words from his 1933 inaugural address:

> Let me assert my firm belief that the only thing we have to fear is fear itself—nameless, unreasoning, unjustified terror which paralyzes needed efforts to convert retreat into advance.[12]

Americans were able to stand in the face of the darkness of the Depression and soon to follow Nazi fascism emerging from World War II as a world leader. From that nameless, unreasoning, unjustified terror Americans created promise of a new and better future—evolving the American republic into a leader-nation of democratic ideals and national might that proved resolute and eventually victorious against the global threat of Soviet communism.

With the victorious defeat of Soviet communism at the dawn of the 1990s, America entered a new world order with it the sole remaining superpower and Americans expecting a well-deserved peace dividend for all of their sacrifices during the preceding 50 years of long war. There was no peace dividend, only an interregnum. The attacks of 9/11 finally gave us the kind of perspective needed to place the first 10–12 years of the post–cold war in its more accurate, albeit tragic, context: another *Interwar Period.*

America and the global community of nation-states are today in another *Long War.* What example has America set for its own posterity as well as that of the community of nations of which the United States is a member and its leader? What kind of example has already been set? Assuredly, these first six years of this new globalwide war bear witness to a flawed American way of war and peace. Again, Iraq is the exemplar. The twenty-first-century reveals a new global environment replete with new security threats. It is also an environment potentially with an equal abundance of opportunities. This new age bears witness to the dawn of a new age of war and peace. While it may be true that the nature of war is eternal and unchanging (see Clausewitz), surely its character is a dynamic thing, ever-changing by the very nature of war's purpose: a form of policy (ways and means) designed for attainment of intended political goals and objectives. War as policy is intended to be an accurate sign of the times reflecting a nation's ideals, security and defense imperatives, and national interests writ-large strategically aligned (ends-ways-means) in such a way as to ensure an effectively balanced nation and grand strategy that proves instrumentally effective, legally right, and ethically (ideationally) just and consistent with American republican principles.

Again, the nineteenth-century military theorist (father of modern Western military thought and practice), Carl von Clausewitz while clearly seeing war as the final word in a conflict or dispute resolution political process as clearly saw fixed limits on that war policy through its subordination to political goals, *ways* and *means* subordinated to (and deriving all relevancy and legitimacy from) political *ends.* As Clausewitz put it, "Its [war's] grammar, indeed, may be its own, but not its logic."[13] That "grammar" is a changing thing—military objectives change, as do the organizations and operational doctrine undergirding those objectives, the specific political purposes of war-policy and strategy change and adjust to altering environmental "atmospherics" and public sentiments, wants, expectations, and mores. The logic of war-policy is the unchanging thing: (1) war as a policy set of ways and means (one of many) deriving all purpose and meaning from a political "object"; (2) that political "object" directing a nation's war-policy always relates and refers to the attainment of a "relative peace" (either through unconditional surrender of an adversary through full application of lethal force or a limited/temporary peace attainment through limited applications of military and other instruments of power). This "logic" is the logic of war and peace that has defined and shaped the U.S./Western way of war-fare throughout the modern era.

Yet what we see, feel, and bear today is a new environment of war and peace—one that demands a new grammar for nation-states' intervention policy that goes well beyond military war applications (i.e., modern war-fare) toward a full and holistic integration of national/community of nation tools and instruments of power (i.e., military, information, diplomacy, economic, etc.) and a conversion of these integrated packages of intervention into joint, interagency-intergovernmental-multinational (JIIM) tools of progress. This new grammar derives from the eternal logic of war, persistent throughout the modern era of war and peace but perhaps more prescient today in this new twenty-first-century, post–cold war (and post-9/11) world: the application of policy toward the attainment of a new status quo post bellum, a better and more legitimate state of stability and peace beyond the combatives—*beyond war*. The sooner we as Americans (and the leading nation of the Westphalian community of nations) can recognize this eternal logic but wildly alter grammar—and think beyond our modern notions of war—the sooner we can begin to act anew and in so doing, as President Abraham Lincoln said during the dark days of 1862, "disenthrall ourselves [of old dogmas of a "quieter past"], and then we shall save our country."[14]

This book is one effort to begin to think beyond and thus inspire us to begin to act anew.

Note on Sources

This is a book of *from-the-field* as well as scholarly observation. The story it tells reflects a gathering of data and lessons collected from a wide and varied body of sources over at least 10 years of formal study and over 20 years of personal experiences. Sources include firsthand observations from participations in military and other-than-military interventions, interviews, diary and journal accounts, data collection as an official war-historian, media accounts, and formal academic research.

In addition to firsthand experiences, observations, and interviews, I also depended on information collected from the many policy reform initiatives underway throughout U.S. government federal agencies (the interagency) relating to U.S. intervention policy. Media coverage of the public debate and discourses on Iraq, foreign and domestic, has also informed the story told here.

Four sources in particular deserve a special recognition for their impact on my understanding of today's predicament in war and peace-policy, but more importantly for the significant role each has had on this nation's current intervention policy situation.

Clausewitz' *On War*

The seminal work on what has become the doctrinal standard in all Western military thought and practice is that of the nineteenth-century Prussian soldier-general and theorist Carl von Clausewitz titled *On War*. The 1984 edited edition by Michael Howard and Peter Paret is regarded by far as the citable source. Clausewitz' work is important to the study and practice of Western, modern (i.e., for the most part, twentieth-century) war-fare because of its transcendence beyond the author's own nineteenth-century experiences with linear-based, Napoleonic-era military battle as a theory and applied art and science for war-fare, its transcendence beyond "Western warfare," and its bringing forward to modern-time and European cultures Eastern ideas and prescriptions of war- and peace-fare dating back 2,500 years to the times and works of the fabled *Sun Tze*. It is noted as well for its transcendence beyond war itself. Clausewitz talks to us in the theoretical books of his work as much about the politics and purpose of war (peace) as he does about the waging of war-fare. As such, his is likely the first comprehensive study on *intervention*. *On War* is also notable for its contribution to the paradox that plagues and stymies Western and American intervention policy—not by what the book offers in its pages, but rather by what we have since its publication chosen to gather and learn from its lessons and dictates. Our paradox is a direct result of getting the lessons of Clausewitz wrong in the first instance, and then, in the second, adding insult to that injury by building our modern ways of war-fare and peace-fare on those errant lessons learned.

The future of a better U.S. intervention policy lies in a renaissance of Clausewitz' *On War*.

Harry Summer's *On Strategy*

Newsweek magazine noted the 1982 publication *On Strategy* by Harry G. Summers, Jr., as "perhaps the most trenchant single post-mortem to date of our defeat in Vietnam . . . a classic."

The story told of America's war-loss during the Vietnam War has been attributed with serving as a catharsis for the U.S. Army and American nation. By drawing out a distinction between the enemy the U.S. Army solidly defeated in battle (the Vietcong) from the enemy the Army lost the war to—a conventional military force, the North Vietnamese Army—Summers helped the army and Americans feel better about themselves in the war-loss. Where we could no longer deny the fact that America had lost the war—its first loss in war as a nation, *On Strategy's* assessment offered a way out of losing to an *unworthy opponent*. By Summer's account, the United States lost the war it was intended for and designed to win (a conventional war) because it was too occupied with fighting a war anathema to itself as a nation and army of that nation—an insurgent's war. *On Strategy* gave us a national answer to the nature of the loss if not to the loss itself; it gave us an "out" from having to evaluate the strategic causes of the loss any further. It provided the beginnings of a blueprint upon which the Army set about re-creating its way of intervening and its designs and capabilities for waging war and peace. Using *On Strategy* as a benchmark, the United States beginning around 1973 initiated a revision in U.S. military thought and practice. This renaissance resulted in the development of Airland Battle Doctrine and the combined-arms forces that waged and won the 1990 Gulf War, the military that we live with today. That renaissance was premised upon exorcising U.S. military doctrine of unconventional war-fare tactics, techniques, and procedures (TTP) and become reborn in conventional war-fare—in the doctrine that attributed to a win in World War II. The lessons learned was that *America's Army* was intended to fight and win a certain kind of war and intended not to engage in other forms of pseudo-war or nonwar.

Those credited with this 1970s and 1980s reformation are today seen as individuals who *saved America's Army*, and America in the process. These saviors, I guess, would all at some point reference Summers's work as the road map beneath their efforts. Summers's *On Strategy* must then, in the end, be given its due credit in helping this nation and its Army rid themselves of the ghost of its war-loss in Vietnam. But the work must also take responsibility for in its role in saving the Army's war-fighting ethos and capacity, advancing its limited understandings of the power and place of war-fare and the military in overall intervention policy. Summers's contribution, in the end, is a mixed bag of wrong lessons gathered and learned. The quagmire that is Iraq today is an unintended offspring of this important piece of literature.

Richard Haass's *Intervention*

Haass's book *Intervention* was first published in 1994 by the Carnegie Endowment for International Peace. The book was important at the time of this first publishing for its early descriptions of what were at the time anecdotal cases of military interventions in the immediate shadow and aftermath of the militarily static cold war. By the time of the second edition in 1999, history had confirmed that the return to an age of diverse and numerous military interventions—the dawn of a new era of complex intervention—was not a historical anomaly emblematic of a contemporary age of war and peace. Haass's work provides us a taxonomy of modern intervention policy *in transition*, and in doing so offers us an important look at and a better understanding and appreciation of the place and purpose of military intervention—and war-fare—in the wider policy domain of intervention. Haass's dissections of the varied modern-age forms and functions of war- and peace-fare (i.e., war-fighting, as compared to peace-keeping, peace-making, peace enforcement, etc.) provide a vital view of the modern division of labor in war-fare and peace-fare, and in doing so sets the conditions for asking the question that is perhaps most important at this juncture, this dawn of a new age of war and peace: *do these distinctions still make sense?* The first step in the taking of a leap of faith away from tradition and standing doctrine is first knowing that doctrine. Haass's *Intervention* provides us with that knowledge and, consequently, sets up the first leap.

Intervention is a work that brings the discussion, debate, and study of war and warfare, peace and peace-fare back into its holistic context; it brings us back full-circle to Clausewitz, and Liddell Hart, and T. E. Lawrence, and Sun Tze before them, and the indirect applications of military power in support of other nonmilitary instruments as a holistic tool of intervention. It brings us back to the reality of war and peace, thesis and antithesis of what it means to intervene, when to intervene, and most importantly why and how to rightly and justly intervene.

Etzioni's From Empire to Community

In the preface to his 2004 best seller, *From Empire to Community*, Professor Amitai Etzioni expressed the following sentiment:

> Whether one favors the U.S. global projection of force or is horrified by it, the question stands—where do we go from here?

This book offered me with the sort of theoretical springboard needed to propel these new ideas of how to better and more legitimately intervene in international politics to a higher level of politics and purpose. As Etzioni puts it, our best, and perhaps natural, next steps Please recheck the year to the avoidance of a *clash of civilizations* (see Huntington's 1996 book) is to de*martialize* our intervention policies, de-*Americanize* our international politics, and assist in the building of a new world order that is truly democratic in a sense that remains consistent with and in community with American goals and interests, but that does not necessarily have to reflect an American face. Etzioni's discussions of the nation-states' inability to effectively attend to what are now rising transnational problems provide substantial evidence supporting the existence of a paradox within not merely America's way of war and peace, but in the intervention capacity of individual nation-states, particularly when they choose to act alone and outside of a community of nation-states.

Certification and validation of the paradox lies in this work. So too do some of the answers to the paradox and, most importantly, to how we can save the relevancy of the nation-system as an effective, just, and worthy force for global justice, humanity, prosperity, and therefore peace and security.

Many other works have contributed to the thoughts and the processes that have formed and framed the offerings of this book, but ultimately it boils down to these four contributions.

What follows is a small but representative listing of books and articles that were also useful as *sources consulted.*

Books

Bell, Gertrude. *The Letters of Gertrude Bell: Vols I and II.* London: Ernst Benn, 1927.

Beer, Francis A. *Meanings of War and Peace.* College Station, TX: Texas A&M University Press, 2001.

Bobbitt, Philip. *The Shield of Achilles: War, Peace, and the Course of History.* New York: Anchor, 2002.

Bush, George, and Brent Scowcroft. *A World Transformed.* New York: Alfred A. Knopf, 1998.

Diamond, Larry. *Squandered Victory: The American Occupation and the Bungled Effort to Bring Democracy to Iraq.* 1st ed. New York: Time Books, 2005.

Durch, William J., ed. *UN Peacekeeping, American Policy and the Uncivil Wars of the 1990s.* New York: St. Martin's, 1996.

Etzioni, Amitai. *From Empire to Community: A New Approach to International Relations.* New York: Palgrave Macmillan, 2004.

Franks, Fred, Gen., (Ret.), USA, and Tom Clancy. *Into the Storm: A Study in Command.* New York: C. G. Putnam's Sons, 1997.

Gordon, Michael R., and Bernard E. Trainor. *The General's War.* Boston, MA: Little, Brown, 1995.

Grant, Michael. *The Fall of the Roman Empire.* New York: Collier, 1990.

Haass, Richard N. *Intervention: The Use of American Military Force in the Post-Cold War World.* Washington, DC: Brookings Institution Press, 1999.

Hammes, Thomas X. *The Sling and the Stone: On War in the 21st Century.* Osceola, WI: Zenith, 2004.

Herodotus. *The Histories.* Trans. Robin Waterfield. Oxford: Oxford University Press, 1998.

Holbrooke, Richard. *To End A War.* New York: Random House, 1998.

Howard, Michael, and Peter Paret, eds. and trans. *Carl Von Clausewitz, On War.* Princeton, NJ: Princeton University Press, 1984.

Huntington, Samuel P. *The Clash of Civilizations and the Remaking of World Order.* New York: Simon & Schuster, 1996.

Keaney, Thomas A., and Elliot Cohen. *Gulf War Air Power Survey Summary Report.* Washington, DC: U.S. Government Printing Office, 1993.

Kretchik, Walter E., Robert F. Baumann, and John T. Fichel. *Invasion, Intervention, Intervasion: A Concise History of the U.S. Army in Operation Uphold Democracy.* Fort Leavenworth, KS: U.S. Army Command and General Staff College Press, 1998.

Lawrence, T. E. *Seven Pillars of Wisdom: A Triumph.* New York: Anchor, 1991.

Liddell Hart, B. H. *The Real War: 1914–1918.* New York: Little, Brown, 1930.

MacGregor, Douglas A. *Breaking the Phalanx: A New Design for Landpower in the 21st Century.* 1st ed. Westport, CT: Praeger, 1997.

Mearsheimer, John J. *Conventional Deterrence.* Ithaca, NY: Cornell University Press, 1983.

Naveh, Simon. *In Pursuit of Military Excellence: The Evolution of Operational Theory.* London: Frank Cass, 1997.

Packer, George. *The Assassin's Gate: America in Iraq.* New York: Farrar, Straus and Giroux, 2005.

Pape, Robert A. *Bombing to Win*. Ithaca, NY, and London: Cornell University Press, 1996.

Schwarzkopf, H. Norman, Gen., and Peter Petre. *It Doesn't Take a Hero*. New York: Bantam, 1992.

Shy, John. *A People Numerous and Armed: Reflections on the Military Struggle for American Independence*. Ann Arbor, MI: University of Michigan Press, 1990.

Snow, Donald M., and Eugene Brown. *International Relations: The Changing Contours of Power*. New York: Longman, 2000.

Summers, Harry G., Jr. *On Strategy: A Critical Analysis of the Vietnam War*. Novato, CA: Presidio, 1982.

Swain, Richard M. *Lucky War*. Fort Leavenworth, KS: U.S. Army Command and General Staff College Press, 1994.

Xenophon, *Anabasis*. Trans. Carleton L. Brownson, Loeb Classical Library. London: Harvard University Press, 2003.

———. *Hellenica, Books 1–4*. Trans. Carleton L. Brownson, Loeb Classical Library. London: Harvard University Press, 2003.

Articles and Periodicals

Adolf, Robert B., Jr., Maj., USA. "PSYOP: Gulf War Force Multiplier." *Army* (December 1992): 18–20.

"Bush's Iraq Rating at Low Point." August 5, 2005. http://http://www.cnn.com/2005/POLITICS/08/05/buh.ap.ipsospoll.ap/index.html (February 2005).

Caldwell, Warren, Jr. "Promises, Promises: The Technical Revolution in Military Affairs May Not Live Up to All the Promises." *Proceedings of the U.S Naval Institute* (January 1996): 54–57.

Cosby, William N., Capt., USA. "BCTP (Battle Command Training Program) Lessons Learned—Battlefield Air Interdiction." *Field Artillery* (April 1990): 40–42.

Crews, Fletcher, Maj., USA. "PSYOP (Psychological Operations) Planning and the Joint Targeting Process." *Special Warfare* 11 (Winter 1998): 16–21.

Curtis, Steven, Lt. Col., USA, et al. "Integrating Targeting and Information Operations in Bosnia." *Field Artillery* (July–August 1998): 31–36.

DeGroat, Arthur S., and David C. Nilse. "Information and Combat Power on the Force XXI Battlefield." *Military Review* (November–December 1995): 56–62.

Durch, William J. "Introduction to Anarchy: Humanitarian Intervention and 'State-Building' in Somalia." *UN Peacekeeping, American Policy and the Uncivil Wars of the 1990s*. New York: St Martin's, 1996, 311–366.

"EW Expands into Information Warfare." *Aviation Week & Space Technology* (October 10, 1994): 47–48.

"Fallujah—Wikipedia." http://www.en.wikipedia.org/wiki/Fallujah.

Gloriod, John A., Col., USA, and Scott E. Nahrwold, Lt. Col., USA. "Targeting—Keeping It Simple." *Field Artillery* (February 1992): 11–14.

Golz, Eugene, Daryl G. Press, and Harvey M. Sapolsky. "Come Home America." *International Security* 21 (Spring 1997): 5–48.

Harner, William E., Lt. Col., USA. "Brigade Targeting." *Infantry* 86 (November–December 1996): 15–17.

Holder, L. D., Lt. Col., USA. "Maneuver in the Deep Battle." *Military Review* 5 (1982): 54–56.

Hollis, Patrecia L. "Deception, Firepower and Movement." *Field Artillery* (June 1991): 31–34.

Ingram, Bernd L., Lt. Col., USA (Ret.). "Joint Targeting for Time-Sensitive Targets: To Boldly Go Where No Army Has Gone Before." *Field Artillery* (May–June 2001): 28–31.

"IO in a Peace Enforcement Environment." Center for Army Lessons Learned Newsletter no. 99–2 http://call.army.mil/call.html. November 7, 2001 (accessed February 7, 2007).

Jablonsky, David. "U.S Military Doctrine and the Revolution in Military Affairs." *Parameters* (Autumn 1994): 18–36.

Jones, David S., Capt., USA, and Paul J. McDowell, Capt., USAF. "To Catch a War Criminal: The United Nations Apprehension of an Indicted War Criminal." Center for Army Lessons Learned http://call.army.mil/. December 11, 2001 (accessed February 15, 2005).

Jones, William A., Lt. Col., USA. "A Warfighting Philosophy." *Field Artillery* 4 (April 1993): 47–53.

Kimmitt, Mark T., Col., USA. "Fire Support in Bosnia-Herzegovina: An Overview." *Field Artillery* 4 (July–August 1998): 29–31.

Krepinevich, Andrew. "Calvary to Computer: The Pattern of Military Revolutions." *National Interest* (Fall 1994): 30.

Layne, Christopher. "The Unipolar Illusion." *International Security* 17 (Spring 1993): 5–51.

Lee, David A., Maj., USA, and John A. Yingling, Col. "Fire Support Planning for the Brigade and Below." *Field Artillery* (March–April 1999): 15–19.

Libicki, Martin. "The Emerging Primacy of Information." *Orbis* (Spring 1996): 261–276.

Mann, Edward, Col., USA. "One Target, One Bomb—Is the Principle of Mass Dead?" *Military Review* (September 1993): 33–41.

Marty, Fred F., Maj. Gen., USA. "Targeting and the D3 Methodology." *Field Artillery* (February 1992): 1.

McEvoy, Richard P., Lt. Col., USA. "Targeting for the Maneuver Task Force." *Infantry* 86 (November–December 1996): 12–14.

Nock, Richard E., Capt., USA. "High Payoff Targets: When to Engage." *Military Intelligence* 19 (April–June 1993): 19–23.

Otis, Glenn K., Gen., USA. "The Airland Battle" (Letter for Distribution). *Military Review* 5 (1982): 1.

Phillips, John, Lt. Col., USA. "Intelligence Targeting in Korea." *Military Intelligence* 20 (January–March 1994): 22–23.

Ralston, David C., Col., USA, and Rodney L. Lusher, Capt., USA. "Exploiting the Effects of Fires: Synchronized Targeting and Execution." *Field Artillery* (January–February 1996): 30–31.

Ricks, Tom. "Army Historian Cites Lack of Postwar Plan for Iraq." *Washington Post*, December 25, 2004, A1.

Rieff, David. "Who Botched the Occupation?" *New York Times Magazine*, November 2, 2003.

Rogers, J. B. "Synchronizing the Airland Battle." *Military Review* 4 (1984): 61–62.

Starry, Michael D., and Charles W. Arneson. "FM 100–6: Information Operations." *Military Review* (November–December 1996): 2–15.

Summe. "Jack N. Maj. USA. PSYOP Support to Operation Desert Storm." *Special Warfare* (October 1992): 9–10.

Von Clausewitz, Carl. *On War*. Trans. and ed. Michael Howard and Peter Paret. Indexed ed. Princeton, NJ: Princeton University Press, 1984.

Wentz, Larry K. "Lessons from Bosnia: The IFOR Experience." http://call.army.mil/. December 11, 2001 (accessed February 15, 2005).

Willbanks, James H. "The Battle for Hue, 1968." GlobalSecurity.org. http://www.globalsecurity.org/military/library/report/202/MOUTWilbanks.html.

Government Documents

24th Mechanized Infantry Division Combat Team Operation Desert Storm Attack Plan Oplan 91–3, January 17, 1991.

Department of Defense. *Conduct of the Persian Gulf War: Final Report to Congress.* Washington, DC: Department of Defense, April 1992.

———. *Undersecretary of Defense (Policy), 1991 Summer Study.* Newport, RI: Office of the Director of Net Assessment, 1991.

U.S. Army. *FM 3–0. Operations.* Washington, DC: Department of the Army, 2001.

———. *FM 3–13. Information Operations* [Draft]. Washington, DC: Department of the Army, 2001.

———. *FM 5–0 (101–5). Army Planning and Orders Production* [Initial Draft]. Washington, DC: Department of the Army, August 1, 2001.

———. *FM 6–0 (100–34). Command and Control.* DRAG Ed. Washington, DC: Department of the Army, March 2001.

———. *FM 6–20–10. Tactics, Techniques and Procedures for the Targeting Process.* Washington, DC: Department of the Army, 1990.

———. *FM 90–2. Military Deception in Army Operations* [Working Draft]. Washington, DC: Department of the Army, March 20, 1997.

———. *FM 100–5. Operations.* Washington, DC: Department of the Army, 1976.

———. *FM 100–5. Operations.* Washington, DC: Department of the Army, 1982.

———. *FM 100–5. Operations.* Washington, DC: Department of the Army, 1986.

———. *FM 100–5. Operations.* Washington, DC: Department of the Army, 1993.

———. *FM 100–6. Information Operations.* Washington, DC: Department of the Army, 1996.

———. *FM 101–5. Staff Organization and Operations.* Washington, DC: Department of the Army, 1997.

———. *FM 101–5–1. Operational Terms and Graphics.* Washington, DC: Department of the Army, 1997.

———. "INFORMATION OPERATIONS: IO in a Peace Enforcement Environment." *Center for Army Lessons Learned NEWSLETTER NO. 99–2.* http://call.army.mil/call.html. November 7, 2001 (accessed February 15, 2005).

VII Corps Archives. Annex H (Psychological Operations) to VII Corps OPLAN 1990–2 (Operation Desert Sabre) VII Corps Archives (Fort Leavenworth, KS, 1991): SG HST AAR3–033.

———. Appendix D (Fire Support) to VII Corps OPLAN 1990–2 (Operation Desert Sabre) VII Corps Archives (Fort Leavenworth, KS, 1991): SG HST AAR3–033.

———. Tab C (Attack Guidance Matrix) to Appendix D (Fire Support) to 3AD OPLAN 91–1 (Operation Desert Spear) (Fort Leavenworth, KS, 1991): SG HST AAR4–332.

"White Paper: Fire Support Planning for the Brigade and Below." Fort Sill, OK: Fire Support Division, Fire Support and Combined Arms Department, September 16, 1998.

U.S. Congress. "Army Transformation: Implications for the Future." July 15, 2004. http://www.house.gov/hasc/openingstatementsand pressreleases/108thcongress/04-07-15 Macgregor.pdf (accessed February 15, 2005).

Monographs, Reports, Theses, and Unpublished Works

Boslego, David V., Maj., USA. "Relationship of Information to the Relative Combat Power Model in Force XXI Engagements." Monograph, School of Advanced Military Studies. Fort Leavenworth, KS: U.S. Army Command and General Staff College, 1995.

Eisen, S. "Network Warfare: 'It's Not Just for Hackers Anymore.'" Thesis. Newport, RI: Joint Military Operations Department, Naval War College, June 1995.

Johnson, Robert C., Lt. Col., USA. "Joint Campaign Design: Using a Decide-Detect-Attack (DDA) Methodology to Synchronize the Joint Force's Capabilities against Enemy Centers of Gravity." Monograph, School of Advanced Military Studies. Fort Leavenworth, KS: U.S. Army Command and General Staff College, 1994.

Metz, Steven. "The Future of Insurgency." Thesis. Carlisle Barracks, PA: Strategic Studies Institute, U.S. Army War College, December 10, 1993.

Schifferle, Peter J., Lt. Col., USA. "Incorporating Enemy Psychological Vulnerability into U.S. Army Heavy Division IPB Doctrine." SAMS Monograph. Fort Leavenworth, KS: U.S. Army Command and General Staff College, 1993.

Schwark, Stuart H., Maj., USA. "Command and Control Warfare and the Deliberate Targeting Process." MMAS Thesis. Fort Leavenworth, KS: U.S. Army Command and General Staff College, 1997.

Smith, Kevin B., Maj., USA. "Crisis and Opportunity of Information War." Monograph, School of Advanced Military Studies. Fort Leavenworth, KS: U.S. Army Command and General Staff College, 1994.

Sullivan, M. P. "Revolution in Military Affairs: Operational Fires on the Future Battlefield." Strategy Research Report. Carlisle Barracks, PA: U.S. Army War College, April 1996, 5.

Notes

Part I Beyond War

1. I have taken literary license in turning a phrase with the lead title of General (Ret.) Wesley Clark's book *Waging Modern War* (New York: Perseus Books, 2001). More than just this play on wording, the ideas that General Clark and others have recently conveyed in their "histories" of recent and/or ongoing military interventions provide characterizations of war and warfare that I regard as "modern," and as such and to a significant degree, no longer the most effective model of warfare given the conditions (challenges and opportunities) of the contemporary operating environment (COE).

Chapter 1 The Paradox of the American Way of War and Peace

1. It is to Pyrrus we owe the expression "a Pyrrhic victory." After having defeated the Romans at Heraclea in 280 BC by inspired use of his elephant corps but otherwise very considerable cost to his own forces, he is reported to have said that one more such victory would lose him the war. Accessed online at http://www.phrases.org.uk/meanings/297150.html (accessed May 29, 2007).
2. The U.S. Marine Corps defines "small wars" as operations undertaken under executive authority, wherein military force is combined with diplomatic pressure in the internal or external affairs of another state whose government is unstable, inadequate, or unsatisfactory for the preservation of life and such interests as are determined by the foreign policy of the United States.
3. Brig. Gen. Robert H. Scales, Jr., *Certain Victory: United States Army in the Gulf War* (Washington, DC: Simon and Schuster, 1992).
4. "Poll Finds Dimmer View of Iraq War," online at http://www.washingtonpost.com/wp-dyn/content/article/2005/06/07/AR2005060700296 (accessed 15 February 2005).
5. Transcript: First Presidential Debate, September 30, 2004 from Coral Gables, FL. Text From FDCH E-Media, online at http://www.washingtonpost.com/wp-srv/politics/debatereferee/debate_0930.html.
6. Patricia Sullivan, "War Aims and War Outcomes: Major Power Military Operations since World War II," unpublished paper presented at the annual meeting of the Midwest Political Science Association, Chicago, IL, April 15–18, 2004.
7. Ivan Arreguin-Toft, *How the Weak Win Wars* (Cambridge: Cambridge University Press, 2005); Stephen Biddle, *Military Power: Explaining Victory and Defeat in Modern Battle* (Princeton, NJ: Princeton University Press, 2004); Dan Reiter and Allan C. Stam III,

Democracies at War (Princeton, NJ: Princeton University Press, 2002); Allan R. Millett, Williamson Murray, and Kenneth H. Watman, "The Effectiveness of Military Organizations," in Millett and Murray, eds., *Military Effectiveness*, vol. 1: *The First World War* (Boston, MA: Allen and Unwin, 1988).

8. Gil Merom, *How Democracies Lose Small Wars* (Cambridge: Cambridge University Press, 2003).
9. This is a reference to Virgil's opening phrase in the *Aeneid*: "I sing a song of arms and the man."
10. Harry G. Summers, Jr., *On Strategy: A Critical Analysis of the Vietnam War* (Novato, CA: Presidio Press, 1982); H. R. McMaster, *Dereliction of Duty: Johnson, McNamara, the Joint Chiefs of Staff, and the Lies That Led to Vietnam* (New York: HarperCollins Publishers, 1997).
11. Dave R. Palmer, *Summons of the Trumpet: A History of the Vietnam War from a Military Man's Viewpoint* (New York: Ballantine, 1978).
12. Summers, *On Strategy*, 1.
13. Ibid., xiv.
14. Ibid., xiii.
15. Ibid.
16. Harry G. Summers, Jr., *On Strategy: A Critical Analysis of the Vietnam War* (Novato, CA: Presidio Press, 1995).
17. Ibid., 1.
18. Bob Woodward, *Plan of Attack* (New York: Simon and Schuster, 2004); Richard Clarke, *Against All Enemies: Inside America's War on Terror* (New York: Free Press, 2004); Paul Krugman, *The Great Unraveling: Losing Our Way in the New Century* (New York: W. W. Norton & Company, 2003); Zbigniew Brzezinski, *The Choice: Global Domination or Global Leadership* (New York: Basic Books, 2004); Fareed Zakaria, *The Future of Freedom: Illiberal Democracy at Home and Abroad* (New York: W. W. Norton & Company, 2003); and Seymour M. Hersh, *Chain of Command: The Road from 9/11 to Abu Ghraib* (New York: HarperCollins, 2004).
19. Gregory Fontenot, E. J. Degan, and David Tohn, *On Point: The United States Army in Operation Iraqi Freedom* (Fort Leavenworth, KS: Combat Studies Institute Press, 2005).
20. The OIFSG was a history-recording and Army Strategic Planning Board-related research initiative formed and missioned by General Eric Shinseki, at the time the chief of staff of the U.S. Army. The OIFSG was formed in early April 2003, a week after the initiation of ground combatives in Iraq. The group was tasked with following U.S. and coalition forces during their historic march up country, conducting interviews with soldiers and their generals along that long hazardous expedition, recording and chronicling what they observed firsthand, including flaws in operational planning and materiel failings and shortfalls that hampered the pure and noble courage of the soldiers in the efforts on the ground. Most of the accounts written on the major combat operation phase of the war have, to date, made use of the over 4,000 gigabytes of data collected and coded by the OIFSG.
21. *Anabasis* is the most famous work of the Greek writer Xenophon. The journey it narrates is his best-known accomplishment. Xenophon accompanied the Ten Thousand, a large army of Greek mercenaries hired by Cyrus the Younger, who intended to seize the throne of Persia from his brother Artaxerxes II. Though Cyrus's army was victorious in a battle at Cunaxa in Babylon, Cyrus himself was killed and the expedition rendered moot. Stranded deep in enemy territory, the Spartan general Clearchus and most of the other Greek generals were subsequently killed or captured by treachery. Xenophon played an instrumental role in encouraging the Greek army of 10,000 to march north to the Black Sea.

Chapter 2 Modern War Revisited: Three Generations of Modern War-Fare

1. Stephen N. Waltz, *Man, the State, and War* (New York: Columbia University Press, 1954).
2. "Student Text" (ST 47) from the U.S. Army Command and General Staff College (CGSC), Fort Leavenworth, KS, 2001–2002.
3. Stephen Peter Rosen, *Winning the Next War: Innovation and the Modern Military (Cornell Studies in Security Affairs)* (Ithaca, NY: Cornell University Press, 1994).
4. Michael Howard, *War in European History* (New York: Oxford University Press, 1976), 49.
5. Thomas E. Griess, *The West Point Military History Series: The Dawn of Modern Warfare* (New York: Avery Publishers, 1984).
6. From Michael Howard and Peter Paret, eds. and trans., *Carl Von Clausewitz, On War* (Princeton, NJ: Princeton University Press, 1976/1984), based on the original in German, *Vom Kriege* (Dummlers Verlag, Berlin, 1832).
7. Carl von Clausewitz, *On War*, trans. and ed. Michael Howard and Peter Paret, indexed ed. (Princeton, NJ: Princeton University Press, 1984).
8. Thomas E. Griess, series ed., *Definitions and Doctrine of the Military Art: The West Point Military History Series* (Princeton, NJ: Avery, 1985), 5.
9. Ibid.
10. Clausewitz, *On War*, 75.
11. Ibid., 127.
12. Donald Snow and Eugene Brown, *United States Foreign Policy: Politics beyond the Water's Edge* (Boston, MA: Bedford/St. Martin's, 2000).
13. Griess, *Definitions and Doctrine of the Military Art*, 5.
14. See M. E. Porter, *Competitive Strategy: Techniques for Analyzing Industries and Competitors* (New York: Free Press, 1980) and M. E. Porter, *Competitive Advantage: Creating and Sustaining Superior Performance* (New York: Free Press, 1985).
15. Henry Mintzenberg, *The Rise and Fall of Strategic Planning* (New York: Free Press, 1994), 27.
16. Edward N. Luttwak, *Strategy: The Logic of War and Peace* (Cambridge, MA: Belknap Press of Harvard University Press, 2001), 2.
17. Clausewitz, *On War*, 177.
18. J. D. Hittle, "Introduction," in *Jomini and His Summary of The Art of War, A Condensed Version*, 387–432, in *Roots of Strategy, Book 2*, ed. with an introduction by Brig. Gen. J. D. Hittle, U.S. Marine Corps, Ret. Harrisburg (Pennsylvania: Stackpole Books, 1987).
19. Sun Tzu, *The Art of War*, ed. Samuel B. Griffith (Oxford: Oxford University Press, 1972), 77–79.
20. B. H. Liddell Hart, *Strategy* (New York: HarperCollins, 1967), 319.
21. Luttwak, *Strategy*, 128.
22. Ibid., 88.
23. Current U.S. and Western military doctrine conceives of the operational domain in very specific geographical ways. See s.v. "joint doctrine" (*Joint Publication 3–0* and *Joint Publication 5–0*, September 17, 2006 and January 25, 2002, respectively); U.S. Army *Field Manual 3–0, Operations*, June 14, 2001, and so on.
24. Dr. James Schneider provides a most useful definition of the operational art of nineteenth-century, Western (European), conventional force-based war-fare. See James J. Schneider, *The Structure of Strategic Revolution: Total War and the Roots of the Soviet Warfare State* (Presidio Press, 1994), 2.
25. Alexandr Svechin's detailed description of the operational art still seems most relevant to and descriptive of the capabilities and limitations of modern, Western conventional force military operations. His understandings of the nuances between a nation's

historical, geographical, cultural, economic, political, social, and military attributes and that nation's strategic goals and availability of resources—and how these factors are or must be combined through a sequencing of intermediate operational goals and objectives—are still informative of logical, purpose-based operational artistry. See Aleksandr Andreevich Svechin, *Strategy*, ed. Kent D. Lee (New York: Eastview Publications, 1992).

26. This point is important not only to the arguments put forward in this study but more importantly to the relationship between strategy and policy, how that relationship has changed over time (due to many factors, not the least of which was the effect of technological advancements on the growing scope and scale of military operations), and how the shift in the relationship can affect war-policy itself. B. H. Liddell Hart makes the point more clearly: "to break down the distinction between strategy and policy would not matter much if the two functions were normally combined in the same person, as with a Frederick or a Napoleon. But as such autocratic soldier-rulers have been rare in modern times and became temporarily extinct in the nineteenth century, the effect was insidiously harmful. For it encouraged soldiers to make the preposterous claim that policy should be subservient to their conduct of operations, and, especially in democratic countries, it drew the statesman on to overstep the definite border of his sphere and interfere with his military employees in the actual uses of their tools." See Sir Basil Henry Liddell Hart, *Strategy* (London: Faber and Faber Ltd., 1954), 319–320. This Hartian notion underpins this chapter and will be addressed more directly later. But suffice it to say now that an effective and legitimate war-policy, balanced between its policy and its strategy, is predicated on a balanced approach to how one educates, trains, and develops its experts in the strategic, operational, and tactical science and art of war-policy. Stovepiped and illogical education in these three domains can lead to an illogical (military policy determining war-policy?) understanding of and approach to the making of war-policy.
27. Ibid., 319.
28. Ironically, the same nonlinearity that one finds in the world of policy and policymaking exists in the realm of strategy, strategic planning, and strategy making.
29. Luttwak, *Strategy*, xii.
30. This is done within normal policy circles through the apparatuses of bureaucracy. In the world of strategy, the contrariness of strategic ends and resources available is rationalized through the use of operational art and science. It is the procedure—the functions and formulas—at the operational level of war-policy that allows for a logical cohesion of strategy and tactics.
31. Randall B. Ripley, *Political Analysis in Political Science* (New York: Wadsworth Publishing Company, 1985).

Chapter 3 The Dawn of the Postmodern Age of War

1. Carl von Clausewitz, *On War*, trans. and ed. Michael Howard and Peter Paret (Princeton, NJ: Princeton University Press, 1976), 605.
2. *The 9/11 Commission Report: Final Report of the National Commission on Terrorist Attacks upon the United States* (New York: W. W. Norton & Company, 2002).
3. For more on the theory of professions, see Andrew Abbott, *The System of Professions: An Essay on the Division of Expert Labor* (Chicago, IL: University of Chicago Press, 1988). For discussions of the U.S. Army as profession, see Don Snider and Lloyd Matthews, *The Future of the Army Profession* (New York: McGraw-Hill, 2005).
4. For details on the fourth generation of war-fare school of thought, go to http://www.d-n-i.net/second_level/fourth_generation_warfare.htm (accessed February 15, 2005).

5. http://www.d-n-i.net/second_level/fourth_generation_warfare.htm (accessed February 15, 2005).
6. Thomas X. Hammes, *The Sling and the Stone: On War in the 21st Century* (Osceola, WI: Zenith, 2004).
7. Samuel P. Huntington, *The Clash of Civilizations and the Remaking of World Order* (New York: Simon and Shuster, 1998).
8. Returns to scale refer to a technical property of production: what happens to output if we increase the quantity of all input factors by some amount. If output increases by that same amount there are CRTS, sometimes referred to simply as returns to scale. If output increases by less than that amount, there are decreasing returns to scale. If output increases by more than that amount, there are increasing returns to scale. See http://en.wikipedia.org/wiki/Economies_of_scale (accessed February 15, 2005).
9. The term and concept are borrowed from Theda Skocpol's *Bringing the State Back In* (Cambridge: Cambridge University Press, 1985).
10. Term and concept borrowed from Amitai Etzioni's *From Empire to Community: A New Approach to International Relations* (New York: Palgrave Macmillan, 2002).
11. Richard N. Haass, *Intervention: The Use of American Military Force in the Post-Cold War World* (New York: Carnegie Endowment for International Peace, 1999).
12. John Lewis Gaddis, *Strategies of Containment: A Critical Appraisal of Postwar American National Security Policy* (New York: Oxford University Press, 1982).
13. "ICRC Neutrality and Neutrality in Humanitarian Assistance," online at http://www.icrc.org/Web/Eng/siteeng0.nsf/iwpList126/FCAC6D3AA091869BC1256B660059F2FB (accessed February 15, 2005).
14. See Amy Zegart, *Flawed by Design: The Evolution of the CIA, JCS, and NSC* (Stanford, CA: Stanford University Press, 1999).
15. Dr. Conrad Crane, presentation delivered at SAIS Conference on Planning and Operations Relating to the Iraq War, Johns Hopkins University, November 2, 2005.
16. Isaiah Wilson, III, "Thinking Beyond War: Civil-Military Operational Planning in Northern Iraq," online at http://www.einaudi.cornell.edu/PeaceProgram/calendar/index.asp?id=3989 (accessed February 15, 2005).
17. Ibid.
18. Gregory Fontenot, E. J. Degan, and David Tohn, *On Point: The United States Army in Operation Iraqi Freedom* (Fort Leavenworth, KS: Combat Studies Institute Press, 2005).
19. Ibid.
20. Ibid. See also Williamson Murray and Maj. Gen. Robert H. Scales, Jr., *The Iraq War: A Military History* (Cambridge, MA: Harvard University Press, 2003).
21. Fontenot, Degan, and Tohn, *On Point.*
22. Ibid.
23. For details on the history, organizational and combat lineage of the 101st Airborne Division, go to http://www.campbell.army.mil/dhistory.htm (accessed 15 February 2005).
24. Ida M. Tarbell, "Life of Abraham Lincoln," in Mabel Hill, ed., *Liberty Documents: With Contemporary Exposition and Critical Comments Drawn from Various Writers* (New York: Longmans, Green, and Company, 1901), 371.
25. U.S. Congress, "Army Transformation: Implications for the Future," July 15, 2004, http://www.house.gov/hasc/openingstatementsand pressreleases/108thcongress/04-07-15 Macgregor.pdf (accessed August 18, 2005). Statement of Col. Douglas MacGregor, USA (Ret.), Testifying before the HASC on July 15, 2004 in 2118 of the Rayburn House Office Building.
26. Douglas A. MacGregor, *Breaking the Phalanx: A New Design for Landpower in the 21st Century*, 1st ed. (Westport, CT: Praeger, 1997).

27. The key concept/entity informing this study is the strategic planner. A critical albeit secondary objective in this project is to progressively develop and refine a definition for and criteria for the development of Army strategic planners. Nevertheless, a baseline for an eventual definition (a vision) is necessary to begin the study. A statement made by General (Ret.) John Galvin some years ago provided the vision of the "strategist in uniform" for the Army then and will provide the baseline for the development and refinement of the definition of the strategic planner in this study. For a full review of General (Ret.) Galvin's thoughts on Army strategists, see John R. Galvin, "What's the Matter With Being a Strategist?" *Parameters* (Summer 1995): 161–186.
28. Clausewitz, *On War*, 605.
29. Stephen, D. Krasner, *International Regimes* (Ithaca, NY: Cornell University Press, 1983), 2.

Chapter 4 On Planning: A New Methodology for Postmodern War-Fare

1. *Chairman, Joint Chief of Staff Manual* (*CJCSM*) 3500.05, pg. 5-II-6, online at http://www.dtic.mil/doctrine/jel/cjcsd/cjcsm/m3500_05.pdf (originally accessed February 15, 2005; accessed May 29, 2007).
2. Suitability (i.e., accomplishes the mission, complies with CJTF's intent, accomplishes essential tasks, meets the endstate, considers centers of gravity and decisive points); feasibility (i.e., availability of force structure to do it, other resources available); acceptability (i.e., worth the risks, within limitations); differentiation (i.e., different and distinct from all other COAs); and completeness (i.e., answers the key questions—who, what, when, where, why, and how). See *CJCSM 3500.05*, dated April 15, 1997.
3. See Randall B. Ripley, *Political Analysis in Political Science* (New York: Wadsworth Publishing Company, 1985).
4. CENTCOM Operation Iraqi Freedom Briefing. Presenter: Brigadier General Vincent Brooks, Deputy Director of Operations. Time: 7:07 AM EST, FRIDAY, March 28, 2003.
5. Isaiah Wilson III, "American Anabasis," in Thomas Keaney and Thomas Mahnken, eds., *War in Iraq: Planning and Execution* (New York: Routledge, 2007).
6. Isaiah Wilson III, "Thinking Beyond War: Civil-Military Operational Planning in Northern Iraq," Peace Studies Program seminar, Cornell University, October 14, 2004.
7. Eric Schmitt, "Pentagon Contradicts General on Iraq Occupation Force's Size," *New York Times*, February 28, 2003.
8. Samuel B. Griffith, ed. and trans., *The Art of War* (New York: Oxford University Press, 1972), 84.
9. Gregory Fontenot, E. J. Degan, and David Tohn, *On Point: The United States Army in Operation Iraqi Freedom* (Fort Leavenworth, KS: Combat Studies Institute Press, 2005).
10. The most recent of an almost 20-year ongoing debate over operational art at SAMS is a debate between myself and a SAMS colleague, Major Joseph McLamb—a series of papers collectively entitled *Operational Art: Will I Know It When I See It?* (Fort Leavenworth, KS: Combat Studies Institute [CSI]: 2001–2002).
11. Shimon Naveh, *In Pursuit of Military Excellence: The Evolution of Operational Theory* (New York: Frank Cass Publishers, 1997).
12. The CPA, CJTF-7, and other divisional plans derived from variations of the 101st plan.

13. Author's researcher notes (OIFSG) and planner journal entries, 2003–2004. Go to http://history.acusd.edu/gen/st/~cshimp/france_1940.htm (accessed February 15, 2005) for a quick description. For detailed accounts, see Marc Bloch, *Strange Defeat: A Statement of Evidence Written in 1940* (New York: W. W. Norton & Company, 1999).
14. See also Robert Doughty, *The Breaking Point—Sedan and the Fall of France 1940* (Hamden, CT: Archon, 1990).

Part II Lessons in Postmodern War: Civil-Military Operations in Northern Iraq

1. Rick Atkinson, *In the Company of Soldiers: A Chronicle of Combat* (New York: Henry Holt & Company, 2004).
2. In August 2005, Lieutenant General Petraeus was renominated by the U.S. president to the rank of lieutenant general and to command of the Combined Arms Center (CAC) at Fort Leavenworth, Kansas. In addition to the traditional roles, functions, and responsibilities of the CAC commander, the secretary of defense has added an additional mission role to Lieutenant General Petraeus as CAC commander: to establish and direct a new institute for the development (formation, education, training) of international security forces—the *Institute for International Security Forces* at Fort Leavenworth, Kansas.

Chapter 5 The Liberation and Reconstruction of Northern Iraq

1. What proved early on and what continues to prove as a useful tool by FRE as an informational (propagandist) justification for anticoalition/antireconstruction activities have been the dilapidated condition of essential service infrastructure and the overall impoverished state of the economy and security situation throughout Iraq since initiation of the war in March 2003. Similar to the Russians, in the difficult days of reconstruction following the demise of Stalin, call for the "good old days of Stalin," the organic threats (particularly FRE and the insurgent base) sought then and continue to seek a situation of continued despair and mediocre improvement of civic life and daily public administration as a means of supporting their baseline claim to the general populace: "[Y]ou are worst off under US occupation than you were under Saddam." Defeat of this informational attack at the tactical (ground, implementation) level is the key to future operational (regional) and strategic (national, international) victory.
2. Makhmur is situated in the southeastern region of Ninevah province, traditionally Kurdish in ethnic majority, though an area subjected to numerous ethnic-based forced migrations (the result of periodic Arabization policies and Kurdification policies—intentional policies within the area throughout the rein of Saddam, designed to maintain a measure of Arab-Kurd imbalance, reinforcing his own regimes' stability).
3. Northern Iraq has traditionally and historically been the de facto homestead of former Iraqi military officers as well as the seedbed of military-based tribal families and clans. With the collapse of the Saddam regime in April 2003 and the dissolution of the Iraqi Army by Ambassador Paul Bremer, the north became a center of rampant and destabilizing former military-based unemployment. In an attempt to help the economy and, moreover, to stave off the potential of former military soldiers taking their martial skills *onto the market*, the 101st created a Veterans Employment Center, similar to the veterans-preference programs in the United States, which actively focused on the

respectful employment of former senior military officers and soldiers throughout the northern regions.

4. It is during this time that I arrived in Mosul to join the 101st Airborne Division (Air Assault) as its chief war-planner.
5. For example, the Security LOO was initially composed of six key tasks: safe and secure environment; Iraqi security forces; weapons caches, military equipment, and ammunition; locate and secure WMD; territorial integrity of Iraq; and information tasks in support of these key tasks.
6. For example, again using the Security LOO to illustrate one of seven initial supporting tasks for security, LOO key tasks 1.1 (safe and secure environment), was determined to *identify neutral and stabilizing elements and their agendas*, as Supporting Task 1.1.5. The measure of effectiveness for this particular supporting task was *the percentage of key business and community elements that are neutral or willing to cooperate with coalition forces.* This was a quantifiable measure of effectiveness by which Division planners could regularly assess, adding to a measurable overall assessment that was then periodically reported to the division commander, key divisional staff, higher headquarters, and local community leaders, once a relative degree of trust was established.
7. David Easton, *The Political System: An Inquiry into the State of Political Science* (New York: Alfred A. Knopf, 1953; 2nd ed., 1971, 1981).
8. The distinction between operational planning "groups" as opposed to "teams" was based largely on the scope and scale of the operational problem, OPGs being larger composites of subject matter experts gathered to work more systemic long-term challenges and issues.
9. These funds were known as Commander's Emergency Response Funds (CERP).

Chapter 6 Patronage Politics in Northern Iraq: The Case of Tribal Engagement in Northern Iraq, June 2003–March 2004

1. Types of tribes in northern Iraq ranged from the Western "stereotypical" notions of Arab tribes (a la the popular rendition of the film *Lawrence of Arabia*) of the western and Tigris River Valley regions (Shammar, Jaburi) to the military and political tribes of the urban areas (Al Tai, Humarabi). The Kurdish "tribes" have become known more as political parties rather than tribes, although tribalism remains an important political and public administrative (control) tool for the Kurdish parties. Moreover, "modern" Kurdish tribalism derives more from a familial lineage than other Arab tribes in Iraq, with the two majority Kurdish "families" being the KDP, under the leadership of the Barzani family and the PUK, under the leadership of the Talabani family. Each "family," or party machine, maintains their own militias known as the *peshmerga* (the KDP maintains a *peshmerga* of approximately 55,000 fighters; the PUK has a *peshmerga* of over 70,000 fighters).
2. As Division planners continued to assess past operations in light of the development of future ones, earlier tactical and operational missteps were seen in a new context, looking through the tribal lenses. Forceful cordon and searches conducted during the summer months soon after occupation could be seen and reassessed as being judged not only as harsh public displays of oppression (justified or not) by the locals, but based on tribal norms, acts of dishonor to family, clan, and tribe, acts that demanded retribution ("eye for an eye"). Further reassessment confirmed a few such instances that, in turn, had resulted unintentionally in the Division triggering "blood feuds." Learning how to "recover" from such instances and to avoid the obligatory "eye-for-an-eye" response was important for protecting the force—U.S. and the Iraqi

population. Writing a monetary check following an incident within a local community was not enough. A public reconciliation—a tribal truce ceremony—had to take place, with unit leadership visiting the offended family/tribe and spending an adequate amount of time (sometimes hours) over numerous pots of *Chi* (tea). The greater the offense, the higher level of Division leadership was "required" to attend the truce. Reassessing some of the previous anticoalition attacks revealed a few instances where a highly ineffective attack on U.S. forces followed either a major operation or an operation-based instance of unintended collateral damage. More than a handful of these former attacks, then judged as lethal attacks against our forces, were able to be reassessed as merely symbolic retribution (honor-bound) by tribal members—kin of the offended, injured, or killed person. By tribal honor, the relative was required to strike in reprisal. Some of the attacks that we originally saw as "poor marksmanship" were likely intentional misses by attackers pro-progress and pro-United States but honor-bound to avenge a perceived wrong that U.S. forces at the time did not know how to appropriately resolve.

3. One of many indirect linkages between the Syrian Ba'athist Party and the former Iraqi Ba'athist Party reside in the Shammar tribe, both by land and by marriage connections.
4. Bruce Russett, *Grasping the Democratic Peace* (Princeton, NJ: Princeton University Press, 1993).
5. Thomas P. M. Barnett, *The Pentagon's New Map: War and Peace in the Twenty-First Century* (New York: Putnam, 2004).
6. For a full explanation see Peter Gourevitch, "The Second Image Reversed: The International Sources of Domestic Politics," *International Organization*, 32 (4) (Autumn 1978): 881–912.
7. Ibid.
8. Kenneth N. Waltz, *Man, the State, and War* (New York: Columbia University Press, 1954).
9. Alexis de Tocqueville, Democracy in America (New York: Signet Classics, 2001).
10. Edward Schatz, *Modern Clan Politics: The Power of "Blood" in Kazakhstan and Beyond* (Seattle and London: University Washington Press, 2004).
11. Charles E. Lindblom, *Politics and Markets* (New York: Basic Books, 1977).
12. Theda Skocpol, *States and Social Revolutions: A Comparative Analysis of France, Russia and China* (Cambridge, MA: Cambridge University Press, 1979).
13. Clinton Rossiter, *The Federalists Papers* (New York: Signet Press, 1999).
14. Theodore J. Lowi, Benjamin Ginsberg, and Kenneth A. Shepsle, *American Government: Power and Purpose* (New York: W. W. Norton & Company, 2002).
15. Gregg B. Walker (Author), David A. Bella (Author), Steven J. Sprecher (Editor), *The Military-Industrial Complex: Eisenhower's Warning Three Decades Later.* American University Studies Series X, Political Science (New York: Peter Lang, 1992).
16. Alvin Toffler, *The Third Wave* (New York: Bantam, 1984); David S. Alberts, John J. Garstka, and Frederick P. Stein, *Network Centric Warfare: Developing and Leveraging Information Superiority* (Washington, DC: CCRP Press, 1999); John Arquilla, Swarming and the Future of Conflict (Santa Monica, CA: Rand Corporation, 2000).
17. Joe Strange, *Centers of Gravity & Critical Vulnerabilities* (Quantico, VA: U.S. Marine Corps Association, 1996), 93–96.
18. Edward Schatz, *Modern Clan Politics: The Power of "Blood" in Kazakhstan and Beyond* (Seattle and London: University Washington Press, 2004).
19. Ibid., 165.
20. Ibid., 167.
21. Ibid., 30; *Small Wars Journal*, online at http://smallwarsjournal.com/reference/culturalintelligence.php.
22. Schatz, *Modern Clan Politics*, 31.

23. 101st Airborne Division Unit History.
24. Schatz, *Modern Clan Politics*, 34.

Chapter 7 My Iraq War: A Postscript

1. "Bush's Iraq Rating at Low Point," August 5, 2005, online at http://www.cnn.com/2005/POLITICS/08/05/bush.ap.ipsospoll.ap/index.html (accessed August 7, 2005).
2. Wikipedia, "Post-Invasion Iraq, 2003–2004," online at http://en.wikipedia.org/wiki/Post-invasion_Iraq%2C_2003-2005 (accessed August 7, 2005).
3. James H. Willbanks, "The Battle for Hue, 1968," GlobalSecurity.org, online at http://www.globalsecurity.org/military/library/report/202/MOUTWilbanks.html (accessed August 7, 2005).
4. "Fallujah—Wikipedia," online at http://www.en.wikipedia.org/wiki/Fallujah (accessed August 7, 2005).
5. Carl von Clausewitz, *On War*, trans. and ed. Michael Howard and Peter Paret, indexed ed. (Princeton, NJ: Princeton University Press, 1984).
6. Gregory Fontenot, E. J. Degan, and David Tohn, *On Point: The United States Army in Operation Iraqi Freedom* (Fort Leavenworth, KS: Combat Studies Institute, 2004).
7. U.S. Department of Defense, *Dictionary of Military and Associated Terms, Joint Publication 1–02*, March 27, 2007, 207.
8. Bard E. O'Neill, *Insurgency & Terrorism: Inside Modern Revolutionary Warfare* (Washington, DC: Brassey's, 1990), 13.
9. John Shy, *A People Numerous and Armed: Reflections on the Military Struggle for American Independence* (Ann Arbor, MI: University of Michigan Press, 1990). See also Ian F. W. Beckett, *Modern Insurgencies and Counter-Insurgencies: Guerillas and the Opponents since 1750* (New York: Routledge, 2001).
10. Beckett, *Modern Insurgencies and Counter-Insurgencies*, 8.
11. Charles Gwynn, *Imperial Policing* (London: Macmillan, 1934).
12. Beckett, *Modern Insurgencies and Counter-Insurgencies*, 44.
13. Robert R. Mackey, *The Uncivil War: Irregular Warfare in the Upper South, 1861–1865* (Oklahoma City, OK: University of Oklahoma Press, 2004).

Chapter 8 Whither Mosul? The Story of Transition Failure and the Rise and Fall of Northern Iraq

1. As commander of the 101st Airborne, Petraeus was a major general (Two-Star). In May 2004, he was elevated to the rank of lieutenant general and given his Third Star.
2. Of the various accounts, one of the more recent and first-person accounts is by David Phillips in his book *Losing Iraq: Inside the Postwar Reconstruction Fiasco* (New York: Westview Press, 2005).
3. Larry Diamond, *Squandered Victory: The American Occupation and the Bungled Effort to Bring Democracy to Iraq*, 1st ed. (New York: Time Books, 2005), 29.
4. Michael R. Gordon, "The Strategy to Secure Iraq Did Not Foresee a 2nd War," *New York Times*, October 19, 2004.
5. "The Strategy to Secure Iraq Did Not Foresee a 2nd War," *New York Times*, October 19, 2004, online at http://www.nytimes.com/2004/10/19/international/19war. html?pagewanted=4&ei=5088&en=7d6bb64ff7591648&ex=1255838400&partner=rssnyt.

6. David Rieff, "Who Botched the Occupation?" *New York Times Magazine*, November 2, 2003, 32.
7. Tom Ricks, "Army Historian Cites Lack of Postwar Plan for Iraq," *Washington Post*, December 25, 2004, A1. This article presented my scholarly assessment of the "failed to plan to win the peace" debates of 2003–2004, arguments that I had presented at the 2004 American Political Science Association (APSA) Annual conference, Thinking Beyond War: Civil-Military Operational Planning in Northern Iraq.
8. Major Isaiah Wilson III, 101st Airborne Division planner's notes/planner's journal, June 2003–May 2005.
9. Ibid.
10. Ibid.
11. Ibid.
12. Ibid.
13. CPA strategic campaign plan, dated January 2003; author's planner notes.
14. Author's planner notes.
15. A military planning technique known as troop-to-tasks allocation and analysis.
16. This delay would prove to be 40–45 days.
17. In military vernacular, these sorts of complex major unit reliefs-in-place and transfers-of-authority are facilitated through a process termed right seat-left seat rides.
18. For doctrinal details refer to U.S. Department of Defense, "Department of Defense Dictionary of Military and Associated Terms," *Joint Publication 1–02*, April 12, 2001.
19. Author's planner notes.
20. Ibid.
21. Ibid.
22. 1–10 CAV from the 10th Mountain Division, Fount Drum, New York, was templated as the augmenting force in this course of action. This course of action was eliminated around November 2003.
23. The size of force, type of force, composition of force, the capability within the force, the training levels of the personnel within the force, and the degree of education with the leadership core of the force, and so on.
24. The physical stationing or positioning of the force, the manner in which the force is employed on missions, and so on.
25. As an example, where the 101st Airborne's plans staff alone was composed of 21 staff officers, skilled in a myriad of war-specialties, the TF Olympia's plans staff was one officer. The lack of a plans staff itself limited the entire TFO campaign approach to tactical management. In effect, by failing to "man" the operation command headquarters adequately, AO North was deprived of an operational command.
26. Army and Joint Doctrine lists the Principles of War (Operations) as offensive, maneuver, massed effects, economy of force, simplicity, surprise, unity of effort, security, morale, objective. That same doctrine offers the following as the Elements of Operational Art: synergy, simultaneity and depth, anticipation, balance, leverage, timing and tempo, operational reach and approach, forces and functions, arranging operations, centers of gravity, direct vs. indirect approach, decisive points, culmination and, finally, termination (*Joint Publication 3–0*, Exec Summary).
27. U.S. Department of Defense, "Department of Defense Dictionary of Military and Associated Terms," *Joint Publication 1–02*, April 12, 2001, 259.
28. Maneuver is more than just the summation of fire and movement. It also includes the dynamic, flexible application of leadership, firepower, and protection. It requires flexible thoughts, plans, and operations and the considered application of the principles of massed effects, surprise, and economy of force. See *Joint Publication 1–02.*
29. Norman M. Wade, in *The Operations and Training Smartbook* (New York: Lightning Press, 2005), 2–25.
30. Ibid., 3–55.

Chapter 9 Fighting to Change, Changing to Fight: The Lessons of Iraq on Army Transformation, *Under Construction*

1. A Department of the Army referenent to the collective organizations of the active Army, National Guard and Army Reserves.
2. Carl Connetta, *Operation Enduring Freedom: Why a Higher Rate of Civilian Bombing Casualties*, Project on Defence Alternatives Briefing Report no.11, January 24, 2002.
3. Fuller was born in 1878, in Chichester, West Sussex, England, and educated at Malvern College and Royal Military Academy Sandhurst from 1897 to 1898. He was commissioned into the Oxfordshire Light Infantry and served in South Africa from 1899 to 1902. He then attended Staff College at Camberley and served as an adjutant to a territorial battalion. During World War I, he was a staff officer with the Home Forces and with 7 corps in France, and from 1916 in the Headquarters of the Machine Gun Corps' Heavy Branch, which was later to become the Tank Corps. He planned the tank attack at Cambrai and the tank operations for the autumn offensives of 1918. His Plan 1919 for a fully mechanized army was never implemented, and after 1918 he held various leading positions, notably as a commander of an experimental brigade at Aldershot.

   In the 1920s, he collaborated with his junior B. H. Liddell Hart in developing new ideas for the mechanization of armies.

   On his retirement in 1933, and impatient with what he considered the inability of democracy to adopt military reforms, he became involved with Sir Oswald Mosley and the British Fascist movement. As a member of the British Union of Fascists, he sat on the party's Policy Directorate and was considered one of Mosley's closest allies. His ideas on mechanized war-fare continued to be influential in the lead up to World War II, ironically more with the Germans, notably Heinz Guderian, than with his countrymen.
4. J. F. C. Fuller, *Generalship—Its Diseases and Their Cure: A Study of the Personal Factor in Command*, reprint ed. (Fort Leavenworth, KS: U.S. Army Command and General Staff College, 1987).
5. Douglas MacGregor, *Breaking the Phalanx: A New Design for Landpower in the 21st Century*, 1st ed. (Westport, CT: Praeger, 1997).
6. Borrowed from Samuel P. Huntington, *The Clash of Civilizations and the Remaking of World Order* (New York: Simon and Shuster, 1998) in style as well as substance.
7. http://www.globalsecurity.org/military/agency/army/101abn.htm.
8. John Shy, "First Battles in Retrospect," in Charles E. Heller and William A. Stofft, eds., *America's First Battles: 1776–1965* (Lawrence, KS: University of Kansas Press, 1986), 327–352.
9. Ibid., 327.
10. Ibid., 328.
11. Ibid., 327.
12. Ibid., 332.
13. The loss of the first battle in the current war against global terrorism, with our national failure to predict and mitigate the terror attacks on the American homeland, September 11, 2001.
14. Paraphrased from Gordon R. Sullivan and James Dubik, *Land Warfare in the 21st Century* (Carlisle Barracks, PA: Strategic Studies Institute, 1993).
15. Shy, "First Battles in Retrospect."
16. A. T. Mahan, *The Influence of Sea Power upon History*, 12th ed. (Boston, MA: Little, Brown, 1980), 2.

17. Eliot A. Cohen and John Gooch, *Military Misfortunes: The Anatomy of Failure in War* (New York: Vintage, 1990).
18. George C. Wilson, *This War Really Matters: Inside the Fight for Defense Dollars* (Washington, DC: Congressional Quarterly Press, 1999).
19. The literature on revolutions in military affairs (RMA) chronicles this history. For more on this debate, see Larry H. Addington, *The Patterns of War since the Eighteenth Century* (Bloomington, IN: Indiana University Press, 1994); Leslie Anders, "Austerlitz: A Clash of Command Systems," *Military Review*, 38 (June 1958); Jonathan B. A. Bailey, "Deep Battle 1914–1941: The Birth of the Modern Style of Warfare," *Field Artillery* (July–August 1998); Jonathan Bailey, "Deep Battle 1914–1941: The Birth of the Modern Style of Warfare," *Field Artillery*, 4 (July–August 1998); David Evans and Mark Peattie, *Kaigun: Strategy, Tactics, and Technology in the Imperial Japanese Navy, 1887–1941* (Annapolis, MD: Naval Institute Press, 1997); Williamson Murray and Alan Millett, eds., *Military Innovation in the Interwar Period* (Cambridge: Cambridge University Press, 1996); Steven Rosen, *Winning the Next War: Innovation and the Modern Military* (Ithaca, NY: Cornell University Press, 1991).
20. Peter Boyar, "A Different War," *New Yorker*, July 1, 2002.
21. Goure, "Army Leads Transformation," *Defense News*, February 26, 2001.
22. General Eric K, Shinseki Intent of the chief of staff, U.S. Army, June 23, 1999, online at http://www.ausa.org/webpub/DeptILW.nsf/byid/KGRG-6EGLXE.
23. Andrew Krepinevich, "Cavalry to Computer: The Pattern of Military Revolutions," *National Interest*, 7 (Fall 1994): 30, emphasis mine.
24. Michael Howard, *War in European History* (New York: Oxford University Press, 1976), 49.
25. See Colonel Douglas McGregor's testimony before the House Armed Services Committee (HASC), online at http://www.iwar.org.uk/rma/resources/army-transformation-hearing/hasc-hearing.htm (accessed February 15, 2005).
26. See my own discussion in "Strategy Revisited," *Military Review* (January/February 2003): 42–49.
27. The 2002 war in Afghanistan is an ample example. See Sean Naylor, *Not a Good Day to Die: The Untold Story of Operation Anaconda* (New York: Berkely Books, 2005) and *The Bear Went over the Mountain: Soviet Combat Tactics in Afghanistan* (Colorado Springs, CO: Institute for National Strategic Studies [INSS]).
28. Visit http://www.army.mil/cmh-pg/books/www/Www2.htm (accessed February 15, 2005).
29. Major Isaiah Wilson III, 101st Airborne Division planner's notes/planner's journal, June 2003–May 2005.
30. Direct liaison authorized (DIRLAUTH) was not granted to Division personnel or TF Modularity personnel. Though I am unable to confirm with official correspondence or DOD/OSD memoranda, the common understanding among all involved at the time, and since, confirms this prohibition for planners at these two separate levels of the early transformation initiative to cross-talk.
31. Author's planner notes, June 2003–May 2005.
32. http://usmilitary.about.com/od/armyweapons/a/gator.htm.
33. See Naylor, *Not a Good Day to Die.*
34. U.S. Congress, "Army Transformation: Implications for the Future," July 15, 2004, online at http://www.comw.org/pda/fulltext/0704macgregor.pdf (accessed August 18, 2005). Statement of Colonel (Ret.) Douglas MacGregor, USA, Testifying before the House Armed Services Committee on July 15, 2004 in 2118 of the Rayburn House Office Building.

Chapter 10 Educating Holistic Warriors

Author's Note: The original version of this chapter first appeared in 2002 as my monograph, part of the matriculation requirements for graduation and receipt of a Masters in Military Art and Science (MMAS) from the U.S. Army School of Advanced Military Studies, Fort Leavenworth, Kansas. The original arguments and propositions were focused on the development of the U.S. Army's new core of strategic planners, FA59 strategic plans and policy officers. Expanding the context of those original propositions beyond one branch of the Army to the entire domain of the nations' traditional and emergent security professions adds a new and powerful relevancy to the original work, making the repeat articulation of it here, justified.

1. This chapter will confine its renderings of the Clausewitzian nature of war and war-fare to the Michael Howard and Peter Paret translation and conceptualizations. See Carl von Clausewitz, *On War*, ed. and trans. Michael Howard and Peter Paret, indexed ed. (Princeton, NJ: Princeton University Press, 1984).
2. The debate over how best to educate, train, and develop military professionals (generalists) for war is as old as war itself. The debate has taken different form and emphasis over time, reflective of changes in war and the ways of war. Practitioners and scholars alike, writing about revolutions in military affairs (RMAs), have identified at least three distinct epochs of "modern" war-fare—the dynastic age of war-fare (ca. 1200–mid-1800s), the industrial age of war-fare (ca. 1800s–1920s), and the mechanized age of war-fare (ca. 1940s–1990s). Evolutions from one epoch to the next reflected changes in all aspects of war. As Morris Janowitz, a renowned political sociologist, has offered, each evolutionary period witnessed reforms in officer education and training. Janowitz identified three essential types of officers—individually and in combination—in war: military technologists, heroic leaders, and military managers.
3. The Office of the Secretary of Defense (Net Assessment) defines RMA as "a major change . . . brought about by the innovative application of new technologies which, combined with dramatic changes in military doctrine and operational and organizational concepts, fundamentally alters the character and conduct of military operations." See Andrew W. Marshall, director of net assessment, Office of the Secretary of Defense, memorandum, August 23, 1993.
4. Amid the plethora of literature on RMAs, there is some consensus on a best definition—one offered by Andrew Krepinevich in "Calvary to Computer: The Pattern of Military Revolutions," *National Interest* (Fall 1994): 30. He argues, "[RMA] occurs when applications of new technologies into a significant number of military systems combines with innovative operational concepts and organizational adaptation in a way that fundamentally alters the character of conflict. It does so by an order of magnitude or greater—in the combat potential and military effectiveness of armed forces." Michael Howard provides a similar thinking on RMAs, one that places an emphasis on the organizational and sociopolitical rather than technological factors of change: "The revolutionary changes associated with the French Revolution and Napoleon were mostly sociopolitical and organizational in nature" (Howard, in Larry H. Addington, *Military Innovation and the Interwar Period* [New York: Cambridge University Press, 1998]). For other seminal works on the subject of RMA, see MacGregor Knox and Williamson Murray, eds., *The Dynamics of Military Revolution, 1300–2050* (Cambridge: Cambridge University Press, 2001); Michael O'Hanlon, "Technological Change & the Future of Warfare: Introduction," Chapter One in *Technological Change & the Future of Warfare* (Washington, DC: Brookings Institution, 2000); Stephen Peter Rosen, *Winning the Next War: Innovation and the Modern Military* (Ithaca, NY: Cornell University Press, 1994).
5. See White House, "The National Security Strategy of the United States of America," online at http://www.whitehouse.gov/nsc/nss.html (accessed May 29, 2007); Office

of the Chairman, Joint Chiefs of Staff, "National Military Strategy, 2002," draft version, as of March 27, 2002, online at http://www.defenselink.mil/news/Mar2005/d20050318nms.pdf (accessed May 29, 2007).

6. See Joint Vision 2010 and 2020, located on the JCS homepage http://www.jcs.mil/ (accessed May 29, 2007).
7. President George W. Bush, Speech, Norfolk Naval Air Station, February 13, 2001, online at http://frwebgate6.access.gpo.gov (accessed November 12, 2002).
8. Keaney, Thomas A., and Elliot Cohen. *Gulf War Air Power Survey Summary Report*, Washington, DC: U.S. Government Printing Office, 1993, 2.
9. For an adequate listing of postmodern "threats," see Robert Kaplan, *The Coming Anarchy* (New York: Vintage, 2001).
10. Ronald H. Cole, *Operation Urgent Fury: The Planning and Execution of Joint Operations in Grenada 12 October–2 November 1983* (Washington, DC: Joint History Office, Office of the Chairman of the Joint Chiefs of Staff, 1997).
11. U.S. Congress, House Armed Services Committee, Panel on Military Education Report (Skelton Report). Report to the Committee on Armed Services House of Representatives, 101st Congress, 1st session, April 21, 1989.
12. Today's joint war-fighting "scorecard" still indicates a joint anemia afflicting the U.S. military, with service-centric education still the dominant key to future career success, and therefore service centricity still dominating officer education.

    However, the shortfall has been identified and actions are currently underway to rectify the problem. What is the current scorecard regarding strategic planner education? Does it reveal an educational gap similar to the joint specialty officer shortfall? If so, what is missing in the current master strategist curriculum and education system?
13. A lack of expertise in the joint integration of service capabilities for joint effects was the specific finding, yet, the more general and substantial learning point that following every major war, the U.S. military was compelled to establish new and/or redesign existing educational programs. After the American Civil War, the U.S. Army established the School of Application for Infantry and Cavalry in 1881, and the U.S. Navy established the Naval War College (1884). During World War II, the Joint Staff created the Army-Navy Staff College, followed up after the conclusion of WWII with the creation of the National War College and the Industrial College of the Armed Forces (ICAF). Positive and negative experiences in the execution (implementation) of war policy have not only led to new institutions and institutional designs; they have also led to new procedures for the education, training, and experience-based learning (hereafter referred to, in combination, as "education") of individual officers and small cohorts of specialized war policy experts. The GNA '86 and the Skelton Panel gave birth to, and have continually emphasized since the late 1980s, the Joint Specialty Officer (JSO). Again, the emphasis has consistently been more about the integration of multiservice effects rather than about joint capabilities themselves.
14. See Colonel Lloyd J. Matthews, *The Future of the Army Profession* (Boston, MA: McGraw-Hill Primus Custom Publishing, 2002).
15. Alvin Toffler, *The Third Wave* (New York: Bantam, 1984).
16. For more on the modern-postmodern divide over professional education, see my SAMS monograph *Educating the Post-Modern U.S. Army Strategic Planner: Improving the Organizational Construct* (Fort Leavenworth, KS: Army Command and General Staff College, School of Advanced Military Studies, 2003), 97. Accession Number: AD-A419795, online at http://handle.dtic.mil/100.2/ADA419795 (accessed February 15, 2005). Abstract: The prevailing U.S. Army professional military education (PME) system reflects the legacy of the twentieth-century, modern, mechanized age of war-fare. The twenty-first-century security environment presents unique challenges to U.S. national security and military strategy. The rise of a new information age of war-fare exacerbates the perpetual dichotomy between strategic

intent and tactical action in war policy. In this new age, perhaps more than ever before, the distinction between periods of peace and episodes of war has become arbitrary; war in this age is increasingly just a "continuation of politics and policy by other (all) means" (87). Yet, the persisting PME continues to separate the martial tactical expert (the war-fighter) from the extramartial operational and strategic expert (the war-thinker), even constructing the career development profile of the Army officer corps in this bifurcated manner. Effective war policy through the integration of the full spectrum of national and multinational (coalitional) capabilities is less effectively learned under such an education and career development system. What the information age of war-fare demands is the education, training, and experience-based learning of uniformed strategic planners: experts well versed in the planning, management, and leadership of full-spectrum, holistic war policy. See http://handle.dtic.mil/100.2/ADA419795 (accessed February 15, 2005).

17. Kenneth Allard, *Somalia Operations: Lessons Learned* (University Press of the Pacific, 2002); Jonathan Stevenson, *Losing Mogadishu* (New York: Airlife Puiblishing, 1995); Col. Lawrence E. Casper, ed., *Falcon Brigade: Combat and Command in Somalia and Haiti* (New York: Lynne Riener Publishers, 2000).
18. The U.S. military has had a difficult time coming to terms with these ideational and contextual changes in postmodern war-fare. Senior military leaders of combat forces in both Somalia and the Balkan campaigns acknowledge the difficulties they faced in integrating military and nonmilitary elements and organizations (capabilities) of power to intended effect. The military achieved "success" in these operations, but more recent studies have concluded that those successes came at perhaps a higher cost than needed and continue to mask lingering problems that will plague military policy implementation if not soon rectified. The United States has not yet found the need for a new round of "Goldwater-Nichols"-type reviews and reforms but the idea for a necessary new round has been circulating within defense and military policy circles for several years. The rising call for a new round of review centers, again, on the issue of force and power *integration*. Though the present integration questions still imply shortfalls in joint effects, concerns with the integration of martial and nonmartial elements of national power and the operationalization of this widening spectrum of national power into war policy dominates the current reform discussion. See Dennis J. Quinn, *The Goldwater-Nichols DOD Reorganization Act: A Ten-Year Retrospective* (Washington, DC: National Defense University Press), 1999.
19. Charles E. Heller and William A. Stofft, eds., *America's First Battles: 1776–1965* (Lawrence, KS: University of Kansas Press, 1986), ix.
20. Ibid., xi.
21. See General (Ret.) John R. Galvin, "What's the Matter with Being a Strategist?" *Parameters* (Summer 1995) (Carlisle: U.S. Army War College): 161–186.
22. General (Ret.) John R. Galvin, online at http://www.fa-59.army.pentagon.mil/ (accessed May 29, 2007).
23. General (Ret.) John R. Galvin, "What's the Matter with Being a Strategist?" *Parameters*, 19 (1) (March 1989): 2–10; H. R. McMaster, *Dereliction of Duty: Johnson, McNamara, the Joint Chiefs of Staff, and the Lies That Led to Vietnam* (New York: Harpers Perennial, 1998).
24. Galvin, "What's the Matter with Being a Strategist?" 2–10.
25. Theodore J. Crackel, "On the Making of Lieutenants and Colonels," *Public Interest* (76) (Summer 1984): 18.
26. The seminal work in this area was edited by Peter B. Evans, Dietrich Rueschemeyer, and Theda Skocpol, *Bringing the State Back In* (Cambridge: Cambridge University Press, 1985). In addition to the works by Evans, Rueschemeyer, and Skocpol and North, other prominent works in the new institutionalism approach include James March and Johan Olsen, "New Institutionalism: Organizational Factors in Political Life," *American Political Science Review*, 78 (December 1984): 734–749; Stephen

Krasner, "Approaches to the State: Alternative Conceptions and Historical Dynamics," *Comparative Politics*, 16 (January 1984): 223–246; Karen Oren and Stephen Skowronek, "Beyond the Iconography of Order: Notes for a 'New Institutionalism,'" in Lawrence Dodd and Calvin Jillson, eds., *The Dynamics of American Politics: Approaches and Interpretations* (Boulder, CO: Westview Press, 1993); and Theda Skocpol, *Protecting Soldiers and Mothers* (Cambridge, MA: Harvard University Press, 1993).

27. The same structural issues reside within the general PME design of the entire U.S. armed forces. However, this chapter limits the majority of it analyses to the U.S. Army.
28. Robert H. Dorff, *Professional Military Security Education: The View From A Senior Service College* (Carlisle Barracks, PA: Strategic Studies Institute, U.S. Army War College, 2001), 22.
29. Ibid.
30. Ibid.
31. Ibid., 25.
32. See Richard A. Chilcoat, *Strategic Art: New Discipline for 21st Century Leaders* (Carlisle Barracks, PA: U.S. Army War College, Strategic Studies Institute, 1995).

    General Chilcoat defines "strategic art" as "the skillful formulation, coordination and application of ends (objectives), ways (courses of action), and means (supporting resources) to promote and defend the national interests" (iii).
33. Dorff, *Professional Military Security Education*, 25.
34. That is, strategy is a policy or specifically a plan or family of plans, what is referred to here as "S"trategy. But it is also a referent to an approach, a particular method, function, or "stratagem. This distinction is important in that a distinction can be made between a national strategy (singular or, rather, one particular policy) and agency-specific national strategies (plans or series of plans) that are part of a policy process that enables the parent Strategy. The U.S. *National Security Strategy* is an example of this multiple meaning; some may call it schizophrenic notion of strategy. There is a resourcing aspect to strategy (again, small "s") and an execution or war-fighting aspect to strategy (perhaps big "S"). So much of strategy is about resourcing. Within military circles, the resourcing functions relating to strategy fall within the domain of Title X functions—congressionally mandated roles and missions for each of the four military services of the United States relating to manning, arming, equipping, maintaining, sustaining, deploying, developing, and training of military forces. These "s"trategic functions are designed to serve the war-fighting domain of "S"trategy—the execution of joint (multiservice), combined (multinational), and interagency/multiagency strategic plans and policies. To simplify and clarify, big "S" refers to the "tooth" of strategy, while small "s" refers to the "tail." Understanding the distinction between service-specific Title X strategy and combatant command strategy is a necessary condition for gaining an understanding of, and appreciation for, the systemic-centered arguments put forward in this chapter. The design of an education system geared to produce this desired "strategic planner" must be approached from this fuller understanding of strategy, the broader sociopolitical context of war as policy. The strategic planner education apparatus must educate, train, and develop the officer in all aspects of strategy: war-fighting, war-providing, war-provisioning.
35. James M. Smith, Daniel J. Kaufman, Robert H. Dorff, and Linda P. Brady, *Educating International Security Practitioners: Preparing to Face the Demands of the 21st Century International Security Environment* (Carlisle, PA: Army War College, Strategic Studies Institute, July 2001).
36. I call these individuals holistic warriors.

37. General (Ret.) John R. Galvin, "What's the Matter with Being a Strategist?" *Parameters*, 19 (1) (March 1989): 2–10; reprinted in the Summer 1995 edition of *Parameters*, 25 (2): 161–168.
38. Morris Janowitz, *The Professional Soldier* (New York: Free Press, 1971), 428.
39. For Janowitz, the "warrior-scholar" is the collective of all three military typologies.
40. Janowitz, *The Professional Soldier*, 428.
41. Ironically, the same nonlinearity that one finds in the world of policy and policymaking exists in the realm of strategy, strategic planning, and strategy making.
42. Edward N. Luttwak, *Strategy: The Logic of War and Peace* (Cambridge, MA: Belknap Press of Harvard University Press, 2001), xii.
43. This is done within normal policy circles through the apparatuses of bureaucracy. In the world of strategy, the contrariness of strategic ends and resources available are rationalized through the use of operational art and science. It is the procedure —the functions and formulas—at the operational level of war policy that allows for a logical fitting together of strategy and tactics.
44. This chapter puts forward an argument. It contends that this natural paradox that always persists between grand and national strategic vision and the means and resources available to any national state or other sovereign entity can only be effectively brought into coherence through the planning processes at the operational level of war policy. Moreover, this lashing together of the ends, ways, and means of war policy must be accomplished by individuals and small bodies of educated, trained, and experienced individuals in all three domains—both dimensions—of war policy.
45. B. H. Liddell Hart, *Strategy* (London: Faber & Faber Ltd., 1954), xx.
46. The contention put forward in this chapter is that as war as policy becomes more complex, the need for a body of experts educated, trained, and experienced in the policy, planning, and execution of war becomes more important.
47. This chapter intends to build support for this latter proposition by first discussing the history of strategy, as theory and practice, from the late eighteenth century to the present. This short histiography of strategy, operations, and tactics will provide a review of the literature surrounding the issue of military strategy and operational art and science. It will also introduce some of the more prominent writings and musings on the subject of how to educate strategists, operational planners, and military tacticians. What is strategy? What is meant by "operational art"? How do the two differ, relate, and inform each other? Answers to these questions take on a particular importance in the context of this study. What these domains of war policy are, separate from and in relation to one another and the tactical realm—execution, inform the alternative approaches to the education, training, and development of specialists, experts in strategy, operational planning, and policy formulation and implementation. Whether (and how) the knowledge, skills, and attributes of strategists differ from the core competencies of operational artists is the question that must form the baseline of any redesign of the strategist education system.
48. This point is an important one not only to the arguments put forward in this study but also to the relationship between strategy and policy, how this relationship has changed over time (due to many factors, not the least of which was the effect of technological advancements on the growing scope and scale of military operations), and how the change can affect war policy itself. B. H. Liddell Hart makes the point more clearly: "[T]o break down the distinction between strategy and policy would not matter much if the two functions were normally combined in the same person, as with a Frederick or a Napoleon. But as such autocratic soldier-rulers have been rare in modern times and became temporarily extinct in the nineteenth century, the effect was insidiously harmful. For it encouraged soldiers to make the preposterous claim that policy should be subservient to their conduct of operations, and, especially in democratic countries, it drew the statesman on to overstep

the definite border of his sphere and interfere with his military employees in the actual uses of their tools." See Hart, *Strategy*, 319–320. This latter, Hartian notion underpins this chapter and will be addressed more directly later. But for now suffice it to say that an effective and legitimate war policy, balanced between its policy and its strategy, is predicated on a balanced approach to how one educates, trains, and develops its experts in the strategic, operational, and tactical science and art of war policy. Stovepiped and illogical education in these three domains can lead to an illogical (military policy determining war policy?) understanding of and approach to the making of war policy.

49. Ibid., 319.
50. Theorizing about war's purposes (grand strategic and national strategic thinking and practice) increasingly fell to civilian leaders, academic/policy experts, and sometimes military theorists (senior military leadership). The practice of war remained the domain of the military officer corps. Operational planning—the development of plans (operations and campaigns) that translate or "operationalize" strategic-level aims into tangible, resourcable, and executable military objectives—was, at best, left to the martial experts; at worst, it was largely ignored, underdeveloped, and misunderstood. The growing complexity of war demanded a professional and bureaucratic specialization in war policymaking, planning, and implementation. Unfortunately, while specialization has been gained, it has come at the expense of coherence and integration.
51. In short, the modern military officer education system truncates the study and experiencing of war for its leaders largely to the tactical and operational domains. Those officers fortunate enough to study and fulfill assignments outside the normal system tend to do so at their own risk—foregoing operational- and tactical-level assignments deemed by the organization as "career-enhancing" in order to study and experience the other-than-military factors of war policy. Those officers able to balance the tactical, operational, and strategic aspects of their education and assignment career are a rarity.
52. Michael Howard, "The Use and Abuse of Military History," *Paramaters* (March 1981): 14.
53. A concept presented by Hart in his book *Strategy*.
54. The reform debates began, justifiably, with the GNA '86 initiatives, and carry forward through the Skelton Panel recommendations, and the Richard B. Cheney studies, conducted by now Vice President Dick Cheney, when he served with the Center for Strategic and International Studies (CSIS) in the mid-1990s.
55. Linda P. Brady, "On Paradigms and Policy Relevance: Reflections on the Future of Security Studies," *National Security Studies Quarterly*, 3 (4) (Autumn 1997): 2–3.
56. *Preparing Global Professionals for the New Century: Issues, Curricula and Strategies for International Affairs Education*, ed. Michele Cisco Titi (Washington, DC: Association of Professional Schools of International Affairs, November 1998).
57. *Preparing Global Professionals for the New Century: Issues, Curricula and Strategies for International Affairs Education*, Michele Cisco Titi, ed. (Washington, DC: Association of Professional Schools of International Affairs), November 1998.
58. Robert A. Vitas, "Civilian Graduate Education and the Professional Officer," *Military Review*, 79 (3) (May/June 1999): 47–59.
59. Morris Janowitz, "Civic Consciousness and Military Performance," in Morris Janowitz and Stephen D. Wesbrook, eds., *The Political Education of Soldiers* (Beverley Hills, CA: Sage, 1983), 76.
60. John W. Masland and Lawrence I. Radway, *Soldiers and Scholars: Military Education and National Policy* (Princeton, NJ: Princeton University Press, 1957), 3.
61. The "new age" Masland and Radway spoke of was the mechanized age of war-fare, ca. 1950s. The shortfall in the civilian side of professional military education is seen by many to still persist and to hinder the military in its ability to more effectively contend with the realities of twenty-first-century war-fare.

62. I supervised such an outreach program for the Department of Social Sciences, USMA, at West Point, from 1998 to 2001. Prestigious international relations, public policy, comparative politics programs in institutions such as Harvard's JFK School, Princeton's Woodrow Wilson School, and Columbia University's School of International and Public Affairs (SIPA) have been quite accommodating in lowering their annual tuition cost—as well as their in-residency degree requirement timelines—to help facilitate military officer attendance. These programs have also adjusted some of their requirements relating to PhD research and dissertation preparation, increasingly allowing student officers to complete these requirements in absentia during their military follow-on utilization tours. The added "time" this provides to officers makes attainment of the masters and PhD more affordable than ever before.
63. I participated in this initiative under the aegis of the then newly formed Office of Homeland Security and the authority of Governor Ridge, who was at the time the advisor to the president on homeland security. This initiative took place between October 2001 and March 2002.
64. "Distributed Learning," Booz Allen Hamilton, online at http://www.boozallen.com/capabilities/Industries/army/658191.

Epilogue: No More Iraqs?

1. A social scientist specializing in the study of government, a social scientist being someone expert in the study of human society and its personal relationships.
2. Dave Richard Palmer, *Summons of the Trumpet: A History of the Vietnam War from a Military Man's Viewpoint* (New York: Ballantine, 1978).
3. Ibid., xi.
4. H. R. McMaster, *Dereliction of Duty* (New York: HarperCollins, 1996).
5. Jeffrey Brown, "Intelligence Report Predicts Dire Future for Iraq's Security," Online News Hour with Jim Lehrer, available online at http://www.pbs.org/newshour/bb/middle_east/jan-june07/iraq_02-02.html (accessed June 1, 2007).
6. The now-sitting U.S. Secretary of Defense Robert Gates at the time of his nomination for SECDEF was a member of the Baker-Hamilton Commission.
7. James A. Baker III and Lee H. Hamilton et. al., *The Iraq Study Group Report: The Way Forward, A New Approach* (New York: Vantage Books, 2006), ix.
8. Grand strategy is a general term for a broad statement of strategic action. A grand strategy states the means that will be used to achieve long-term objectives. Examples of business grand strategies that can be customized for a specific firm include concentration, market development, product development, innovation, horizontal integration, divestiture, and liquidation. In a government context, Paul Kennedy defines grand strategy as "the capacity of the nation's leaders to bring together all of the elements [of power], both military and nonmilitary, for the preservation and enhancement of the nation's long-term (that is, in wartime and peacetime) best interests." From this perspective, grand strategy requires the articulation of both policy goals and interim objectives as well as a broad definition of power that extends beyond the use of the military forces. Military strategist B. H. Liddell-Hart defined grand strategy as a plan "to co-ordinate and direct all the resources of [an organization] towards the attainment of . . . [a] goal defined by fundamental policy." Sources: P. Kennedy, *Grand Strategies in War and Peace*, (Hartford, CT: Yale University Press) 1991, also Profs. K. C. Johnson and S. P. Remy, CUNY; B. H. Liddell-Hart, "Fundamentals of Strategy and Grand Strategy," *Strategy* (1967): 322. Check Chris Wells at http://www.yale.edu/iss/ Grand-Strategy-Bureaucracy-Wells.pdf, available online at "Planning Skills: A Web-based Knowledge Repository," http://planningskills.com/glossary/38.php (accessed June 1, 2007).

9. See David Ignatius, "Achieving Real Victory Could Take Decades," *Washington Post*, December 26, 2004, for CENTCOM Combatant Commander General John Abizaid's views on what he calls "The Long War."
10. General (Ret.) Barry McCaffrey, After Action Report—General Barry R McCaffrey USA (Ret) VISIT IRAQ AND KUWAIT 9–16 March 2007, available online at http://www.iraqslogger.com/downloads/McCaffreyIraq.pdf (accessed June 1, 2007).
11. Ibid.
12. Source: Franklin D. Roosevelt, Inaugural Address, March 4, 1933, as published in Samuel Rosenman, ed., *The Public Papers of Franklin D. Roosevelt, Volume Two: The Year of Crisis, 1933* (New York: Random House, 1938), 11–16.
13. Jonathan Schell, *The Unconquerable World: Power, Nonviolence, and the Will of the People* (New York: Metropolitan Books, 2003), 24.
14. Excerpt from Abraham Lincoln's second inaugural address to Congress, December 1, 1862. Source: "The Lincoln Museum," available online at http://www.thelincolnmuseum.org/new/about/others_say.html (accessed June 1, 2007).

Index

PART I

Beyond War

Chapter 1

PART I

Beyond War

Chapter 2

PART I

Beyond War

Chapter 3

PART I

Beyond War

Chapter 4

PART II

Lessons in Postmodern War: Civil-Military Operations in Northern Iraq

Chapter 5

PART II

Lessons in Postmodern War: Civil-Military Operations in Northern Iraq

Chapter 6

PART III

Lessons Gathered but Not Yet Learned

Chapter 7

PART III

Lessons Gathered but Not Yet Learned

Chapter 8

PART IV

Past as Prologue

Chapter 9

Part IV

Past as Prologue

Chapter 10